THE PLAYS OF W. B. YEATS

The Plays of W. B. Yeats

Yeats and the Dancer

Sylvia C. Ellis
University of Wales, Bangor

M

St. Martin's Press

First published in Great Britain 1995 by
MACMILLAN PRESS LTD
Houndmills, Basingstoke, Hampshire RG21 2XS
and London
Companies and representatives
throughout the world

A catalogue record for this book is available
from the British Library.

ISBN 0–333–60498–9

10   9   8   7   6   5   4   3   2   1
04 03 02 01 00 99 98 97 96 95

Printed and bound in Great Britain by
Antony Rowe Ltd
Chippenham, Wiltshire

First published in the United States of America 1995 by
Scholarly and Reference Division,
ST. MARTIN'S PRESS, INC.,
175 Fifth Avenue,
New York, N.Y. 10010

ISBN 0–312–12047–8

Library of Congress Cataloging-in-Publication Data
Ellis, Sylvia C.
The plays of W. B. Yeats : Yeats and the dancer / Sylvia C. Ellis.
p. cm.
Includes bibliographical references and index.
ISBN 0–312–12047–8
1. Yeats, W. B. (William Butler), 1865–1939—Dramatic works.
2. Yeats, W. B. (William Butler), 1865–1939—Knowledge—Dancing.
3. Salome (Biblical figure)—In literature.   4. Dancing in
literature.   5. Dancers in literature.   6. Japan—In literature.
I. Title.
PR5908.D7E43 1995
822'.8—dc20
                                                        93–38847
                                                             CIP

Contents

To the memory of Alan Barnes

List of Plates

The author and publishers wish to acknowledge, with thanks, the Trustees of the Theatre Museum (Victoria and Albert Museum) for the illustration on p. xiii and the following photographs:

Preface

This study seeks to investigate the manner in which the drama of W. B. Yeats was influenced by the notion of dance and the figure of the dancer by considering the increasing interest that they aroused in the 1890s in France and England. It examines the way in which a scholarly writer like Mallarmé responded to music-hall performers such as Loïe Fuller in prose of a highly theoretical nature, the argument of which linked the view of the dancer as embodying the fusion of humanity with abstraction, emotion with intellect and the tenets of *Symboliste* poetry. The credo of the French poet was taken up by English and Irish writers: Wilde, Arthur Symons, Craig and W. B. Yeats himself all produced their own tributes to dance and dancers.

Consequently, in response to *fin-de-siècle* fervour for them, the following prevalent preoccupations of *Symbolisme-Décadence* are observed: the fascination for the biblical dancer Salome in literature from the 1840s up to Yeats's transformation of this figure in his own dance plays as late as the 1930s; the voguish mania for Japan and her art and artefact, especially for Noh drama with its central dance; the significance of the solo female dancer in performance exhibited both in music hall and in Diaghilev's *Ballets Russes*; and, lastly, an account of the theorising on dance itself as an aesthetic form current both at the time of Yeats's writing and that of our own age precedes an appraisal of the results of these investigations to the plays of the Irish writer. There the role of the dancer progressively increases until she finally becomes the central character. Hence, the last section of this study dwells at some length on each of Yeats's dance plays and discusses how dialogue is transformed into dance therein and then examines how theory is put into practice in the performance of some of the plays.

Acknowledgements

This study has been fifteen years in the conception and making and I have incurred many debts along the way. I should particularly like to extend warmest thanks to my supervisor at the University College of Wales, Bangor, Professor William Tydeman, for his direction, enthusiasm and support over my three years as his postgraduate student. Gratitude is also due to Professor Gabriel Pearson of Essex University who, when I was an undergraduate, gave me a love which never fails for the study of literature and who astutely suggested that I should pay some attention to the plays of W. B. Yeats as, despite the then-current critical judgement, he believed them to be worthy of scrutiny. I also thank Professor Christopher Salvesen of Reading University for his interest and staunch support. My thanks go, too, to Professor Geoffrey Hunter of the University of Wales, Bangor, for his suggestions on the philosophy of dance, and to Ms Melanie Christoudia of the Theatre Museum, Covent Garden, for her great help in tracking down relevant journals and illustrations. Dr John Stokes of Warwick University read the thesis text and kindly and meticulously made many valuable suggestions, while Dr John Kelly of Oxford University very generously helped me with the locating of material in Yeats's unpublished letters. I willingly avow a more recent and deep indebtedness to Martin Wright of Warwick who has been unfailingly kind and generous with his time and great knowledge of ballet and dance. He has provided many fascinating sources of information and indicated numerous rewarding avenues of enquiry and has always made his enthusiasm for the project clear and committed. I am profoundly grateful to him.

Acknowledgements are owed too to the energy and good humour of the late Garfield Gwynne and those who knew him will understand how much and how well he deserved the gesture. On a personal note I thank my dear friends for their unstinting affection and support, and especial gratitude goes to my mother for her constant encouragement and to my brother for his selfless help at every stage. Without these people I would never have got this far.

The author and publishers wish to thank the following for permission to use copyright material.

The Council of Trustees of the National Library of Ireland.

Oxford University Press for the extracts from the *Collected Letters of W. B. Yeats*.

Introduction

In this study I have sought to establish the context in which Yeats's work as a playwright can most helpfully be seen and distinguished from the many aesthetic creeds and practices prevailing around him. In the four chapters into which the investigation is divided, research into general context – the vogue for artistic treatments of the biblical dancer Salome, the contemporary fascination with things Japanese, the significance of the dancer in performance, exhibited both in music hall and in the *Ballets Russes*, a consideration of the theorising on dance by both Yeats's own contemporaries and those of the present age – precedes an application of the results of these searches to the dance dramas of the Irish writer. The subtitle 'Yeats and the Dancer' indeed involves a scrutiny of current thinking on dance and dancers as well as a focussing on Yeats's own dance plays in which the dancer figures significantly. The demands of space as well as limits imposed by the subject-matter dictated my concentration on the plays only; almost all consideration of Yeats's poetry is necessarily precluded, even where it treats of dance and dancers as aesthetic images. The contemporary public – consumers of the writers' productions – may have maintained a modish concern and fervid admiration for famous dancers, but the poets adopted as an image of ordered spontaneity the dance itself.

Any reader of Frank Kermode's *Romantic Image* (1957) will become instantly aware of where my researches began. While I would highlight my indebtedness to Professor Kermode, nevertheless I have developed in some detail those points that remain merely adumbrated in his admirable study because the nature of his investigation precluded a deeper and more intense concentration on them. Indisputably, however, it was he who established an approach which a work such as that offered here could adopt with confidence and it is on his hints that I have proceeded.

This account of Yeats's plays does not include his entire dramatic *oeuvre*. My analysis focusses on dance and the dance plays since it is shaped by the increasing interest in the dancer shown among artists of the *fin de siècle*, particularly in France, and the manner in which English and Irish writers such as Arthur Symons, Wilde and Gordon Craig as well as Yeats himself were influenced by this very marked preoccupation. Many of Yeats's plays contain a dance but in my view not all of them qualify for inclusion under the heading 'dance play'. An examination of their shortcomings in this respect need not prove negative, however, since it throws light on the strengths of the dance plays themselves and helps analysis of just what constitute genuine examples of the mode. For these reasons importance has been attached to *The Land of Heart's Desire* (1894), *Where There is Nothing* (1902), *Deirdre* (1907), *The Player Queen* (1922) and *The Herne's Egg* (1938) as instances of experimentation with such dance-play features as mask, chorus or movement, and *On Baile's Strand* (1904) because, although it contains no dance, it provides in embryo a model for the later *Four Plays for Dancers* (1921). *At the Hawk's Well* (1917), *The Dreaming of the Bones* (1919), *The Only Jealousy of Emer* (1919), *Calvary* (1920), *The Cat and the Moon* (1926), *The Resurrection* (1931) and three last plays – *A Full Moon in March* (1935), *The King of the Great Clock Tower* (1935) and *The Death of Cuchulain* (1939) – are treated as achievements fulfilling the criteria identified as central to the dance play proper. None the less, because Yeats had a passionate and contradictious heart, only a suggested schema for cataloguing or classifying a dance play is drawn: he crafted moulds and then broke and transcended them without a qualm where the needs of staging, action or even mood required it. For this reason each play has been considered individually since the force and function of no two dances are ever quite identical.

Yeats's drama mirrors contemporary obsessions while being simultaneously supremely innovative and his pronouncements on theatre and theatrical method prove him to be a theoretician of great sensitivity and insight. He was also iconoclastic: he rejected thoroughly the current fervour in some circles for Ibsen and what he perceived to be the banalities of Naturalism. In proposing another method, one employing ritual, mask, dance and constituting an 'unpopular theatre', time has revealed Yeats as influencing not only such playwrights as Samuel Beckett, but also very many of those whose work or passion provokes them to meditate on theatre: writers, designers, producers, critics, actors and audiences.

Programme cover for Charles B. Cochran's League of Notions, produced and staged by John Murray Anderson at the New Oxford Theatre January 1921

NEW
OXFORD THEATRE

Proprietors   ·   ·   ·   The OXFORD Ltd.

"CHARLES B. COCHRAN'S

LEAGUE OF NOTIONS"

The Entire Production Devised and Staged

by

JOHN MURRAY ANDERSON.

PROGRAMME.

1

The Figure of the Dancer: Salome

Before embarking on the principal concern of this chapter, an examination of versions of the legend of Salome which emerged after Heinrich Heine's publication of *Atta Troll* in 1841, reached a climax in the 1890s and continued, in a transformed manner, in the works of W. B. Yeats, echoing even in the last plays of 1935 and 1939, I shall first discuss the figure of the dancer as a concept of great significance to the movement of *Symbolisme-Décadence* and why she so captivated the *fin-de-siècle* consciousness of writers, painters and musicians. The gender of the dancer was indeed automatically assumed to be female, a legacy, as shall be made plain in Chapter 3 on the dancer in performance, from Romantic Ballet and the Marie Taglioni tradition: it is only with the advent of Diaghilev's *Ballets Russes* as late as 1909 in Paris and 1911 in London and, in particular, the very Russian phenomenon of Nijinsky – set, as he is, in a tradition which emphasised the importance of the male dancer – that the tyranny of the female dancer began to loosen its grip. The discussion of several works with the Salome story as theme will entail a brief investigation into the historical perspectives of the critics cited in this chapter and it will then be brought to a close by paying some attention to the modern critical debate on sexual politics and the fascination for the girl-dancer in those terms. It is no coincidence that the vogue for Salome should manifest itself simultaneously with the growing prominence of the 'New Woman'.

Initially, however, it may be of use to define the terms 'Symbolism' and 'Decadence' as aesthetic creeds and to place them historically, thereby enabling a discovery of the manner in which they were viewed both by their practitioners and by their contemporary admirers. In the *Oxford English Dictionary* there is an entry from the *Contemporary Review* of May 1866 which states:

1

By Symbolism in art, poetic or pictorial, we understand the attempt to suggest higher, wider, purer, or deeper ideas by the use of simpler, humbler, or more familiar thoughts or objects.

In 1898 R. N. Bain in *Literature*, 12 November, 453:1 proffers:

Symbolism is the name given by French critics to that revolt against the dryness and photographic exactness of naturalism, which ... is characterized, at its best, by a ... somewhat dreamy poetry, and half-naive, half-mystical attempts to interpret the moods of nature through the medium of human sensations.[1]

One of the aims of Symbolism was that of a unity of all the arts, while another was that of an aspiration to the state of music, where synthesis of form and content would be achieved. In his book *The Symbolist Aesthetic in France, 1885–1895*, A. G. Lehmann[2] considers both 'musicality' and 'total art' in relation to the Symbolists. He also comments on the privacy of the symbol which is employed in quite another way by the Symbolists from that of the Romantics. He discovers, as indeed he must, solipsism: a vision in which received symbolism has broken down, where the poet is using images which make sense to himself alone and, thus, render the writing Self-rather than Other-directed.[3]

When Rimbaud devised a system of interpretations of vowels according to the colours that they evoked for him, it is clear that the only reality in which his images were grounded was that of his own mind. Baudelaire in his poem 'Correspondances', a work seminal to Symbolism, claimed:

> La Nature est un temple où de vivants piliers
> Laissent parfois sortir de confuses paroles;
> L'homme y passe à travers des forêts de symboles
> Qui l'observent avec des regards familiers.[4]

He is demoting reality and promoting the appropriation of it by the individual consciousness which provides corresponding meanings from a personal repertoire. As Edmund Wilson suggests in *Axel's Castle*:

what the symbols of Symbolism really were, were metaphors detached from their subjects – for one cannot, beyond a certain point, in poetry, merely enjoy colour and sound for their own sake; one has to guess what the images are being applied to. And Symbolism may be defined as an attempt by carefully studied means – a complicated association of ideas represented by a medley of metaphors – to communicate unique personal feelings.[5]

Rimbaud, in 'Hallucinations', expressed his frustration with language as the mode of conveying the visions obtained by his 'dérèglement de tous les sens'[6] and Mallarmé pleaded for deliberate vagueness of expression:

> Exclus ... si tu commences
> Le réel parce que vil
>
> Le sens trop précis rature
> Ta vague littérature.[7]

If we consider the work of Stéphane Mallarmé to be the *locus classicus* of the tenets of Symbolism, it would be useful to acknowledge what Lehmann has to say about this writer's poetic method of proceeding:

> Starting with brute language, where palpably unsatisfactory expressions abound on all sides and go unnoticed in ordinary discourse, he held it to be the poet's task to eliminate the disorder and replace it by language in the highest degree 'musical'; that is to say, knit together, flowing, the 'words' interacting to the point where they are comparable to a melody in which the alteration of a single note would destroy the effectiveness of the whole sentence.[8] From the point of view of the poet, the one quality that runs through all language in its amorphous brute state is randomness, lack of complete appropriateness; or as Mallarmé calls it, 'Le Hasard'.[9]

We may note two further quotations which Lehmann selects from Mallarmé's work on this desired-for musicality:

> Toute âme est une mélodie, qu'il s'agit de renouer; et pour cela, sont la flûte ou la viole de chacun.[10]

This is taken from the latter's *Divagations* and the following is from an article, 'Enquête', published in the *Figaro* of 3 August 1895:

La Poésie n'est que l'expression musicale et suraiguë, emotion-
nante, d'un état d'âme; le vers libre est cela. En résumé peu mais
bon.[11]

Lehmann explains the Symbolists' belief in the significance of
music as allied with their desire for total art:

The symbolist obsession with 'Music' results from the chance
encounter of three important events in the history of art: first,
Wagner's personal solution of the operatic problem of combining
music and libretto in continuous recitative, and the enormous
impression it made on the world of letters, then as always relatively ignorant in matters of music; secondly, an extension of
verbal experiment, especially marked in the last fifty years of the
century; and thirdly, the realization that poetry, for all the interest
of these new verbal resources, is not merely a trick, an arbitrary
variation on the normal didactic or informative discourse, but in
some sense connected with an emotional activity – either expressive, or emotive, or mystical, but at any rate lyrical – and in that
sense closer to music than to social science; in short, that poetry is
intent to 'reprendre à la musique son bien'.[12]

In 1899, Arthur Symons dedicated his influential book *The
Symbolist Movement in Literature*[13] to W. B. Yeats as 'the chief representative of that movement in our country'. Much has been written
on Yeats as Symbolist, focussing particularly on the dreamy, vague
quality of many of his early verses such as those collected in *The
Wind Among the Reeds* of 1899. Yeats, in later years, saw himself as
one of 'the last romantics'[14] and this may be a more justified opinion
than that of Symons in the 1890s. Where Yeats coincides with the
Symbolists is in his desire to forge mystical imagery and in his wish
to produce a 'brief, dreamy, kind delight'.[15] Where Yeats differs from
the Symbolists, however, is in his lack of solipsism. Although he
was greatly influenced by the French writers, as an examination of
the 'Byzantium' poems would show, however heavy the burden of
the personal that they may carry, his symbols remain received. A
rose is a symbol of passion, of beauty, of mystical purity; it retains its
traditional associations. For a Symbolist, a rose can represent anything that the poet chooses from his own store of signification. It
must therefore be deciphered by the reader through an attempt to
enter and decode the writer's individual consciousness. In Yeats's

writing reality is not appropriated and engulfed by the Self in such a manner: he is closer to Wordsworth or Shelley in his relating of symbol to reality and they permit Nature to remain supremely Other.

So, whether Symons is right or partly right about classing Yeats as a Symbolist is an interesting but perhaps vexed question. In his plays Yeats was certainly an amateur of 'total art' and he struggled for many years to produce it on stage, as his keen support for the experiments of Edward Gordon Craig in 1911 bear witness. His masked dance plays produce a mingling of theatrical genres, as do his presentations of verse spoken to the psaltery, drum or gong, flute or zither. Yeats was also allied to Symbolism in his desire for musicality and in his reaction against Naturalism; he saw the strengths of Ibsen's plays but hated them for their lack of mystery and the mundane qualities of their dialogue.

In France the Symbolist movement is often dubbed *Symbolisme-Décadence* and after this brief digression on attempts to define Symbolism it may be of use to examine some definitions of Decadence. This will lead us back to our consideration of the dancer.

The *Oxford English Dictionary* refers to 'Decadent' in a manner in which we may recognise some of those characteristics attributed above to Symbolists. The *Dictionary* quotes the *Figaro* of 22 September 1885:

> Le décadent n'a pas d'idées. Il n'en veut pas. Il aime mieux les mots. C'est au lecteur à comprendre et à mettre des idées sous les mots. Le lecteur s'y refuse généralement. De là mépris du décadent pour le lecteur.

On 8 November 1889, the *Daily News* uses the word 'decadent' in the following way:

> A wonderful piece of 'decadent' French, in a queer new style, as if Rabelais's *Limousin* had been reborn, with a fresh manner of being intelligible.

And the *Saturday Review* of 22 November 1890 places the movement very firmly in France:

> The very noisy and motley crew of younger writers in France ... naturalists, decadents, scientific critics, and what not.[16]

It is evident from these dates that Decadence did not replace Symbolism but rather existed contiguously with it and one of the several preoccupations of Decadence was that of the *femme fatale*, who was often the dancer.

Contemporary writers such as Mallarmé and Symons wrote explications of the dancer's art, Mallarmé in his notes 'Crayonné au théâtre' where he presented the article 'Ballets' in 1886 and Symons in his essay 'The World as Ballet' of 1898 and in his very numerous reviews in theatrical periodicals such as the *Sketch*. Mallarmé saw the dancer in linguistic terms as sign, as metaphor:

> A savoir que la danseuse *n'est pas une femme qui danse*, pour ces motifs juxtaposés qu'elle *n'est pas une femme*, mais une métaphore résumant un des aspects élémentaires de notre forme, glaive, coupe, fleur, etc., *et qu'elle ne danse pas*, suggérant, par le prodige de raccourcis ou d'élans, avec une écriture corporelle ce qu'il faudrait de paragraphes en prose dialoguée autant que descriptive, pour exprimer, dans la rédaction: poème dégagé de tout appareil du scribe.[17] [Mallarmé's emphasis]

Mallarmé was not alone in taking as read the female gender of the dancer and Symons follows him in his exposition published in *Studies in Seven Arts* of 1906 where, speaking of the central role of ballet, he wrote:

> And something of the particular elegance of the dance, the scenery; the avoidance of emphasis, the evasive, winding turn of things; and above all, the intellectual as well as sensuous appeal of a living symbol, which can but reach the brain through the eyes, in the visual, concrete, imaginative way; has seemed to make the ballet concentrate in itself a good deal of the modern ideal in matters of artistic expression. Nothing is stated, there is no intrusion of words used for the irrelevant purpose of describing; a world rises high before one, the picture lasts only long enough to have been there: and the dancer, with her gesture, all pure symbol, evokes, from her mere beautiful motion, idea, sensation, all that one need ever know of event. There, before you, she exists, in harmonious life; and her rhythm reveals to you the soul of her imagined being.[18]

As well as embodying both form and meaning the dancer occupies the periphery between Art and Nature, a territory scrutinised closely by the writers of the Decadence. Huysmans, in what is a curious amalgam of manifesto and critique of Art for Art's sake, *A Rebours* of 1884,[19] endeavoured to render Life as Living Artefact by having des Esseintes, his apostle of Decadence, set precious stones into the shell of a tortoise. The fact that the poor animal died did nothing to attenuate the force of the motivation to dispense with Naturalness, since Decadence found it vulgar. The dancer is neither Nature nor Art but a combination of both: while she is human flesh and blood, her dance is not. The dance has structure and yet it is not external to her: form can only be made real by performance and only through performance can its meaning be produced. As we noted in Mallarmé's remarks on 'Ballets' of 1886, he saw the dancer as projecting an 'écriture corporelle'[20] which could only be reproduced by the writer in his particular medium by pages of descriptive prose. The dancer eliminates 'hasard' through the shape and discipline of her dance and in so doing becomes an art form. As Frank Kermode writes in *Romantic Image* of Mallarmé,

> for whom, at one period, the dancer was the emblem of identical form and meaning, 'l'incorporation visuelle de l'idée'. The Dance signified the artist's effort 'à vêtir l'idée d'une forme sensible'; we should remember that 'l'idée ' is here used in a limited sense, meaning a truth inaccessible to unaided intellect.[21]

The 'truth' perceived is not one arrived at through language, it is, rather, apprehended as vision by the imagination. Just as Symons saw the dancer's gestures as pure symbol, so too does Mallarmé perceive the dancer as a purveyor of meaning. Lehmann examines the link between dance and poetry:

> It will be remembered that Mallarmé has defined the dance as a language which describes briefly what speech would take paragraphs to describe. This is a comparatively early judgement; in time he comes to turn it round, though not contradict himself. The dance – as gesture – is to be not described, but transcribed, taken up into poetry. Speech has absorbed music – or at least all that it is fit to take; now it is to absorb dance in its march towards 'total art'. Of course, it is speech rhythm in the worst sense that is to do this; and to register the refinements of the excessively stretched rhythmical sense, there is the notation of *Un Coup de Dès*.[22]

Mallarmé never ceased in his efforts to bring what he called the languages of poetry and dance together through his endeavour to produce musicality in his verse and drama. His fascination with the dancer was not limited to the music-hall dancer, Loïe Fuller, about whose presence in Paris he wrote in *The National Observer* of 13 March 1893, under the title 'Considérations sur l'art du Ballet de la Loie Fuller'. He had also begun, in 1866, a verse drama, 'Hérodiade', in which he portrayed the character of Salome. As will be made apparent below, the French poet spent from 1866 to his death in 1898 struggling to complete 'Hérodiade'; it was abandoned in play form and rewritten as a long poem and we are left with some fragments of the latter which are precious and coldly beautiful. But the Loïe Fuller phenomenon was treated with exactly the same degree of commitment and seriousness and she was described with Mallarmé's usual erudition. When an intellectual figure of this stature devoted such attention to a music-hall dancer – albeit one who performed in highly respected venues and was admired by many a contemporary highbrow – we realise the level of significance with which writers and artists, both French and English, perceived dance in all its manifestations during the historical period under investigation. Mallarmé is portraying here what he called 'l'ensemble d'un art':[23]

Au bain terrible des étoffes se pâme, radieuse, froide la figurante qui illustre maint thème giratoire où tend une trame loin épanouie, pétale et papillon géants, déferlement, tout d'ordre net at élémentaire. Sa fusion aux nuances véloces muant leur fantas-magorie oxyhydrique de crépuscule et de grotte, telles rapidités de passions, délice, deuil, colère: il faut pour les mouvoir, prisma-tiques, avec violence ou diluées, le vertige d'une âme comme mise à l'air par un artifice.[24]

What is perhaps most remarkable about this depiction of Loïe Fuller dancing is the poet's stress on her as, paradoxically, a mechanical abstraction which, none the less, conveys passion: he avoids emphasis on the human aspect of the dancer. Such an appraisal would have given Fuller reason to congratulate herself; she was aiming at this very achievement of the primacy of artifice over the formlessness of mere life.

Arthur Symons too wrote of music-hall dancers. The poems grouped under the title *Amoris Victima* of 1 March 1896,[25] were the result of his love affair with a dancer and the celebrated Jane Avril is the heroine of 'La Mélinite: Moulin Rouge', written in Paris in 1892.[26] In the sixth stanza he presents her thus:

> And, enigmatically smiling,
> In the mysterious night,
> She dances for her own delight,
> A shadow smiling
> Back to a shadow in the night.

As noted above, the dancer in performance will be considered in a later chapter where the art of Fuller and Jane Avril will be examined more closely. The writings on dance and dancer of both Mallarmé and Symons now lead us to the figure of Salome, the particular fictional dancer so often depicted by subscribers to the movement, *Symbolisme-Décadence*.

> Salome was the subject of poems by Mallarmé and Symons, as well as many lesser poets. ... Salome was a heroine of the Decadence; Beardsley's illustrations to Wilde's *Salomé* set the tone, and there is ample evidence of the degree to which she appealed to artists in search of a fantastic 'Decadence'. But Yeats transformed her entirely, and gave her a place in his aesthetic and historical systems. As a dancer she represented the idea of the Image as non-discursive, without separable intellectual content; as the woman who demanded the head of a saint, she emblematized the cost of the artist's achievement. She haunts the works of Yeats down to the last plays.[27]

Frank Kermode states clearly here that a continuum of interest in the theme of Salome existed from the 1840s onwards. In investigating these works on this figure, I hope that the rich background to Yeats's own obsessions with the dancer will be revealed and that the manner in which he transformed the *fin-de-siècle* presentation of the image will be thrown into relief. He was himself familiar with some of the versions of the story, for example he knew Oscar Wilde's *Salomé* of 1893 and he had read the 'Hérodiade' of Stéphane Mallarmé (1866), because it was translated into English by his friend Arthur Symons in 1896.

In her book *The Legend of Salome and the Principle of Art for Art's Sake* (1960), Helen Grace Zagona[28] considers the way in which the

vogue for this dancer has come into prominence at different
historical periods and how the treatment of her story has differed
accordingly:

> Giving the legend's history a sweeping glance, we note that in its
> twenty-one-hundred-year course it has hit three peaks of interest:
> the first, in the period of the Roman decadence; the second, in the
> Middle Ages; and the third in the post-romantic era, notably in
> France where the development of that frame of mind which even-
> tually branded itself 'décadent' was to provide the ideal esthetic
> climate for our subject. Whether or not it will enjoy another
> period of high interest in literature, one cannot say. Certainly,
> after the first decade of this century it has declined considerably
> as a source of inspiration for major writers.[29]

Some of the writers depict Salome herself, others focus their
attention on Herodias, her mother. At the time of the Crusades, one
of the historical peaks of interest in the dancer because of the
contemporary concern with John the Baptist, confusion arose over
the girl's name. Some writers called her Salome, some mistook
her for her mother, Herodias, others used the Egyptian name,
Pharaildis.[30] This confusion continued into the nineteenth century
where both Mallarmé and Banville named her 'Hérodiade' and
Heine, in the original version of his poem written in German in
1841, called his heroine 'Herodias', but he did seem to be speaking
of the mother of Salome, Herod's wife. In the French translation
which he undertook himself and which appeared in Paris in 1847,
his protagonist's name is 'Hérodiade'. While the Hérodiade of
Mallarmé and Banville is clearly Salome, it is less evident that this
is the case for Heine's queen and I disagree with Zagona here
where she states that the German poet is in fact portraying
Salome.[31] A consideration of the relevant part of *Atta Troll* should
later show that Heine is portraying Herodias. Zagona does switch
from speaking of Heine's 'Herodias' to 'Hérodiade' without comment or explanation.[32]

Let us consider the actual titles and dates of the various works on
the Salome-Herodias legend from the 1840s onwards to the period
dubbed 'Décadence' and from thence to Yeats. The list may be hefty
but is not, I fear, exhaustive: suffice it to explain that I have
attempted to appraise the more immediately accessible of the
works, but cannot pretend to have paid due attention to every

instance in the startlingly copious collections of versions of this theme. Heine's *Atta Troll* appeared in 1841, J. C. Heywood's *Salome, the Daughter of Herodias* appeared anonymously in 1862, was published as *Herodias: A Dramatic Poem* under his own name in 1867 in Cambridge, Massachusetts and was then published in London in 1884 under the same title, Mallarmé's 'Hérodiade' in 1866, Banville's poem 'La Danseuse' in 1870 and his 'Hérodiade' in 1874, Flaubert's 'Hérodias' in 1877, the opera *Hérodiade* by Paul Milliet and Henri Grémont with music by Massenet was first produced in Brussels in 1881, Jean Lorrain's anthology 'La Forêt Bleue' containing poems on the theme appeared in 1883, Huysmans' *A Rebours*, which includes vivid descriptions of Gustave Moreau's two famous paintings of the dancer, in 1884, Laforgue's '*Salomé*' in 1887, Wilde's *Salomé* in 1893, Symons's 'The Dance of the Daughters of Herodias' in 1897 and Sudermann's *Johannes* in 1898.[33] While Yeats himself never wrote a version of the Salome–John the Baptist legend, he does claim that 'Emer must dance, there must be severed heads' in his last play of 1939.[34] We shall investigate in depth in the final chapter on Yeats's dance plays the manner in which he perceived the dancer and what she stands for in his aesthetic. Meanwhile, our concern is with the structural differences in the various Salome narratives here appraised as well as an estimation of the extent of Yeats's personal knowledge about them.

A consideration of the New Testament versions of the Salome story may now serve as a useful yardstick with which to compare what came later: the Herod of the narrative was Herod Antipas (son of Herod the Great), Tetrarch of Galilee from 4 BC to AD 39 and sometimes known as Herod the Tetrarch. Herodias was his wife, formerly married to his brother Philip by whom she had a daughter. John's death at the order of Herod occurred sometime between the years AD 27 and 30. The account is presented as a short episode in the Gospels of Mark, 6: 14–29, and Matthew, 14: 1–12, and the former's treatment is as follows:

> And King Herod heard of him [Jesus]; (for his name was spread abroad:) and he said, That John the Baptist was risen from the dead, and therefore mighty works do shew forth themselves in him.

Others said, That it is Elias. And others said, That it is a prophet, or as one of the prophets.

But when Herod heard thereof, he said, It is John, whom I beheaded: he is risen from the dead.

For Herod himself had sent forth and laid hold upon John, and bound him in prison for Herodias' sake, his brother Philip's wife: for he had married her.

For John had said unto Herod, It is not lawful for thee to have thy brother's wife.

Therefore Herodias had a quarrel against him, and would have killed him; but she could not:

For Herod feared John, knowing that he was a just man and an holy, and observed him; and when he heard him, he did many things, and heard him gladly.

And when a convenient day was come, that Herod on his birthday made a supper to his lords, high captains, and chief estates of Galilee;

And when the daughter of the said Herodias came in, and danced, and pleased Herod and them that sat with him, the king said unto the damsel, Ask of me whatsoever thou wilt, and I will give it thee.

And he sware unto her, whatsoever thou shalt ask of me, I will give it thee, unto the half of my kingdom.

And she went forth, and said unto her mother, What shall I ask? And she said, The head of John the Baptist.

And she came in straightway with haste unto the King, and asked, saying, I will that thou give me by and by in a charger the head of John the Baptist.

And the King was exceeding sorry; yet for his oath's sake, and for their sakes which sat with him, he would not reject her.

And immediately the King sent an executioner, and commanded his head to be brought: and he went and beheaded him in prison,

And brought his head in a charger, and gave it to the damsel: and the damsel gave it to her mother.

And when his disciples heard of it, they came and took up his corpse, and laid it in a tomb.[35]

St Matthew's later account is the more succinct of the two and it is interesting to note which details in St Mark's narrative are omitted as well as general differences in emphasis:

At that time Herod the tetrarch heard of the fame of Jesus, And said unto his servants, This is John the Baptist; he is risen from the dead; and therefore mighty works do shew forth themselves in him.

For Herod had laid hold on John, and bound him, and put him in prison for Herodias' sake, his brother Philip's wife.

For John said unto him, It is not lawful for thee to have her.

And when he would have put him to death, he feared the multitude, because they counted him as a prophet.

But when Herod's birthday was kept, the daughter of Herodias danced before them, and pleased Herod.

Whereupon he promised with an oath to give her whatsoever she would ask.

And she, being before instructed of her mother, said, Give me here John Baptist's head in a charger.

And the King was sorry: nevertheless for the oath's sake, and them which sat with him at meat, he commanded it to be given her.

And he sent and beheaded John in the prison.

And his head was brought in a charger, and given to the damsel: and she brought it to her mother.

And his disciples came, and took up the body, and buried it, and went and told Jesus.[36]

Clearly, in each case, the relating of the decollation is told in flashback and both versions stress Herod's guilty belief that Jesus the Messiah is none other than John the Baptist, Herod's erstwhile victim, arisen from the dead. While both writers present the imprisonment of John after his public denunciation of Herod's incestuous marriage to Herodias, St Mark is unique in stating that Herodias wanted his death. In both accounts the dancer's mother instructs the unnamed girl what to request: in the earlier version of St Mark she refers to her mother's decision after dancing, while in the St Matthew story Salome is tutored by Herodias *before* her performance to demand John's head as reward, so confident is Herod's wife about the probable outcome of the dance. The latter version thus exhibits more premeditation on the part of Herodias (a detail later reproduced and developed by Flaubert), while the former makes the gruesome plea seem more like a spur-of-the-moment grotesque whim. St Mark's portrayal of Herod dwells more on his reluctance to make good his oath out of his genuine respect for the man to be beheaded: 'he heard him gladly' and among later writers, both Flaubert and Oscar Wilde focus on Mark's rendering of Herod's personal anguish.

The details of the relationship between king and prophet are omitted in St Matthew's more concise account. As a final distinction between the two narratives, the episode according to St Mark accentuates the role of an executioner sent to the prison to fetch back the head. Flaubert, Wilde and Laforgue use this incident to produce an element of suspense in the proceedings. Matthew simply states, 'And he sent, and beheaded John in prison'. Absent in the Biblical models, but conspicuous in later versions, is the presence of a love relationship between the prophet and one of the women, Herodias or her daughter, a passion sometimes rejected and sometimes reciprocated by John. Thus, the Gospels provide the pattern which subsequent writers and painters employ to varying degrees of faithfulness.

As we see and it is of great significance the Bible portrays Salome as less of a temptress than as a docile girl and the responsibility for John's death lies firmly with Herodias. But it is the figure of Salome, the dancer, which took on dimensions of immorality as time went by until she is discovered as *femme fatale* of the Decadence amid trappings that become frankly barbaric and culminate in the grotesque.

The publication of Heine's *Atta Troll* introduced a new era of fascination with Salome:

> The post romantic era, which saw traditional styles founded on reason and logic give place to a great extent to thoroughly individualized modes of expression was to prove the most fertile in production of Salome works. From the point of view of variety of perspective, originality of treatment and profundity of insight into humanity's spiritual complexities, this period is incomparable. No longer rendered in simple terms and turned to the understanding of the many, the episode took on an esoteric character. Salome became a symbol of a philosophy of beauty entirely devoid of moral significance. From Heine to Wilde, she treaded [sic] her mysterious way and left a trail of plays, tales and poems giving witness to the power of her fascination over a certain breed of artist – for whom art was all that she was: coldly beautiful, cruel, unrelenting, existing gratuitously, with no need for justification, with no purpose but to be admired.[37]

Atta Troll, a long poem, was published in German in 1841 and appeared in Paris in the author's translation into French in 1847. Heine spent his last years living in France where he gained more popularity than in his native Germany. The French version was widely read and highly influential: Banville, Lorrain and Gautier were familiar with it and Mallarmé referred to its portrayal of Herodias in his notes before attempting his own poem 'Hérodiade'. This may well be Yeats's source of information about Heine's work. The initial avowed intention of the German poet was to write political polemic directed against rising nationalism, but he became more concerned with attacking the contemporary wave of Utilitarianism in art which he perceived as bourgeois philistinism. As Zagona indicated, Heine was among the first to applaud the gratuitously beautiful and to indict the current concern of employing art as a tool in the struggle for social progress.

The story of *Atta Troll* – 'a dream of a summer's night' – is long and complicated and I intend to concentrate simply on the section of the poem which deals with our theme. 'Atta Troll' is a dancing bear who escapes his captor and is hunted through a truly impressive landscape of ravine and forest by ghostly figures from mythology. The focus of our interest in the 'Wildjagd', the wild hunt, rests on the three feminine hunters: Diana, transformed from the customary picture of Goddess of chastity and the moon into a sensual figure epitomising pagan Greece; secondly, the mysteriously and essentially Celtic Fay Abunda, like Diana, forced into hiding by Christianity; and, thirdly, the Semitic Herodias. Heine is most attracted to this third figure because she is filled with spirit and ardour of living and she symbolises for him the soul of gratuitous art. The depiction of the cavalcade of ghosts who make up the wild hunt is the most achieved part of the ballad and Heine took the idea from old German legend. He, however, transformed the sombre chase of the original into a wild, noisy, rollicking affair in which the three feminine hunters mentioned are accompanied by riders who have also been damned by conventional bourgeois morality, such as King Arthur, Goethe and Shakespeare. Supreme in Heine's esteem and affection is Herodias because,

> Embodied in the Judean queen is all of the color and intensity which [Heine] thought lacking in poetry of Christian–nationalist tradition.[38]

As the poet himself said of Herodias,

> Si c'était un ange ou un démon, c'est ce que j'ignore. On ne sait jamais au juste chez les femmes où cesse l'ange et où le diable commence.[39]

The portrayal of Herodias in Heine's original German version is as follows:

> Wirklich eine Fürstin war sie,
> War Judäas Königin,
> Des Herodes schönes Weib,
> Die des Täufers Haupt begehrt hat.

This is surely a presentation of Herodias, not Salome, since the girl was never described as 'Königin' nor was she ever wife to Herod. Heine introduces an element not present in the Bible episode – the love of Herodias for John the Baptist:

> Dieser Blutschuld halber ward sie,
> Auch vermaledeit; als Nachtspuk
> Muß sie bis zum Jüngsten Tage
> Reiten mit der wilden Jagd.

> In den Händen trägt sie immer
> Jene Schüssel mit den Haupte
> Des Johannes, und sie küßt es;
> Ja, sie küßt das Haupt mit Inbrunst.

> Denn sie liebte einst Johannem –
> In der Bibel steht es nicht,
> Doch im Volke legt die Sage
> Von Herodias' blut'ger Liebe.[40]

The rhythm gallops jerkily along at a pace suggestive of the wild hunt; the language is simple and redolent of a folk tale or ballad, as the conversational repetition of 'sie küßt es' preceded by the colloquial and emphatic 'Ja' illustrates: 'und sie küßt es / Ja, sie küßt das Haupt mit Inbrunst'. Zagona maintains that there were many versions of the Herodias–Salome story in popular legend of medieval Germany and that several forms of it had developed in German folk lore by the 1830s and 1840s.[41] It is possible that Heine took the texture of his writing from these and, hence, the structure and tone of folk tale suggestive of an oral tradition of verse. Typically, therefore, he projects himself into his creation by swearing his own love for Herodias:

Ja, ich liebe dich! Ich merk es
An den Zittern meiner Seele.
Liebe mich und sei mein Liebchen,
Schönes Weib, Herodias!

Liebe mich und sei mein Liebchen!
Schleudre fort den blut'gen Dummkopf
Samt der Schüssel, und genieße
Schmackhaft bessere Gerichte.[42]

Once again in these stanzas quoted above the writing is plain and forthright, reminiscent of ballad in its colloquial style. It debunks the seriousness of the legend by its irreverence, 'den blut'gen Dummkopf', and by its matter-of-fact simplicity, 'Liebe mich und sei mein Liebchen'. He omits the dance before Herod, the oath and the subsequent execution: Heine presents the reader instead with a *fait accompli*. He races through the events as related in the Bible in the three lines establishing Herodias's pedigree as Queen of Judea and fully-developed *femme fatale*:

War Judäas Königin,
Des Herodes schönes Weib,
Die des Täufers Haupt begehrt hat,

and then proceeds to add elements of his own derived from folk lore to a poetic concoction which subsequently had such impact on a number of writers.

With the publication of *Atta Troll*, however, the legend was reintroduced into the world of artists and it was recast over and again by English, French, American and Irish poets. One of these was J. C. Heywood, whose *Salome, the Daughter of Herodias* appeared anonymously in 1862 in Cambridge, Massachusetts, and was later published as *Herodias: A Dramatic Poem* in 1867. In common with Heine, Heywood portrays Herodias, the mother who clamoured for his death, kissing the head of the dead prophet.

This play opens with a preface from the Gospel of St. Matthew and a prologue in which John is already imprisoned but is none the less joyfully celebrating the coming of Jesus Christ:

My work is finished; way made for the Word.
Earth heareth silent Thine approach, O Lord.[43]

Salome enters the dungeon having escaped from the palace to bring John refreshment. Her greeting reveals her relationship to him: 'All hail! Good master. ...'; she loves him as a child does a father or teacher and she promises to try to set him free. John, speaking enigmatically, replies, 'And thou shalt do it'.[44] Unlike his innocent young follower, he knows that salvation is at hand for him, but he sees freedom in a different way: he is expecting death which, ironically, Salome herself will precipitate. He asks her three times whether she loves him and enjoins her to keep his words which, she promises, 'are enshrined' in her.[45] In this play the dance is anticipated by Salome's parting lines to the prisoner:

> I leave thee now, but take with me thy words;
> For, as thou know'st, King Herod with his lords
> Keepeth a feast, and in the revelry,
> Against my will, I must a sharer be.[46]

The following scene is set in the banqueting room in Herod's palace where the king, Herodias and all the company of lords, captains and courtiers are expecting the promised appearance of Salome:

> SECOND LORD: Here, where elysian joys invite the soul
>   To revel in an ecstasy of bliss,
>   I waiting stand, unblessed, till I behold,
>   Transcendant fair, like shell-borne Aphrodite,
>   The crowning glory of the feast appear.[47]

Heywood, faithful here to the Bible original, does not provide explicit details of the dance itself, he merely offers a stage direction, '*Salome glides in dancing*',[48] but her manner of performing is described by the effect that she produces on the onlookers:

> FIRST CAPTAIN: Dost note the sad expression of her face?
>   The downcast, curtained eyes? She looketh as
>   She came to dance for pity more than praise;
>   Led on by sorrow, not by vanity.[49]

By a similar technique, the audience is informed of the impression that the dance exerts on the king by a guest's interpretation of his facial expression:

FIRST CAPTAIN: Look at the king! His fierce, admiring eyes
Devour her every motion. Would'st thou think
His head could easy rest upon his couch
This night?[50]

Herod reacts by promising Salome whatever she wants, even to a half of his kingdom, 'We swear it by the ever-loving gods',[51] and on this oath the banquet ends. In this case Herodias does not instruct Salome what to ask, nor does her daughter herself make any request. But one detail of the scene which tallies with other versions including those of the Gospels is the news herein imparted that John is indeed in jail on the orders of Herodias.

Where Heywood differs from other accounts is in his introduction of a Roman soldier, Sextus, who loves and is loved by Salome and of Antonius, father of Salome by Herodias whom he knew as Livia. Salome's first intuition is to ask Herod for a princeship for Sextus, her second, to request the release of John the Baptist. But she had reckoned without Herodias. She receives tuition from her mother and the tenor of the lessons is that of the manner in which a woman's power may be employed: it reads like a manifesto:

Thou art strong when thou art loved,
For then thou rulest; weak when thou dost love,
For then thou art ruled...
... love them not. Their love,
Make it an engine built against themselves,
And batter them; the missiles which they send
Burn not on thine own hearth for warmth, but cast them
Envenomed back. What's sense of love compared
With sense of sway, the tyranny of will? ...
Tempt, tempt, yea tempt always, for men aye love
Temptation more than that which tempteth them.
Let nothing tempt thee save desire to tempt ...
Yet so thou be temptation thou must be
Never fruition, therefore thou must be
A Proteus in thy skill to escape and change
Thy seeming, with a siren's voice and lures ...
Seem to be all things but that which thou art,
And seem to seem not, all unconscious seem.
Ruling herself a woman may rule all
If she of seeming know the perfect use ...[52]

Herodias's educating of her child in the ways of the world as she sees it forms a grotesque parody of the instructing of Salome by John the Baptist. The mother explains from whence she has gleaned her bitter philosophy: she was abandoned when Antonius went to war and was informed of his death. Herod made advances to her which she reciprocated and she bore his child. When Antonius finally returned to give the lie to rumour, he fled on seeing her as part of Herod's household. Herodias strangled the offspring fathered by Herod who proved to be then 'A kingly villain in a god-like form'[53] who mistreated her, scorned and humiliated her. She now seeks only revenge and is jealously and eagerly guarding Herod as her own property on which to wreak it. She is not to be cheated of this ambition by her daughter, however great the lust her husband feels for Salome:

> he is mine
> Till I deliver him to furies. She
> Who weakeneth admiration in his heart,
> And looseneth thus my vengeful hold on him,
> Cannot escape my wrath and punishment.[54]

Herodias has devised a plan whereby she will be avenged upon her daughter, John the Baptist and the king himself; she orders her child to write on some tablets to her dictation: 'Presently after midnight let me have, / Upon a charger, John the Baptist's head'.[55] Utterly against her will Salome is forced to comply because her mother is holding Sextus to ransom. As she inscribes John's name she sees a cold, bright flame following her hand. The monstrous deed is accompanied by storms and omens of bloodshed. Salome is brought the severed head which seems to smile at her in understanding and forgiveness, but, so horrified is she by the events in which she has been instrumental, if not instigator, that she forswears her love for Sextus and will express her penitence by becoming a Christian vestal. As she bids Sextus farewell she insists that she could not have done otherwise than save his life.

The head is left for the enjoyment of Herodias:

> At length I am avenged! Drink, drink, my soul
> The sweet conviction, drink till thou be drunk!
> The king, smitten of god before his time,
> Eaten alive of worms, in torment howleth,

> Calleth for death that cometh not ...
> Salome, from the world self-banishèd,
> Seeketh to find her exile in the world,
> And by self-punishment to make amends ...[56]

She fondles the head and kisses it, caressing it, she claims, out of hatred:

> Thou threatened me with judgment and with hell,
> Yet thou art mine! I can embrace thee even,
> And weave my lily fingers in thy hair,
> And stroke thy temple, fondle thee, and hate!. ...
> Come, let me taste thy virtuous, scornful lips –[57]

As she does so, a voice is heard echoing through the chamber: 'Go to thy place!', and it is with these words reverberating through her obsessed brain that she dies, refusing to ask for forgiveness. Hell claims her:

> I come! I come! world for a space, good-night,
> Hail! Pluto, hail! infernal horrors! hail![58]

and Heywood has made certain that everyone has met fit punishment, but in so determining has strayed far from his model. He went to great lengths to present Salome as innocent and helpless on all counts: she could not do other than as she did. He wrote two more plays around the figure of the girl, *Antonius* and *Salome: A Dramatic Poem*, both published in the late 1880s. The latter is sequel to *Herodias* examined above and deals with the fortunes of Salome as a Christian and the conversion of Sextus to her new faith. While Heywood's plays are ingenious and energetic, they are not convincing or aesthetically pleasing. He is of interest, however, as a member of the artistic fraternity who took up the challenge of the Salome legend, but the liberties that he took with the original are manifold. His influence is limited, but there is something of his version of Salome to be discerned in that created by Milliet and Grémont in their libretto of *Hérodiade* produced in 1881. Oscar Wilde knew Heywood's *Salome* which he reviewed in 'The Poets' Corner' of the *Pall Mall Gazette* of 15 February 1888, where he judged it to be 'a triumph of conscientious industry' but a 'very commonplace production indeed'.[59]

Chronologically, the next appearance of the Herodias–Salome theme is that of the existing sections of Stéphane Mallarmé's 'Hérodiade', begun in 1864 and published incomplete in 1866. The poet attached great significance to this creation and he struggled with its complexities until the end of his life in 1898. It was an ambitious work, one in which Mallarmé wished to discover a new kind of poetic; as he wrote of it to his friend Henri Cazalis in October 1864 when he was still drafting it out as a play for the theatre:

Pour moi, me voici résolument à l'oeuvre. J'ai enfin commencé mon *Hérodiade*. Avec terreur car j'invente une langue qui doit nécessairement jaillir d'une poétique très nouvelle, que je pourrais définir en ces deux mots: Peindre *non la chose, mais l'effet qu'elle produit*. Le vers ne doit donc pas, là, se composer de mots, mais d'intentions, et toutes les paroles s'effacer devant les sensations ...[60]   [Mallarmé's emphasis]

In November 1865 another letter to Cazalis revealed that the poet had changed his plans for 'Hérodiade':

Je commence *Hérodiade*, non plus tragédie, mais poème ... parce que j'y gagne aussi toute l'attitude, les vêtements, le décor et l'ameublement, sans parler du mystère.[61]

Hérodiade is the girl known to us as Salome and Mallarmé explained in his preface to *Les Noces d'Hérodiade, Mystère*, a collection crafted from the unfinished manuscripts by Gardner Davies,[62] why the poet decided to retain this name:

J'ai laissé le nom d'Hérodiade pour bien la différencier de la Salomé je dirai moderne ou exhumée avec son fait-divers archaique – la danse, etc., l'isoler comme l'ont fait des tableaux solitaires dans le fait même terrible, mystérieux – et faire miroiter ce qui probablement hantra, en apparue avec son attribut – le chef du saint – dût la demoiselle constituer un monstre aux amants vulgaires de la vie.[63]

In his introduction to *Les Noces d'Hérodiade* Davies discusses contemporary aesthetic influences on Mallarmé and claims that the poet was inspired by paintings on the subject, those of Henri Regnault, whom the writer knew personally and who exhibited a

Salomé in 1870 and of Gustave Moreau whose work appeared in 1874.[64]

> Quoi qu'il en dise sur le choix du nom d'*Hérodiade*, Mallarmé a certainement voulu que sa héroine incarne à la fois la beauté légendaire de la danseuse et la froide raison de la mère, dans le fusion de ces deux êtres qui devaient réclamer la tête de saint Jean.[65]

Davies has gathered together all the writings that Mallarmé produced on Hérodiade and has discovered the rudiments of a dance which will be investigated below. First, a consideration of the parts of the poem that were published in 1866 and which are to be found in the Pléiade edition of the *Oeuvres Complètes* shows that a 'Scène' was completed at this early date, a conversation between the girl and her nurse, and that this was followed by 'Le Cantique de St Jean' in which the saint's head tells of the sensation of execution. Preceding these two documents, but not published until 1926 and not added to *Poésies* until the Pléiade collection of 1945, was an 'Ouverture Ancienne d'Hérodiade' which took the form of a solitary incantation by her nurse.

The most important section of the manuscripts is the 'Scène', the dialogue between Hérodiade and her nurse, where we witness vividly contrasted the simple human warmth of the old woman and the girl's fierce, virginal beauty. There is an obvious affinity between this encounter and that of Shakespeare's Juliet with her garrulous old nurse, though the subject of their discourse is tellingly different. Here the old woman wants to kiss Hérodiade's fingers, to offer her perfume, to bind up a loose skein of her hair. In every case her gesture is repugnant to the girl who at first orders her 'Reculez' and later maintains that physical contact between them would be a 'crime':

> Reculez.
> Le blond torrent de mes cheveux immaculés
> Quand il baigne mon corps solitaire le glace
> D'horreur, et mes cheveux que la lumière enlace
> Sont immortels, ô femme, un baiser me tûrait
> Si la beauté n'était la mort …[66]

Were she not already 'dead' through her exceptional beauty, the cold incarnation of virginity, the human warmth of a kiss would kill her. Throughout the poem Mallarmé refers to her lustrous hair along with gold, precious stones, particularly diamonds, metals and reflected light:

> The hair symbol, repeated much in *Hérodiade* and in the poet's work as a whole, is ... significant. As jewels and metals, which it resembles in its cold, golden smoothness, the hair also reflects the perfection of the infinite, and does not partake of the transient, mortal character of the rest of the body.[67]

In an unexpected touch of ingenuous childishness Hérodiade asks the nurse, 'Nourrice, suis je belle?',[68] but when the woman moves to correct the falling tress which is marring the girl's perfection, Hérodiade ferociously forbids her, speaking first, as noted above, of 'crime' and moving from this notion to that of 'sacrilège'. She is violent in her rejection of the human aspects of life:

> Arrête dans ton crime
> Qui refroidit mon sang vers sa source, et réprime
> Ce geste, impiété fameuse: ah! conte moi
> Quel sûr démon te jette en le sinistre emoi,
> Ce baiser, ces parfums offerts et, le dirai-je?
> O mon coeur, cette main encore sacrilège,
> Car tu voulais, je crois, me toucher, sont un jour
> Qui ne finira pas sans malheur sur la tour ...
> O jour qu'Hérodiade avec effroi regarde![69]

This day, which the young princess apprehends with terror, is the one on which John will be beheaded.

The nurse, not unnaturally, asks the girl for whom she is preserving her jealously-guarded virginity:

> et pour qui, dévorée
> D'angoisses, gardez-vous la splendeur ignorée
> Et le mystère vain de votre être?
> HERODIADE: Pour moi ...
> Oui, c'est pour moi, pour moi que je fleuris, déserte![70]

She lists the old gold and precious stones which are hidden from sunlight, and she wants her own beauty to be at one with them, concealed and apart:

J'aime le horreur d'être vierge et je veux
Vivre parmi l'effroi que me font mes cheveux
Pour, le soir, retirée en ma couche, reptile
Inviolé sentir en la chair inutile
Le froid scintillement de ta pâle clarté
Toi qui te meurs, toi qui brûles de chasteté,
Nuit blanche de glaçons et de neige cruelle![71]

Hérodiade will accept only two gestures of attentiveness from her nurse, the first, that the old woman should hold a mirror so that the girl can comb her incomparable hair – she says that she stares at herself as at an idol with her clear, diamond gaze – and, next, that the nurse close the shutters to obliterate the 'azur' which she detests. This detail, the shutting out of the blue sky, places her firmly on the side of Artifice against Life. Much has been written about Mallarmé and 'l'azur' and what it represented for him. He lived and wrote trying to capture or emulate this 'azur', the 'Ideal' towards which he was constantly striving. What he attained in his own estimation was 'l'Ennui', boredom, spleen, mediocrity and he managed at great cost to survive artistically between the two extremes. In this case, however, 'l'azur' represents Life, the sun, the world of the Natural, all of which the princess rejects. The scene with the nurse is brought to a close with Hérodiade's realisation that childhood is over and she is to be separated from its preciousness:

J'attends une chose inconnue
Ou peut-être, ignorant le mystère et vos cris,
Jetez-vous les sanglots suprêmes et meurtris
D'une enfance sentant parmi les rêveries
Se séparer enfin ses froides pierreries.[72]

It is not evident from the poems in the *Oeuvres Complètes* whether Hérodiade has met John the Baptist, the only hint being where, as we have remarked, she claims to be terrified of what that particular day may bring. It is made very apparent from the unfinished manuscripts of *Les Noces d'Hérodiade* that he has looked on her and that she wants his head. I shall reproduce the notes which seem to be concerned with a dance and with the severed head in their original typographical sequence. Their striking eroticism maintains the weight and order of the earlier verse discussed above; these existing fragments are comparable in their

heaviness and portentousness. In the draft of a 'Scène Intermédi-
aire', which was projected to appear directly after the dialogue
with the nurse, there is the suggestion that Hérodiade has seen the
Precursor, has been disturbed by his glance and that the only way
for her to regain her equilibrium is by having him killed. The draft
of the episode is this:

> Le message de traits
> Du fiancé que mal je connaîtrais
> Va pour sa peine
> Dût son ombre marcher le long du corridor
> M'en apporter le chef tranché dans un plat d'or.[73]

The sketch of a solitary dance intimates that she has the head before
her:

> l'ambiguité d'Hé –
> rodiade et de sa
> danse ...
> elle maîtrise cette
> tête révoltée
> qui a voulu
> penser plus haut –
> où s'éteint l'idée
> inouie et [ ] ...[74]

> II
> se penche-t-elle d'un
> côté – de l'autre –
> montrant un
> sein – l'autre

> et surprise
> sans gaze[75]

> et cela fait – sur
> un pied l'autre,
> eux-mêmes
> sur les pieds
> seins

une sorte de danse
effrayante esquisse
– et sur place, sans
bouger
– lieu nul[76]

She kisses the dead lips and in so doing declares that she is no longer the capricious child whom we saw depicted in the dialogue with the nurse.[77]

The second series of notes presents another dance in which she is nearly naked, because, 'le glaive qui trancha ta tête a déchiré mon voile',[78] and she is subsequently portrayed with the severed head on her thighs, the purple blood dripping from it and staining her skin. The verse is again weighty and portentous, but whether we can justifiably comment on its studied hesitations is not sure; these are merely drafts after all:

Ah! qu'importe la mort et les morts
je ne sais[79]

– idée
saigne – sang sur ses cuisses
pourpre des cuisses
et leur royauté.[80]

Finally, at the moment of the setting of the sun, she throws the head out of the open window into a fountain and,

danse un moment
pour elle seule ** – afin d'être
à la fois ici là – et que
rien de cela ne soit arrivé

** pour la première fois
yeux ouverts –[81]

Instead of the familiar trappings of the Bible account we are presented in Mallarmé's 'Hérodiade' with a cold, virginal, fierce young princess surrounded by glass and mirrors, cold metals and precious stones. It has been said of this poem that it is, 'de tout point et absolument le poème de l'absence'[82] and the absence is that of humanity.

Hérodiade is unwilling, in her haughty, guarded purity, to enter the flow of life. Love inspires her only to cruelty: John's glance awakens her nascent sexuality and arouses forces in her own psyche which threaten her self-contained invulnerability. She has to kill in order to win back the equilibrium of her childish days when such impulses in her remained dormant. She, who could walk with lions and survive untouched,[83] is marked by being observed by the prophet and she evades her own part in the encounter by dubbing the offender 'sacrilegious' and by punishing him with death.

The lines from the drafts quoted above reveal another kind of 'absence' at the level of the poetry itself. This is the lack of a vibrant warmth or of any vital energy which is not already transmuted by the heaviness of Mallarmé's verse into stasis. The poet wrestled with this work all his life because he was concerned to portray Beauty – the 'Absolu', as Mallarmé often terms Beauty – and to do so he chose the way of cold but perfect sterility, a depiction as frozen but flawless as a diamond:

> the mystery of Hérodiade's being is fruitless. However, what the nurse does not comprehend is that it is this very gratuitousness which in Hérodiade's eyes gives her being its highest significance and value. Suggested certainly is the poet's principle of the gratuity of Beauty and by extension, Art; particularly when the heroine tersely replies that it is for herself that she exists.[84]

Into this perfect barrenness, the incomplete manuscripts suggest, was projected a dance which is not the familiar one of the performance before Herod. In this version Herod and Herodias are absent so that the girl is impelled to action solely by her own decisions and instincts: the nurse has no influence upon her. Hérodiade's is a solitary dance with only the severed head for spectator and gruesome witness:

> Cette danse, sur la quelle devait probablement se terminer le Mystère des *Noces d'Hérodiade*, symbolise également aux yeux de Mallarmé l'assujettissement réciproque du génie et de son rêve de beauté, qui est la condition de l'oeuvre pure.[85]

In 1870 Théodore de Banville dedicated his poem 'La Danseuse' to Henri Regnault whose painting *Salomé* was exhibited in Paris that year. Banville's stanzas describe the dancer of Regnault and reveal a different kind of heroine from the docile, obedient girl of Heywood or from the narcissistic virgin of Mallarmé; in this instance we discover once more the sadism displayed in Heine's *Atta Troll*, but here the investigation of the depths of the dancer's character plumbs areas untouched by Heine's account. Zagona's analysis of the painting is of use as preamble to Banville's poem:

> Regnault's painting of the dancer was one of the first to interpret the subject in terms of sadistic self-indulgence. Callous and thoroughly sensual, Salome is seated, her dark hair flowing over her smiling face, anxiously awaiting the head of the Baptist. One hand rests arrogantly on a luxuriously draped hip while the other leans on a gleaming gold tray held in readiness for the trophy.[86]

In response to Regnault's portrayal Banville wrote:

> Salomé, déjà près d'accomplir son dessein,
> Sous ses riches paillons et ses robes fleuries
> Songeait, l'oeil enchanté par les orfèvreries
> Du riant coutelas vermeil et du bassin.
>
> Son chevelure éparse et tombant sur son sein,
> La Danseuse au front brun, parmi ses rêveries,
> Regardait le soleil mettre des pierreries
> Dans les caprices d'or au fantastique dessin,
>
> Mêlant la chrysoprase et son fauve incendie
> Au saphir, où le ciel azuré s'irradie,
> Et le sang des rubis aux pleurs du diamant,
>
> Comme c'est votre joie, ô fragiles poupées!
> Car vous avez toujours aimé naivement
> Les joujoux flamboyants et les têtes coupées.[87]

Banville emphasises the wilful irresponsibility of the dancer, an element which will occur again in later versions of the legend by Flaubert and Wilde and which appeared in the earlier Biblical models. This insouciance is accentuated by the grotesque absurdity in the rhyming of 'poupées' and 'coupées' of the last stanza. It is the only true, perfect rhyme of the poem and is shocking in its trenchant finality. The rhymes of the other stanzas are slightly dislocated and produce distorted echoes: 'dessein/bassin/sein/dessin', 'fleuries/

orfèvreries/rêveries/pierreries/s'irradie'. The rhyme scheme seems to be abba abba bbcdcd, though whether it is justified to discern any element of rhyme between 'incendie' and 's'irradie' is open to question. It is a disturbing, disorienting scheme which undermines in its quirkiness the settled richness and calm expectancy of the atmosphere.

The sensuality of this Salome is suggested through the luxury of the fabrics and the precious stones with which her world is ornamented and it is in such surroundings that the decorated bloody sword promises yet another trophy with which to bedeck the palace, that of a severed head. Salome is tranquil because she is simply accomplishing her destiny as mechanically as the doll to which she is likened; she has performed her dance and the consequences follow automatically in obscene sequence. And she does not rebel from her role in the undertaking; she seems to be complete mistress of herself and to take her horrible desires as accepted procedure. As has been suggested, the vital energy of this figure is akin to that of Heine's Herodias, even though Salome's actions in this poem are merely 'songeait', 'rêveries' and 'Regardait'. The implication is that the energy and sensuality are controlled during this brief respite, only to break out anew when the trophy is finally granted.

Banville's next poem on the subject, his 'Hérodiade' of July 1874, depicts a figure more closely related to the princess created by Mallarmé, although the preface is, interestingly, a quotation from *Atta Troll*:

Car elle était vraiment princesse: c'était la reine de Judée, la femme d'Hérode, celle qui a demandé la tête de Jean-Baptiste.[88]

'Hérodiade' appears twelfth in a series of poems about twenty princesses whose beauty has now disappeared from the earth. Before her come Hélène, la Reine de Saba and Cléopâtre and she is followed by Messaline, Marie Stuart and others from history and legend. The wild exuberance of Banville's princess allies her with Heine's Herodias, but her cold contempt for the rest of humanity brings her close to Mallarmé's heroine:

Ses yeux sont transparentes comme l'eau du Jourdain.
Elle a de lourds colliers et des pendants d'oreilles;
Elle est plus douce à voir que le raisin des treilles,
Et la rose des bois a peur de son dédain.

Elle rit et folâtre avec un air badin,
Laissant de sa jeunesse éclater les merveilles.
Sa lèvre est écarlate, et ses dents sont pareilles
Pour la blancheur aux lys orgueilleux du jardin.

Voyez-la, voyez-la venir, la jeune reine!
Un petit page noir tient sa robe qui traine
En flots voluptueux le long du corridor.

Sur ses doigts le rubis, le saphir, l'améthyste
Font resplendir leurs feux charmants: dans un plat d'or
Elle porte le chef sanglant de Jean-Baptiste.[89]

The rhymes are again the slightly distorted ones of 'La Danseuse': 'Jourdain/dédain/badin/jardin' are not true rhymes and they fit the disturbing nature of the poem. For this princess makes us anxious in the description of her which juxtaposes the translucent beauty of her eyes to the more clichéd account of her scarlet lips and teeth as white as lilies. She is a bizarre combination of earthiness and arrogant disdain and we are right to be perplexed because, in a calm, matter-of-fact manner, appears the statement,

> dans un plat d'or
> Elle porte le chef sanglant de Jean-Baptiste

and this is shocking in its impassivity and abruptness. No mention is made here of the dance. In both poems by Banville it is already accomplished and we are simply presented with the performer resting on her laurels, her mission fulfilled. Through the very tenor of his writing, this poet explores the idiosyncrasies of Salome's character and portrays her as amoral and unthinkingly cruel.

There is, however, the hint of an added dimension in Banville's presentation, that of generalisation: in depicting what is after all a conventional study of sensual beauty, this poet suggests, for perhaps the first time in the legend's history, that his heroine's characteristics are common to all women. Salome thus becomes a kind of everywoman who is, by her nature, cruel. And this piece of innuendo will be taken up by writers and artists who follow Banville until it reaches crisis point in some very overtly anti-feminine art and literature.

It might have been anticipated that this new avenue, that of Salome's callous sensuality, would have been further explored by all the versions of the episode that follow from Banville in 1870, but Gustave Flaubert's novella 'Hérodias' eschews that path and adheres faithfully to the Biblical model of the Gospel according to St Mark. In this version the princess is quite different from the heroines of Heine, Mallarmé or Banville who precede her, neither is she the little plotter of Sudermann's later account, nor the rejected lover portrayed by Oscar Wilde. Unlike Heywood's Salome, who is blackmailed into signing John's death warrant and who makes herself responsible for all that ensues, this is an insouciante little girl who has no idea of the import of what she is doing. She is a pawn in her mother's game, never having met Herod until the birthday banquet and having been brought up in Rome, far from Machaerous where his citadel is located. She dances because Herod is celebrating and Herodias has told her to, and that is all that she knows. Salome is not aware of how her dancing is affecting the tetrarch, her mother's husband, but Herodias has correctly predicted what influence her daughter will have on the ageing monarch:

> Elle avait fait instruire ... Salomé sa fille, que le Tétrarche aimerait; et l'idée était bonne.[90]

This detail, the mother's premeditation, derives directly from the Bible account.

Flaubert's Salome enters the feasting room unannounced, unexpected and unknown: Herod has only glimpsed her twice before and had no notion of his stepdaughter's existence in his palace. The dance is described in a very detailed manner since it is the culmination of the narrative. The writer lovingly portrays her costume in all its delicacy:

> Sous un voile bleuâtre lui cachant la poitrine et la tête, on distinguait les arcs de ses yeux, les calcédoines de ses oreilles, la blancheur de sa peau. Un carré de soie gorge-pigeon, en couvrant les épaules, tenait aux reins par une ceinture d'orfèvrerie. Ses caleçons noirs étaient semés de mandragores, et d'une manière indolente elle faisait claquer de petites pantoufles en duvet de colibri.[91]

From the moment that Salome, quite simply and without warning or introduction, 'se mit à danser',[92] Flaubert depicts her performance as an erotic dance, and the maturity of her gestures is in contradistinction to the dancer's youth and naïveté. She seems to call to someone who is ever fleeing before her; she sighs languidly as if in the embrace of a god; her eyes are half-closed in ecstasy; she dances, unwittingly, like an Indian princess who dances the unsatisfied love of her idols:

> Ses attitudes exprimaient des soupirs, et toute sa personne une telle langueur qu'on ne savait pas si elle pleurait un dieu, ou se mourait dans sa caresse. Les paupières entre-closes, elle se tordait la taille, balançait son ventre avec des ondulations de houle, faisait trembler ses deux seins, et son visage demeurait immobile, et ses pieds n'arrêtaient pas ... Puis ce fut l'emportement de l'amour qui veut être assouvi. Elle dansa comme les prêtresses des Indes, comme les Nubiennes des cataractes, comme les bacchantes de Lydie. Elle se renversait de tous les côtés, pareille à une fleur que la tempête agite.[93]

The contrast between the biddable young girl doing her best to please and the sensuality of her dance is telling. As child–woman she has a power as murderously innocent as the sea, for Herod, in a trance of desire, offers her half his kingdom. Salome, remembering her mother's tutelage, goes to Herodias to be further instructed and on her return makes her request. At first, so great is her lack of interest and complicity in all the momentous events in which she is entangled that she forgets the name of the man whose death she is demanding:

> en zézayant un peu, [elle] prononça ces mots d'un air enfantin:
> – Je veux que tu me donnes dans un plat, la tête ...
> Elle avait oublié le nom, mais reprit en souriant:
> – La tête de Iaokanann![94]

Flaubert follows St Mark once more in portraying Herod's great reluctance in granting her wish,

> For Herod feared John, knowing that he was a just man and an holy, and observed him; and when he heard him, he did many things and heard him gladly.[95]

None the less, as in the Bible, he feels constrained by his oath and the number of witnesses present and he gives the order for the execution. Here, once the severed head has been displayed to the guests by the executioner, the banqueting chamber is vacated and Antipas remains alone, tears streaming down his cheeks, 'les mains contre ses tempes, et regardant toujours la tête coupée ...'[96] Meanwhile Salome is indifferent to the outcome of her actions: in Flaubert's version there is no love relationship between her and the prophet, nor is she, as elsewhere, grief-stricken by what she has done. As such, as total instrument of her mother's will, she is as terrifying as the shadowy damsel of the Gospel accounts and as indomitable, because she is too young to be prepared to care.

Flaubert presents the fullest description of the dance of all the forms of the story considered here, a portrayal unsurpassed by anything written before or after. His novella inspired two librettists, Paul Milliet and Henri Grémont in their opera *Hérodiade* with music by Massenet, first produced in 1881, just four years after Flaubert's work. In this instance the name 'Hérodiade' refers to Herodias, not to Salome and surprisingly absent in this case is the dance before Herod, although four ballets are performed.

The libretto opens with Salome in distress searching for a mother whom she has never met:

> Sans cesse, je cherche ma mère! ...
> Une voix me criait: Espère,
> Cours à Sion! ... – Je ne l'ai pas trouvée, hélas!
> Et je reste seule ici-bas.[97]

She knows and loves John the Baptist and her love is eventually returned:

> Le prophète est ici! ... C'est vers lui que je vais! ...
> Il est doux, il est bon; sa parole est sereine,
> Il parle, tout se tait ...[98]

Neither Herod nor Hérodiade is any more knowledgeable about Salome's identity than is the girl herself, but Herod has seen her in Jerusalem and his desire has been aroused:

> Salomé, Salomé! C'est ma voix qui t'implore!
> Une ivresse ineffable illumine mes cieux!
> Mon rayon de soleil c'est l'éclat de tes yeux!
> C'est toi, toi que j'attends! Ah! reviens, je t'adore![99]

Hérodiade has been insulted by John the Baptist; he has labelled her 'Jezebel' and cast doubt over the legitimacy of her marriage to Herod. She demands that her husband avenge her, insisting, 'C'est sa tête que je réclame!'[100] and, thus far, we recognise details which tally with the traditional narrative and others which differ from it. The final scene of the first act is quite innovatory, however, since Salome falls down before John and, embracing his knees, swears eternal love to him:

> Loins de toi je souffrais et me voilà guérie!
> Dans ton regard est ma patrie;
> Mon visage est baigné de larmes, et mon coeur
> Tressaille de bonheur![101]

John endeavours to repulse his ardent admirer, explaining that, while Salome, still a child, finds herself in the 'season of love and kisses and fearless vows', his destiny is quite different. The girl persists,

> Non, l'amour n'est pas un blasphème
> Et c'est ton amour que je veux!
> Qu'à tes genoux, ô toi que j'aime,
> S'épande l'or de mes cheveux![102]

We note with interest that this version of Salome follows that of Mallarmé in breaking with tradition by insisting on her hair being blonde; she is not the conventional dark Semitic princess.

The second act opens with one of the ballets performed by slaves before Herod while he is still yearning for Salome. A love philtre is administered to him which will make him dream of her. The atmosphere of luxurious perversity is indebted to Flaubert's portrayal of the corrupt ambience of Herod's palace, as is the description of the political events which provide the context of the Salome episode, since, as the king is obsessed with purely personal matters, outside his court his people are shouting for the Messiah and his surest allies have just surrendered to the Romans. A revolt is anticipated among Herod's subjects who are demanding independence from Rome and the arrival of Vitellius and his army in Jerusalem is announced. The figure of the Roman leader is also an imitation of Flaubert. John, revered by the people, enters Herod's sanctuary and is accompanied by Salome whom the tetrarch recognises as the object of his passion. When Hérodiade realises that her husband desires this girl she instantly embarks on a scheme of jealous plotting, ironically, perhaps tragically, ignorant that Salome is her own daughter:

> Il connaît cette enfant! Il pâlit à sa vue!
> D'où vient elle?[103]

She consults Phanuel, the Essenian first encountered in Flaubert's version of events and asks him to interpret from the stars the future of the rival who threatens to supplant her in Herod's affections, merely to have it revealed that Hérodiade's own constellation is covered with blood. To her delight the queen takes this sign to mean that her scheme of vengeance over John the Baptist will be realised. Just as Phanuel is reminding her that she is a mother as well as being woman and wife, Hérodiade glimpses Salome entering the temple and she expresses her intention also to wreak revenge on the child. With dramatic irony, since Hérodiade does not know her own daughter, Phanuel exclaims:

> Reine impitoyable et fatale!...
> Et tu disais que tu l'aimais!...
> Va ! tu n'es qu'une femme ... une mère jamais![104]

Salome attempts to join John who has been imprisoned: she announces to the executioner that should the prophet be put to death she will share his fate. Herod initially decides to spare his captive, however, in order to use him as part of a plot against the invading Romans. On meeting Salome the king pledges his love to her anew, believing her to be one of his own slaves.

It will by now be evident that, unlike its predecessors, this libretto by Milliet and Grémont can make no claim to being high art. The verse is mechanical and the rhymes facile: Herod's wooing of Salome is no exception; it verges on doggerel:

> Faveur suprême
> Du ciel en ce jour!
> Esclave, je t'aime
> Et veux ton amour!
> ... Vois quelle aurore
> S'ouvre devant toi!

C'est moi qui t'implore
Et je suis le roi.[105]

It can only be hoped that Massenet's music remedied the flagrant
weaknesses of the libretto. As for the melodramatic vagaries of the
imperfect plot, when Herod discovers that Salome's love is not for
himself but for John, he resolves to have them both put to death.

A third ballet – a 'Danse sacrée' – is performed before the High
Priest and his acolytes who are demanding the death of John as a
rebel and a false prophet. The priests are compelling Herod to deal
with the problem of the Baptist and Vitellius, too, wants a judgement
on the man who has been stirring up the people by his preaching:

Achève donc ton oeuvre en condamnant un homme
Qui prêche la discorde et méconnaît ta loi:
Il pervertit le peuple et des Juifs se dit roi ...
Rends la paix au royaume en frappant cet impie!...[106]

The crowd, swayed by the priests, also calls for John's death; they
want to crucify 'ce faux Messie'[107] and Hérodiade clamours along
with them, 'A mort! mort!...Mort à l'impie!...'[108] Yet, when Herod
orders the execution of both John and Salome, Hérodiade discovers
a strange feeling of tenderness in her heart for the girl, 'Quelle
étrange pitié saisit mon âme!...'[109] but none the less insists that John
be led to torture.

In common with more customary versions, Herod's birthday is also
celebrated here, but by the presentation of a ballet. Salome is dragged
in from the dungeon shared with John and begs both Herod and
Hérodiade for his life. She does not dance before the king, he swears
no oath, nor does the queen instruct Salome to demand John's head;
this libretto parts company considerably with tradition. The girl does
almost succeed in softening Hérodiade, especially through her emotional plea which bears a significance of which she is unaware:

O reine, vois mes larmes!
Une femme comprend de pareilles alarmes!...
Pitié! si tu fus mère![110]

but just at the moment of her succumbing to Salome's supplications,
the executioner appears with a blood-stained sword. In despair the
girl pulls a dagger from her belt and rushes at Hérodiade,

Il est mort de ta main...
Tu mourras donc aussi!... Tu m'implores en vain![111]

The queen suddenly recognises her own daughter, 'Pitié! Je suis ta mère',[112] and Salome, horrified at this disclosure, turns the dagger on herself:

Ah! reine détestée,
S'il est vrai que tes flancs odieux m'aient portée,
Tiens! reprends ton sang et ma vie. (*Elle se frappe.*)[113]

This version is unique in avoiding the encounter of either Hérodiade or Salome with the severed head, in making John reciprocate the love which Salome bears him, in failing to depict Salome's dance. It will be evident that the plot is a melodramatic conglomerate in which only the more coherent details owe their inception to an imitation of Flaubert: the tone of the entirety, however, reveals unfortunately no debt to the French novelist, nor does the general looseness of the writing. The plot, in all its convolutions, perhaps recalls more closely the efforts of the American, J. C. Heywood, especially in its profound insistence on Salome's innocence and helplessness amid the horror of the events which surround her.

Jean Lorrain's poems in his anthology *La Forêt Bleue* of 1883 hark back to Heine in that they portray once more a hunt of the damned in which heroines from antiquity ride; the whole displays a deep indebtedness to *Atta Troll*. Lorrain himself, however, dedicated his poems 'Diane', 'Hérodiade' and 'Dame Habonde' from the collection 'Le Pays des Fées' to Théodore de Banville and it is clear that he was also inspired by the latter's list of the fabulous princesses of old. In his version of 'Hérodiade' Lorrain emphasises the punishment meted out to her once the dreadful beheading has taken place. The wild hunt is termed the 'Hérodiade hunt' and Lorrain stresses his heroine's Semitic roots: 'Chrétiens, voici la chasse Hérodiade',[114] while her torment takes the form of being forced to wander as a spectre through the sky above Israel:

Au fauve appel des cors, au bruit rageur des cistres
La grande Hérodiade et ses nymphes sinistres
Sur des balais fourbus chevauchent en plein ciel.

Des démons accrochés aux crins de leurs cavales,
Elles vont, ventre à terre, au dessus d'Israël
Et la haine implacable, éclair froid et cruel,
Luit dans leurs grands yeux morts, emplis de larmes pâles.[115]

Lorrain does not achieve the focussed precision attained in the studies by Heine and Banville, nor does he probe the characters of his heroines and explain their motivation except to portray the implacable hatred which spurs the spectres on. In a later poem, however, which Lorrain dedicated to Gustave Flaubert, from a collection called 'Lunaires', he discloses a hint of information which shocks in the same manner as Banville's matter-of-fact conclusion to his own 'Hérodiade' discussed above. There, the latter, after a detailed, if conventionalised, portrait of his heroine, delivered the final blow almost as an afterthought: 'dans un plat d'or / Elle porte le chef sanglant de Jean-Baptiste'. Lorrain, his successor, subsequent to a vignette of an unnamed woman, closes on a shock of recognition:

Dans un grand vase d'Hébron,
L'oeil rêveur et satanique,
Une femme sans tunique
Fait bouillir l'eau du Cédron,

Et dans l'ombre du chaudron
Monte en reflets d'améthyste
Le sang de Saint Jean Baptiste.[116]

His technique is quite evidently similar to that of Banville: also here we discover the distorted rhyme effected by juxtaposing 'Hébron' and 'Cédron' with a parallel which overspills into the next stanza, that of 'chaudron'. This unease prepares emotionally if not logically for the gruesome surprise, that the anonymous woman must indeed be Hérodiade because she is concocting a potion which contains John's blood.

　　Lorrain nowhere dwells on the details of the legend and the background story; he simply portrays a heroine who is deserving of the punishment which she is undergoing. While acknowledging his debts both to Heine and Banville, he creates a deliberately hazy and impressionistic picture of a criminal which lacks the sensuality and colour and, most significantly, the admiration felt by the two previous exponents of the theme. Lorrain's work remains essentially derivative, however and I am unable to discern any direct influence on his successors.

Let us now turn to the golden book of Decadence, J. K. Huysmans's *A Rebours*, (*Against Nature*), of 1884, in which he discusses two paintings by Gustave Moreau, *Salomé*, an oil, and *L'Apparition*, a watercolour, both of which were exhibited at the Spring Salon in Paris in 1876. Huysmans's protagonist is des Esseintes, a model of the Decadence, who wants to furnish his house with every kind of luxury that artifice can provide; books, paintings, jewels, perfumes and in his search for correctly 'décadent' pictures he requires,

> pour la délectation de son esprit et la joie de ses yeux, quelques oeuvres suggestives le jetant dans un monde inconnu, lui dévoilant les traces de nouvelles conjectures, lui ébranlant le système nerveux par d'érudites hystéries, par des cauchemars compliqués, par des visions nonchalantes et atroces.
>
> Entre tous, un artiste existait dont le talent le ravissait en de longs transports, Gustave Moreau.[117]

These two paintings answer his needs for 'une peinture subtile, exquise, baignant dans un rêve ancien, dans une corruption antique, loin de nos moeurs, loin de nos jours'[118] and they are analysed lovingly in a way which eschews objectivity and presents the reader with the mental impressions of des Esseintes himself as he gazes at them.

The first oil painting depicts Salome dancing before an old, yellow and withered Herod and she is portrayed frozen forever in her provocative stance. Des Esseintes's enjoyment of it depends upon its perversity:

> Dans l'odeur perverse des parfums, dans l'atmosphère surchauffée de cette église, Salomé, le bras gauche étendu, en un geste de commandement, le bras droit replié, tenant à la hauteur du visage, un grand lotus, s'avance lentement sur les pointes, aux accords d'une guitare dont une femme accroupie pince les cordes.[119]

The description of her dance recalls that of Flaubert in its attention to detail, but, because the figure is of course static, des Esseintes's account is in effect a mere inventory of arrested movement; all of her actions are in fact imagined by him. His narrative, however, is so energetic that it succeeds in investing the girl's jewels and ornaments with vitality:

La face recueillie, solonnelle, presque auguste, elle commence la lubrique danse qui doit réveiller les sens assoupis du vieil Hérode; ses seins ondulent et au frottement de ses colliers qui tourbillonnent, leurs bouts se dressent; sur la moiteur de sa peau les diamants, attachés, scintillent; ses bracelets, ses ceintures, ses bagues, crachent des étincelles; sur sa robe triomphale, couturée de perles, ramagée d'argent, lamée d'or, la cuirasse des orfèvreries dont chaque maille est une pierre, entre en combustion, croise des serpenteaux de feu, grouille sur la chair mate, sur la peau rose thé, ainsi que des insectes splendides aux élytres éblouissants, marbrés de carmin, ponctués de jaune aurore, diaprés de bleu d'acier, tigrés de vert paon.[120]

Clearly the immobility of the portrait is undercut by the aggressive vividness of the verbs and participles; 'tourbillonnent', 'scintillent', 'crachent', 'croise', 'grouille', all convey an impression of activity as if the gems are a living, burning fire. The description is deliberately overwrought and excessive in order to reflect the mental condition of its fascinated onlooker.

Salome dances concentratedly, like a somnambulist, her eyes fixed in front of her but seeing nothing. And this version of the girl which haunts artists and poets has obsessed des Esseintes for years. For him nothing in the Bible story suggests 'les charmes délirants, ... les actives dépravations de la danseuse';[121] she is only accessible,

aux cervelles ébranlées, comme rendues visionnaires par la névrose ... incompréhensible pour tous les écrivains qui n'ont jamais pu rendre l'inquiétante exaltation de la danseuse, la grandeur raffinée de l'assassine.[122]

Nowhere previously has Salome been labelled 'assassine' and it is simple to perceive that this account of the dancer is very different from those which have preceded it. She would not be out of place in Baudelaire's anthology of anti-feminist portraits, *Les Fleurs du Mal*, particularly when des Esseintes plunges into excess in seeing her as the goddess of Decadence:

la déité symbolique de l'indestructible Luxure, la déesse de l'immortelle Hystérie, la Beauté maudite ... la Bête monstrueuse, indifférente, irresponsable, insensible, empoisonnant ... tout ce qui l'approche, tout ce qui la voit, tout ce qu'elle touche.[123]

The poisonousness and depravity of this rendering of the girl are not to be found in Flaubert, where she is powerful and irresponsible, but not perverse. The essence of Mallarmé's creation is cold purity and Banville's princess is shocking as she holds her golden dish and its gory contents, but curiously uncorrupt. Because des Esseintes is bewitched by a painting and nothing there depicted can be changed, Huysmans's prose adopts an element of implacability, of inexorability, which serves to accentuate the cruel resolution of the dancer. The various interpretations of Salome seem to move in a crescendo presenting a study of an increasing depravity.

All of this is disconcerting enough for the reader, but des Esseintes goes on to claim that the second picture, *L'Apparition*, is more terrifying still:

> Tel que le vieux roi, des Esseintes demeurait écrasé, anéanti, pris de vertige, devant cette danseuse, moins majestueuse, moins hautaine, mais plus troublante que la Salomé du tableau à l'huile.[124]

In this picture Salome is standing, transfixed, still ornamented for her dance, in the palace of Herod. The murder is accomplished and the executioner waits impassively for further orders, his hands on the pommel of his long, blood-stained sword. Herod and Herodias sit seemingly immobile on their thrones: the spectacle which, according to des Esseintes, is terrifying the girl is invisible to them. The severed head of John has risen from the charger on which it was carried from the prison and is gazing down at Salome with an expression of supreme, otherworldly forgiveness. Des Esseintes's reading of the picture is that the dancer is trying to fend off the vision with her outstretched left arm while her right hand clutches convulsively at the heavy necklace which seems to be choking her. I accept this interpretation because her stance appears to be one of pure dread: the angle of her head suggests to me that she is incapable of raising it to meet the prophet's steady but compassionate gaze. But the painting has been decoded differently by, for example, Bram Dijkstra,[125] an American critic to whose work on sexual politics and *fin-de-siècle* art I shall refer below. He claims that Salome is reaching out to the head in ecstatic hunger. The details of the painting seem, however, to give such a reading the lie. Salome is transfixed, still poised on the points of her toes from her dance and her body too, now rigid in terror, suggests a choreographed pose. A mosaic of light surrounds the bleeding head and this is in turn encircled by an aureole which illuminates all the jewels encrusting Salome's body. These ornaments now appear extraneous; they are embossed growths on her nakedness. The saintly tenderness of the prophet's expression throws the girl's depravity into sharp relief. Des Esseintes perceives her as essentially and stereotypically *fin-de-siècle*; she is hysterical, neurotic, ardent in her cruelty and quite as corrupt as her mother, Herodias. And yet in this study she is vanquished by the mercy in John's dead face and all trace of the goddess of the first oil painting has left her:

> Dans l'insensible et impitoyable statue, dans l'innocente et dangereuse idole, l'érotisme, la terreur de l'être humain s'étaient fait jour; le grand lotus avait disparu, la déesse s'était évanouie; un effroyable cauchemar étranglait maintenant l'histrionne, extasiée par le tournoiement de la danse, la courtisane, pétrifiée, hypnotisée par l'épouvante.[126]

This is the first time that Salome has been called 'courtisane' and we here perceive that Huysmans presents a goddess of Decadence, a debauched *femme fatale*. This creation is quite aware of what she has done and of the price; out of her own poisonousness she has conceived the ghastly vision of the severed head which haunts her alone. She is also portrayed as a statue, an idol and as such she is totally and completely the figure of Artifice,

> une grande fleur vénérienne, poussée dans des couches sacrilèges, élevée dans des serres impies.[127]

All Naturalness has been extracted from her and what remains is unforgettably perplexing, the emblem of an aesthetic movement summed up in all its brilliance, luxury and perversity.

It is with some relief that we turn from this *tour-de-force* by Huysmans to Laforgue's 'Salomé' of 1887 which is a parody. Jules Laforgue, who died at the age of twenty-seven, directed his iconoclasm against the Salomes of Mallarmé, Flaubert and Huysmans and we may cling to the fact that he felt the need to do so as a small sign of health in a prevailing mood of widely generalised and violent anti-feminism. His princess, Herod's daughter, not his stepdaughter, instead of dancing, strikes a little black lyre and chants philosophy – principally, anachronistically, that of Hartmann on the manner in which the Unconscious becomes Conscious. There is no mention of Herodias and in this instance John, a bespectacled scholar, has been jailed for distributing political pamphlets. Herod's title here is 'Tétrarche Emeraude-Archetypas' and he rules over 'les Iles Blanches Esotériques' which are all artifice and an obvious attack on Mallarmé's preciosity. As we shall see, Flaubert's copious mass of detail is parodied in Laforgue's depiction of the banqueting hall and the feast in weighty encumbrances of description. The whole novella is one long literary joke in which Laforgue, through his self-consciously ironic and knowing tone, also satirises his own pretentiousness as a writer. He too had striven after Absolutes and been attracted to the very tenets which Mallarmé held so dear. It is therefore with a touch of self-mockery that he dubs his little princess 'la petite Immaculée-Conception' and portrays her as an intellectual.

As in Flaubert's 'Hérodias', this short story too opens with a surveying of the country surrounding Herod's citadel. And this tetrarch is paid a similar official visit, this time from two princes of the North, the erstwhile home of the imprisoned John the Baptist. They show no sympathy for their compatriot, however and, visiting him in his dungeon, are content to leave him to his fate with no intercession on their part. They even rain anachronistic curses upon his head:

> Ah! ah! te voilà, idéalogue, écrivassier, conscrit réformé, bâtard de Jean-Jacques Rousseau. C'est ici que tu es venue te faire pendre, folliculaire déclassé! Bon débarras.[128]

The tone of the story is equally ironic, especially where Laforgue satirises his own literary heritage and personal writing skills within it:

> Devant lui la mer, la mer, toujours nouvelle et respectable, la Mer puisqu'il n'y a pas d'autre nom pour la nommer[129]

and the use of the capital letter is a sly thrust against his Symbolist predecessors, particularly against Mallarmé, whose tendency was always to give a more profound degree of abstraction to conceptions and objects through employing capitals as a partially-concealed code to his fellow initiates in the mysteries.

The tetrarch's thoughts are all of John, 'un monsieur de génie après tout',[130] and the monarch has so far refrained from having the prophet put to death because of the pleas for mercy from his daughter, Salome:

> Heureux encore! et cela grâce aux inexplicables intercessions de sa fille Salomé, de n'avoir pas dérangé le bourreau de sa traditionnelle sinécure honoraire, en l'envoyant vers Iaokanaan avec le Kriss sacré![131]

John has not been jailed for condemning Herodias as an adulteress; he is a political rebel in his own country publically accused of sedition. Herod has put him in prison for stirring up the people with his printed matter and for his own safety, because the crowd finally turned on him and threatened to stone him to death. This portrait of John is of a feeble, inept and fatalistic scholar.

It is evident that Laforgue's version of the Salome theme is very different from, but dependent upon, accounts which preceded it. He presents the preparation for the feast in a manner which directly echoes and parodies Flaubert: of the projected banquet we are informed:

> la table fut à peindre, dans l'arrangement léger, parmi les cristaux, de ses quelques artichauts callipyges nageant en des gousses de fer hérissées et à charnières, asperges sur claies de jonc roses, anguilles gris-perle, gâteaux de dattes, gammes de compotes, divers vins doux.[132]

This description is even more precious than that on which it is based and the satire derives from the utter impossibility of the adjectives: 'callipyges', 'hérissées et à charnières', all push the account towards the esoteric, while the inventory-like list recalls unmistakably Flaubert. When Laforgue thus dabbles in ridicule of his masters, nobody is exempt from his thrusts.

As the tetrarch contemplates the activity around him he meditates on the twenty peaceful years of his reign and on his daughter; she is obviously intended to remind the reader of Mallarmé's fiercely aloof virgin:

> Et puis Salomé lui restait, qui ne voulait pas entendre parler des douceurs de l'hymen, la chère enfant![133]

The girl enters the narrative in a manner which is familiar to the reader of Flaubert: as the princes of the North are conducted around the palace they catch a glimpse of her retreating to her own apartments. Thus did Flaubert's Herod distinguish from a distance Salome's arms and the nape of her neck and the sight disturbed him. The princes glance momentarily at her once again as she disappears among the corridors of the Hanging Park and she is seen briefly near John's prison. Each time she is described thus:

> une jeune forme hermétiquement emmousselinée d'arachnéenne jonquille à pois noirs ...[134]

Both palace and princess are all artifice: even the swans wear 'boucles d'oreilles vraiment trop lourdes pour leurs cous fuselés'.[135] Where, in Mallarmé's poem, Hérodiade is ornamented with heavy necklaces, here it is the swans which are similarly bedecked – birds so beloved of the older poet as symbols of purity, natural grace and transience.

The entertainment for the tetrarch's banquet includes three clowns who represent the Idea, the Will and the Unconscious. Laforgue's passion for philosophy is here manifested since he introduces, satirically, the ideas of Schopenhauer and Hartmann, particularly the latter's notion of Consciousness, a state which cannot be expected in the immediate future because the evolution of the Unconscious is a very slow process.[136] Such concepts are life-blood to the tetrarch; his sole real interest is philosophy and when Salome arrives at the feast she does not woo him by dancing but by her chanted discussion of abstractions and in her treatise she shows herself to be learned beyond her years. It is surely significant that in Laforgue's version the sensuality and physicality of a portrayal of a dance is replaced by a show of intellectual prowess and metaphysical speculation: this is what Herod finds sexually stimulating and exciting. Laforgue's parody is perhaps making a statement about an increasingly complex and subtle source of arousal as opposed to the banal and flagrant attractions of dances and shed veils and pyrotechnics of the body. In doing this he may approach an appreciation of the attributes of the 'New Woman'. While he does indeed also dwell on the visible charms of the young girl, as we shall discover, Laforgue interestingly demonstrates that her true power over her father lies in her mental capacities and she is very well aware of this.

As does Flaubert's princess, this one too enters the chamber unannounced and unexpected:

Elle entre, descendant l'escalier, raide dans son fourreau de mous-
seline; d'une main elle faisait signe qu'on se recouchât; une petite
lyre noire pendait à son poignet; elle détache au bout des doigts
un baiser vers son père.[137]

The description of her dress and allure recalls both Flaubert and
Huysmans; it is equally detailed and the narrative is even more
dense than theirs. Laforgue deliberately punctuates the account in a
manner which makes for accumulation of fact and subsequent
breathlessness:

Hermétiquement emmousselinée d'une arachnéenne jonquille à
pois noirs qui, s'agrafant ça et là de fibules diverses, laissait les
bras à leur angélique nudité, formait entre les deux soupçons de
seins aux amandes piquées d'un oeillet, une écharpe brodée de
ses dix-huit ans et, s'attachant un peu plus haut que l'adorable
fossette ombilicale en une ceinture de bouillonnés d'un jaune
intense et jaloux, s'adombrait d'inviolable au bassin dans
l'étreinte des hanches maigres, et venait s'arrêter aux chevilles,
pour remonter par derrière en deux écharpes flottant écartées,
rattachées enfin aux brassières de nacre de la roue de paon nain
en fond changeant, azur, moire, émeraude, or, halo à sa candide
tête supérieure ...[138]

The eroticism penetrates through the mass of information about costume and jewellery and it is quite evident whom Laforgue has
adopted as his literary mentors. His manifest debt does not prevent
him from subtly satirising the high solemnity with which those
masters penned their versions of this scene and he proves himself
an apt, if ironical, pupil.

Her father leans forward, pupils dilated, longing to catch every
gesture, every word uttered. She satisfies his desire by striking
her little black lyre and chanting her improvisations on the theme
of the Void, the 'Vie latente',[139] which is Hartmann's Consciousness, on a statement of the development of the Unconscious into
the Conscious. The joke derives from the total seriousness with
which the young girl serves up digested and half-digested philosophies and aesthetic theories and in so doing inflames her
father, king of the Esoteric Islands. For her, love is simply a
mania for not wanting to die,[140] the active Essential loves itself
dynamically, more or less at its pleasure[141] and touches on the

characteristics of the Great Creative Virtue.[142] As a result of the sensuality of her intellectual games the tetrarch is left moaning for more. Following the pattern of other versions, here too he makes an oath:

> – Oh! continue, continue, dis tout ce que tu sais! ... ma parole tétrarchique! tu auras tout ce que tu voudras, l'Université, mon Sceau, le culte des Neiges? Inocule-nous ta grâce d'Immaculée-Conception.[143]

Thus pressed to continue, she takes up again her treatise of abstractions. Here is the typical tenor of the prose:

> C'est l'état pur, vous dis-je! O sectaires de la conscience, pourquoi vous étiqueter individus, c'est-à-dire indivisibles? Soufflez sur les chardons de ces sciences dans le Levant de mes Septentrions! ... Plongeons donc, et dès ce soir, dans l'harmonieuse mansuétude des moralités préetalies; flottons aux dérives, le ventre florissant égaré à l'air; dans le parfum des gaspillages et des hécatombes nécessaires; vers le là-bas où l'on n'entendra plus battre son coeur ni le pouls de la conscience.[144]

It is at this point in her abstruse incantation that her Unconscious has slowly ripened into Consciousness and she makes her abrupt and unanticipated demand for John's head. Now she brings her exposition to a close, breaks the lyre over her knee and states in a hard, matter-of-fact voice:

> – Et maintenant, mon père, je désirerais que vous me fassiez monter chez moi, en un plat quelconque, la tête de Iaokanann. C'est dit. Je monte l'attendre.[145]

Herod tries briefly to dissuade her but, seeing that his guests, who include the princes of the North, show no signs of remonstrating, he simply tosses his seal to the Administrator of Death as signal to perform the beheading. In this account there is no Herodias to drive the girl on out of her own hatred of the prophet and his insults; Herod here is no anguished monarch trying to avoid a killing which fills him with horror. The final words of this section of the narrative pay ironical tribute to Flaubert in echoing the impassive ending of his novella:

Déjà les convives se dispersaient, causant d'autre chose, vers le bain du soir.[146]

And yet there is a little more in Laforgue's account: we still have to witness what the princess will do with her trophy and Part Four leads us into the observatory to partake in a ritual conceived and performed by Salome herself, a ceremony modelled on Mallarmé's version of events. It is a splendidly starry night and the girl, in order to mirror the sky, has covered her hair and body with diamonds. The head of John reposes on a cushion beside her:

la tête de Jean (comme jadis celle d'Orphée) brillait, enduite de phosphore, lavée, fardée, frisée, faisant rictus à ces vingt-quatre millions d'astres.[147]

She has made frenzied attempts to revive the head by caressing it and exposing herself naked before it; she does not, however, dance. Having failed in her endeavours, she gently places the opal of Orion in John's dead mouth like 'une hostie' and carefully kisses him. We recognise from preceding accounts the sadism which so often plays its part in Decadent literature, but despite such actions, Laforgue's Salome is never presented as corrupt or perverse; she is too dignifiedly amoral to be so. She placidly goes on performing the next act in a ritualistic sequence of events of her own devising.

Like her predecessor in Mallarmé, she takes the perfumed head in her hands and tosses it over the parapet into the sea. In a typically Decadent preoccupation with aesthetics at the expense of humanity or morality, she comments on the pleasing 'noble parabole'[148] of its descent. But even such an intellectual heroine is not exempt from human error; she seriously miscalculates her swing and she tumbles over the parapet and ricochets from cliff to cliff, yelping as the diamonds with which she adorned herself pierce her flesh. Laforgue remarks on this 'cri enfin humain'[149] as the sole note of naturalness in the aloof coldness and mystery of this parody of Mallarmé's princess. Laforgue's laconic concluding notes about his creation are typically tongue-in-cheek; he makes a final intrusion into his narrative in an attempt to sum up his Salome, with necessarily inadequate results. It is as though he has thrown up his hands in despair at ever comprehending either his own protagonist or those whom she resembles. In pretending that a successful explanation of her behaviour would be beyond his powers, Laforgue is once again satirising his own pretensions as a writer and laughing at himself for having been attracted to *Symbolisme-Décadence*:

> Ainsi connut le trépas, Salomé, du moins celle des Iles Blanches Esotériques; moins victime des hasards illettrés que d'avoir voulu vivre dans le factice et non à la bonne franquette, à l'instar de chacun de nous.[150]

As we see, he blames it all on Artifice.

What is interesting about this parody, as well as the obviously significant fact that it was one, is that 1886, one year before the posthumous publication of *Moralités Légendaires*, the collection of short stories in which 'Salomé' appears, saw the foundation of the movement *la Décadence* by Leo d'Orfer and René Ghil and the printing of Moréas' manifesto of Decadence in the 18 September supplement of *Figaro*.[151] Laforgue was, typically, already criticising a movement and exposing its absurdities before it had ever become fully established: he had in his art and life already probed its ultimate conclusions in his own personal search for Absolutes and the Ideal and had found them wanting. Hence, the satire, also self-directed, in his 'Salomé'.

Oscar Wilde's *Salomé*, published in 1893, is perhaps the best known of the various versions of the legend because it attracted so much publicity in its own time and has continued to do so since. Initially it too was taken quite seriously to be a parody, that of Maeterlinck's curiously child-like and repetitive style, all short sentences and liquid cadences. Wilde was not being consciously ironic, however; his acknowledged model of the prose was the incantatory Song of Solomon and the echoes of the Biblical lyricism and imagery are insistent. There is controversy over its inception – whether it was first written in English or French, where it was written and whose translation was retained. Wilde himself claimed that its first version was in French, begun in 1891 and translated into English by Lord Alfred Douglas. Wilde modified this translation but still attributed the work to Douglas, much to the latter's resentment.[152]

There were huge and notorious problems over the production of the play as it was refused a licence in England by the Lord Chamberlain, censored, as was standard practice at that period, because Biblical characters could not be portrayed on stage. It was first performed in Paris at the Théâtre Libre on 12 February 1896, by

Lugné-Poë when Wilde was in prison in Reading: this was the only performance that he knew of in his lifetime. *Salomé* had great success in Germany where it was produced in 1901; in Berlin it played for two hundred nights. Eventually the work was privately staged in English by the New Stage Club in May 1905 at the Bijou Theatre, Archer Street, under the direction of Yeats's friend Florence Farr and a second private performance was given on 10 June 1906, by the Literary Theatre Society. Charles Ricketts designed the setting and costumes but the production met with press refusals to review it or to reproduce photos. A licence to perform the play in England was not granted until 1931 and the first public performance after the ban was lifted was at the Festival Theatre, Cambridge, on 23–28 November. Constant Lambert composed the music and Ninette de Valois was responsible for the choreography. Yeats was also involved with these figures prominent in the contemporary theatre: Ricketts designed costumes for his *The King's Threshold* and the poet had asked de Valois in 1927 when she was working with her cousin, Terence Gray, and his productions at Cambridge, whether she would set up a ballet school at the Abbey Theatre for the choreography of Yeats's own dance plays. De Valois also danced the part of the Queen in Yeats's *The King of the Great Clock Tower* in 1935.

The popularity of Wilde's *Salomé* in Germany was made much of, to its detriment, by Noel Pemberton-Billing in a celebrated court case of 1918. Pemberton-Billing, a Member of Parliament, had accused the Canadian music-hall dancer, Maud Allan, who was to play the part of Salome and J. T. Grein, founder and Literary Manager of the Independent Theatre and would-be producer of the play, of promulgating unEnglish filth. On a personal level, he 'accused' Allan of lesbianism and Grein of homosexuality. The play, argued Pemberton-Billing, was such stuff as sapped the patriotic feelings of the English, loosened their moral fibre and threatened to attract them to the German side in the war. He claimed that Allan and Grein were both among the '47,000', a list of people in an ominous and notorious black book, miscreants whose immoral tendencies or other affiliations were likely to render them German sympathisers. Allan, who had been dancing as Salome since her appearance in Vienna in 1903, and Grein lost their libel action against Pemberton-Billing, such was the tenor of feeling at the time. The whole absurd business is documented in Michael Kettle's *Salome's Last Veil*.[153] At the centre of the mounting horror and accumulation of stupidities was Oscar Wilde's play, the heroine of which was judged by Pemberton-Billing and his cohorts to be 'guilty of sadism'.

Identifying influences is often a somewhat nebulous affair, but critics of Wilde have applied themselves to the task with gusto. It is clear that Flaubert's 'Hérodias' inspired Wilde, particularly in the time sequence of the events: Wilde reduces the French novelist's duration of the action from twenty-four hours to the amount of time taken to perform the play. In tone, as we have remarked, the inspiration is from Maeterlinck; so closely does Wilde reproduce the timbre and staccato sentences of the Belgian playwright that some critics, Mario Praz[154] among them, believed it to be an intentional and straightforward parody. *Les Sept Princesses* and *La Princesse Maleine* are considered by Praz to have been particularly influential.

Wilde's Salome is at first a cold, aloof young girl who, when meditating on the moon, praises chastity:

> How good to see the moon. She is like a little piece of money, you would think she was a little silver flower. The moon is cold and chaste. I am sure she is a virgin, she has a virgin's beauty. Yes, she is a virgin. She has never defiled herself. She has never abandoned herself to men, like the other goddesses.[155]

But Salome is also passionate and wilful and her cruelty derives from rejection. She has heard John's curses against her mother emanating from his prison and has been fascinated by his scorn and anger; when she eventually sees the prophet she falls violently in love with him. Rebuffed, she turns to obsessional revenge.

In the versions by Flaubert and Laforgue, Salome slips onto the scene unannounced and unanticipated as a surprise for Herod at his feast. In Heywood's play the whole court is awaiting her arrival and this, too, is Wilde's method here: from the very first line Salome is under scrutiny long before she actually appears. The opening words are spoken by Narraboth, the young Syrian Captain of the Guard, who loves the princess and will subsequently kill himself through his passion for her: 'How beautiful is the Princess Salomé tonight!'[156] Heywood also introduced a lover for Salome, Sextus, the Roman soldier, but with the difference that, while Sextus is beloved in return, Wilde's heroine feels nothing but contempt for Narraboth and will merely manipulate his feelings in order to make him bring

John to her from prison, thereby flouting the express orders of Herod.

The dialogue of the Syrian captain and the young page of Herodias with which the drama begins displays a curious stilted preciousness which characterises much of the writing. The touch of Maeterlinck is evident:

THE PAGE OF HERODIAS: Look at the moon. How strange the moon seems! She is like a woman rising from a tomb. She is like a dead woman. You would fancy she was looking for dead things.

THE YOUNG SYRIAN: She has a strange look. She is like a little princess who wears a yellow veil, and whose feet are of silver. She is like a princess who has little white doves for feet. You would fancy she was dancing.[157]

These words contain, part-concealed within them, a veiled warning of how the play will end: both death and dancing are foreshadowed.

One of the main themes of *Salomé* is that of people looking at others and of being looked at in their turn; Narraboth is rebuked by the page for looking too much at Salome, Herodias chides Herod for always staring at her daughter, Salome's first complaint on entering the scene is,

Why does the Tetrarch look at me all the while with his mole's eyes under his shaking eyelids ? It is strange that the husband of my mother looks at me like that. I know not what it means. In truth, yes I know it.[158]

When Salome in turn looks at John she conceives a great passion for him and expresses it in simile after simile, Wilde thus investing his text with an incantatory quality:

It is thy mouth that I desire, Jokanaan. Thy mouth is like a band of scarlet on a tower of ivory. It is like a pomegranate cut with a knife of ivory. ... Thy mouth is like a branch of coral that fishers have found in the twilight of the sea, the coral that they keep for kings ...! It is like the vermilion that the Moabites find in the mines of Moab, the vermilion that the kings take from them. It is like the bow of the king of the Persians, that is painted with vermilion, and is tipped with coral. There is nothing in the world so red as thy mouth. ... Let me kiss thy mouth.[159]

Both words and images are redolent of the Song of Solomon:

> Thy lips are like a thread of scarlet, and thy speech is comely: thy
> temples are like a piece of pomegranate within thy locks[160]

and the Old Testament rhythm is reproduced in its weightiness and
fullness. The prophet rejects Salome as an incarnation of sin, as is
her adulterous mother and he elects to return to his prison:

> Back daughter of Sodom ! Touch me not. Profane not the temple
> of the Lord God.[161]

When Herod emerges from the banqueting hall onto the terrace in
order to find Salome who has so far managed to elude him, he slips
in the blood of Narraboth. The young Syrian, unable to endure witnessing Salome's sexual overtures to John, stabbed himself to death.
The violence suggested by the moon at the beginning of the play has
been realised. Herod is terrified of the blood and sees it as an ill-
omen, but his fear does not prevent him from importuning his stepdaughter. He presses her to drink wine so that he can drain the cup,
to bite into a fruit so that he can finish it, to dance before him. In this
detail Wilde's version of the story is quite different from its predecessors. There the dance was usually Herodias's idea, but in this
instance she attempts to thwart the performance and she similarly
abstains from turning Herod's oath to her own personal use here,
whereas elsewhere she profits to the utmost from his actions. Here
he makes his promise before Salome has danced and, as in other
versions including those of the Bible, he offers her half his kingdom.
Herodias does not instruct her daughter what to demand; she is
simply delighted when Salome, her dance completed, requests the
head of John on a silver charger, but the notion is the girl's alone. In
Flaubert's narrative the Queen planned the dance and its consequences. There and in Huysmans's account, as has been demonstrated, the dance is described in loving detail. Here, ironically
enough amid all his characteristic wordiness, Wilde's stage direction is strangely sparse:

> (*Salomé dances the dance of the seven veils*),[162]

and the detailed delineation of the dancer's dress found elsewhere
is absent in this case.

Wilde's Herod is the most strenuous in his attempts to dissuade his stepdaughter from her grisly demand. He offers her magic jewels, white peacocks, sandals encrusted with glass and even the veil of the sanctuary which he has had stolen from the Temple of the Jews. He is as terrified as is Flaubert's tetrarch of having the prophet killed:

> Salomé, think of what you are saying. This man comes perchance from God. He is a holy man. The finger of God has touched him. God has put into his mouth terrible words. ... Furthermore if he died some misfortune might happen to me.[163]

When Laforgue's Salome ordered the head of John to be conveyed to her chamber she seemed to be performing some macabre *acte gratuit* because there had been no indication that she had ever met, let alone loved, the man. She had been glimpsed in the vicinity of the prison, but that was the sole information offered. And yet she, too, wished to kiss dead lips. Such a desire for the decapitated head is, however, quite consistent with the nature of Wilde's princess since she wants revenge on the man who refused her, the only one whom she had ever loved herself and whose appearance transformed her from a haughty, cold girl into a sensuous woman making known her passionate pleas. When the prophet was alive she insisted that she would kiss his mouth: now after his death she will not be hindered:

> Ah! thou wouldst not suffer me to kiss thy mouth, Jokanaan. Well! I will kiss it now. I will bite it with my teeth as one bites a ripe fruit. ... Ah! I have kissed thy mouth, Jokanaan. I have kissed thy mouth. There was a bitter taste on thy lips. Was it the taste of blood ... ? But perchance it is the taste of love. ... They say that love hath a bitter taste. ... But what of that? I have kissed thy mouth, Jokanaan.[164]

Herod, on witnessing her action with the dead head, orders his soldiers to crush her to death with their shields, for he judges her to be perverted and monstrous. Wilde's is the only version to terminate in the little princess being put to death for her alleged depravity by someone who is arguably more corrupt than she herself.

As quotation demonstrates, this is the most wordy Salome: Wilde devised a lyrical style from a blending of Maeterlinck and the Song of Solomon which is either overripe and fetid or genuinely powerful and sensuous according to taste. With the death of John, Salome moves from simile to metaphor in her eulogies: her comparisons are thereby less transparent and child-like:

> Thy body was a column of ivory set on a silver socket. It was a garden full of doves and silver lilies. It was a tower of silver decked with shields of ivory. ... Thy voice was a censer that scattered strange perfumes, and when I looked on thee I heard strange music.[165]

And the theme of perceiving the essential self of the other is prolonged to the end of the play: the girl says of John,

> If thou hadst seen me thou wouldst have loved me. I saw thee, Jokanaan, and I loved thee. ... Ah! ah! wherefore didst thou not look at me, Jokanaan?[166]

Herod finally orders complete darkness to cover all:

> I will not look at things, I will not suffer things to look at me. Put out the torches![167]

Wilde establishes at the outset a certain number of images, the moon being one of the more potent of them and weaves them as *Leitmotivs* through his play. This gives it a unity which is pleasing in such a relatively short work and his echoing of Biblical cadences as well as imagery brings a roundedness and plenitude to the prose. The work was enormously influential. Richard Strauss, using the translation by Hedwig Lachman, took Wilde's version as a model for his own opera produced in 1905. Diaghilev's *Ballet Russes* presented *The Tragedy of Salomé* in 1913 with Karsavina in the title role. Yeats bore Wilde's rendering of the legend in mind when crafting his last plays and noted with pleasure his own originality in having his queen, unlike that of Wilde, dance with the severed head in her hands. But Yeats disliked his compatriot's prose intensely. He remarked of it in a letter to Sturge Moore of 6 May 1906, 'The general construction is all right, is even powerful, but the dialogue is empty, sluggish and pretentious. It has nothing of drama of any kind, never working to any climax but always ending as it began.'[168]

Wilde's version was only one of a plethora of works on the Herodias–Salome theme in the 1890s, however, and Arthur Symons,

as early as 1897, was haunted by it when he devised his long poem
'The Dance of the Daughters of Herodias', and he manifests his debt
in a clear echo from Wilde:

> Here is Salome. She is a young tree
> Swaying in the wind, her arms are slender branches,
> And the heavy summer leafage of her hair
> Stirs as if rustling in a silent wind;
> Her narrow feet are rooted in the ground,
> But when the dim wind passes over her,
> Rustlingly she awakens, as if life
> Thrilled in her body to its finger tips. ...
> They dance, the daughters of Herodias,
> With their eternal, white, unfaltering feet,
> And always, when they dance, for their delight,
> Always a man's head falls because of them.
> Yet they desire not death, they would not slay
> Body or soul, no, not to do them pleasure:
> They desire love, and the desire of men;
> And they are the eternal enemy.[169]

The detail of the 'white, unfaltering feet' surely derives from
Wilde, while the suppleness suggested by the image of the 'young
tree' seems to owe its inception to both Flaubert and Laforgue and
their insistence on the sinuous, youthful form of their heroines. The
whole picture of the dancers' desiring love, not death, is taken from
Wilde's version of the legend rather than elsewhere, because it is the
only one of the preceding works on the theme to focus on Salome's
demands of love from the prophet. In the libretto by Milliet and
Grémont that love is returned and it is not the princess who requires
John's execution but Herodias. In Heywood's early play Salome
loves John as would a child; there is no revenge motive stemming
from unrequited passion. While Symons is certainly influenced by
Wilde's rendition, he models the wilful irresponsibility of the
dancer,

> Yet they desire not death, they would not slay
> Body or soul, no, not to do them pleasure

on Flaubert, St Mark and St Matthew. We must also bear in mind
that Symons had translated Mallarmé's 'Hérodiade' and had it

published in *The Savoy* in December 1896 and so hints of aloof, cold amorality are to be expected.

As a poet of the Nineties Symons certainly made his mark and what is relevant to our topic here is the fact that he did write on the Herodias–Salome theme and returned to it much later, in July 1920, when he produced a collection of poetry called 'Studies in Strange Sins' with the following schema: I: 'The Woman in the Moon', II: 'Design for the list of pictures', III: 'Salome's lament', IV: 'John and Salome', V: 'Enter Herodias', VI: 'The eyes of Herod', VII: 'Danse du Ventre', VIII: 'The Dancer's Reward'. Symons took as his source for these studies the illustrations done by Aubrey Beardsley in 1894 which were inspired by Wilde's play. It is also of some significance, I think, that Symons went on to write a poem 'for des Esseintes'. I do not wish to examine these verses in this chapter as they are situated rather too far away from *fin-de-siècle* investigations. It is quite simply noteworthy that, as in the case of Yeats, Symons's bewitchment by the Salome story carries across many years and he cannot totally put it behind him; it resurfaces in his writings over and again.

In a letter of September 1902, to Lady Gregory[170] Yeats mentions his familiarity with the work, in translation, of the German playwright Hermann Sudermann. The latter indeed wrote his own version of the Salome episode in 1898, *Johannes*, and, while German was not a language in which Yeats was competent, it is interesting to note that he was aware of Sudermann's plays. In fact, a review of a production of *Johannes* which took place in Berlin on 16 January 1898, appeared in *The Times* the next day.[171] In this play, John is perceived by the people as a rabbi teaching of and awaiting the coming of the Messiah. The play opens with news of the forthcoming marriage of Herod and Herodias, but in this instance, as elsewhere, Philip, Herodias's present husband and Herod's brother, is still living. John's reaction to what he considers to be an adulterous and incestuous union is that the two perpetrators should be stoned to death. The prophet continues to spread unrest among the citizens of Jerusalem with his prediction of the coming of Jesus, and now he adds to it in his railing against Herodias.

Salome sees John in the market place and is drawn to him without knowing his identity: 'Es gehen Blitze aus seinem Auge. Mutter, sieh!'[172] The princess confides in her playmates that she has already looked at Greek men and found them beautiful. She claims,

Ich fürchte mich vor keinen Männern ... [sic] Sie sind mir recht so,
wie sie sind. Ich lieb' sie, wie sie sind.[173]

She speaks of herself and her own loveliness with the same degree
of lyricism as when she describes the Greeks of Antioch:

> da sah ich bleiche Jünglinge mit goldbraunem Gelock, die trugen
> rote Schuhe und dufteten ... Das seien Griechen, sagte mein Vater,
> wirkliche Griechen aus Hellas.[174]

Of herself she employs a formula echoing the Song of Solomon: 'I
am the rose of Sharon, and the lily of the valleys'[175] which becomes
slightly modified to: 'Ich bin eine Blume zu Saron, und eine Rose in
Thal'.[176] This resonance is curious in the mouth of a pagan princess
and we must conclude that Sudermann owes a debt to Wilde in imitating the latter's use of Biblical prose models.

This girl has noticed, as does her counterpart in Wilde, that
Herod has been stealing glances at her behind her mother's back
and Sudermann's princess also understands what such looks
import. She is more worldly-wise than Wilde's creation; she is probably the most sexually aware and mature Salome of those discussed
here, for she has just realised, unlike her predecessors, that her
beauty bestows power upon her, a quality she admires in others.
When she catches sight of John from her window surrounded by a
crowd of his followers she is delighted to note that he never hum-
bles himself by bending to anyone. Similarly, and this has a slight
though unfocussed parallel in Wilde, it is his obdurate criticism of
her family that attracts her perversely to him. She intends to break
him:

> Sei ers wie er sei ... Schaut, wie das Volk ihn flehend umdrängt!
> Habt ihr von eurem Thale her je einen Felsen gesehen sich
> neigen? Er neigt sich nicht – hahaha. Der nicht ... Nur – wenn –
> vielleicht – (*Sie reckt die Arme.*)[177]

Sudermann emulates Huysmans in portraying her wilfulness
along with her cruelty. Herodias orders John to be brought before
her in order to negotiate. No longer able to endure his abuse, she
will try to buy his silence, if necessary with the offer of her own
daughter, Salome. The girl thrills at the prospect of such a meeting
because she knows of her own capacity for skittish corruption:

SALOME: Vergieb, Mutter! Wir sind nicht wie die anderen! ... Wir stechen, wenn wir lieben.

HERODIAS (*leise*): Und wen wir hassen?

SALOME (*leise*): Den küssen wir.[178]

When she eventually comes face to face with John she throws armfuls of roses at him, begs him to be Sun King to her Queen and asks whether he finds her lovely among 'the daughters of Jerusalem'.[179] He undermines her brazen advances by addressing her constantly as 'Jungfrau', speaking down to her as 'Du' – thereby insisting that he also perceives her as the child–woman witnessed in earlier versions – and enquiring whether she is as guilty as the other members of her family. He warns her, ironically echoing her own phrase:

Du bist lieblich unter den Töchtern Jerusalems. Sie werden weinen um dich.[180]

He bans her from his sight announcing that he has been sent as a scourge to exterminate her. All that Salome perceives, however, is that once again he has refused to bend.

John is imprisoned for threatening to stone Herodias outside the temple; at length he let fall the stone destined to hit the queen. Salome hears of his jailing quite by chance when the ball with which she is playing is mistakenly directed over the wall into the prison yard. This incident surprises us: we have just witnessed her throwing roses at the prophet and demanding his love. Now Sudermann bewilders us by depicting the same ardent young woman in childish pursuits and, while we are hardly prepared for this new dimension, it reminds us yet again that we are confronted, as in Flaubert, with the child–woman and all her disturbing power.

It is precisely with this species of innocence that rapidly becomes knowledge that she proposes to Herod: 'Ich kann auch tanzen, Herr'[181] and we almost shiver in apprehension as we hear her fateful offer. She is employing her beauty and her seductive skills in dancing as a tool with which to plead on John's behalf against the death penalty. In her intercession she recalls Laforgue's heroine. Flattering Herod knowingly, she persuades him that the people will revere him for his act of mercy. While seeing the strength of her argument, he sets his own terms for complying; Salome must unveil herself. Salome, tasting again that particular kind of power, claims that Herod's act of mercy will make her proud because of her own part in the event: 'Er that nach [meinem] Rat'.[182] As she leaves him she moves her veil a fraction.

Herod keeps his word and the prisoner is unchained and at liberty to wander in the jail and yard. Salome, all obedience, goes to him ostensibly in order to be taught. But she has known power and, to our horror, we learn that she has had her playmate, Miriam, put to death for listening to John's preaching. Salome will allow nobody near him but herself. It is disgusting that her whim should have been pandered to and horrific that she should have conceived of such a scheme at all. She proceeds to astound us; she has prepared her bedchamber for John and now she offers herself. Her language is characteristically Biblical:

Ich will dir geben meinen jungen Leib, du wilder unter den Söhnen Israels.[183]

To her utter astonishment the prophet rejects her; she is dangerous to him, he says, for she is Sin Incarnate.

In this version, one in which reader or audience deems Salome as morally repugnant as in Huysmans's portrayal of her from Moreau's *L'Apparition*, the girl begs her mother to be allowed to dance at Herod's birthday feast. Sudermann follows Flaubert and St Mark in having Herodias decide what she must claim as reward and, uniquely here, Herodias also instructs her daughter on the manner of her performance. Salome, the damsel who played ball in the garden, wants to request trinkets – jewellery for her hair, soft shoes or, most coveted of all, a pretty mirror – but Herodias has other plans:

Keinen Spiegel sollst du fordern, keinen Haarschmuck, auch keine sämischen Schuhe. Sondern daß man ihr bringe auf einer Schüssel das Haupt jenes, den sie nennen Johannes den Täufer.[184]

Salome does not demur except to wonder whether the charger will be of gold.

This seeming irrelevance emphasises her amorality and youth. Other versions of the account have presented her as irresponsible for her actions to a greater or lesser degree, but Sudermann, in the longest and most comprehensive of them, is able to examine the princess in all her contradictions. It is curious and slightly maladroit that the German playwright insists that Salome had no plans for taking John's head, particularly when he stressed the prophet's violent rejections of her advances. His Salome thus has a motive for revenge that is not used. We never fathom why Laforgue's heroine demanded the execution; there is no hint in the story that she had any reason to do so. Flaubert's princess merely obeys orders, while Wilde's must have the head to serve her bloody vengeance. Sudermann's giddy creation would rather have a mirror and her skittish, arbitrary wilfulness will be taken up again in the dance, while her brushes with irrationality will conclude the play.

Salome's entrance into the banqueting hall is fully expected since Herod has already promised her as the newest sensation to his guests. She is accompanied, deeply veiled, by her mother who has tutored her to dance modestly, the blush of shame on her cheeks. But Salome, impatient and rebellious, wrenches herself from Herodias's arm and performs, spurred on by the shouts of delight and admiration of the spectators. The dance is described in a long, explanatory stage direction:

> *(Salome hat sich aus den Armen der Herodias gelöst und, von unwillkürlichen Ausrufen der Bewunderung und des Entzückens begleitet, zu tanzen begonnen. Ihr Tanz wird wilder, sie löst allgemach den Schleier, verhüllt sich wieder in wollüstiger Scham und löst ihn aufs neue, bis sie gänzlich schleierlos mit scheinbar unverhülltem Oberkörper dasteht, dann sinkt sie halb in Erschöpfung, halb um ihm zu huldigen, vor Herodes nieder, der auf rechten Seite der Tafel steht.)*[185]

This performance is similar to the accounts in Flaubert and Huysmans but with none of their detail of costume and gesture. It is rather a stereotyped 'Eastern dance' and disappointing in being such a cliché. This is the most willing dancer; she abandons herself to her movements in a bizarre mixture of pudency and a voluptuous shamelessness which disobeys Herodias's prescriptions. She can never resist exercising sexual power.

When asked what she now desires in return, however, she mechanically follows commandments:

> So bitt' ich und begehr' ich, daß du mir gebest auf einer Schüssel das Haupt Johannes, des Täufers.[186]

Here too Herod tries to dissuade his stepchild as he clearly recognises the influence of Herodias in her gory plea, but when he tries to reason with the girl, she merely amends her words by adding 'gold-enen' in front of 'Schüssel'. Yet she is destined to be disappointed: she will indeed be granted the head, but what she really yearned for, to see John on his knees begging her for mercy – to see him bend – will be denied her. The prophet accepts his fate calmly and stoically. Salome urges,

Meister, siehst du wohl, wie mächtig ich bin? Nun bitte mich![187]

but her mother predicts that if John did indeed entreat her daughter, she would simply be moved to laughter. Salome agrees: 'Vielleicht. Wer kann wissen, was meine Seele will? ...'[188] She remains capricious and perverse and takes a delight in not being able to foresee her own reactions.

Once the severed head on its charger is delivered, Salome seizes it and dances, but she does not emulate some of her notorious predecessors in kissing it. Instead, something seems to break inside her and she repeats in a crazed, automatic manner the now wholly inappropriate words, 'ich bin eine Blume zu Saron und eine Rose im Thal'.[189] Herodias's daughter loses her wits and the play closes on her mouthing banalities like a clockwork doll. She is led away by a fondly smiling mother whom we suspect to be as mad as she is herself. As does Wilde, Sudermann has his heroine pay the cost of what, after all, begins as a natural if unreciprocated adolescent passion.

And so, finally, to Yeats's place in this sequence, a position open to analysis and discussion, since, although he was aware to a greater or lesser degree of his celebrated predecessors and the current zeal for representing Salome as the figure of the dancer, he did not himself adopt any one stance. The image of the dancer develops in Yeats's oeuvre over the years until she is transformed into a more complex and sophisticated figure than any produced by his forbears, illustrious and able though they were.

In Yeats's work, the notion of human sacrifice as the price of the symbolic dance is deeply and curiously embedded. From very early days he associates Salome with the Sidhe.[190]

As early as 1899, one year after Sudermann's play, Yeats published a book of poetry, *The Wind among the Reeds*. Already here, in the first poem, 'The Hosting of the Sidhe' – the Sidhe are gods and goddesses of ancient Ireland – a link with the customary portrayal of Salome is revealed:

> Empty your heart of its mortal dream,
> The winds awaken, the leaves whirl round,
> Our cheeks are pale, our hair is unbound,
> Our breasts are heaving, our eyes are agleam,
> Our arms are waving, our lips are apart;
> And if any gaze on our rushing band,
> We come between him and the deed of his hand,
> We come between him and the hope of his heart.[191]

The images hark back to a legendary 'Wildjagd', possibly to the specific version of Heine's *Atta Troll* which Yeats probably knew through his acquaintance with the works of Mallarmé and where Herodias was one of the huntresses. Yeats's own comment on this poem is telling:

> [The Sidhe] still ride the country as of old. Sidhe is also Gaelic for wind, and certainly the Sidhe have much to do with the wind. They journey in whirling wind, the winds that were called the dance of the daughters of Herodias in the Middle Ages, Herodias doubtless taking the place of some old goddess.[192]

Yeats may well have discovered a source for the association of whirlwind, Sidhe and the daughters of Herodias in Jacob Grimm's *Teutonic Mythology* published in 1882. Here legend states that certain goddesses became the 'wind's bride' and that the dancing Herodias was of their number. Grimm provides the following information to the Herodias/Salome–John the Baptist narrative:

> She was inflamed by love for John, which he did not return; when his head is brought in on a charger, she would fain have covered it with tears and kisses, but it draws back, and begins to blow hard at her; the hapless maid is whirled into empty space and there she hangs for ever. ... There is no doubt whatever that quite early in the Middle Ages the Christian mythus of *Herodias* got mixed up with our native heathen fables: those notions about dame *Holda* and the 'furious host' and the nightly jaunts of sorceresses were grafted on it, the Jewish king's daughter had the part of a *heathen*

goddess assigned to her, ... and her worship found numerous adherents [Grimm's emphasis]

In a note on this text Grimm states:

This reference to the *turbo* (the whirlwind of [John's] blast), looks mythical and of high antiquity ... to this day (such) a wind is accounted for in Lower Saxony (about Celle) by the dancing Herodias whirling about in the air.[193]

Grimm then goes on to forge the link between Herodias and the Sidhe to which Yeats alludes above:

But the whirlwind appears to be associated with *Phol* also, and with an opprobrious name for the *devil* (... sow's tail) to whom the raising of the whirl was ascribed ... as well as to witches. It was quite natural therefore to look upon some female personages also as prime movers of the whirlwind, the gyrating dancing *Herodias*, and *frau Hilde, frau Holde* ... in Celtic legend it is stirred up by *fays*, and the Irish name for it is *sigh gaoite* (O'Brien), *sighgaoithe* (Croker III i xxi). [Grimm's emphasis][194]

So the first mention of Salome-like figures appears in Yeats's work in 1899, precisely at the time when the dancer was much in vogue, as has been demonstrated, but the image of the dancing girl surfaces again and again in the poetry and drama, until, in the last plays, she becomes central, as a later chapter will fully show.

However, she is subtly transformed from the figure which has been examined in the 1840s and onwards: for example, as early as 1894, Yeats inserted a dance into his play *The Land of Heart's Desire*. This was a slight foretaste of a Salome dance: a little girl, a faery child, dances to lure a young farmer's wife out of her comfortable home to join her in Faeryland. The child succeeds in her seduction although she is almost vanquished by the forces of Christian religion represented by a country priest. The sexual element is well-nigh obliterated and there is no severed head as trophy, but we do discover, in embryonic form, Yeats's association of the female dancer with power and an important transition occurs in the use of that authority. Instead of the figure as the castrating woman of some previous versions of the legend we find the dancer as seducer. Yeats's shift in emphasis here is telling and, while he indeed progresses in later plays also to presenting the dancer as assassin procuring the severed heads of male wooers for her own delight, in this early work the focus is firmly on the dance as bewitchment and its intended object is a woman.

In his essay 'The Tragic Generation' of 1910 in which he portrays the writers and artists of the *fin de siècle*, the poet makes it clear that he knew Mallarmé's 'Hérodiade' through Symons's translation of 1896. Yeats makes the following comment on his own work:

> Yet I am certain that there was something in myself compelling me to attempt creation of an art as separate from everything heterogeneous and casual, from all character and circumstance, as some Herodiade of our theatre, dancing seemingly alone in her narrow moving luminous circle.[195]

In Yeats's 'system', *A Vision*, where he classifies the character and personality of friends and historical personages according to the phases of the moon in which they flourish, the poet makes Salome emblematic of the perfect work of art, the Fifteenth Phase, 'perfect unity of being, with the moon at the full',[196] and it is not surprising that, for example, the dancer figures in such poems as 'To a Child Dancing in the Wind' and 'Among Schoolchildren', where she is stripped of all the Decadent trappings attached to her by Moreau and Wilde, and in the poem 'Nineteen Hundred and Nineteen', where she is not. She is then, most importantly for our present purposes, rediscovered in the dance plays.

In *At the Hawk's Well* of 1916, Cuchulain, the young warrior hero, is lured away from his goal by the dance of the Hawk Woman, a woman of the Sidhe and, three years later, in *The Only Jealousy of Emer*, Cuchulain's deserted wife, Emer, complains of the same type of woman:

> I know her sort.
> They find our men asleep, weary with war,
> Lap them in cloudy hair or kiss their lips;
> Our men awake in ignorance of it all
> But when we take them in our arms at night
> We cannot break their solitude.[197]

But it is in the last plays of the 1930s that we discover dancers and severed heads. Here, however, the Queen who dances is the object of the man's desire – she is the trophy to be bestowed on him who sings his passion best. In *A Full Moon in March* of 1935 the wooer is a foul and ugly swineherd who has had the temerity to come to court in order to plight his troth. The Queen, insulted by his impertinence, orders his execution, but, once in possession of the severed head, she holds it in her hands and sings to it. When she places it tenderly upon the throne and dances to it, the head begins to sing. At this point, dialogue is dispensed with and dance takes over, as is evident from Yeats's comprehensive stage direction in which he choreographs her second dance:

> (*Queen takes up the head and lays it upon the ground. She dances before it – a dance of adoration. She takes the head up and dances with it to drum-taps, which grow quicker and quicker. As the drum-taps approach their climax, she presses her lips to the lips of the head. Her body shivers to very rapid drum-taps. The drum-taps cease. She sinks slowly down, holding the head to her breast. ...*)[198]

In common with Wilde's play, Laforgue's story and Heine's poem we rediscover here the prominence of the act of kissing the dead lips; in contradistinction to previous versions, however, we find a reversal of the familiar passionate-woman and indifferent-male pattern. In this case the woman punishes because the man has the insolence to love her ardently: elsewhere she seeks revenge for being rejected.

The Queen in *A Full Moon in March* clearly owes something to Mallarmé's Hérodiade. She says of herself that,

> I am crueller than solitude,
> Forest or beast. Some I have killed or maimed
> Because their singing put me in a rage,
> And some because they came at all. Men hold
> That woman's beauty is a kindly thing,
> But they that call me cruel speak the truth,
> Cruel as the winter of virginity.[199]

The conscious echo of Hérodiade's revelation of her own tyrannical nature to her nurse is impossible to ignore.

The King of the Great Clock Tower, also of 1935, presents us with another severed head and a plot almost identical to that of the play discussed above. A later chapter will demonstrate at greater length the subtle differences between the two. This time a stroller has arrived to woo the silent Queen and the King has him beheaded for his impudence. This head, too, is laid upon the throne, the Queen sings and dances to it and in turn it sings its own song. Yeats's stage direction for the Queen's dance is as follows and we shall be able to see in a projected study of the details of these plays that the similarities between this performance and that of *A Full Moon in March* are deceptively superficial:

> (*When the song has finished, the dance begins again, the Clock strikes. The strokes are represented by blows on a gong struck by Second Attendant. The Queen dances to the sound, and at the last stroke presses her lips to the lips of the head. The King has risen and draws his sword. The Queen lays the head upon her breast, and fixes her eyes upon him. He appears about to strike, but kneels, laying the sword at her feet. ...*)[200]

In the prologue of his last play, *The Death of Cuchulain*, Yeats has an old man explain of Emer, Cuchulain's abandoned wife:

> I wanted a dance because where there are no words there is less to spoil. Emer must dance, there must be severed heads – I am old, I belong to mythology – severed heads for her to dance before.[201]

When her warrior husband is finally vanquished in a ludicrously unequal battle against Maeve, his old enemy, Cuchulain's head is taken. It is represented on stage by a parallelogram of wood and Emer, grief-stricken, is moved to dance before it. The stage direction indicates:

> (*She moves as if in adoration or triumph. She is about to prostrate herself before it, perhaps does so, then rises, looking up as if listening. ...*)[202]

Why does Emer move 'in adoration or triumph'? The former passion stems from the all-encompassing, self-sacrificing love for her husband illustrated in the earlier play, *The Only Jealousy of Emer*, where she selflessly renounced all claim to him as the price exacted by the forces of the sea in return for bringing Cuchulain back from the edge of death. And she expresses triumph in her movements because she has finally ousted all her rivals, her husband's young mistresses and, in performing the rituals of a wife in mourning, has reinstated herself as the woman to take priority in his death if not in life. But it must also be recognised that her dance of triumph manifests the celebration of the destruction of the man who betrayed and humiliated as well as loved her. She makes a strange Salome figure, this, Yeats's last dancer, a domesticated, mature wife still caught in the trammels of the power struggle between herself and her husband which has not abated with his death.

Thus, we discover here, in Irish theatre, the continuation of the fascination with Salome. Kermode claimed (p. 9) that the Irish poet never completely freed himself of the mark made by the girl-dancer and her image changed, developed and was transformed according to the idiosyncrasies and demands of the various works in which she figured.

One of the versions of the biblical account of the story that Yeats certainly knew is that of Oscar Wilde's *Salomé*. As the investigation of this work revealed (p. 56), Yeats professed to despise it, but Katharine Worth, in her chapter on *Salomé* and *A Full Moon in March*, perceptively questions the violence of Yeats's hatred. She believes that, while Yeats protests too much in his desire to distance himself markedly from Wilde's study of the dancer, there are indeed links to be perceived between the former's late 'severed head' dance plays and the Wilde version, although Yeats always denied any possible influence and was at pains to emphasise this. The parallels which Worth draws are convincing, centring, as they do, on the relation of both writers to French ideas of art then current, particularly *Symbolisme* and, most tellingly for my own purpose here, on the function of the dance. Worth has her reasons for electing to examine *A Full Moon in March* rather than *The King of the Great Clock Tower* and I choose to follow her in her selection for mine, namely that the former is the more achieved version of the intense, passionate episode which it relates, as Yeats himself agreed.

Salomé is different from Yeats's Queen even though both women cast the man as simultaneously victim and beloved in their personal dramas. Both Queen and princess are complicated in their virginity – they desire fiercely, but while Salomé openly and passionately makes her feelings known and is then profoundly damaged by rejection, Yeats refrains from portraying the Queen as a child newly-aware of her sexuality; she is rather depicted as holding genuine power which has been transformed into tyrannical whim. The contrast between the two women is epitomised in the style of their dances and this disparity is what interests me here.

Salomé does not dance in order to please, or even to woo, the object of her love, but simply as pay-off in the bargain with her lecherous stepfather. Does her performance smack simply of an exotic strip-tease, what Yeats called 'a mere uncovering of nakedness'?[203] I think not. While Wilde gives away very little in his bald stage direction, audience or reader cannot fail to respond to the insistence of the clamouring voices which lead up to the dance, most notably the scornful castigations of Jokanaan. It is in response to these attacks as much as to the constant importunate pleas of Herod that Salomé is finally moved to perform and, of course, the girl has silently and secretly made her own pact – in her own way she is as obdurate as Herod in her promise to herself that she will kiss Jokanaan's mouth. The dance before the king and its outcome are her means of fulfilling her own oath and she fully accepts that her reward will appear in a barbarous and grisly form.

Wilde's child–woman has already employed her only partly understood sexual power to manipulate others: nowhere does she even comment on the young Syrian captain's suicide for love of her, a love which she exploited to the full when cajoling him to let her see Jokanaan. How much of her partial and recently acquired knowingness goes into the dance? How much of the performance is simply a mechanical piece of titillation to give Herod what he wants? And how great is the element of genuine heartfelt passion inflamed in the dancer by the curses emanating from Jokanaan's prison – a complicated passion, but one which none the less contains both violent possessive love and the fury of being spurned? In his response to the dance Herod gives no inkling of its nature: he is simply pleased to have scored a point against Herodias who had forbidden Salomé to dance at all. As for the little princess, she merely replaces the earlier obsessive incantation about kissing Jokanaan's mouth with an equally determined claim for his head. The fact of the performance of the dance, the displaying of her body, does not seem to have changed her: she has understood no more of herself through her compliance to supply exotic revelations and their results. Had Salomé been dancing before Jokanaan himself, perhaps a true seductiveness would have been discovered and a degree of comprehension of what she was doing. Understanding is indeed vouchsafed to her, however, when she finally holds the severed head and kisses the dead lips. But Wilde's strength is, in his silence, to present something enigmatic – a dance that is in part a burdensome duty and, thus, inhibiting to the revelation of self, part sincerely expressive – but certain to fascinate the audience on stage as well as off, as onlookers try to decode the extent of the adolescent girl's awareness of her own power and its nature.

The nuances of interpretation are perplexing, but the virgin herself claims that she has lost her chastity, has gained sexual knowledge, through demanding a murder. Despite such a bizarre defloration, however, and because of it, she is doomed to remain the child–woman, even though Herod's last command, 'Kill that *woman*' [my emphasis] would suggest that dancing and bargaining and kissing dead lips have led her to reach maturity. His words are rather an indictment of her sex than an attack on an individual representative of it. But in so commanding, the king robs Salomé of her self-hood and of any insight which she may briefly have gained. Indeed, the genre of Wilde's dance, like his chosen language in this play, conceals as much as it reveals in its luxuriant but ordered ceremonial stiltedness.

Yeats's version of the dance of sex is complex too, but in a different manner. His Queen knows herself and that her own set of idiosyncratic rules have nothing to do with logic or justice: 'None I abhor can sing'.[204] She is seen to be in control of what goes on in her court and it is quite fitting that she is addressed as 'lady', an epithet which never comes to mind in reference to Wilde's princess. The Queen's challenge is to any man who can move her to passion by his song and the poetry of his professions of love. Should one do so, she will dance for him and kiss his lips. What she is longing for is a release from control; she awaits the very mastery of her own skittish wilfulness. Salomé is already caught in the toils of such power – she is besotted by Jokanaan's beauty and loses sense of herself. It is only through violence that she can regain a measure of control, but her revenge is barbaric and short-lived. Yeats's Queen finds a master; she luxuriantly abandons self-domination, but she, too, demands the price of a head.

It is through the Queen's dances that the extent of her sexual attraction to the Swineherd is perceived and through that, her naked, vulnerable self. To some degree Salomé was acting in her dance: she was *performing* a task. The Queen, on the other hand, surprises herself through and in her dancing; she discovers abandonment and delight, but she is too regal to wish to admit that she has been won at last. In her fear of being humiliated by reciprocating love, and to such an object of it, she must destroy the bearer or forfeit that self-possession which she wishes to guard yet, at the same time, to surrender.

Salomé desires revenge for not being loved and her dance-as-instrument serves to further that aim: she will possess the object of her love and she will punish him for his violent rejection of her expressions of passion for him. The Queen also reveals herself as an avenger. Salomé wanted to be seen: the Queen is thoroughly seen and the seer must be destroyed for his temerity in having made himself privy to her most secret self. This dancer knows herself in a way that Salomé never does. The Queen's dances disclose that she indeed achieves the orgasmic delight for which she was waiting and which she demanded as her right, but she is none the less piqued at the Swineherd's utter confidence that he can please her. The genuineness of her power over her court is dangerous and we witness her abuse of it. She treacherously plays the tease – she leads her suitor in conversation to reveal his intention and then, once articulated and made public, she proclaims his wooing as insults upon her person. For all her dishonest, wily cunning, her hypocrisy, trickery and lies, her dance is terrifyingly truthful. Despite her heavy veil, he has seen her and she, too, a moment before his execution, has looked on him: 'Begone! I shall not see your face again.'[205] As he goes to his death she drops her veil that he may clearly feast his eyes on the vengeful object of his passion as well as on her unquestionable beauty.

Yeats's Queen too obtains her lover's severed head and the blood dripping from it not only horribly stains her dress and hands but also mysteriously impregnates her. Her dances as she holds her trophy are revelatory but complex. Her accompanying song discloses her own self-knowledge – she combines maternal tenderness with virgin's cruelty – she was compelled to have the Swineherd destroyed because she 'loved in shame'.[206] Now anxious to make amends and also brave in wishing to make public his real power over her, she places the head on her throne as fitting tribute to his royalty of spirit. Her dance to this newly found equal is one of sexual titillation: will she yield or not? Her laughter is a combination of cruel glee at the killing and of surprised delight in having discovered her master and her subsequent dance of adoration combines sexual frenzy, as she kisses the dead mouth, with *caritas*, when she cradles the head on her breast.

Yeats choreographs his Queen's dances in an explicit manner which is quite absent from Wilde's version. Yeats explores the manifold complexities of his dancer's psyche as well as charting the perplexing attributes of love which reconcile 'Crown of gold or dung of swine',[207] the instinct of preserving the self's integrity at the very moment of longing to surrender it. Yeats's protagonist is dangerous in knowing herself and of what cruel deeds she is capable: Wilde's creation is dangerous in her lack of self-knowledge. Salomé is motivated solely by unmediated instinct and is just on the point of realising what power is hers through her beauty and nascent sexuality when she is put to death. Both dancers are fascinating in their differing degrees of ability to articulate passion.

Yeats was right to insist on the distinctions to be drawn between his Queen and Wilde's Salomé, but, as Worth has so admirably pointed out, wrong to dismiss Wilde's version of the dance so peremptorily. Wilde served to clarify Yeats's ideas by providing an example of what the latter was striving against and what he believed himself to wish to reject. And yet it cannot be denied that, years later, Yeats remembered *Salomé*, as his letters demonstrate, and whatever he claimed to think of it, the dance had engraved its curious metres on his consciousness.

In investigating certain of the different versions of the legend of Salome in circulation at roughly the turn of the century we have seen how they have coincided with or differed from the original Bible account in the Gospels of Mark and Matthew. It has also been evident that they influenced each other or, perhaps more correctly, that artists were aware that they were part of a continuum of interest. They created the fashion for Salome, but they were also consumers of that same vogue. As far as critics studying this *fin-de-siècle* mode are concerned, they, too, are clearly dependent on their own temporal and historical place; Frank Kermode's account of the phenomenon of Salome-fervour, written in 1957, is quite different from that of Bram Dijkstra in 1986. The latter does cite a work to which I am deeply indebted, Helen Grace Zagona's book *The Legend of Salome and the Principle of Art for Art's Sake* (1960), but neither Kermode, writing his influential *Romantic Image*, nor Zagona herself, mention the cult of the dancer in terms of men and women and what could loosely be termed in today's jargon 'sexual politics'. Dijkstra remedies this lack by perceiving the individual treatments of the girl and the Decadence in general very much in terms of a deeply anti-feminine culture. This is perhaps only to be expected from someone writing when the passions incited by twentieth-century Feminism have shown no signs of abating.

So too must the opinions of Kermode and Zagona, working at the first cutting edge of the Sixties, have been coloured by their perspectives. In both cases these critics are discussing the dancer as art and while they relate their observations to the contemporary culture of the individual writer on Salome, they are primarily interested in the aesthetic phenomenon of Decadence, perceiving it from within the cultural and political dimensions of their own times – the approaching of the Sixties with its economic boom and its consequent two trends in art: the frivolity of multiples – throw-away soup-can paintings – on the one hand, and the beginnings of the protest movements inspired by the war in Vietnam, on the other. Kermode in particular, with the hectic materialism of the post-war fifties just behind him and the Bay of Pigs ahead, uses the same terms as does Yeats himself to talk of the role of the dancer and the purpose of art as a force for integrating the Self which had been divided for centuries, certainly since the onset of Materialism, and disintegrated in a precise manner since Freud. Significantly enough, R. D. Laing's very influential study *The Divided Self* was published in 1959. For Kermode, paraphrasing Yeats, the subject of his study in *Romantic Image*, the dancer is the image of unified body and soul: she is the great reconciler containing life in death, death in life, movement and stillness, action and contemplation, a healer of the split in personal integrity which occurred when philosophers declared that mind and body were separate entities. As he states in his essay 'Poet and Dancer before Diaghilev',

> The peculiar prestige of dancing over the past seventy or eighty years has, I think, much to do with the notion that it somehow represents art in an undissociated and unspecialized form – a notion made explicit by Yeats and hinted at by Valéry. The notion is essentially primitivist; it depends upon the assumption that mind and body, form and matter, image and discourse have undergone a process of dissociation, which it is the business of art momentarily to mend.[208]

This was clearly the aim of Symbolism in its desire for total art and its attempts to make all art approximate to the condition of music. Kermode forges the link between this wish for a unity of sensibility and the figure of Salome:

Although Yeats associated his cult of the inward-looking, or expressionless face with Blake, it is a recurring feature of Romantic poetry and painting, and Mario Praz studied it, more or less under the aspect of Romantic pathology, in his *Romantic Agony*. It is, however, important to see it as rather more than that. Throughout this tradition, the beauty of a work of art, in which there is no division of form and meaning, no overplus of 'littérature', is more or less explicitly compared with the mysterious inexpressive beauty of such women, and perhaps particularly with that of Salome.[209]

However, in investigating the significance of the dancer in *fin-de-siècle* culture we discover that she is not only answering an intellectual desire for the unity of form and meaning in art, but that, emotionally and sexually, she fills the need for the dangerous *femme fatale*, the castrating woman of the Decadence. To paraphrase Bram Dijkstra, men had gone to war cn women. Even where the version of Salome presents a sympathetic girl, as in Heywood's plays, she is still compelled to demand the death of John the Baptist. She may repent profoundly – in the libretto by Milliet and Grémont she stabs herself to death once John is killed – but she is none the less, to a greater or lesser degree, instrumental to the taking of his life. However much the form of the dance may suggest all that Kermode claims, its function or its outcome is ultimately destructive, although Salome herself may not always be held totally and personally responsible for the violence which results.

Writing in 1960, Helen Zagona saw the preoccupation with Salome among the *Symbolistes-Décadents* as a blow for 'The Principle of Art for Art's Sake' – that the dancer, in direct contrast to the nineteenth-century ethos of utilitarian art or of a bourgeois functionalism, was gratuitously beautiful and that her demand for the head of the saint was part of her amorality, an absurd gesture. It is not, however, as if the writers dealt with in her study were apolitical or asocial: she makes it clear that they were

Idealists at heart, but possessing a sufficient degree of insight to see that the regeneration of humanity was not going to proceed automatically from social and political reform, they directed their lofty sentiments elsewhere. Heine, Flaubert, Banville, Mallarmé, Huysmans, Laforgue, Wilde all found their chief worldly delights and aspirations bound with the cultivation of beauty and tended to put as much distance as possible between their art and the banal, futile strife of the time.[210]

Thus, Heine satirises in *Atta Troll* the bourgeois philistinism of his age and creates a heroine whose morality is the extreme opposite to prevailing social values. Mallarmé's Hérodiade is similarly at odds with contemporary standards and her concern is to transform the material into the spiritual, banal mediocrity into the mysticism of the Absolute and Ideal. As does Heine with his heroine, Mallarmé presents a figure whose beauty and whose very self are both gratuitous:

> For him, Hérodiade, as unacceptable to the utilitarians as Heine's heroine, is the incarnation of that disinterested, sacred conception of beauty without which a glimpse of the 'Absolute' is impossible.[211]

Flaubert and Huysmans, in their concentration on the dance of Salome, depict the extremes of luxury and sensual gratification and indulge further than their predecessors in current misogyny. Less idealistic than Mallarmé or, indeed, Yeats, they do not focus on the dance as fusion of movement and stasis, form and meaning, but rather on the erotic but child-like powers of the dancer. Banville, too, emphasises Salome's calm sadism which he states as a self-evident fact; she is merely pursuing her destiny as a woman. Even in parody the amorality of Laforgue's heroine is very keenly felt. She is arbitrary in all that she says and does; there is no causal link between her actions and her demand for the prisoner's head and her own death is characteristically absurd. Wilde's combination of a variety of factors from preceding artists leads him to present a heroine whose cruelty is only to be outdone by Sudermann's princess and, perhaps, by the later creations of W. B. Yeats. Wilde's play is so deeply immersed in all that is *fin-de-siècle* that it is almost pushed to the point of caricature. It may not be too far-fetched to suggest that this work goes to such an extreme that it it may collide with its opposite, an 'anti-Decadence', for Salomé is aesthetically, though not morally, innocent. She is responding to John's cold beauty warmly and passionately without any of the unhealthy, perverse desires of Sudermann's heroine to humiliate him. She is killed by Herod for the full-blooded expression of her passions and may be seen as his victim, 'martyred' to conventional-mindedness.

Sudermann's version would correspond closely to Dijkstra's notion of the prevalent myth of the castrating *femme fatale*; she wished to make John beg for mercy.

Not surprisingly, for he was always highly receptive to contemporary trends of thought, it is Arthur Symons who best illustrates Dijkstra's hypothesis in his manifesto-like poems. He put the problem most nakedly when he stated of Salome and her fictional sisters, 'And they are the eternal enemy', thus making prevalent anti-feminine feeling most apparent. His heroines are portrayed as self-deceiving viragos who claim that they merely seek love.

These creatures, heroines of the Decadence, are all creations of male writers and painters and as such they reveal that the minds of men at the turn of the century had bred a curious set of monsters:

> we witness turn-of-the-century culture completing its long, fantastic, ritualistic indictment of woman for crimes she never planned, and for outrages she only committed in the skittish, nerve-wracked minds of economically ever more marginalized men.[212]

This is Dijkstra's analysis in 1986 of the treatment of women in art at the end of the nineteenth century. Reviews and newspapers of the 1890s such as the *St James Gazette* or the *Sketch* reveal an obsession with the figure of the 'New Woman' who is portrayed in a series of very cruel cartoons in which she is shown as a dowdy, bespectacled blue-stocking and, thus, not interesting sexually, but she was financially independent of men. Was her self-sufficiency really so threatening? It certainly seems to have aroused male resentment. They had been better satisfied with the image of women which they had fabricated for her in the middle years of the century, 'The Angel in the House' or what Dijkstra calls 'The Household Nun' and men's subsequent discovery that women were not the idealised specimens which the myth made them out to be seems to have provoked terror. Salome became the favourite scapegoat of men who had to find a source for the wrongs that they imagined were being done to them and the responsibility for the creation of the *femme fatale* myth was theirs alone:

> Symbolic castration, woman's lust for man's severed head, the seat of the brain, that 'great clot of seminal fluid' Ezra Pound would still be talking about in the 1920s, was obviously the

supreme act of the male's physical submission to women's predatory drive.[213]

This is simply the substitution of one set of images of women for
another, equally false, and all are creations of a patriarchal society.
Dijkstra's prose becomes extravagant here, but the point is made:

> No longer the personification of the warm, inviolate womb of
> domestic bliss, of motherly self-negation, woman became the
> womb of the earth, the all-encompassing, all absorbing, indis-
> criminate receptacle of masculine vitality, the dark grotto of phys-
> ical temptation opening mysteriously and wide before the
> terrified spiritual adolescence of man.[214]

Elaine Showalter in her study of 1990, *Sexual Anarchy: Gender and
Culture at the Fin de Siècle*,[215] cites Dijkstra's work of four years before
in her own analysis of Salome-as-New-Woman. While she discusses
Wilde's version in depth, she does not touch on those Salome-
inspired plays of Yeats's which follow, possibly because the major
part of the latter's work lies outside Showalter's *fin-de-siècle* concerns. She informs us, interestingly, however, that the term, 'The
New Woman' was familiar by 1894, the year which not only witnessed the first London performance of Sidney Grundy's play of
that name[216] (which later travelled to Dublin) but also the appearance of Yeats's first dancer in *The Land of Heart's Desire*.

Thus, Salome, particularly in those instances where she is
depicted as a figure of depravity, found her secure place in male
masochistic fantasy; a dancing adolescent with a viraginous mother
and a taste for power and blood. We should perhaps, sanely, bear in
mind at this point that, while Sacher-Masoch had created his *Venus
in Furs* in 1870, Ibsen's Nora slammed the door of *A Doll's House*
behind her in 1879 and was not chastised by everyone for being an
unnatural wife and mother. She was certainly a force of which
neither men nor women could be ignorant and the possible strategy
on their part of a retreat into complacency was henceforth out of the
question.

Yeats, in his prejudice against Ibsen's Naturalism, perceived the
Norwegian playwright as presenting a method of expressing the
phenomenon of woman's redefinition of her traditional role which
Yeats himself considered unsuitable for his own personal emulation;
he was equally aware of the treatment of the same issue by the

Decadence. The focus of the latter rested on an eccentric and sometimes grotesque anti-feminism and while Yeats shared with the Decadents his recognition that Salome haunted contemporary consciousness, he parted from their company by refraining from portraying all of his dancers as predators. His images derive from something more than an easy misogyny; his fascination with the dancer stems more from a preoccupation with meaning, whether that conveyed by language or that which may conceivably be expressed in dance. More important to Yeats than mere head-chopping was the figure of the dancer in performance of her dance, since she was there the living representation of the aesthetic significances with which he was obsessed. The dancer and particularly Salome as Yeats perceived her, with her impassive face, cannot be detached from the execution of the dance measures and if that dance is indeed capable of expressing meaning, it is of one synonymous with its form. Yeats's most celebrated articulation of the phenomenon appears, not in a play, where it finds its actualisation, but in the poem 'Among Schoolchildren',

> O body swayed to music, O brightening glance,
> How can we know the dancer from the dance?[217]

This discussion of the works centred on Salome's dance achieved by his predecessors and contemporaries may serve to supply the context and terms in which Yeats's own reflections on the dancer have a place.

NOTES

1. *Oxford English Dictionary*, X (Oxford: Clarendon Press, 1933; rpt. 1978), p. 364. Hereafter cited as *OED*.
2. A. G. Lehmann, *The Symbolist Aesthetic in France, 1885–1895* (Oxford: Basil Blackwell, 1950; rpt. 1968). Hereafter cited as Lehmann.
3. Lehmann, p. 74.
4. Charles Baudelaire, *Oeuvres Complètes*, texte établi, présenté et annoté par Claude Pichois (Paris: Gallimard, 1975): 'Les Fleurs du Mal' (1861), p. 11.
5. Edmund Wilson, *Axel's Castle* (London & Glasgow: Charles Scribner's Sons, 1931; rpt. London: Fontana, 1967), p. 24.
6. Arthur Rimbaud, 'déréglement de tous les sens', letter to Demeney, 15 May 1871, pp. 61–2. Quoted in Lehmann, p. 96. 'Puis j'expliquai

mes sophismes magiques avec l'Hallucination des mots.' 'Saison en enfer', Délires II, 'Alchimie du verbe', Lehmann, p. 97.

7. Stéphane Mallarmé, *Oeuvres Complètes*, texte établi et annoté par Henri Mondor et G. Jean-Aubry (Paris: Librairie Gallimard, 1945; rpt. Bilbliothèque de la Pléiade, 1951): 'Toute l'âme résumée ...', p. 73. Hereafter cited as Mallarmé, *Oeuvres Complètes*.

8. Lehmann explains in a footnote that the comparison is Bergson's.

9. Lehmann, p. 159.

10. Mallarmé, *Divagations*, p. 241; quoted by Lehmann, p. 151.

11. Quoted by Lehmann, p. 188.

12. Lehmann, pp. 174–5.

13. Arthur Symons, *The Symbolist Movement in Literature* (London: Heinemann, 1899), p. v.

14. W. B. Yeats, *Collected Poems of W. B. Yeats* (London: Macmillan, 1933; rpt. 1973), p. 275. 'Coole Park and Ballylee, 1931', 'We were the last romantics – chose for theme / Traditional sanctity and loveliness.' Hereafter cited as *Collected Poems*.

15. *Collected Poems*, p. 87. 'Never give all the heart'.

16. *OED*, IV, p. 318.

17. Mallarmé, *Oeuvres Complètes*: 'Crayonné au Théâtre', p. 304.

18. Arthur Symons, *Studies in Seven Arts* (London: Martin Secker, 1906; rpt. 1924), p. 246. Hereafter cited as Symons, *Seven Arts*.

19. J. K. Huysmans, *A Rebours*, first transl. as *Against the Grain*, John Howard (New York: Lieber & Lewis, 1922); transl. as *Against Nature*, Robert Baldick (Harmondsworth: Penguin, 1959). Hereafter cited as Huysmans.

20. Mallarmé, *Oeuvres Complètes*, p. 304.

21. Frank Kermode, *Romantic Image* (London: Routledge & Kegan Paul, 1957; rpt. Fontana, 1971), p. 85. Hereafter cited as *RI*.

22. Lehmann, pp. 235–36.

23. Mallarmé, *Oeuvres Complètes*, p. 309.

24. *Ibid.*, p. 308.

25. Arthur Symons, *Poems* (London: Martin Secker, 1906; rpt. 1924), I, p. 273. Hereafter cited as Symons, *Poems*.

26. *Ibid.*, pp. 190–1.

27. Frank Kermode in W. B. Yeats, *Images of a Poet*, ed. D. J. Gordon (Manchester: Manchester University Press, 1961), p. 121.

28. Helen Grace Zagona, *The Legend of Salome and the Principle of Art for Art's Sake* (Genève: Librairie E. Droz, 1960; Paris: Librairie Minard, 1960). Hereafter cited as Zagona.

29. *Ibid.*, p. 22.

30. *Ibid.*, p. 20.

31. *Ibid.*, p. 20.

32. *Ibid.*, p. 30.

33. Heinrich Heine, 1797–1856; J. C. Heywood, d. 1900; Stéphane Mallarmé, 1842–1898; Théodore de Banville, 1823–1891; Gustave Flaubert, 1821–1880; Paul Milliet, 1858–n.d.; Henri Grémont, d. 1900; Jules Emile Frédéric Massenet, 1842–1912; Jean Lorrain, 1856–1906; Joris Karl Huysmans, 1848–1909; Jules Laforgue, 1860–1887; Oscar

Wilde, 1854–1900; Arthur Symons, 1865–1945; Hermann Sudermann, 1851–1928.
34. W. B. Yeats, *Collected Plays of W. B.Yeats* (London: Macmillan, 1934; rpt. Papermac, 1982), *The Death of Cuchulain*, p. 694. Hereafter cited as *CP*.
35. The Holy Bible (London: The British and Foreign Bible Society, n.d.), St Mark, Chapter 6, 14–29, p. 1016. Hereafter cited as Bible.
36. *Ibid.*, St Matthew, Chapter 14, 1–12, p. 987.
37. Zagona, p. 22.
38. *Ibid.*, p. 29.
39. Heinrich Heine, *Poèmes et légenæes*, p. 51. Quoted by Zagona, p. 29.
40. Heinrich Heine, *Gedichte* (Paris 1859; rpt. Munchen: Winkler Verlag, 1972), *Atta Troll*, I, p. 383. Hereafter cited as Heine, *Atta Troll*.
41. Zagona, p. 35.
42. Heine, *Atta Troll*, p. 387.
43. J. C. Heywood, *Herodias. A Dramatic Poem* (New York: Hurd and Houghton, 1867; rpt. London: Kegan Paul, Trench & Co., 1884), p. 7. Hereafter cited as Heywood.
44. *Ibid.*, p. 11.
45. *Ibid.*, p. 11.
46. *Ibid.*, p. 14.
47. *Ibid.*, p. 19.
48. *Ibid.*, p. 20.
49. *Ibid.*, p. 21.
50. *Ibid.*, p. 20.
51. *Ibid.*, p. 29.
52. *Ibid.*, pp. 83–6.
53. *Ibid.*, p. 93.
54. *Ibid.*, p. 97.
55. *Ibid.*, p. 100.
56. *Ibid.*, p. 131.
57. *Ibid.*, p. 133.
58. *Ibid.*, p. 157.
59. Oscar Wilde, 'The Poet's Corner', *Pall Mall Gazette*, XLVII: 7128. February 15, 1888, pp. 291–2. Richard Ellmann deals briefly with Heywood's trilogy in 'Overtures to Salome', *Yearbook of Comparative and General Literature*, No.17, 1968, pp. 17–28 where he mentions Wilde's review.
60. Mallarmé, *Oeuvres Complètes*, 'Notes et Variantes', p. 1440.
61. *Ibid.*, p. 1442.
62. Stéphane Mallarmé, *Les Noces d'Hérodiade, Mystère*, ed. Gardner Davies (Paris: Gallimard, 1959). Hereafter cited as Mallarmé, *Noces*.
63. *Ibid.*, p. 51.
64. *Ibid.*, p. 15.
65. *Ibid.*, p. 15.
66. Mallarmé, *Oeuvres Complètes*, p. 44.
67. Zagona, p. 51.
68. Mallarmé, *Oeuvres Complètes*, p. 45.
69. *Ibid.*, p. 45.
70. *Ibid.*, p. 46.

71. *Ibid.*, p. 47.
72. *Ibid.*, p. 48.
73. Mallarmé, Noces, p. 73.
74. *Ibid.*, p. 111.
75. *Ibid.*, p. 113.
76. *Ibid.*, p. 114.
77. *Ibid.*, p. 117.
78. *Ibid.*, p. 136.
79. *Ibid.*, p. 137.
80. *Ibid.*, p. 138.
81. *Ibid.*, p. 139.
82. Jean Royère in Mallarmé, *Oeuvres Complètes*, p. 1446.
83. Mallarmé, *Oeuvres Complètes*, p. 44.
84. Zagona, p. 59.
85. Mallarmé, *Noces*, Gardner Davies's introduction, p. 44.
86. Zagona, p. 91.
87. Théodore de Banville, *Choix de poésies* (Paris: Bibliothèque-Charpentier, 1923), p. 259.
88. Théodore de Banville, *Oeuvres de Théodore de Banville*, 'Les Exilés et Les Princesses' (Paris: Alphonse Lemerre, 1875; rpt. 1890), p. 241. Hereafter cited as Banville, *Oeuvres*.
89. *Ibid.*, p. 241.
90. Gustave Flaubert, *Trois Contes*, 'Hérodias' (1877; Paris: Louis Conard, Librairie-Editeur, 1921), p. 185. Hereafter cited as Flaubert.
91. *Ibid.*, p. 184.
92. *Ibid.*, p. 184.
93. *Ibid.*, p. 185.
94. *Ibid.*, p. 187.
95. St Mark 6:20.
96. Flaubert, p. 190.
97. Paul Milliet and Henri Grémont. Musique de J. Massenet, *Hérodiade, Opéra en quatre actes* (Paris: Calmann-Lévy, éditeurs, 1911), p. 8. Hereafter cited as Milliet and Grémont.
98. *Ibid.*, p. 8.
99. *Ibid.*, p. 10.
100. *Ibid.*, p. 11.
101. *Ibid.*, p. 13.
102. *Ibid.*, p. 14.
103. *Ibid.*, p. 26.
104. *Ibid.*, p. 32.
105. *Ibid.*, p. 36.
106. *Ibid.*, p. 40.
107. *Ibid.*, p. 42.
108. *Ibid.*, p. 42.
109. *Ibid.*, p. 44.
110. *Ibid.*, p. 53.
111. *Ibid.*, p. 54.
112. *Ibid.*, p. 55.
113. *Ibid.*, p. 55.

114. Jean Lorrain, *La Forêt Bleue* (Paris: Alphonse Lemerre, 1883), p. 13. Hereafter cited as Lorrain.
115. *Ibid.*, p. 14.
116. *Ibid.*, p. 160.
117. Huysmans, p. 104.
118. *Ibid.*, p. 104.
119. *Ibid.*, p. 105.
120. *Ibid.*, p. 105.
121. *Ibid.*, p. 106.
122. *Ibid.*, p. 106.
123. *Ibid.*, p. 106.
124. *Ibid.*, p. 109.
125. Bram Dijkstra, *Idols of Perversity: Fantasies of Feminine Evil in Fin-de-Siècle Culture* (New York: Oxford University Press, 1986). Hereafter cited as Dijkstra.
126. Huysmans, p. 109.
127. *Ibid.*, p. 109.
128. Jules Laforgue, *Moralités légendaires* (Paris: Mercure de France, 1902; rpt. 1964), p. 138. Hereafter cited as Laforgue.
129. *Ibid.*, p. 125.
130. *Ibid.*, p. 127.
131. *Ibid.*, p. 127.
132. *Ibid.*, p. 130.
133. *Ibid.*, p. 128.
134. *Ibid.*, p. 132.
135. *Ibid.*, p. 133.
136. See Zagona, p. 115.
137. Laforgue, pp. 143–4.
138. *Ibid.*, pp. 144–5.
139. *Ibid.*, p. 146.
140. *Ibid.*, p. 146.
141. *Ibid.*, p. 147.
142. *Ibid.*, p. 148.
143. *Ibid.*, p. 148.
144. *Ibid.*, pp. 149–50.
145. *Ibid.*, p. 150.
146. *Ibid.*, p. 151.
147. *Ibid.*, p. 153.
148. *Ibid.*, p. 154.
149. *Ibid.*, p. 154.
150. *Ibid.*, p. 154.
151. See Zagona, footnote, p. 119. She continues, significantly: 'It was only two years earlier (December 1884), in *Les Taches d'encre* of Maurice Barrès, that "décadent" was first used to characterize a literary group. The term had already been used by Gautier, Flaubert, and Goncourt in the general sense of literary refinement, but not until 1884 was it used to specify a special group of artists "qui se complaisent dans le rare et poussent l'amour de l'unique jusq'au culte du décadent." Among the first to be classed in this group were Verlaine, Mallarmé (despite him-

self) and Huysmans. Later Moréas, Laforgue, Vignier, and Fénéon were added (Jacques Plowert, *Petit glossaire pour servir â l'intelligence des auteurs décadents et symbolistes* (Paris, 1888), p. 27f).

152. See Zagona, p. 122.
153. Michael Kettle, *Salome's Last Veil* (London: Hart-Davis, Macgibbon, 1977).
154. See *The Romantic Agony*, p. 298, quoted by Zagona, p. 129.
155. Oscar Wilde, *Complete Works* (London: Collins, 1948; rpt. 1967), p. 555. Hereafter cited as Wilde.
156. *Ibid.*, p. 552.
157. *Ibid.*, p. 552.
158. *Ibid.*, p. 555.
159. *Ibid.*, p. 559.
160. The Song of Solomon, 4,3. Hereafter cited as Song. Sol.
161. Wilde, p. 559.
162. *Ibid.*, p. 570.
163. *Ibid.*, pp. 571–2.
164. *Ibid.*, pp. 573 and 575.
165. *Ibid.*, p. 574.
166. *Ibid.*, p. 574.
167. *Ibid.*, p. 574.
168. *W. B. Yeats and T. Sturge Moore: Their Correspondence 1901–1937*, pp. 8–9. Letter of 6 May 1906. Quoted in Katharine Worth, *The Irish Drama of Europe from Yeats to Beckett* (London: The Athlone Press, 1978), p. 114. Hereafter cited as Worth.
169. Symons, *Poems*, II, p. 36.
170. *The Letters of W. B. Yeats*, ed. Allan Wade (London: Rupert Hart-Davies, 1954), p. 380. Hereafter cited as *Letters*.
171. *The Times*, January 17, 1898, 6c.
172. Hermann Sudermann, *Johannes* (Stuttgart: Verlag der J. G. Cotta'schen Buchhandlung, 1898), p. 43. Hereafter cited as Sudermann.
173. *Ibid.*, p. 46.
174. *Ibid.*, p. 46.
175. Song. Sol. II, 1.
176. Sudermann, p. 47.
177. *Ibid.*, p. 49.
178. *Ibid.*, p. 51.
179. See Song. Sol. I, 5. 'I am black, but comely, O ye daughters of Jerusalem.' I, 7. 'I charge you, O ye daughters of Jerusalem, by the roes and by the hinds of the field, that ye stir not up, nor awake my love, till he please.'
180. Sudermann, p. 67.
181. *Ibid.*, p. 118.
182. *Ibid.*, p. 118.
183. *Ibid.*, p. 127.
184. *Ibid.*, p. 140.
185. *Ibid.*, p. 146.
186. *Ibid.*, p. 147.
187. *Ibid.*, p. 149.

188. *Ibid.*, p. 149.
189. *Ibid.*, p. 157.
190. *RI*, p. 89.
191. *Collected Poems*, 'The Hosting of the Sidhe', p. 61.
192. *Collected Poems*, note to 'The Hosting of the Sidhe', p. 524.
193. Jacob Grimm, *Teutonic Mythology*, transl. James Steven Stallybrass, 4 vols (London: George Bell & Sons, 1882), I, p. 285. Hereafter cited as Grimm. I am indebted to John Stokes for directing me to this source which he located in Ian Fletcher, 'Symons, Yeats and the Demonic Dance', *The London Magazine*, ed. John Lehmann, June 1960, vol. 7, no. 6, pp. 57–8. Hereafter cited as Fletcher.
194. Grimm, II, p. 632.
195. W. B. Yeats, *Autobiographies* (London: Macmillan, 1955; rpt. 1973), 'The Tragic Generation', p. 321.
196. W. B. Yeats, *A Vision* (1925; London: Macmillan, 1969), p. 135. Hereafter cited as *A Vision*.
197. *CP, The Only Jealousy of Emer*, p. 290.
198. *Ibid.*, p. 629.
199. *Ibid.*, p. 624.
200. *Ibid.*, p. 640.
201. *Ibid.*, p. 694.
202. *Ibid.*, pp. 703–4.
203. *Letters*, p. 827.
204. *CP*, p. 625.
205. *Ibid.*, p. 626.
206. *Ibid.*, p. 628.
207. *Ibid.*, p. 622.
208. Frank Kermode, *Puzzles and Epiphanies, Essays and Reviews, 1958–61* (London: Routledge and Kegan Paul, 1962), 'Poet and Dancer before Diaghilev', p. 2. Hereafter cited as 'Poet and Dancer'.
209. *RI*, p. 74.
210. Zagona, p. 133.
211. *Ibid.*, p. 134.
212. Dijkstra, p. 398.
213. *Ibid.*, p. 375.
214. *Ibid.*, p. 237.
215. Elaine Showalter, *Sexual Anarchy: Gender and Culture at the Fin-de-Siècle* (New York: Viking Penguin, 1990). Hereafter cited as Showalter.
216. *Ibid.*, p. 171.
217. *Collected Poems*, p. 245.

2

Japan, *Japonisme* and *Japonaiserie*

It is quite untrue, by the way, that Fenollosa and Pound introduced the Noh plays; interest in them is at least as old as this century.[1]

Frank Kermode makes the above assertion in his essay 'Poet and Dancer before Diaghilev', although it is customarily believed that W. B. Yeats was introduced to Japanese Noh theatre when Ezra Pound was preparing the manuscripts of Ernest Fenollosa for publication in 1913, while he and Yeats wintered together at Stone Cottage, Coleman's Hatch, Sussex, with Pound serving as Yeats's secretary. It is noteworthy that the majority of critics, among them Kermode himself elsewhere in *Romantic Image*,[2] assumes this collaboration to be the origin of the older poet's interest in the Noh. Yeats had met Pound – this 'queer creature'[3] – in 1909, knowing him then as a scholar versed in Provençal troubadour poetry. It is certainly true, as his letters make evident, that Yeats believed the Noh to be the dramatic form for which he had been searching and his relief and pleasure in finding the genre are expressed in a letter of 1916, written just before the performance of *At the Hawk's Well* in Lady Cunard's drawing-room. He told Lady Gregory on 26 March of that year, 'I believe I have at last found a dramatic form that suits me',[4] and in a subsequent letter to John Quinn of 2 April 1916, the day on which the play was acted at Cavendish Square, Yeats remarked most significantly:

If when the play is perfectly performed (musicians are the devil) Balfour and Sargent and Ricketts and Sturge Moore and John[5] and the Prime Minister and a few pretty ladies will come to see it, I shall have a success that would have pleased Sophocles. No press, no photographs in the papers, no crowd. I shall be happier than Sophocles. I shall be as lucky as *a Japanese dramatic poet at the Court of the Shogun*.[6] [my emphasis]

86

A few days earlier, on 14 March, he had written to his father, the painter John Butler Yeats:

I have just been turning over a book of Japanese paintings. Everywhere there is delight in form, respected yet varied, in curious patterns of lines, but these lines are all an ordering of natural objects though they are certainly not imitation. In every case the artist one feels has had to *consciously* and deliberately arrange his subject.[7] [Yeats's emphasis]

Such remarks appearing, as they do, after 1913 and Pound's work on the Fenollosa manuscripts, would seem to suggest that the usual view of Pound as instigator of the interest in Japan may legitimately be upheld. I shall endeavour to demonstrate in this chapter, however, that Yeats already knew something of Japanese culture and art and had been moving instinctively in the direction of the Noh for some years before being made familiar with the Fenollosa writings. When Pound introduced him to the manuscripts and discussed the problems of translation, he was tapping a vein of interest which, as I hope to show, had been present for some time in the older poet, ever since Yeats had been experimenting with dramatic form, stage scenery and the figure of the dancer.

The most cursory glance at the years preceding the composition of *At the Hawk's Well* of 1916 reveals that it would have been difficult for Yeats to be unaware of things from Japan, were they handcrafted artefacts or theatrical productions, and an investigation here of the varied available material dealing with *Japonisme* and *Japonaiserie* from their introduction to a Europe eager to receive them will reveal a vogue that was widespread and pervasive. A brief survey of the Japan craze and the reactions it aroused will create a background in which to set a more detailed study of the Japanese Noh theatre which so excited Yeats.

The European enthusiasm for *Japonaiserie* started in the 1850s following the arrival in Japan of the American Commodore Perry in 1853 to discover a medieval, feudal society that had cut itself off from all foreign influence. This fervour stretched up to and beyond the mania of the 1880s, when a Japanese village was built in Knightsbridge, London, numerous trade treaties were negotiated between Britain and Japan and the demand for Japanese products reached massive proportions. It is of great interest to examine some of the ways in which Japan was studied, presented and admired from the 1850s onwards. The picture in England was one of constant exhibitions, lectures, the founding of the Japan Society in 1891 and the publication of magazines about Japanese art and craft, while at the same time in France Japanese prints, *ukiyo-e*, were exerting enormous influence on artists:

> Oriental art seems to have been known to some Parisian artists in the middle 1850s. The periodical *Once a Week* started to publish an account of Japan in July 1860, and this article was illustrated by prints, while Sherard Osborn's *Japanese Fragments*, London, 1861, also contained reproductions of prints. In 1854 an exhibition of Japanese applied art had been held in London in the gallery of the Old English Water Colour Society in Pall Mall, though the impact of the applied arts was, in England, to be felt somewhat later than that of the prints. Japanese lacquer, bronze and porcelain were shown in London at the 1862 Exhibition. In the earlier 1860s, Whistler and Rossetti were enthusiasts in the collection of Oriental china. ... Porcelains, screens, and prints had been available from the 1880s at Farmer and Rogers' Oriental Warehouses in Regent's Street; Liberty's was founded in 1875 at the height of the Japanese mania.[8]

The above quotation is drawn from an article written by Ian Fletcher on Bedford Park, the 'Aesthetes' Village', which was the London home of the Yeats family from 1876 until 1880 and again from March 1888 for many years. The passion for *Japonisme* and *Japonaiserie* was apparent in the structure and decoration of the houses – in that famous asymmetry which is characteristic of Japanese prints and paintings. Indeed, the suburb was even satirised for its preciousness in the 1860s by a contemporary poet, who invited his audience to Bedford Park to 'read Rossetti (there) by a Japanese lamp'.[9] W. S. Gilbert's *Patience* also parodied the Aesthetic Movement and its concomitant *Japonisme*, while his *Mikado* of 1885 drew a formal protest from the Japanese ambassador for so misrepresenting Japanese life. Yeats therefore found himself surrounded at Bedford Park by the manifestations of the prevailing cult long before his publishing of what he termed his 'Noh plays'.[10]

During and after the writing of these, from 1916 onwards, Yeats had much to say about Japan and her theatre and his accounts will be considered later in the second half of this chapter. The important task is first to establish the poet's sources of information which preceded the creation of the 'Noh' plays and, by means of an examination of the material on Japan which would have been available to Yeats before 1913 and the work with Pound, it may be possible to piece together an overall background picture, an atmosphere enclosing the older poet which, consciously or unconsciously, stimulated him into absorbing Japan and her art as inspiration. I hope to be able to demonstrate that Yeats was anything but insensitive to the prevailing *Zeitgeist*.

The mania for *Japonaiserie* of the late years of the nineteenth century has already been briefly mentioned. As we saw, no artist in France from the 1850s onwards could have ignored the existence of Japanese prints – '*ukiyo-e*', literally, 'the floating world'. Exhibitions followed each other in Paris while those in London were well previewed and documented by *The Times* and I intend to cite this newspaper and its articles on Japan as record of the current British thinking on that country. J. A. Michener, in his book *The Floating World*, offers a clear exposition of the impact of the prints on the French Impressionists:

> From 1850 on Paris was aware of the brilliantly coloured, artistically arranged Japanese print, for during this decade Felix Bracquemond, a young and gifted etcher, fell under the spell of Utamaro and Hiroshige, forming, from sources that are unknown, an extensive exhibition of *ukiyo-e*. He also became a moving spirit of the Japanese Society, which met in the home of the director of the Sèvres porcelain factory, where Bracqemond insisted that everyone eat with chopsticks and drink saki. His work immediately reflected Japanese motifs, for he borrowed from Hiroshige and was for some time a one-man propaganda agency. ...
>
> In 1867 the Paris Exposition Universelle exhibited enough prints to make a powerful impression on artistic circles. Journals of that time reflect the impact of Japanese flat color on the Western mind and from this time on the reputation of ukiyo-e was firmly established. Other exhibitions followed until there was no artist working in Paris who could have remained unaware of Japanese influence. ...
>
> The most famous exhibition of ukiyo-e in Paris occurred in 1890, when the first prints from many private collections were shown at the Ecole des Beaux Arts. Among those who attended were Degas, Camille Pissarro and an American artist Mary Cassatt, sister to the austere president of the Pennsylvania Rail

Road. ... The effect of this 1890 exhibition was greatest however on Pierre Bonnard ... but the artist who seems to have digested the ukiyo-e influence with the most satisfying and lasting results was Toulouse Lautrec, whose big posters promptly took on a Japanese system of design, line and color.[11]

In England the first manifestations of a Japanese style appeared in the early 1860s. In 1859, when Whistler had arrived in London from France, his passion for Japanese prints and fabrics impressed the Rossettis. E. W. Godwin, Gordon Craig's father, the aesthetic architect, decorated his home in the Japanese fashion of bare floors with white rugs and a sparseness of ornament and dressed his wife in a kimono. It was indeed in 1860 that Godwin began to devote himself to the study of Japanese art and its principles and his designs for bamboo furniture as well as his patterns for wallpaper, some of which represented sunflowers or birds in flight, reflected his interest. He examined minutely the construction of Japanese artefacts such as lanterns, umbrellas and boxes as well as houses and he was the first in England to use Japanese prints as wall-decorations.

In its issues from July 7,1860, on, the British magazine *Once a Week* devoted considerable space to a report of a trip through Japan and illustrated it with woodcut reproductions of ukiyo-e, Hiroshige's landscape predominating. The next year, Sherard Osborne [sic] published in London a book called *Japanese Fragments*, in which ukiyo-e prints were described, and from then on their presence in European cultural life can be taken for granted.[12]

The second Great Exhibition of 1862 in London provided the first occasion in Europe for Japanese art to be displayed in an organised and methodically instructive fashion. A painting, *La Princesse du Pays de la Porcelaine*, appeared in 1864 and there Whistler produced a study in rose and silver which was crowded with Japanese detail but owed little to the vision and technique of Japanese prints. The artist's passion for oriental blue and white china had developed by the 1860s and he and his rival, Rossetti, compiled collections in attempts to outdo each other. Another painting of 1864 incorporates samples of his china – *Purple and Rose: The Lange Lijzen of the Six Marks* – in which his mistress, Joanna Hiffernan, dressed in a magnificent Chinese robe, is shown in the act of painting a pot. The title refers to the elegant female figures often found on these jars and the 'Six Marks' to the potter's seals. Despite the accoutrements of *Japonaiserie*, the painting is more Victorian than oriental, even though Whistler has attempted to imitate the fluidity and assurance with which Japanese and Chinese potters drew on their jars.[13] *Symphony in White No. 2: The Little White Girl* was also painted in 1864 and is the most famous of Whistler's portraits to employ Japanese themes to enliven an essentially Victorian subject. The model is again Joanna Hiffernan and she is surrounded by a Japanese fan, pink magnolia blossom and a Japanese vase.[14] 1865 saw the painting of *Harmony in Blue and Silver: Trouville* in which the influence of Japanese art can be felt in the high horizon which flattens the composition and the use of thinner paint: all is hazy space and the solitary foreground figure stands out, as in *ukiyo-e,* from the vastness of the background of nature.[15] *Symphony in Blue and Pink* of about 1868 portrays four ladies dressed in long robes suggestive of kimonos, one of them carrying a parasol, who are being buffeted by a strong wind while pink blossoms are shed on the ground.[16] *Variations in Flesh Colour and Green: The Balcony* was begun in 1864 and completed in 1870 and was derived from a woodcut of Kiyonaga (1752–1815), called *The Sixth Month* from a collection, *Twelve Months in the South* (1784). As in the original, two female figures lie or sit languidly on a balcony, one of them fanning herself, the other playing a musical instrument, while a third figure, seen from the back, leans on the railing to meditate on the view: this standing woman is used to unite the foreground and the distant horizon. The painting also contains oriental details: a tray with a saki jar and cups, Japanese screens in one corner to help frame the composition and blossom and the kimonos of the three women, but here, unlike in the portraits of 1864, we do not find a Victorian painting simply ornamented with *Japonaiserie,* instead we are presented with a composition which is redolent of its Japanese model.[17] Finally, the famous *Nocturnes* of the early 1870s, of which *Nocturne in Blue and Gold: Old Battersea Bridge* of about 1875 is perhaps the most well-known, show the possible influence of Hiroshige prints on their form.[18] In 1867 Whistler had painted his notorious 'peacock room' at W. R. Leyland's house at 49, Prince's Gate, London, an ambitious swirling oriental design in gold and black, but he was now discovering new interests apart from *Japonaiserie* and after about the mid-1870s the hitherto substantial influence of Japan on his painting subsided.

A new wave of Japanese influence manifested itself in art in the 1880s and 1890s. In Paris a Japanese exhibition at the Galerie Georges Petit in 1883 was followed by the *Exposition historique de l'art de la gravure au Japon* at the Galerie Bing three years later and another important exhibition was held at the Galerie Durand-Ruel in 1893. This second phase differed in a significant manner from that of the 1860s and 1870s:

> Whereas the artists of the Impressionist generation had been interested in Japanese prints mainly for technical reasons and pillaged them for compositional and other devices to help to solve their own artistic problems, the Post-Impressionists were interested in them stylistically. The Japanese influence is therefore more profound, though less obvious, in Post-Impressionist paintings.[19]

Van Gogh himself organised an exhibition of *ukiyo-e* at the Café le Tambourin in 1867. Gaugin, in 1884, had made a painting of a Japanese fan, but a more genuine influence of Japanese art on his work can be perceived after the spring of 1888 when he began to experiment in *cloisonnisme* or *synthétisme*.

The sheer bulk of writing about Japan both in France and England is made apparent when we discover, slightly earlier in 1882, Christopher Dresser in the preface to his *Japan: Its Architecture, Art, and Art Manufactures* apologising,

> for adding to the number of our books on Japan. We have heard of the ways of the Japanese, of the peculiarities of their manners, of their feasts and festivals, of the food they eat, and of the aspect of the country in which they live.[20]

He none the less justified his undertaking by explaining, less than modestly perhaps, that:

> My excuse for writing is a simple one – I am a specialist. An architect and ornamentalist by profession, and having knowledge of many manufacturing processes, I went to Japan to observe what an ordinary visitor would naturally pass unnoticed[21]

and he proceeded to satisfy contemporary demand by presenting a detailed analysis of Japanese artefact, particularly the lacquer ware and porcelain which had become by then in 1882 familiar to his public. His initial apology remains, however, indicative of the current high levels of curiosity and knowledge in England about Japanese affairs.

The making of such artefacts as those described by Dresser was one of the most vital attractions of the Japanese village built in Knightsbridge in 1884 and heavily patronised by delighted English visitors. At this time Yeats was living and working in London and the opening of this community attracted much publicity in *The Times.* The newspaper presented a series of articles about it, praising the ingenuity of the Japanese craftsmen who had been brought to London to demonstrate the creation of their wares, examining the beauty of the finished objects and even announcing coming attractions to the Theatre Nippon built within the village gates. On 31 May 1887, for example, feats of Japanese jugglery were promised and 'droll dances' by five little Japanese girls in native costume.[22] The press showed enthusiasm and much respect for this artistic centre in Knightsbridge and registered its popularity with the millions of visitors. The very construction of such a place demonstrates the esteem with which Japanese life and craft were then held in London and this respectful fascination came as a prelude to the Japanese–British alliance of a few years later in 1902 and to the grand Japanese–British Exhibition in 1910 in the English capital. The relationship between the two countries remained close and mutually honoured for many years. *The Times,* significantly perhaps, proved itself capable of reporting atrocities inflicted by the Japanese during the war in Formosa with the Chinese or, later, with Russia, in the same matter-of-fact way as descriptions of the intricate excellence of lacquer ware or bronzes.[23] The newspaper's code of ethics seems not to have been disturbed by any possible dilemma here.

The Times of 26 June 1889 carried an article on 'A New Japanese Art' – that of flower-arranging – 'new' meaning 'new to the West'.[24] Centuries-old skills were just being discovered by an awed and receptive Europe, but it was feared that the price of such popularity to Japan herself would be high. In reporting, on 15 March 1890, the coming National Exhibition which was to take place in Tokyo (this one having been preceded by two others held in the capital in 1877 and 1881), the newspaper recorded the crisis in art in Japan which had come about as a result of Westernisation.[25] The end of feudalism had brought with it the disappearance of patronage and Japanese artists and craftsmen had begun to produce work of inferior quality for export because they were, for the first time, obliged to enter a competitive market. Meanwhile the European demand for *Japonaiserie* reached monstrous proportions:

> The rise and decline of japonaiserie forms one of the most surprising interludes in the history of nineteenth-century taste. The vogue began in about 1856; by 1878 it had reached such heights of popularity that a critic complained 'Ce n'est plus une mode, c'est de l'engouement, c'est de la folie'; and within another thirty years it was all but extinct. Brief though the fashion had been, its influence was extraordinarily potent and penetrated all the decorative arts in France and England.[26]

The dilemma – native excellence or mass production for the West – has a curiously modern ring about it. It was also prominent in 1863 when the Japanese government found itself compelled to suppress the xenophobia on the part of the samurai which had been stirred up by the signing, in 1858, of a long-wanted trade agreement with the West. By 1866 Japanese ambassadors in bowler hats and morning coats were a common sight in most of the capitals of Europe. Today Japanese students and intellectuals set themselves on fire or ritualistically disembowel themselves as a modern protest against 'Coca-colonisation'.

Among this generalised fervour was exhibited great interest in Japanese theatre as well as in trade and art and this was demonstrated by *The Times* of the period 1870–1920. Japanese Noh theatre was first mentioned in England in 1871 in a discussion in A. B. Mitford's *Tales of Old Japan*.[27] Early October 1876 saw the publication of a translation of a Noh play, *Honekawa*, with some introductory remarks by Basil Hall Chamberlain in the *Cornhill Magazine*. On 16 July 1890,[28] a Japanese actor was interviewed by *The Times*'s journalist and he commented on the stage as a profession and on 15 June 1893, the paper printed an account of the technique and the philosophy of the art of acting by Japan's currently leading actor of the popular stage:

> The greatest Japanese actor of modern times is Ichikawa Danjuro, and he is usually regarded as one of the greatest ornaments that the Japanese stage has ever possessed.[29]

Danjuro explained that when he played a villain he absorbed his role into himself and became the most consummate villain that ever lived; moreover, although he was then fifty-six years old, he was about to play the part of a seventeen-year-old girl.

The previous year, 1892, had seen the publication in England of a play based on the Japanese. Sir Edwin Arnold's *Adzuma: The Japanese Wife* presented a story of a woman's loyalty to her husband: she gladly and bravely sought her own death in order to prove her fidelity and to protect his life. Arnold had discovered a formula for success by mixing elements of a plot relying on stereotypes of Japanese characters – evil samurai, honourable warriors and seemingly flower-frail ladies – with Indian notions of *karma* served up in a popularised form. The whole appeared to English audiences to be accessible and exotic at the same time.

The 1894 Declaration of War with China and the ensuing 1898 alliance between that country and Japan were both precisely documented by *The Times,* while the next year of note from the point-of-view of a study of Japan and her art is 1900, when the context is that of Japanese theatre in London. Osman Edwards, in his *Japanese Plays and Playfellows* to be published the following year, showed his delight with the performance at the Coronet Theatre in the spring. He applauded

> The celebrated Japanese Court Company from Tokyo, of which the leading stars, Mr Otijiro Kawakami and Madame Sada Yacco, were freely described as the Henry Irving and Ellen Terry of the Far East.[30]

Charles Ricketts also witnessed this memorable performance and wrote an acute analysis in his journal for 22 June 1900.[31] As we have remarked, Ricketts was a friend of Yeats and his journal and letters were compiled and collected by another friend of the poet, T. Sturge Moore. Yeats's own personal writings make no mention of seeing the play himself; he was usually at Coole Park for that part of the summer every year, only returning to London in October or November, but June 1900 did see him, exceptionally, at Woburn Buildings but wishing himself at Coole.[32] He may not have attended the performance in the company of Ricketts and their mutual friend, Charles Shannon, but it could have been discussed in the circles which Yeats frequented.

Ricketts found the Japanese play enchanting and some of his perceptions are worthy of communication. Although he mentioned dances, it is probable that what he saw was not a Noh play but

Kabuki or a piece of popular theatre since there is no allusion to
mask and it is clear that a woman was acting, not a man.

> We found the Japanese plays curiously coherent and direct,
> though interspersed with obbligato dances executed for their own
> sake, and only slightly related to the general action. ... During
> elaborate scenes of facial expression the body will remain almost
> immobile or kept in cramped or curtseying positions. Other
> scenes of violent altercation will be mirrored with violent gestures
> and distortions of face and body, and with lightning rapidity, and
> with fantastic poses of the legs. ...
>   Sada Yacco, the actress, is entrancing; curiously natural in her
> acting, she also at times lapses into vague entranced movements
> of the eyes – a downward squint – odd, tremulous movements of
> the mouth, and marionette actions of the arms. ... As a dancer she
> has a wild 'electric' grace, something of a wave or tiger by
> Hokusai. In a scene of despair where she runs amuck, she appears
> dishevelled like a Hokusai ghost, and moves – almost slides –
> across the stage with an ecstatic face, with eyes revulsed. Her face,
> lit by flashes of expression, will become pallid and vacant. She
> dies really gasping for breath and hunted down from within.[33]

Ricketts records pleasurable surprise in finding the plays 'coherent and direct' since he had obviously anticipated a degree of
incommunicability. Interestingly, after his account of the very
strangeness of the body movement expressing violent emotion, he
depicts Yacco's acting style to be 'curiously natural'. This opinion
would seem to be given the lie by the statement which follows
about 'marionette actions of the arms'. Ricketts has manifestly been
led by the Japanese performance to revise some of his previous
assumptions about naturalistic acting: he is quite prepared in this
case to accept the stylisedly violent and excessive interpretation of
the action of the play which coincides, paradoxically, with under-
statement when it came to facial expression; 'vague entranced
movements', 'odd tremulous movements'. While applauding the
accessibility of the event to a London audience he nevertheless
emphasises its alien qualities, especially those of the dances which
were unconnected with the plot. Perhaps the most striking feature
of Ricketts's reading of the performance is the absence of any comment on the manner of using language, except to assert that 'violent
altercation' was mirrored by appropriate gesture. But the play

seems not to have relied on dialogue at all and it thereby forced
Ricketts to a reappraisal of contemporary expectations of theatre in
the West.

In 1901 this company returned to London and their arrival was
remarked by *The Times* for 13 June of that year:

> A series of representations will be given at the Criterion Theatre
> this month by Mme. Sada Yacco, Mr Otojiro Kawakami, and The
> Imperial Court Company from Tokio. These artists appeared at
> the Coronet Theatre last year, where, it will be remembered, they
> had great success.[34]

This is the performance reviewed by Max Beerbohm and recorded
in his *Around Theatres*. On this occasion he refrained from employing his usual implements of satire and vituperation but, under the
title 'Almond Blossom in Piccadilly Circus', praised the beautiful
fragility of the Japanese play and contrasted it with the vulgarity of
the location of its theatre in contemporary London. He had expected
an equal coarseness from Japan, believing that country to have been
occidentalised – infected by the cheapness and ostentation of the
West – but he was glad to have been proved wrong:

> Straight from the prints and drawings of Utamaro and Hokusai
> these creatures have come to us. Those terrific men, bristling with
> hair, and undulating all over with muscle and showing their teeth
> in fixed grins; those pretty little ladies, with their little sick smiles,
> drooping this way or that as though the weight of their great sleek
> head-dresses were too much for them – here they all are, not out-
> lined on flimsy paper, but alive and mobile in the glory of three
> dimensions.[35]

Beerbohm too was obviously impressed by the extreme artificiality of Japanese theatre with its dependence on the presentation of
certain archetypal characters which he dubs 'creatures', thus stressing their participation in what was, for their English audience, an
alien ritual. Both Ricketts and Beerbohm reveal currently accepted
notions about theatre by the fact of their emphasis on the very
unnaturalness of certain aspects of the Japanese model.

Shannon and Ricketts also went to see the company again on
9 July 1901; once more Sada Yacco, Kawakami and, this time,
Makumoto took the leading parts. The play that Ricketts described

was *The Shogun* in which Sada Yacco was called on to go mad with
grief and her insanity was portrayed by dances:

> Sada, in this scene, followed by peasants, wanders into several
> broken dances, I had almost said, snatches of dances, doubtlessly
> oddly contrasted and chosen to the Japanese mind; one felt that,
> unacquainted with the usual dance formulas, it was difficult to
> value the dramatic side of this performance. (These broken
> dances probably are equivalent to the snatches of songs sung by
> Ophelia.)[36]

On a far less sublime note, the year witnessed the bouts of Japanese
wrestlers visiting Britain and demonstrating their art at the Tivoli
and *The Times* reported the ritualistic battles of Tami of Tokyo and
Uyenisti of Osaka.[37] Japan by now seems to have exported and
exhibited everything with which we have later come to associate
her: flower-arranging, wrestling, mythic theatre and prints of geisha
and Fujiama.

   More exhibitions of Japanese art and craft were noted in September
1901, in Japan,[38] in April 1902, in London[39] and in July 1902 at the
Whitechapel Art Gallery.[40] 1902 was the year of the Anglo-Japanese
alliance, but there is surprisingly little coverage of the *entente* in *The
Times*. This alliance proved to be very popular with both countries,
even though it became problematic when, in 1904, Japan went to war
with Russia and it was mooted that Britain should enter the fray to
support her ally. The war elicited poetry printed in *The Times*, verses
praising Japan in her struggle and drawing similarities between the
two allied groups of islands. James Bernard Fagan published 'Dai
Nippon' in the paper of 2 January 1904: the last two stanzas were as
follows, and their tone is typical of the rest of the poem:

> I, too, am outpost of the deep,
> And a sentry to the seas;
> And my dead, too, in thousands sleep
> Where never stirs the breeze;
> And my land, too, like to thine own,
> A conqueror's foot has never known,
> Nor slept in servile ease.
>
> Brother give me thy helping hand,
> Brother, stand thou by me.

We are the vanguard of the land,
And the first-born of the free,
I in the East, as thou in the West,
We are twin – we are twin, and our mother's breast
Is the civilising sea.[41]

The links between the two allied countries would seem to be more substantial than merely those forged by jingoistic poetry, however. There was certainly great respect for Japan from the British side; whether it was reciprocated is difficult to judge without documentation of the way in which Japan considered Britain, but *The Times* correspondents writing from Tokyo did suggest that Britain was viewed with approval.

A collection of armour, gathered and presented in July 1905 by the Japan Society and exhibited at the gallery of the Royal Water Colour Society in Pall Mall East proved popular. The arms of Old Japan, as beautifully ornamented as to be expected in any Japanese artefact, stood side by side with the equipment of the contemporary soldier fighting China or Russia. *The Times* reporter commented:

Naturally enough, it is the decoration that attracts European collectors, who find in this beautiful metal work the same qualities that charm them in fine lacquer boxes and in the drawings of Hokusai.[42]

This exhibition took place in a month which also witnessed honours bestowed by the British King upon the Prime Minister of Japan and on the Minister for Foreign Affairs of his Majesty the Emperor of Japan.[43] The same day, the newspaper published a poem by Henry Newbolt, an elegy on the Japanese war dead, 'Sacramentum Supremum', along with a report of a military officer on the Battle of Mukden.[44] The twenty-fifth of November saw the alliance fetes in Tokyo celebrated in the Kabukiza Theatre by dances and one, called 'chigo no chigiri', meaning 'ever-lasting union', was executed by thirty young girls to the music of twenty-two female performers. The dancers suddenly underwent a change of costume and appeared with the Union Jack on one shoulder and the Rising Sun on the other and the Tokyo correspondent commented thus on their dance:

No one who has witnessed Japanese dancing at its best will require to be told how inexpressibly refined and picturesque were the many movements of these dainty girls, but it has fallen to the lot of few foreigners to witness such a perfect display of the art as that which elicited a storm of applause in the Kabukiza theatre on Alliance Night. Underlying the beauty of the performance there could be read a graceful sentiment that the dancing of fair women most fitly typified an international union having for its main objective the blessing of peace.[45]

The war with Russia provided the Tokyo stage with a play about a heroic young commander, Hirose. The article by Mrs Hugh Fraser, reporting on the performance from the Japanese capital on 15 December 1905, appeared in *The Times* of 22 January 1906 and analysed that country's philosophy towards death and self-sacrifice, the themes which were presented in this piece for the popular theatre. Mrs Fraser's three-column account fully explored the trends of old and new in Japan's theatre and, in considering the old, touched on the Noh. This appears to be the first mention of the theatrical genre by the newspaper, despite the multiple articles on drama of preceding years. Noh is examined again in years to come, but this report of 1906 seems to be *The Times's* introduction to the topic so significant for writers such as Yeats and Pound; even the earlier interview with Danjuro of June 1893 did not deal with Noh or Kabuki as theatrical forms. Mrs Hugh Fraser wrote:

No one would openly question the weight of Court opinion, but it seems to tell very little on the prosperity of the theatres. The handful of aristocrats who condemn the stage can be counted out of the audiences without being missed. They admit no form of drama less exalted than the semi-religious 'No,' taking this diversion sadly and solemnly; the attendance at the Kudan Temple, where the performances are given, presents a most interesting spectacle to any who wish to study the fast disappearing type of the Japanese Grandee. The 'No' represents in Japanese ritual very much the element of the ancient 'Mystery' in Europe, and certainly has an enthralling interest of its own; but the mass of the people care little for it. They follow the more moving popular drama with frank delight. To them their favourite actors are idols and heroes, adored in life and honoured in death.[46]

Information about the Noh had at last reached a wide audience.

In 1907 a Japanese education exhibition was held at the Victoria and Albert Museum which coincided, felicitously, with the visit of Prince Fushimi to London. The newspaper correspondent was as enthusiastic as usual about this and all attributes of Japan and his report seems to represent the current mass opinion of the British about their ally:

It is true that there is nothing here that will cause much surprise; we have ceased to be astonished at anything Japanese, after realising, in the late war, the swift perfection with which that people had assimilated and mastered everything that the West had to teach them. But what this exhibition shows is the patient, methodical way in which the whole people is being taught, the universality of the system, the scientific fashion in which the teaching is graded, and the automatic manner in which one stage leads on to another, from kindergarten to high school. ...

One foreign language is taught almost universally, and that language is English. Six hours in school is the weekly allowance in the middle schools for this, which is deemed by the Japanese authorities to be an absolutely indispensable subject. ... The drawings of even the youngest children show that the idea of the English alliance is familiar and very popular; for one of the favourite subjects of a 'spontaneous' drawing is the Union Jack, either by itself or crossed with the Rising Sun.[47]

A meeting of the Japan Society was reported in *The Times* of 13 March 1908, at which Mr Lawrence Binyon lectured on some phases of Japanese painting. The Society, which met at 20, Hanover Square, London, continued to thrive as it had done from its establishment by Arthur Diosy in the early 1890s and provided a wealth of information on very many aspects of Japanese life and culture. As for this particular lecture by Mr Binyon, some interesting distinctions between Japanese and Western art were drawn:

Japanese art differed from European art in that where the latter began with man as its centrepiece and dealt with the glory of the human body and all its surroundings, the former did not treat the body for its own sake, but rather dealt with the presence of the powers outside in nature, the augustness of mountain peaks, and the glory and colour of valleys and trees as they were presented in their natural state. Japanese painting was first derived from China, and in the eighth century began the first of its great periods when the whole of the paintings consisted of landscapes and subjects at rest. In the twelfth century a new force and vivacity was introduced into the works of the artists, and figures in motion were for the first time portrayed. ... Throughout the whole course of the growth of Japanese art there had been a stream of artists, and while each phase possessed some peculiarity of its own, the main characteristics noticeable were great buoyancy, frankness, fine movement and dramatic sense.[48]

1910 was an important year for the continuing interest in Japan in that it saw the great Japanese–British Exhibition at Shepherd's Bush. *The Times* of 28 April announced the projected opening on 12 May and remarked, most interestingly,

> The magnificent Ro-mon, or gateway of the Kasuga shrine at the ancient capital, Nara, has been reproduced at the Wood Lane entrance. Here, too, is a platform where the famous No dance will be performed.[49]

As we have discovered, the newspaper had mentioned Noh only once before, in the article by Mrs Hugh Fraser in 1906, so it had not itself been very instrumental in making the genre 'famous'.

The coverage of the exhibition in *The Times* was vast and exhaustive; not only were there many accounts about it, among them a special one on 16 May about the pictures there displayed,[50] but also a weighty supplement on Japan accompanied the newspaper on 19 July, dealing with art and craft:[51] included were 'The Japanese Drama – A Stage Reform Movement';[52] Walter Dening writing on 'Japanese Modern Literature';[53] Professor Y. Takenob on 'Japanese Novelists and their Work';[54] and 'The Social Status of Japanese Women'.[55] Yeats himself had contributed an article to the newspaper of 16 June 1910, on 'Irish National Theatre',[56] just a month before the publication of the comprehensive supplement.

The report of 16 May 1910 on the Japanese pictures drew forth some astute judgements about the paintings and an impressive show of learning about the painters:

> In fact, the formulae of design in Oriental painting have much the same function as metre in poetry. They are systematized means of expression, and no more hamper originality than metre does. The

works of Masanoba, the father of Motonobu, are rare, but two of them are in this Exhibition, both landscapes with figures. The 'Angling on a Wintry Lake' has that perfect harmony between figure and landscape which is scarcely found in European painting except in the works of Giorgione. Here the old man fishing in his boat is homely enough, and yet there is no discord between it and the beautiful solitary landscape. And this harmony is not obtained by any generalizing of the figure, as in many of the works of J. F. Millet. The old man is almost a portrait and seems to be painted straight from real life. In fact, the whole picture has the vividness and precision of a sketch direct from reality; yet it is not a sketch, but a finished, calculated, and balanced work of art, and its harmony is obtained not by a lucky chance, but by a deliberate system of selection.

There is one whole room given up to Ukiyoyé, the Japanese term for genre pictures, and three works are shown by Matabei, the rare and famous originator of genre in Japan. ... In works of this kind the Japanese genius seems to be most original, and the Ukiyoyé school has lasted from the sixteenth century without a break up to our own time.[57]

The Times's multiplicity of articles about Japanese painting as well as those on Japanese theatre is worthy of note and I am concerned to direct some attention to these reports for two reasons: firstly, as will be demonstrated later in the second section of this chapter, the prints are crucial to an understanding of Yeats's preoccupation with stage scenery and, secondly, the paintings provided 'images' or visual metaphors, without any form of moralising – Japan's art seemed to be for art's sake – and thus, as in *haiku* poetry which so tellingly marked the work of Pound and the Imagists, they presented no narrative or discursive statement but simply a technique which conveyed tone and meaning alone. The paintings had exerted great influence on French and English artists during the second half of the nineteenth century and by now, in 1910, they were well-known, appreciated and collected.

On 14 July 1910, *The Times* announced the advent of a new illustrated monthly periodical published in Tokyo, *The Japan Magazine*, which was intended for English readers interested in Japanese art and thought and which resembled English monthly magazines in appearance. The first number of February that year had contained a poem by the Empress of Japan with a translation into English.[58]

This new source of information must have added to the ever-growing huge bulk of material inspired by the fervour for Japan and her culture. *The Times* continued to supply many articles and reports and in its special supplement of 19 July 1910, it illuminated for its readers subjects of all possible interest including theatre and literature. Page 56 of this supplement presented an account of a stage reform movement which included information on Noh drama:

> Those who seek the origin of the Japanese drama in the singing and dancing of antiquity will find little to reward them for their researches. Japan possessed its own singing and dancing even in remote antiquity, but the relations of the popular drama to the Nō are very indefinite. Like the ancient Greek tragedies, the Nō performances were at the time of their institution associated with religion. Those who managed and acted in the Nō-Shibai occupied a much higher social position in the community than the actors of the Kabuki Shibai, or popular theatre. It is well known that the latter, until the Theigi period, were regarded almost as social outcasts. An effort is being made in Japan to revive the Nō, or lyrical drama. The writer recently attended a notable performance of this kind, given under the auspices of a descendant of a samurai at a Tokyo club.[59]

It is gratifying to discern that by 1910 documentation about the Noh was beginning to establish itself in the Times, thirty-nine years after the genre was first recorded in England.

The whole of page 6 of *The Times* of 29 July 1910, was devoted to an advertisement for the Japanese–British Exhibition and 10 September brought another article on Japanese painting. Here the writer evaluated the influence of the art of Japan on the European artists of the previous decades dating from the explosion of *Japonisme* on the Western world in the 1850s and 1860s. This report sounded an unexpected note of reserve and caution that is new and incongruous to the customary fervour:

> Scarcely a generation has passed since Whistler was moved to enthusiasm by the Japanese colour print and praised the daintiness and exquisite frivolity of Oriental art. And we further know that this more serious art of theirs was mainly an imitation of a still greater Chinese art of which Whistler and the earlier European admirers of Japanese design were quite ignorant. ... We

have seen no Japanese or Chinese picture that seems to us to express so much as Michelangelo's 'Creation of Adam' or Titian's last 'Pietà' or Rembrandt's 'Supper at Emmaus'. They are all poorer in content than these great works, as a single lyric is poorer than a great drama. They lack the cumulative power which only exists with a very full statement, whether in literature or in art. ... They seem, indeed, to be a nation with a genius for imitation, imitating with the zest and force of originators, divining at once the innermost secret of their models and making it their own. ... Our painters cannot specialize in this way; they are too conscious of the relation between all objects and phenomena. The Japanese eye sees more singly because the Japanese mind can isolate its interest in particular things. But this power of isolation must surely be coming to an end now that Japan is open to all the science of the West. It may be that it will be ruined. Her artistic future is as obscure as her political, and as full of interest.[60]

Contained in this article are a number of assumptions and value judgements which are of significance in elucidating the artistic creeds of 1910, at least those promulgated by *Times* reporters. It is indeed open to question whether a 'single lyric' is 'poorer' than a 'great drama' even 'in content' and the writer seems to estimate as pusillanimity that quality perceived by Whistler as 'daintiness'. The entire piece is charged with prejudice rather than analysis and it would certainly appear that the hitherto unquestioning admiration of Japan was waning. To explain, however, the Japanese technique of specialisation, isolation of aesthetic interest, in terms of Japan's geographical parochialism seems simple-minded, as do the tacit cultural assumptions behind the choice of the works of Michelangelo, Titian and Rembrandt as sole yardsticks with which to measure art. One finds also the hint of disapproval supporting the explanations of Japanese talent as that of imitation whereby is divined 'at once the innermost secret of their models'. While any praise is grudgingly bestowed, the report fascinates by its self-confidence and its novel and perhaps refreshing refusal unequivocally to laud its object of scrutiny.

Also published this year, 1910, was Marie Stopes's book, *A Journal from Japan* which included her account of a visit to a Noh play. An earlier description of such a play by Osman Edwards had been published in 1901 and Yeats may have been familiar with it (see p. 126 below). Stopes's perspective is worthy of note: it was written in

1907, appeared in print in 1910, and provides a very personal reaction to the play along with some insights into the Noh phenomenon as a whole:

> November 3, 1907.   Dr. *H*- took me to a Nō performance. These are extremely interesting old plays, some of them written about 300 years ago, and they are still acted in the same way as they were originally. The intonation (which is most peculiar), dress, steps, even the movements of the hands, are all according to prescribed rules, and all are so highly specialised and conventionalised that it is hard even for most Japanese to understand them. The arrangements of stage, actors, chairs, musicians, etc. remind me partly of the old Greek plays and partly of the original Shakespearean style of acting. There is no scenery, but one pine tree and a few necessary implements; the music-makers and chorus sit on the stage at the back and side, and chant in unison with the 'dancing' (which by the way is a series of slow and very stiff poses, not dancing at all in our sense of the word). The stage is square, and projects out so that the audience sits on three sides of it. The performance began at nine in the morning, but I was there soon after half-past-eight to see the audience come in. There was no artificial light, and as it poured with rain it was at times rather dark, and the rain came in in places. I left at 3.30 and it was still going on – not being over till 4.30. This was not all one piece, but a series of about six short plays, each representing only one incident or situation, and quite disconnected. As the Japanese themselves do not fully understand it without years of study, I could not expect to, but was most interested nevertheless ... the Nō is totally different from the Japanese theatre proper, and is only visited by refined or highly cultivated people who study it deeply. Dr. *Mk*-, who was to interpret for me, went to sleep! Dr. *H*- has studied the pieces for years and knows them well, but can explain very little to me about them. All the pieces are contained in half a dozen volumes, and therefore the study is a possible one, just as the study of Shakespeare is possible, but may take a lifetime. None of the pieces are less than 150 years old.[61]

1910 was thus an *annus mirabilis* for *Japonisme* and *Japonaiserie* in Britain and the indication in Yeats's writings is that he too admired Japan, which he perceived as an aristocratic and aesthetic society, as this chapter will go on to disclose. He contributed an article, 'The Tragic Theatre', to the journal *The Mask* of October, 1910, edited by E. Gordon Craig. Yeats's account appears on page 77: the plate which faces page 76 of the publication portrays *Benkei on the Bridge (No Dance)*. The coincidence may be startling but it still does not allow of any conclusion that Yeats drew information on Noh either from the picture or from the review of the book which it illustrated, *The Japanese Dance* by Marcelle Azra Hinckes, which appeared on page 90 and dealt extensively with the genre.[62]

Many royal and distinguished Japanese guests visited London the following year to attend the coronation of George V and their travel arrangements were assiduously chronicled by *The Times*, as were the meetings of the Japan Society and the subjects of the speeches delivered by those invited. An official report on the Japanese–British Exhibition of the previous year and its development and progress was published; on 14 March 1912, the Japan Society hosted a lecture by Professor Ito on Japanese painting;[63] on 25 May of the same year the Society celebrated its twenty-first annual dinner;[64] and 29 August witnessed a special article on 'The Spiritual Problem of Japan: Difficulties in the New Era'.[65] On 14 September a lengthy report on the funeral ceremony of the Emperor of Japan was printed and, along with it, a brief account of the suicide of Count Noji and his wife in sympathy and out of honourable respect for the Emperor's demise. *The Times*'s readers were assuredly being kept informed about Japanese life in very many of its aspects.

In the winter of the following year, 1913, Yeats was certainly made familiar with examples of Japanese Noh plays through his friendship with Ezra Pound and after December of that year he made up for any previous *lacunae* by beginning to write extensively about Japan and the Noh and to create his own 'Noh plays'. Before considering the end of his long itinerary, let us first conclude the perusal of the information that *The Times* was continuing to offer its readers on Japanese art and theatre. From this we can glean the sort of material that was available for popular consumption, estimate how informed Yeats's potential audiences were and compare the newspaper's version of Japanese culture with the poet's own which is examined below.

During the First World War *The Times* applauded the unstinting support given to Britain by her ally and the newspaper went on reporting on Japanese trade, industry and art up to and including the 1920s. Mr Yone Noguchi, Professor of English Literature at the

Keiogijiki University, Tokyo, became a well-known and popular speaker at the meetings of the Japan Society and elsewhere[66] and he would go on to publish in 1918 three translated selections from Noh drama. On 15 January l914, *The Times* noted his lecture on Japanese poetry in which he discussed *haiku*, a genre which became as profoundly influential on a generation of poets as did the Noh on playwrights and stage-designers. Noguchi spoke of the 'poetry of silence':

> Mr Noguchi said that the very best poems were left unwritten or were sung in silence. The real test for poets was how far they resisted that impulse to utterance or to the publication of their work; not how much they had written, but how much they had destroyed. As instances of great poets he quoted the names of Basho Matsumo, the seventeen syllable *hokku* poet of 350 years ago, and Mallarmé, the French poet, who, he said, united in the point of denying their hearts too free play, with the result of making poetry living and divine, not merely 'words, words, and words'.[67]

Noguchi knew both W. B. Yeats and Arthur Symons. He visited Yeats and Pound in Sussex in January 1914, went on to publish an article in *The Bookman* in June 1916, on 'A Japanese Poet on W. B. Yeats' and his book, *Japanese Hokkus*, published in Boston in 1924 was dedicated to the Irish poet.[68] On 11 March 1914, Mr Noguchi delivered a lecture to the Royal Asiatic Society on 'the "No" drama, the Japanese Plays of Silence'. The correspondent noted the following:

> today there is a strong revival of the art, which is in effect a religious art of spiritual contemplation, Buddhistic in its origin, in which the audience, or what Mr Noguchi called the appreciators, take their part as well as the actors. The stage is never larger than 25 ft. square, and the scenery is of the simplest. The orchestra consists of a flute and two tambourines, and besides the three or four acting characters, one of whom is often a dancer, a chorus, drawn up in two rows with their side-faces to the audience, helps in the interpretation of the play. There are about 300 of these 'No' plays in existence. They deal largely with the connection between mankind and the animal and vegetable worlds, and reflect the tragedy rather than the lighter side of life. The audience, who may be provided with books in which they can follow the story, listen to them, or rather watch their action, in absolute silence; and even

the actors rarely speak their words. To know them by heart, so as to be able to recite them, and still more to have played them upon the stage, is in Japan the ambition of the properly educated man. Yet, though they are thus a part of the education of Japan, as well as of its art, their real value lies in their spirituality, and in the silent magnetic intercommunion of thought and ideal between actors and audience.[69]

We can observe that by this date in 1914 information on the Noh had become more readily available and this accessibility may be contrasted with *The Times*'s silence on this topic up until the relatively late year of 1906.

A glance at the contents of a special Japan Supplement published in June and July 1916 reveals articles on subjects which we have by now come to expect because of their similarity to reports appearing in preceding editions of *The Times* as well as their intrinsic popularity. On 3 June 1916, Zoë Kincaid wrote on 'The Japanese Stage: Value of the Art of Kabuki'[70] and on 15 July 'The Great Actors of Japan' were discussed.[71] Later, on 2 September, the newspaper carried a report about 'Imperial Theatre: Character of its Performances'[72] and on the same day an account of 'Imperial Poetry Party'[73] was printed, along with 'Songs of the Geisha: Her Role as a Society Entertainer' by Dr J. I. Bryan[74] and 'Japanese Women and the War: Ideals and Aspirations'.[75] On 14 October 'Japanese Flower Groups: Ancient and Graceful Art'[76] and lastly and perhaps most interestingly, a study of 16 December called 'A Dream of Masks', was presented.[77] The selection of such topics was obviously made from an understanding of the role and importance in Japanese culture of aesthetic and artistic matters.

In October 1918 a Japanese play at the Coliseum was reviewed:

> Mme. Hanako, who used to make us smile in her quaint comedy at the Ambassadors, leads a small company of Japanese players in a wordless tragedy called *Ki Musume*. The acting is conventional but grim, and tiny Mme. Hanako scores a great personal success [78]

but this was evidently not a Noh play. An article on 'Japan and the West: The Culture of the Orient' appeared on 12 November of the same year and it informed readers that a special society for the promotion of a better understanding of Japan in the West had been created in Tokyo:

There has recently been started in Tokyo a very important propaganda movement for the communication of Japanese national culture to the West, called the Yamato Society, with a group of Japan's leading men as founders, which indicates that the East desires to speak for itself in no uncertain tones, and to convey to the West an interpretation of the chief characteristics of the life, psychology, and art of Japan.[79]

Japan evidently felt the need to correct any misrepresentation of her culture in the West and the founding of this body indicated a desire for even better relationships with the Occident than was previously the case, excellent though such contact had been.

The Times of 1919 produced three important accounts on 'The Theatre in Japan', one on Kabuki, the next on the revival of the Noh and the third on Doll Theatre. It had the following to say about the Noh:

It is several hundred years older than the realistic Kabuki and the marionettes of the doll-theatre, but this ancient and aristocratic ancestor has had great influence upon the younger and more democratic theatres. The No is above all a unity of the arts. In it movement, gesture, speech, song chorus, rhythm, and colour are moulded together to form an organic whole – and show conclusively that the Eastern stage craftsmen have unconsciously made use of a unity of the arts in such a manner as to have come nearer the real source of theatre art than their Western contemporaries. ...[80]

This insistence on the 'unity of the arts' sounds very similar to the *Symbolistes'* ideal which they believed Wagner to have fulfilled, and echoes of the theories of Godwin, Wilde and Craig are all quite noticeably present. *The Times* continues:

As evidence of the growing importance of the No and its present popularity as opposed to its former conservatism, when it was reserved for the pleasure of the chosen few, there have been erected two large No theatres with seating capacity to accommodate the greatly increased number of patrons. One of these, the most beautiful No theatre in Japan, has been constructed near Tennoji, Osaka's ancient Buddhist temple. ...

The West has been so busy teaching the East that it sometimes forgets or overlooks the fact that there are some things to learn in

Japan. It is undeniable that the No holds much inspiration for a new Western theatre.[81]

The last article on 'The Art of the Doll' reflects the aesthetic creed of both W. B. Yeats and his collaborator, Edward Gordon Craig, stage designer and theatrical producer, whose theories of the *Ubermarionette* will be dealt with below because they exerted a strong influence on the poet's theatrical work. This third form of Japanese drama, 'Bunraku', had existed for more than two hundred and fifty years:

> To call them dolls is hardly fair, for they are so full of dignity and grace, their movements so suggestive of the whole gamut of human emotions, that they are far removed from the trivial and banal with which the name of puppet is so widely associated in the West. ...
>
> The actors of the theatre proper in Japan have long gone to the doll actors for inspiration, and the dramas written for the dolls are today the most popular pieces played on the stages of Tokyo and Osaka. The western actors need the dolls to bring them to a clearer recognition of themselves. ... The marionettes of the West need all the support and encouragement their elder brothers and sisters in Japan can give them, and it would not be surprising if this old art, buried in Japan for centuries, should one day inspire the actors of the world – if ever the time should arrive when what is true and sincere in the art of the theatre be given recognition.[82]

The links with Gordon Craig and his writings on mask and *Ubermarionette* are firm and, as we shall discover, even the proselytising tone is redolent of that of Craig. The designer's prophecies about the return of mask to theatre had been made in 1905 and 1907, however: Yeats had become acquainted with his notions as early as 1902 when he had first met Craig. These *Times* reports above appeared only in 1919 and informed readers about ideas that, though centuries old, had been struggling for rebirth in the West.

A lecture given at the Japan Society on 18 December of 1919[83] by Mr W. Heinemann mentioned Marie Stopes's book on the Noh. Finally, in 1920, the newspaper offered another article on Tokyo's theatre in which it again pleaded with the West to follow what the East had to teach.[84] Perhaps such a plea was almost unnecessary; the

West had proved itself well and truly willing to receive what Japan had to give and, for a time, this willingness had amounted to mania.

In observing the coverage of *The Times* alone, it is tempting to suggest very tentatively that Yeats could have heard of a phenomenon called 'Japanese Noh theatre' before Pound's introduction of 1913 and that the latter had simply provided specific examples of the plays; but even this modest proposal is not hard fact: there is no mention of Noh in any of Yeats's writings until after 1913 and a prior acquaintance with the genre, however tenuous, would contradict his own statements that he discovered the form through Pound's work on the Fenollosa manuscripts. It would also preclude his excited comments of 1916 that he had finally found a model of theatre that suited him.

Yeats had, however, referred to Japan in several different manners in the years preceding 1913 and while some of them have been noted above, others will be examined in the second part of this chapter. Earl Miner believes that Yeats 'absorbed Japan scarcely without knowing it'[85] and we have considered several of the latter's possible sources of information. All that can be said with any degree of certainty is that the poet made reference to Japan, though not to the Noh, before he met Pound and, as we shall see below, in his drama he was working, coincidentally, on very similar lines to the methods of this type of theatre. Naturally, after its discovery, writing on the Noh abounds:

> After a period of studying no with Pound, references to Japan and its culture begin to appear casually, naturally one might say, in his writing. But not all of his allusions are related to no; most perhaps are not, so the question arises where the other information came from. No sure answer can be given, but one or both of two explanations must be true. *Either Yeats had been reading more about Japan before he met Pound than one assumes,* or else Pound stimulated him to read a great deal about Japan in the years of the First World War when they spent lengthy periods of time together. At any event, Yeats seems to have acquired certain kinds of knowledge about Japan that Pound never had and to have created in his mind certain images of Japan which were different from Pound's.[86]   [my emphasis]

The next section will deal with four points. Firstly, it will summarise the characteristics of classic Japanese Noh in order to enable a comparison of these with Yeats's early preoccupations in the theatre. Secondly, it will examine the poet's pre-1913 writings on stage design, mask, archetype, chorus and dance, all of which, though he probably did not know it, are Noh features. Thirdly, two early plays of 1894 and 1907 will then be considered where they also exhibit certain attributes of Japanese Noh. Finally, Yeats's own post-1913 'Noh plays' will be discussed along with his prose writings on Noh and, where relevant and possible, the plays will be linked with their Japanese sources that were made available through the Pound–Fenollosa studies of 1913. In addition, importance will be attached to the dance in the Yeatsian versions as well as that manifested in the Japanese Noh and this will prepare for a discussion of the performance dimension, so far not touched upon, in the concluding chapter of this study.

YEATS AND THE NOH

Before listing certain elements in Yeats's early and late plays and labelling them 'Noh', we must first establish what constitutes a classic Noh play: an analysis of the characteristics of this genre will act as reference and yardstick with which to measure the poet's own writings.

There are five different types of Noh play and the classification is usually as follows:

(i)   *Shin,* 'god' – a god play, or a play of prayer in which the chief character is a god.

(ii) *Nan,* 'man' – a battle-play in which the chief character is a warrior who, in most cases, is tortured in the Buddhist Purgatory after death.

(iii) *Nyo,* 'woman' – a 'wig' play, or a female play in which the chief character is a woman who wears a wig.

(iv) *Kyo,* 'madness' – a play of madness in which the chief character is a mad woman.

(v)   *Ki,* 'demon' – a demon-play in which the chief character is often a supernatural being, either friendly or hostile to human beings.

A full day's programme would include one example from each of these categories, with *kyogen* – 'mad words' (farces) – interpolating the other serious plays as comic relief.

The hero or protagonist is called the *shite* – the 'doer' or 'actor'; his companion or assistant is the *tsure* and the balance of the story is preserved by a sort of deuterogonist called the *waki* – his name implies an assistant who 'stands aside' – and he may also have his *tsure*. While the *shite* performs his principal dance, the *waki* usually looks on silently and the chanting of the former during his dance is undertaken by a chorus made up of ten or twelve actors seated motionless at the side of the stage. The music of a high sharp flute, two hand-drums and sometimes a stick-drum played by three uncostumed musicians at the back of the stage accompanies the incantation of the chorus.

The principal plot outline for the majority of the plays is that of a journey which may be quest or pilgrimage and, to signify travelling, the *waki* will take a few steps and relate the features of the landscape around him; he thus conjures up a setting by his words. The characteristic of Noh that Yeats was to find so laudable was the absence of painted stage-scenery since a pine tree is simply delineated on a backdrop and three small living pine trees in pots are arranged down the side of the stage:

> The painting of the pine tree on the back is most important. It is a congratulatory symbol of unchanging green and strength. ... The three real little pine trees along the bridge are quite fixed; they symbolize heaven, earth, and man. The one for heaven is nearest the stage, and then comes the one which symbolizes man. They are merely symbols like the painted pine tree. Sometimes when a pine is mentioned the actors look toward it.[87]

There are few properties and these are usually of a highly conventionalised kind: both a boat and a chariot can be denoted by an open framework of bamboo, while any building, be it palace, cottage or hovel, is represented by four posts covered with a roof. The fan which the actor carries can be used to suggest several objects; knife, brush, cup, paper, pen and so on. Weapons are usually real – the short-sword, belt-sword, pike, spear and Chinese broad sword are carried, as are bows and arrows.

As we have noted, most Noh plays involve a journey which the *shite* or the *waki* undergoes in order to find some person or to fulfil some duty or religious objective and, while travelling, he passes some famous place. There the living person meets a god in disguise or the ghost or reincarnated spirit of the dead or perhaps the desolate wreck of someone once of high estate. The hero does not recognise him and innocently discusses with him the stories and events for which the locality is famous. Finally the ghost will reveal his identity as the spirit of the departed person who renders the place now legendary and, as the traveller is often a priest, he may console the ghost by his prayers and exorcism:

> The primary point to be remembered in the analysis of a Noh play is that action is generally recollected and that the plot hinges on an event that has already taken place in the past. This means that the dramatic situation is not necessarily acted realistically before one's eyes. Rather it is poetically recalled and discussed by the characters and chorus, and their movements become dreamlike glosses to the idea carried by the words.[88]

There is generally some moral teaching implicit in the story with the hero or ghost signifying filial or paternal duty, patriotism or other loyalty:

> The Nō are frankly didactic. Piety, reverence, martial virtues are openly inculcated, though never in such a way as to shock. Artistic sensibilities, Beauty and taste go far to disguise all structural deficiencies.[89]

The Buddhist teaching throughout adds to the dimension of the plays as 'moralities' in its stressing of the transitoriness of human life, the predominance of suffering which must be endured and overcome by stoicism and of a philosophy which states that the world is a dream and that its pain can be escaped by the enlightened spirit.

As well as the moral precepts contained in the play, its object is to create *yūgen*, a perception of beauty which brings about meditation and trance:

> The difficult term *yūgen* ... is derived from Zen literature. It means 'what lies beneath the surface;' the subtle, as opposed to the obvious; the hint, as opposed to the statement. It is applied to the natural grace of a boy's movements, to the gentle restraint of a

nobleman's speech and bearing. 'When notes fall sweetly and flutter delicately to the ear,' that is the yugen of music. The symbol of yugen is 'a white bird with a flower in its beak.'[90]

Two elements which contribute to the production of *yūgen* are mask and dance because they bring about serene distantiation. The use of mask is confined to the main actor (*shite*) and to his subordinate (*tsure*) or companion (*tomo*); neither *waki* nor his *tsure* nor any of the other characters ever wear masks. The *shite* is always masked if playing the part of a woman or old man; women's roles are always taken by men who preserve their natural voice. Boy actors – '*Ko-gata*' – always play the part of emperors or kings which would otherwise be considered irreverently realistic if performed by adult men.

Every Noh play includes a *mai*, a dance characterised by slow steps and solemn gestures, a surprising phenomenon for Western writers, as we have noted, because it did not fulfil the usual expectancies and properties of 'dance'. The most important feature of the rendering of the dance or mime – in five movements for the *shite* and in three for the *tsure* – is the stamping of beats made by the stockinged foot.

This is the Noh as Yeats came to understand it, a genre which had changed little since the fifteenth century and for the preservation of which two men were responsible, Kwanami Kiyotsugu (1333–1384) and his son, Seami Motokiyo (1363–1444). Kwanami was a priest of the Kashuga Temple near Nara when, about the year 1375, he was seen performing at the New Temple of Kumano in the province of Kii by the Shogun Yoshmitsu who was so moved that he became his protector and patron. Seami wrote a series of *Works* – 'Kadensho' – theories of drama only discovered in 1907 and translated into English by Arthur Waley. In these he gave the history of the Noh along with directions about certain parts of the performance. For example, the *Works* include pages of minute instructions about the foot stamping and its relationship with the main rhythm and expression of the beat. His writings also tell us that the chorus did not exist from the beginning of Noh: it appeared in 1430 and the distinguishing factor between the plays of the fourteenth century and those of today lies in its inclusion. Kwanami and Seami belonged to the Yusaki family, one of the four families who traditionally managed the Nara stage; they owned a small estate and, after gaining the Shogun's patronage for their Noh, transformed and developed the genre into extremely popular court entertainment. Throughout the Tokugawa era (1602–1868), every Daimyo with the means to do so maintained a troupe of Noh players. Original costumes, masks and music were preserved and the plays performed by the resident company were considered instructive in understanding the beliefs and values of the medieval era from which they derived.[91]

This brief account of classic Japanese Noh reveals the principal characteristics of the genre and, by reference to it, enables a study of Yeats's own interests in stylisation of stage design, mask, chorus, music and dance for their own sake and in order to establish how similar were the features of his theatre to those of the Noh. These preoccupations were evident in Yeats's work long before 1913 and the information from Ezra Pound and I shall now consider these early perceptions of what the older poet wanted for his drama. For many years he was groping his way towards the dramatic realisation of this series of abstract ideas and experimenting on how to actualise them on the stage and, unwittingly, he was treading a theatrical path in parallel with that of the Noh.

Yeats addressed a letter to 'Fiona Macleod'[92] from Paris in January 1897 and it revealed, significantly, that he had already begun to formulate what he demanded of stage scenery: we can clearly identify what he required as being very akin to what Japanese Noh provides:

> My own theory of poetical or legendary drama is that it should have no realistic, or elaborate, but only a symbolic and decorative setting. A forest, for instance, should be represented by a forest pattern. And not by a forest painting. One should design a scene which would be an accompaniment not a reflection of the text. ... The acting should have an equivalent distance to that of the play from common realities. The plays might be almost, in some cases, modern *mystery plays*.[93] [my emphasis]

We note that the comparison between Noh and the mysteries was also made by Mrs Hugh Fraser on page 100 in her article in *The Times* of 1906. Yeats too, though much earlier in 1897, was seeking a moral didactic component in some of his own drama and these same dimensions are commonly attributed to Noh: Noguchi is reported to have commented on the spirituality of the Japanese plays in 1914 (p. 108), and Fenollosa on the force of their ethics (pp. 132–3). This perception of the pieces as approaching medieval mysteries would seem to indicate that Western audiences apprehended the 'foreign' and religious qualities of Noh by translating them into the terms of their own dramaturgical history. And Yeats here, interestingly, had already expressed a need for such elements in his theatre many years before he discovered them in Noh.

A letter of 27 January 1899, to the Editor of *The Daily Chronicle* discloses, even as early as his struggles with *The Countess Cathleen*, an initial search for a certain kind of scenery, a difficulty which was partly resolved by Yeats's meeting with Craig some three years later and was totally solved by his introduction to Japanese Noh a decade hence:

> I would have such costumes as would not disturb my imagination by staring anachronism or irrelevant splendour, and such scenery as would be forgotten the moment a good actor had said, 'The dew is falling,' or 'I can hear the wind among the leaves.' Sometimes a shadowy background, a pattern of vague forms upon a dim backcloth, would be enough, for the more the poet describes the less should the painter paint; and at the worst one but needs, as I think, enough of scenery to make it unnecessary to look at the programme to find out whether the persons on the stage have met indoors or out of doors, in a cottage or in a palace. ... Such scenery might come, when its makers had mastered its mysteries, to have a serene beauty, such as one finds in Egyptian wall paintings, and it would be more beautiful, even at the beginning, than the expensive scenery of the modern theatre, even when Mr Tree has put into the boughs in the forest those memorable birds that sing by machinery.[94]

It was to Japanese prints that Yeats turned in his profound analysis of the problems of scenery, probably to examples of the *ukiyo-e* which had made such a deep mark on French Impressionist painters. In 1904 he wrote to Lady Gregory of a stage wing designed and constructed by her son:

> Robert's wing will be very good for a remoter play like *The Shadowy Waters*, but it is too far from realism to go with comedy or with any ordinary play. I am very glad to have it. I have found out that the exact thing I want is *the sort of tree one finds in Japanese prints*. If Robert could find time to look up some prints and to make me a wing of this sort in the next three or four days I would be very glad.[95]   [my emphasis]

He had possibly examined Japanese prints even before this date, however, since Earl Miner suggests most persuasively that the poet was introduced to Japan and her art and culture by Arthur Symons well before Yeats's meeting with Craig. Symons certainly acquainted Yeats with the work of the French *Symboliste* poets, Mallarmé and Verlaine and their *Japonisme* as early as the 1890s:

> Since Symons reiterated Jules de Goncourt's idea that 'the triumph of *Japonisme*' was one of the three most important literary and artistic movements of the second half of the nineteenth century, it is possible that he introduced Yeats to Japan. Yeats wrote in his introduction to *Certain Noble Plays of Japan* (1916) of his 'memory of theatrical colour-prints' which he had seen some years before in the British Museum; and if he had been encouraged to look at them before the War, it must have been under Symons' urging.[96]

While considering here Yeats's problems of stage scenery it is interesting to compare two later comments, one of 1902 and the other of 1908, both, again, before the collaboration with Ezra Pound. Yeats is once more waging war on imitation in stage design and advocating anti-realistic suggestion. Here are the two opinions written within six years of one another:

> [1902] Last year I saw *Dido and Aeneas* and *The Masque of Love*, which is to be given again this year, and they gave me more perfect pleasure than I have met with in any theatre this ten years. I saw the only admirable stage scenery of our time, for Mr Gordon Craig has discovered how to decorate a play with severe, beautiful, simple effects of colour that leave the imagination free to follow all the suggestions of the play. Realistic scenery takes the imagination captive and is at best but bad landscape painting, but Mr Gordon Craig's scenery is a new and distinct art. It is something that can only exist in the theatre. It cannot even be separated from the figures that move before it. ...[97]

> [1908] We believe words more important than gesture, that voice is the principal power an actor possesses; and that nothing may distract from the actor, and what he says, we have greatly simplified scenery. When we wish to give a remote poetical effect we throw away reason altogether, and we are content with

suggestion; this is the idea of the Japanese in their dramatic art; they believe that artificial objects, the interior let us say of some modern house, should be perfectly copied, because a perfect copy is possible; but that when you get to sea and sky you should only suggest, and when they wish to suggest a sea they are content to put before you merely a pattern of waves.[98]

In this second remark – from a speech to the British Association – we are given, firstly, a clear indication that Yeats was familiar with Japanese theatre and stagecraft in 1908 and, secondly, an identification of the poet's own dramatic method of proceeding with that of Japan.

A *Journal* for 9 August 1909, informs us that Yeats was still preoccupied with Japanese painting and that he knew Lawrence Binyon's work on that subject:

I had been talking of the literary element in painting ... and turning over the leaves of Binyon's book on Eastern painting in which he shows how traditional, how literary it is.[99]

The book was *Painting in the Far East*, published in 1908 and, as was observed above from *The Times*, Binyon addressed the Japan Society on this topic in the same year. Yeats had already in 1904 instinctively gone to Japanese prints and paintings when attempting to identify what he wanted for his stage design and the interest was evidently a continuing one. The painting indeed prepared for a new way of thinking about decor. The prints depicted natural scenery in their own terms of stylisation and convention, dimensions which translated well into a theatre set conveying simply pattern as suggestive, rather than representative, of landscape. The bold strokes and use of colour were features which were transferrable to the broader canvas of stage design, as was the absence of depth and perspective.

Craig had invented and constructed a series of screens as theatrical scenery and Yeats saw it not only as a revolutionary method of doing away with painted backdrops, but also as something that would be admirably suited for his own theatre. The screens were first used at the Abbey in 1911 for a production of *The Hour Glass* and two plays by Lady Gregory, and Yeats wrote to *The Times* on 11 September 1912 that 'They gave out beautiful effects, light and impressive form'.[100] Between them, Japan and Craig had gone a long way to remedying the ills of realistic stage scenery that Yeats wished so passionately to avoid and yet he had still not been introduced to Noh.

As well as that of stage scenery and design, another very important feature of classic Noh is that of mask and this was to become a vital concept and symbol in Yeats's poetry and prose as well as drama. Gordon Craig gathered together his theories on the mask into 'A note on Masks' of 1910 and Yeats was in agreement with what was there prophesied:

> The mask will return to the theatre; of that I grow ever more and more assured; and there is no very great obstacle in the way, although there is some slight danger attached to a misconception of its revival and a mishandling of its powers.[101]

Craig's reason for desiring the return of the mask was because

> Masks carry conviction when he who creates them is an artist, for the artist limits the statements which he places upon these masks. The face of the artist carries no such emotion; it is over-full of fleeting expression – frail, restless, disturbed and disturbing.[102]

Yeats did not put his enthusiasm for mask into dramatic practice until 1910, in October of which year he submitted his essay 'The Tragic Theatre' to Craig's journal *The Mask,* and, as we discovered (p. 107), this publication carried a review and three illustrations dealing with Japanese dance and including material on Noh. The importance of this year for Japanese art and culture in Britain has already been remarked upon: it was the year of the great Japanese–British Exhibition. Yeats wrote to Lady Gregory on 21 October referring to a revival of his play *The Hour Glass:*

> I am very much excited by the thought of putting the fool into a mask and rather amused at the idea of an angel in a golden domino. ... Craig evidently wants to keep what is supernatural from being inhuman. If the masks work right I would put the fool and the blind man in *Baile's Strand* into masks. It would give a wildness and extravagance that would be fine. I should also like the Abbey to be the first modern theatre to use the mask.[103]

Masks would strip the actors of their humanity and would imbue them with an element of divinity and a mythic dimension which would destroy any illusion of the realism which Yeats rejected in his theatre.

The poet was similarly impressed with another prophecy by Craig, that of the *Ubermarionette*, a notion linked to that of the mask. Years later, in the introduction to his *Four Plays for Dancers* of 1921, Yeats instructed his actors to move a little 'gravely and stiffly' like marionettes and by that date he would know that such ceremonious gravity of movement was typical of a Noh player or dancer. In 1907 Craig had given the following account of 'The Actor and the Ubermarionette':

> The actor must go, and in his place comes the inanimate figure – the Uber-marionette we may call him, until he has won for himself a better name. ... Today in his least happy period many people come to regard him as a rather superior doll – and to think he has developed from the doll. This is incorrect. He is a descendant of the stone images of the old temples – he is today a rather degenerate form of a god. ... The Uber-marionette will not compete with life – rather will it go beyond it. Its ideal will not be the flesh and blood but rather the body in trance – it will aim to clothe itself with a death-like beauty while exhaling a living spirit. ... I pray earnestly for the return of the image – the Uber-marionette to the theatre; and when he comes again and is but seen, he will be loved so well that once more will it be possible for the people to return to their ancient joy in ceremonies – once more will Creation be celebrated – homage rendered to existence – and divine and happy intercession made to death.[104]

We remember encountering very similar sentiments in the previous section of this chapter when commenting on *The Times* of 1919 where a correspondent from Tokyo praised Japanese *Bunraku* – the doll theatre. Craig was too cranky and recondite for most people to accept his theories, but they were life-blood to Yeats when he first came to know the designer in 1902: they answered many of the poet's own questionings on theatre and its relationship to ritual.

Craig's concept of the *Ubermarionette* is also related to another feature of Japanese Noh, that of hero as archetype of mythic dimension rather than simply as character: the *shite* represents more than the mere limits of his human identity. In the Japanese plays he may well be a god in disguise and there also, as in Yeats's own drama, he is 'character isolated by a deed'[105] – the intricacies and contradictions of his 'humanity' are subsumed into the one memorable action by which he is known: he becomes the principal protagonist in a ritual woven around himself. Yeats pleaded for this dimension in the *Mask* article of 1910, 'The Tragic Theatre'; he saw 'character' in drama as an element of comedy, but too banally personal to be the stuff of tragedy. What he wanted was the very absence of such 'character' to be the emblem of the tragic art that he desired for his theatre. Part of Yeats's essay is as follows:

> if we are painters, we shall express personal emotion through ideal form, a symbolism handled by the generations, a mask from whose eyes the disembodied looks, a style that remembers many masters that it may escape contemporary suggestion; or we shall leave out some element of reality as in Byzantine painting, where there is no mass, nothing in relief; and so it is that in the supreme moment of tragic art there comes upon one that strange sensation as though the hair of one's head stood up. ...
>
> Tragic art, passionate art, the drowner of dykes, the confounder of understanding, moves us by setting us to reverie, by alluring us almost to the intensity of trance. The persons upon the stage, let us say, greaten till they are humanity itself.[106]

It is almost unnecessary to point out how close are the poet's ideas to the notions of archetype, trance and meditation of classic Noh or that this article was written before the collaboration with Pound of 1913; Yeats was still unfamiliar with the Noh. Already in 1908, however, Craig had started to link his own dramatic theories with those of Oriental theatre. The critic James Flannery has this to say about these years:

> Ezra Pound is credited with having introduced Yeats to Japanese Noh drama. Here again, however, Craig may have played a larger role than is generally suspected. As early as 1908 Craig began to relate his theories to Oriental Theatre. In 1910 *The Mask* concerned itself with Noh drama. With its emphasis on symbolical gesture and its subordination of accidental traits of 'character' to essential passion, Noh drama provided Craig with yet another ancient manifestation of what he had been pursuing through his theory of the *übermarionette.*
>
> It is significant to note how closely Yeats's ideas paralleled those of Craig when he came to discuss Noh drama. Writing in

1916, he declared that in the Noh he had discovered an ideal dramaturgical model that would synthesize the 'pulse of life' with the 'stillness of death'.[107]

Yeats's theorising on character and archetype of 1910 appears three years after his own writing of the type of drama which he was advocating, *Deirdre*, of 1907. Moreover, this play contained his first use of another element which he would later come to find mirrored in the Noh, that of the chorus. *Deirdre* thus manifested both the employment of musicians as a chorus and archetypal protagonists placed in a situation of such tragic inexorability that they 'greaten till they are humanity itself'.

In the play the chorus comments on the action and supplies necessary background information on what is taking place. The musicians are not masked as they are in the later dance plays, nor do they yet perform the ritual of the unfolding and folding of the cloth to signify the opening and closing of the play: they are 'comely women of about forty'[108] and this is the first time in his theatre that Yeats has presented such figures.

Deirdre treats of the tragic events resulting from the love of Deirdre and her young warrior, Naoise and their seven years of wandering together. The chorus of musicians impart the knowledge that Conchubar, the High King, an old and scheming man, was betrothed to Deirdre in her younger days, but she chose to flee with Naoise to escape the clutches of the monarch. Conchubar's passionate jealousy has not abated in the intervening years and, promising pardon, he entices the young lovers back onto his territory and into his treacherous power. Naoise is trapped like a wild animal and put to death, while Conchubar has had a bridal chamber prepared for himself and Deirdre; she manages to escape him one last time, however, by tricking him into allowing her to see the dead body of her lover. While behind the curtain which conceals herself and Naoise's corpse, Deirdre takes her own life using a knife previously snatched from one of the musicians.

In his retelling of this legend – there are many versions including those of J. M. Synge and Lady Gregory – Yeats eschews realism and invests his play with mythic dimension through his presentation of the archetypal opposition of youth and age, his use of songs and poetry chanted by a chorus, his choice of the unrealistic stage design of a pattern representing branches of forest trees, thus avoiding the idea of a precise, mapped locality and, lastly and most essentially, by means of protagonists who gain in majesty as they come to the realisation that death awaits them both. As well as a linear narrative about jealousy and revenge, the play is a ritual of sacrifice and as such takes on the forces of tragedy in its inexorability. It is thus linked to Japanese Noh by several traits, but these features of archetype and tragedy are particularly significant: had *Deirdre* been a classic Japanese Noh play it might well have portrayed Deirdre's calm before her suicide as a dance, because narrative has been transformed into one single moment of passion and language is only inadequate in the expression of it.

Deirdre is not one of Yeats's 'Noh plays' since it is much too early and the poet was not yet using the concepts involved consciously. We may still, however, discern elements which are amazingly similar to those of Japanese Noh. It is not surprising that Kermode remarks in *Romantic Image*:

> Much of his earlier thought on the drama must have seemed to him a steady, though unwitting, progress in the direction of the Nō; he almost invented it himself.[109]

Let us now consider dance as perhaps the most important of Yeats's preoccupations, one which dates from his beginnings as a playwright. On 5 May 1890, John Todhunter's *A Sicilian Idyll* was staged at the Club, Bedford Park delighting Yeats by the acting of Florence Farr and the inclusion of a dance. The poet himself introduced dance into his own dramatic work as early as 1894 in *The Land of Heart's Desire*, although the function of the dance in this play is, as we shall examine, more significant in terms of plot than is the case in the Japanese genre. Yeats may have known something of the dance in Noh later, in 1901, through an acquaintance with Osman Edwards that is worthy of note. On 1 January 1898, Yeats wrote from 18, Woburn Buildings, for many years his rooms in London, inviting Mrs Dorothea Hunter to his 'at-home' and telling her that he expected Osman Edwards, 'a rather well known critic of French literature'.[110] As was remarked in the previous section above, this guest went on to publish *Japanese Plays and Playfellows* in 1901 and dedicated it to Yakumo Koizumi and Lafcadio Hearn, the latter being a fanatical Japanophile who left the United States of America to set up home in Japan, married a Japanese wife and produced a considerable number of extremely popular books on the spirit and customs of that country without, however, ever directing his attention to her theatre. Edwards described his visit to a Noh play, *Koi no Omone, The Burden of Love*, one of the very works examined by Ezra Pound from Ernest Fenollosa's manuscripts and I shall briefly summarise the plot so that the context of the dance may be comprehensible.[111]

The play, said to be by the Emperor Gohanozuno (1429–65), relates the story of the emperor's gardener who fell in love with a court lady. To win the lady's love, he had to carry a light and richly-brocaded burden on his back many thousands of times around the garden, but the load proved deceptively heavy and he died trying to lift it. The lady was moved to pity by the greatness of his passion and subsequent death and her song of grief conjured the ghost of the gardener, who reproached her for her previous seeming cold-ness. Edwards gave an account of the ghost and his dance:

> His feelings are better conveyed by the dirge-like song and lugubrious posturing which poverty of language compels one to miscall a 'dance'. Full of dignity and fine gesture is the ghost's rebuke. Slowly revolving on his heels, or tossing back his streaming, silvery hair, now dashing his staff upon the ground, now raising his *kimono* sleeve slowly to hide his face, one felt that this weird figure was expressing elemental passion in a language more elemental than speech.[112]

This perceptive analysis of the Noh dance was made by the man whom Yeats knew as a critic of French literature as early as 1898.

Yeats's own first use of dance in 1894 was also to express 'elemen-tal passion in a language more elemental than speech' but it had another function too and such is the case in all his dance plays, those which are claimed as 'Noh plays' and that which was written well before Yeats's introduction to the Japanese genre. Once again a summary of the action of *The Land of Heart's Desire* will throw the purpose of its dance into focus.

The play presents a sensitive and impressionable peasant woman who, after reading the story of Princess Edain and her spiriting away to Faery Land on May Eve, dreams of following her there. The action of Yeats's play also takes place on May Eve and Mary Bruin is more than disposed by her dreamy nature to exchange her rich and loving peasant husband and his parents for the folk of the other world. Along with Father Hart, a country priest, the family fights to save Mary from the toils of Faery and performs ancient superstitious rites to keep away enchantment, but she, on the other hand, encourages the Faery people, giving milk to an old woman dressed in green who comes to the door and fire to an old man for his pipe. A child of that magical country is heard singing outside in the forest and is brought into the sanctity of the home by Maurteen, Mary's father-in-law and is offered milk and honey by his wife. The child is about to dance when she glimpses the crucifix hanging on the wall and retreats in terror. She is able to continue only after the priest has removed the cross from her sight; in so doing he abrogates his spiritual power and transfers effective authority in the house to the child. The dance is performed at this moment in the play and we must hence assume it to be one of victory as well as seduction: the dancer is luring Mary away. In the ensuing struggle for dominance over Mary's soul between the forces of good and those of Faery, the stricken woman dies, torn between wishing to accompany the little girl and remaining with her loving young husband.

The plot is slight, perhaps, but the fact of the dance is significant because it occurs as the climax of the play and is instrumental in the action that follows; Mary is won over by it and Maurteen, too, almost succumbs. The dance here is a precursor to those of Yeats's later 'Noh' plays in its representation of a supernatural power which cannot be gainsaid by any action; as such, any attempts to combat it by either speech or gesture fail and in this it is clearly redolent of the *mai* found in Japanese Noh.

Yeats's interests in stage design, mask, ritual, chorus and dance all date from the 1890s and received a boost from his meeting with Craig in 1902 and continued to be developed, adjusted and polished in the ensuing years until his discovery of Noh in 1913. From examining his perceptions of these early years and by reading these two important plays, *The Land of Heart's Desire* and *Deirdre*, we can clearly identify designs which come to realisation in *Four Plays for Dancers* of 1921 and in some later plays where the characteristics of classic Noh are at last being used knowingly and consciously. Glad as we are that the search was over in 1913, a mystery still remains, namely the reason why Yeats took so many years of personal striving and experimentation before he finally came upon Noh: one might have expected him to have encountered the genre well before this date because evidence of Japan as a country and Japanese aesthetic activity was so manifest in the contemporary political and artistic worlds around him. A mass of information existed and Yeats proved that he was receptive to some, if not all, of it by making many references to Japan and her art over the years preceding 1913, perceiving the culture as an example of an aristocratic society in which artist and poet had a precise and valued role; he was not ignorant of *Japonisme*, having been introduced to it in literature by Arthur Symons in the 1890s; he lived in Bedford Park where he was surrounded by *Japonaiserie*; he studied Japanese colour prints in the British Museum, many of which were portraits of actors in various roles, some of them masked; he would have been aware of Whistler and the Impressionists and he certainly knew the work of Aubrey Beardsley which was heavily influenced by the Japanese print; a parody like *The Mikado* of 1885 was being performed on London stages, as was Owen Hall's *The Geisha* of 1896; his friends Ricketts and Shannon were visiting Japanese plays in London theatres as early as 1900 and 1901; the play on which Puccini's opera was based, David Belasco's *Madame Butterfly*, was staged in London in 1900;[113] records of travellers to Japan existed, some of which described Noh drama, among them Yeats's acquaintance of the 1890s, Osman Edwards; Craig's theories of theatre forged very strong links with Oriental theatre and his journal, *The Mask*, of 1910 printed an article on the Noh; hardly a month went by from 1870 onwards in which *The Times* did not report on some aspect of Japanese life and art and so continued until the international unrest of the 1930s; and, finally and most importantly, as we have perceived above, Yeats's own theatre had been innovating the very techniques which were those of classic Japanese Noh. It is almost unbelievable that he did not stumble across the genre much earlier than was the case and all that can be said is that, in the world of ideas, coincidence plays a larger part than may at first be suspected: certain concepts are 'in the air' and thus can be found running parallel with no notion of their influencing each other.

Katherine Worth makes clear the great attraction of the form once Yeats had indeed discovered it:

> Nō was a totally musical structure such as the Symbolists had dreamed of; low toned, oblique, a chamber form, but one that worked with Wagnerian force. Yeats instantly seized on one vital notion; the presentation of the drama by the musicians. This was certainly one of Nō's greatest gifts to him. Another revelation was the dance; for the first time he encountered a drama where dance had a central place and was expressive in just the way he had imagined in *The Land of Heart's Desire*. The Nō dance too was a

ghostly communication between man and supernatural being, coming to the point where words fail, offering a transcendental experience.[114]

After 1913 Yeats's theorising about art and theatre became the knowledgeable account which is demonstrated in his introduction to 'Certain Noble Plays of Japan' where his admiration for the Japanese aesthetic sense remained profound:

> In neglecting character which seems to us essential in drama, as do their artists in neglecting relief and depth, whether in their painting or in arranging flowers in a vase in a thin row, they have made possible a hundred lovely intricacies.[115]

This absence of character was an idea very close to Yeats's dramatic heart and we remarked his pleading for it in the essay of 1910 on 'The Tragic Theatre', but by now he had found authority for his instinctive wishes and model for the kind of drama he had long desired to write.

It was in April 1916 that the poet's sisters asked him to devise an introduction to their edition of the Noh plays, 'translated by Ernest Fenollosa and finished by Ezra Pound'.[116] Through Pound, Yeats was made familiar with Fenollosa's work, scholarship and life: like Pound, Fenollosa was a graduate of Harvard and he had gone to Japan in 1878 as a professor of economics at Tokyo Imperial University. He ended his career in Japan as Imperial Commissioner of Arts, having discovered cultural treasure of the significance of which no Japanese had been aware and having made that people conscious of its own heritage. He saved hundreds of *ukiyo-e* from destruction as rubbish and reinstituted Noh theatre into the canon of cultural life when it was on the verge of extinction. As Ezra Pound suggests of Fenollosa's massive contribution to Japan's aesthetic existence:

> It may be an exaggeration to say that he had saved Japanese art for Japan, but it is certain that he had done as much as any one man could have to set the native art in its rightful pre-eminence and to stop the apeing of Europe.[117]

On Fenollosa's return to the United States of America in 1890 he became curator of Oriental Art at the Boston Museum of Fine Arts and when he died suddenly in England in 1908, the Japanese government sent a warship to take his ashes to Japan where they were buried by priests within the sacred enclosure at Miidera. He was a scholar of Chinese and Japanese art of great repute, a leading figure in the translation of Noh plays into English and was known in America for his service to various museums as well as being revered in Japan.

Yeats recognised his own good fortune in finally having the Noh works made accessible and in his introduction to his sisters' Cuala Press collection he dwells on the mask, stage scenery, music, acting conventions, dance and the Japanese Noh, most of which are the old preoccupations which had obsessed him in previous years. A large part of what he has to relate had already been gleaned from Craig and his work, but the new note of authority that we perceived above comes from gaining legitimacy for his own less-than-popular notions from a theatre established five centuries before:

> Instead of the players working themselves into a violence of passion indecorous in our sitting-room, the beauty of form and voice all come to climax in pantomimic dance.
>
> I have invented a form of drama, distinguished, indirect and symbolic, and having no need of mob or Press to pay its way – an aristocratic form.[118]

In his meditation on dance Yeats gives an account of the skill of Michio Ito, the Japanese dancer discovered for him in London in 1915 by Pound and who performed the part of the hawk in the 1916 production of *At the Hawk's Well*:

> My play is made possible by a Japanese dancer whom I have seen dance in a studio and in a drawing-room and on a very small stage lit by an excellent stage-light. In the studio and in the drawing-room alone where the lighting was the light we are most accustomed to, did I see him as the tragic image that has stirred my imagination. There where no studied lighting, no stage picture made an artificial world, he was able, as he rose from the floor, where he had been sitting crossed-legged or as he threw out an arm, to recede from us into some more powerful life. Because that separation was achieved by human means alone, he receded, but to inhabit as it were the deeps of the mind. One realised anew, at every separating strangeness, that the measure of all arts' greatness can be but in their intimacy.[119]

'Certain Noble Plays of Japan' contains several ideas with which Yeats had been struggling for many years, and here he presents the following thoughts on the mask:

> it is natural that I go to Asia for a stage convention, for more formal faces, for a chorus that has no part in the action, and perhaps for those movements of the body copied from the marionette shows of the fifteenth century. A mask will enable me to substitute for the face of some commonplace player, or for that face repainted to suit his own vulgar fancy, the fine invention of a sculptor, and to bring the audience close enough to the play to hear every inflection of the voice. A mask never seems but a dirty face, and no matter how close you go is yet a work of art; nor shall we lose by stilling the movement of the features, for deep feeling is expressed by a movement of the whole body.[120]

In this essay Yeats proceeds to give a short history of the Noh theatre of Japan and, most essentially for our purposes, analyses the Noh dance. It is of interest to compare his version of this crucial phenomenon to those of travellers previously considered:

> No 'naturalistic' effect is sought. The players wear masks and found their movements upon those of puppets. ... They sing as much as they speak, and there is a chorus which describes the scene and interprets their thought and never becomes as in the Greek theatre a part of the action. At the climax, instead of the dis-ordered passion of nature, there is a dance, a series of positions and movements which may represent a battle, or a marriage, or the pain of a ghost in the Buddhist Purgatory. I have lately studied certain of these dances, with Japanese players, and I notice that their ideal of beauty, unlike that of Greece and like that of pictures from Japan and China, makes them pause at moments of muscular tension. The interest is not in the human form but in the rhythm to which it moves, and the triumph of their art is to express the rhythm in its intensity. There are few swaying move-ments of arms or body such as make the beauty of our dancing. They move from the hips, keeping constantly the upper part of their body still, and seem to associate with every gesture or pose some definite thought. They cross the stage with a sliding move-ment, and one gets the impression not of undulation but of continuous straight lines.[121]

His perceptive account of the Noh dance may be added to those of Osman Edwards and Marie Stopes that have been mentioned: Yeats's interpretation is perhaps the most complete in its minute attention to choreography and gesture. While both Edwards in 1901 and Stopes in her 1907 journal commented on the 'dancing' as being either 'lugubrious posturing' or 'a series of slow and very stiff poses', Yeats complements their descriptions by depicting it too in terms of 'a series of positions and movements', but goes further to analyse the aesthetic demands upon the dancers and the artistic assumptions actualised in the manner of representing those passions which the dance seeks to express. Thus, every gesture is associated with 'some definite thought', 'human form' is less significant than 'the rhythm to which it moves' and, in order to attain their concept of beauty, the dancers' bodies must 'pause at moments of muscular tension'. Yeats insists on the essential discipline and sense of order achieved by the Japanese performers and goes on to cite specific Japanese Noh plays – *Hagoromo* and *Nishikigi* – to which the Fenollosa translations had given him access and examines the typical plot:

> The adventure itself is often the meeting with ghost, god, or goddess at some holy place or much-legended tomb; and god, goddess, or ghost reminds me at times of our own Irish legends and beliefs, which once, it may be, differed little from those of the Shinto worshipper.[122]

'Certain Noble Plays of Japan' of 1916 thus represents an end and a beginning in Yeats's art and thought: the conclusion of a long quest for dramatic form and the consequent new approach to the writing of plays in the light of an old tradition in an admired culture.

Before considering *Four Plays for Dancers* as the instances of the poet's plays in which he derived plot, structure or some image from known Japanese sources, let us combine the various strands of information on the Noh from different writers and travellers by summarising it in the words of Ernest Fenollosa, that honorary Japanese citizen:

> The beauty and power of Noh is in the concentration. All elements – costume, motion, verse, and music – unite to produce a single clarified impression. Each drama embodies some primary human relation or emotion; and the poetic sweetness or

poignancy of this is carried to its highest degree by carefully excluding all such obtrusive elements as a mimetic realism or vulgar sensation might demand. The emotion is always fixed upon idea, not upon personality. The solo parts express great types of human character, derived from Japanese history. Now it is brotherly love, now love to a parent, now loyalty to a master, love of husband and wife, of mother for a dead child, or of jealousy or anger, of self-mastery in battle, of the battle passion itself, of the clinging of a ghost to the scene of its sin, of the infinite compassion of a Buddha, of the sorrow of unrequited love. Some one of these intense emotions is chosen for a piece, and, in it, elevated to the plane of universality by the intensity and purity of treatment. Thus the drama became a storehouse of history, and a great moral force for the whole social order of the Samurai.[123]

Here, then, is the tradition and genre on which Yeats drew for his own 'Noh' and much work has been undertaken by scholars in attempting to relate his plays to original Japanese models. It is very clear, for example, that *The Dreaming of the Bones* of 1919, the second of the *Four Plays for Dancers*, owes its inception to the Noh play *Nishikigi* by Seami Motokiyo which was translated by Fenollosa and published in the Cuala Press edition. Although this is not chronologically in its correct place, I shall give an account of this play first because it is the one that is closest to its source.

The *'nishikigi'* of the title are painted and carved wands used as a love charm and which the man had offered nightly to his beloved for three years; she, out of coquetry or ignorance, never opened her door to him but went on weaving a cloth made of grass, *'hosonuno'*. These two people have long been dead but the rift between them has still not been bridged in the afterlife and they appear to a travelling priest, the *waki*, as ghost lovers who are longing to be united. Guiding the priest to the cave in which the rejected lover was buried along with his carved wands, they seek blessing and exorcism that they may be joined at last:

TSURE   [in this case, the woman.]
   Hear soothsay,
   Now there is meeting between us,
   Between us who were until now
   In life and in after-life kept apart.
   A dream-bridge over wild grass,

Over the grass I dwell in.
O honoured! do not awake me by force.
I see that the law is perfect.[124]

Their union is celebrated by a dance:

> SHITE: Happy at last and well-starred,
> Now comes the eve of betrothal;
> We meet for the wine cup.
> CHORUS: How glorious the sleeves of the dance,
> That are like snow-whirls!
> SHITE: Tread out the dance.
> CHORUS: Tread out the dance and bring music.
> This dance is for Nishikigi.
> SHITE: This dance is for the evening plays,
> And for the weaving.
> CHORUS: For the tokens between lover and lover:
> It is a reflecting in the wine-cup.[125]

The coming of the dawn causes the two ghosts to flee away leaving
the sleeping priest to find himself alone in a cave in the middle of a
field: 'A wild place, unlit, and unfilled'.[126]

It would be extraordinarily difficult to comment upon the
dialogue of this Japanese play – it is so very exotic and alien to our
dramatic and literary experience – but the manner in which the
dance is produced by language as well as by gesture seems to be
worthy of note. The chorus conjures a metaphor of great beauty in
the 'sleeves of the dance' and, indeed, the speeches themselves
hinge on this technique: 'A dream-bridge over wild grass'. This
employment of metaphor makes the writing highly dense and com-
pact; it needs to be deciphered just as the dance must be decoded:
'This dance is for the evening plays, / And for the weaving'. As
Yeats himself remarked in his essay 'Certain Noble Plays of Japan', a
central image seems to exist which recurs as *Leitmotiv*; here it is the
image of grass, the same grass which the girl continued to weave in
life.

Yeats's own version of this story is *The Dreaming of the Bones* of
1919, also a 'ghost play', which takes its theme from Irish legend
and contemporary history and its inspiration from the Japanese.
Once again two lovers, here Diarmuid and Devorgilla, are condemned to wander for centuries after death to do penance for their

betrayal of their country, Ireland, into the hands of the conquering Norman. They haunt the scenes of their earthly life in the hope of discovering a fellow countryman to forgive them and, thus, bring peace to their errant souls and they meet in a remote place a young man of Aran, a nationalist fighter, fleeing from the British soldiers after the 1916 Easter Rising. The ghosts relate their story: their eyes may meet but never their lips:

> YOUNG GIRL: Their manner of life were blessed could their lips
> A moment meet; but when he has bent his head
> Close to her head, or hand would slip in hand,
> The memory of their crime flows up between
> And drives them apart.[127]

The lovers seek forgiveness of the young Irishman:

> YOUNG GIRL: If someone of their race forgave at last
> Lip would be pressed on lip[128]

but he is adamant:

> O never, never Shall Diarmuid and Devorgilla be forgiven[129]

and the two ghosts weave their infinite suffering into a dance which begins with their eyes meeting and culminates with the dancers separating and leaving the stage apart. The young man, who was so tempted by the strangeness of the place and by their passion that he almost pardoned them, makes good his escape. The musicians close the play with their songs 'for the folding and unfolding of the cloth' and end on a symbol of betrayal fitting to the story of the two ghostly lovers:

> But now the night is gone.
> I have heard them far below
> The strong March birds a-crow.
> Stretch necks and clap the wing,
> Red cocks, and crow![130]

The folding and unfolding of the cloth are not Noh features; Yeats perhaps invented this ceremony which replaces the opening and closing of the front curtain of commercial theatre when he found himself 'thinking of players who needed ... but to unroll a mat in some Eastern garden':[131] the cloth may replace the mat in signifying that the place denoted is 'theatre'. Yeats's play sets the action in a time and place of recent history and thereby reduces some of the universality of the original Japanese. In common with its source, however, *The Dreaming of the Bones* employs heroic masks for the stranger and the young girl and the musicians have their faces made up to resemble masks, it terminates in a dance which is one of hopeless resignation and separation and the story-telling and commentary on the action is allotted to the chorus of musicians who remain on stage throughout. In its theme this play follows the Japanese version most faithfully and yet, even here, Yeats has made the form his own by investing it with the current and specific rather than the universal.

The first play of *Four Plays for Dancers* (1921), was *At the Hawk's Well*, performed in 1916 and published in 1917. As has been noted, *The Dreaming of the Bones* was second, followed by *The Only Jealousy of Emer* (1919) and *Calvary* (1921). These plays are all 'Noh' plays according to Yeats's criteria and personal treatment of the genre in that, in every case, they present musicians, masks, dance and the communication of a moment of emotion rather than linear narrative. Such is also true for some plays which were written later than these four, including the very last.

At the Hawk's Well is the first of Yeats's dramatic works to appear after his collaboration with Ezra Pound of 1913. It is based very loosely on a Japanese origin, *Yoro* (The Sustenance of Age) by Seami,[132] but its debt is certainly not as great as is that of *The Dreaming of the Bones* to *Nishikigi*. *At the Hawk's Well* repeats the use of mask first attempted in 1910 under the influence of Craig and of dance and musicians employed many years previously in *The Land of Heart's Desire* and *Deirdre*. In this case the three musicians and the guardian of the well have their faces made up to resemble masks, while both the old man and the young warrior, Cuchulain, wear genuine masks. In accordance with Yeats's wishes, this play was first performed in a drawing-room with no stage lighting and with the musicians expressing the beginning and ending of the piece by means of their folded cloth; properties were very few and a stage direction informs us that the well was represented by a square of blue cloth. The musicians create the landscape through their song and the story which ensues is simple and immediate and closely approaches Japanese Noh by being one episode of a passionate moment.

Cuchulain, the young, impetuous warrior of Irish legend has undertaken a quest to the Hawk's Well to drink the waters of immortality furnished by a spring when it flows; most of the time the well is dry. It is guarded by a Hawk Woman, a woman of the Sidhe, whose task is to prevent the drinking of the waters by which mortals would overcome death: she is the force of the supernatural which is also presented by Japanese Noh. The young man is not alone at the well, since an aged man has spent his life there trying to catch some drops of the water which has so far eluded him; on several occasions he has fallen asleep and woken too late only to discover the pebbles and leaves wet but the flow of the miraculous waters ceased. Cuchulain believes that he will not share the old man's fate because his 'luck is strong',[133] but the guardian of the well dances. In so doing, she entices the warrior away from the well and hides herself, so that, when he returns from following her, it is to find that he too has been cheated: the waters splashed momentarily but the old man was asleep and Cuchulain was elsewhere chasing and hunting the beautiful and powerful Hawk Woman. Although he does not yet realise it, the young hero has condemned himself to a life of strife and restlessness by his impulsive pursuit of the guardian of the well, but this becomes evident when we learn that a battle is already at hand: the warrior woman, Aoife, has been incited to fight by the Hawk Woman and, along with her troops, is seeking out Cuchulain to kill him. (From their encounter will result the birth of his only son whom Cuchulain kills unknowingly, as chronicled by Yeats's much earlier play of 1904, *On Baile's Strand*.) Aoife's challenge is accepted and the warrior leaves the well and the stage without a backward glance, while the musicians close the play.

In the Japanese work, *Yoro,* on which this is partly based – it also owes something to William Morris's *The Well at the World's End* (1896) – a father and son, both peasants, are interrogated by a court official about the miraculous properties of a fountain which he has been sent to investigate. This is not a very convincing parallel to Yeats's version, however, especially as the two men reveal themselves as gods and dance a blessing on the land and the emperor, an action which has nothing in common with *At the Hawk's Well*; thus only some slight details of plot would seem to have been derived broadly from the Japanese original. The poet had none the less created a new style of theatre, non-representative and non-illusionistic, which answered the demands which he had placed upon drama and upon himself.

At this point, Yeats's plays are being considered necessarily in a simple form as plot synopsis and structure because, in his 'Noh', the dance is related to the action: it is linked to the events which precede it and affects those that ensue. These plays will be examined more closely as dialogue and poetry in a later chapter, but for the moment an outline of their themes will have to serve in order to draw their similarities to the Japanese, if such exist, and to be able to delineate the function and context of their dances. Yeats does not use the dance in the same manner in every play; there is a progression in the degree of importance attached to it and subtle differences in its nature: the dance gradually becomes more crucial until, in some of the late works, it comprises the action itself.

The Only Jealousy of Emer, published in 1919 and first performed in 1922, also presents a dance as its climax. It is different from that in *At the Hawk's Well*, however, where it is principally a dance of seduction, a ruse to entice Cuchulain away from the well or that in *The Dreaming of the Bones*, in which it summarises the action of the story and is a pained exposition of frustration and desperation to be repeated to infinity. Here the dance seduces, certainly, but also provokes action in the form of heroic self-sacrifice.

Once again the scene is set by the musicians:

> I call before the eyes a roof
> With cross-beams darkened by smoke;
> A fisher's net hangs from a beam,
> A long oar lies against the wall.
> I call up a poor fisher's house.[134]

Cuchulain lies death-like from the insane fight with the sea resulting from his frenzy on discovering that he has unwittingly killed his own and Aoife's son (as in *On Baile's Strand*). Emer, his wife, is attempting to win back his spirit because the body on the bed is not inhabited by the soul of Cuchulain but by a usurping sea god, Bricriu, the bringer of discord. The soul of the warrior is embodied elsewhere, in the ghost of Cuchulain crouching near the front of the stage. Emer is prepared to use almost any weapon, including her husband's love for his young mistress, Eithne Inguba, in order to oust the powers that have taken Cuchulain captive and are killing him. Her enemies are the supernatural forces, the Sidhe, the gods of the sea and her last stratagem, which she flinches from employing, is none the less demanded of her: to renounce her love of her husband for ever. A woman of the Sidhe, Fand, is seducing the ghost of the genuine Cuchulain by her dance; she wishes to take him back to the ocean as her consort. It is only the memory of Emer which is restraining him and, eventually, he is lured into following Fand outside the hut to her chariot. In haste and panic Emer renounces her love for him and, with it, her last fond hope that she and her husband will grow old together. Cuchulain, restored to himself, awakes convinced that he has been rescued by his mistress's kiss rather than by the sacrifice of his wife of which he remains ignorant.

There is some indication that this play was influenced by the text of the Noh, *Awoi no Uye,* which Yeats knew from the Pound–Fenollosa work. The Japanese original, by Ujinobu, also relates a story of rivalry in love: the court lady, Awoi, one of the wives of Genji, is jealous of the others and the violence of her passion renders her mad. As Ezra Pound explains:

> The play opens with the death bed of Awoi, and in Mrs Fenollosa's diary I find the statement that 'Awoi, her struggles, sickness, and death are represented by a red-flowered kimono, folded once length-wise, and laid at the front edge of the stage'.[135]

The force of her jealousy conjures up a form for it, that of Princess Rokijo, a rival for Genji's love but, as an exorcism proceeds, the essence is driven out of this personal ghost to appear in its own demonic form. A footnote in Yeats's essay 'Swedenborg, Mediums and the Desolate Places' of 1914 indicates that the poet had been impressed by this demon who is represented by a dancer wearing a 'terrible mask with golden eyes'.[136] Awoi is the author of her own ghosts and demons; Emer is not – Fand and Bricriu are not the result of her own violent passion and Eithne Inguba is real flesh and blood – but there are echoes of the Japanese play at the level of staging and structure. Both accounts also deal with death beds, exorcisms and the great love of mortal woman for mortal man while surrounded and beleaguered by supernatural forces. Nevertheless, Yeats did not imitate *Awoi no Uye* very closely; instead, as in *At the Hawk's Well,* he created a differing dramatic form implementing elements of the Noh model according to his own theatrical wishes. Where these coincide with Noh is in his construction of a drama of passion and poetry and image, far removed from realistic narrative, a portrayal of character raised to archetype by one overriding emotion.

Calvary, the fourth of the dance plays, was written in 1920 and once again all the characters, including the musicians, wear masks or mask-like make up. The chorus sets the scene, this time by introducing the Christ story. This play contains a dance the nature of which has not been previously encountered in Yeats's work, one of acceptance of inexorability and of the individual's own personal role in violent action.

While carrying His cross to be crucified, Christ is confronted by Lazarus who bears Him a terrible grudge for having been deprived of death: he has come to claim Christ's imminent death for his own, since Lazarus can no longer endure the miracle which Christ performed on him and its consequences. Next, Judas presents himself and explains that he betrayed the Messiah in order to be free of His power. As the betrayal and all the elements of the Christ story including this crucifixion itself have been ordained from the beginning of the world, Judas has not succeeded in liberating himself: he has merely endorsed the part mapped out for him in the casual comedy. A *refusal* to accept the role of traitor might have signified the achievement of freedom. The three Roman soldiers have the capacity to explain their actions in advance because they know themselves simply to be carrying out what is expected of them in a plot over which they have no control but which has inevitability as its overriding dimension: its conclusion too has been ordained. Thus, they announce that they will first gamble for Christ's old cloak and then will wheel about His cross in a dance. Their steps are calm and stately because no further action is possible; Christ is dead. At the same time, however, their dance is the means of expression of those people who do not seek to know why they must act in a certain way, those who are resigned to perform the measure allotted to them by some unquestioned authority and who also accept that such passivity may involve them in violence, as it has in this particular plot.

Some critics, among them Richard Taylor, have suggested that the Pound–Fenollosa version of *Kakitsubata* by Motokiyo might have acted as structural model for *Calvary,* but this would seem to be a very tenuous link as the two plays do not appear to me to share a common construction.[137] The Japanese Noh tells of Kakitsubata, a place famous for its magnificent water iris. A travelling priest visits the marsh to see the blooms in season and meets a local girl. She is, typically, a flower spirit in disguise and she relates the story of Narihira. He was a nobleman, a favoured courtier, who fell from grace and was punished by exile. The girl doffs her disguise and reveals herself, transformed, as the spirit of the iris, Kakitsubata. In her splendid robes and hat she performs the dance of the flowers before the imagined audience of Narihira. She has been driven to manifest herself to the travelling priest in this place because her lord passed that way centuries before and, while contemplating the flowers, turned his meditations to his beloved, the spirit of the iris. Her dance completed, she fades away into the aether leaving behind her only 'the cracked husk of the locust'.[138] Whether the structure of this play bears any similarity to that of *Calvary* seems to me to be open to question and I confess to difficulty in relating the two at all meaningfully.

This consideration of the dance plays of 1921 and their connection, where possible, to specific models from the Pound–Fenollosa collection has of necessity been brief; a more thorough examination will take place elsewhere. Even such a glance, however, can indicate with what delight Yeats greeted the Japanese Noh and the high degree of impact that it exerted on his work, particularly on his employment of dance. Some of his later plays show Noh traces too and they will now be examined below both for their indebtedness to Noh and for the function of their individual dances.

The Cat and the Moon was written in 1917 at the time of *Four Plays for Dancers* but was not published until much later in 1924. Although it was conceived to be a *kyogen*, a comic interlude between two Noh plays, it has a similar structure to the dance plays and incorporates such aspects of Noh as an initial travel song and a journey represented by a circuit of the stage. The musicians are made up and the two main characters, the blind man and the lame man, wear grotesque masks; the lame man is visited by the supernatural apparition of the saint; the plot is restricted to one significant episode; and, perhaps most importantly, a stage set is presented which is again one of suggestion:

> The scene is any bare place before a wall against which stands a patterned screen, or hangs a patterned curtain suggesting Saint Colman's Well.[139]

The play contains dances, both of which form part of the action: the first represents a beating that the newly-cured blind man inflicts on the newly-blessed lame man for having stolen the former's black sheep skin and the second dance is one of joy as the lame man, carrying the invisible saint on his back, celebrates choosing to be blessed rather than cured and the consequent spiritual enlightenment.

The Japanese source of *The Cat and the Moon* may be the single *kyogen* translation among the works of Fenollosa that Yeats studied, *Kikazu Zato*, in which two men, one blind and one deaf, discover ways to torment each other according to their respective handicaps, but Yeats's version also obviously owes something to J. M. Synge's *The Well of the Saints* of 1905. A French source also exists with which the poet may have been familiar, *Moralité de l'aveugle et du boiteux* by André de la Vigne (ca. 1457–ca. 1527).[140] Of course, Yeats had already introduced two similar figures in his creation of the fool and the blind man in *On Baile's Strand* (1904).

The Resurrection of 1931, dedicated to Junzo Sato who presented Yeats with a Japanese warrior's sword, also portrays three musicians, a masked figure of Christ but an absence on stage of dance. The poet stipulated in his directions that his play may be performed in a studio or drawing room, like the previous dance plays, with the musicians unfolding and folding the cloth or in a theatre, in which case they would employ the proscenium curtain. The characters are nameless, simply labelled 'the Hebrew', 'the Greek', 'the Syrian' and they represent different religions and philosophies.

The Hebrew believes that Christ was not the Messiah but simply the best man that ever lived who, as a mortal being, had to die a human death. For the Greek, however, Christ is a god and, as a phantom, cannot die or be killed: the crucifixion was thus a meaningless farce. The Syrian alone is disposed to believe in miracle and to interpret the resurrection of Christ in a manner which is closest to Christian orthodoxy: Christ overcomes death as a god but is still of human flesh and blood. While the tumult of the dances of Dionysus can be heard in the street outside, Christ enters and crosses the stage towards an inner room where His disciples await Him; His ceremonial path replaces the dance of the Noh. Each of the three witnesses, the Hebrew, the Greek and the Syrian, reacts according to his own interpretation of the event and the climax of the play is formed by the piercing scream of the Greek when he discovers the beating heart of Christ, whom he believed to be a phantom.

The Resurrection is in prose except for the songs of the musicians and this shifts the play towards more realistic drama. It does contain elements of the *Four Plays for Dancers* and, thus, of the Noh plays, however, in its presentation of characters as archetypes who represent the varying world-views of different races and its staging is once again sparse and austere with merely a system of curtains to suggest an inner room. Although no claims seem to have been put forward to link *The Resurrection* with any Japanese source, it is none the less evident that it forms part of Yeats's 'Noh' theatre because of these factors noted above.

Three of the last plays, *A Full Moon in March* (1935), *The King of the Great Clock Tower* (1935) and *The Death of Cuchulain* (1939) display Noh features in a highly developed form although they do not seem to owe their inception to any classic Noh origin. While they are thus different from the *Four Plays for Dancers* in not being linked to sources found in Pound–Fenollosa, they are similar in the characteristics that they retain in common; musicians called 'attendants', mask, unity of image and, most essentially, dance. In these final plays the dance takes on even greater significance than was previously the case:

> More and more Yeats had come to use the dance not merely as an extraliterary device to express a complex emotion for which words alone would not suffice, but rather as a means of actually furthering the narration directly or of summarising and therefore establishing it as a theatrical image.[141]

A Full Moon in March demonstrates the constituents of Noh in a very sophisticated manner, while its plot is the slight one of a foul and ugly swineherd making his way to court to woo a coldly beautiful queen. The attendants/musicians, an elderly woman and a young man, break all possible illusion of a realistic, well-made play by initially questioning each other in a Pirandellian way about the roles they are supposed to take and the songs that they are expected to sing:

> FIRST ATTENDANT: What do we do ?
>   What part do we take ?
>   What did he say ?
> SECOND ATTENDANT: Join when we like
>   Singing or speaking.[142]

The swineherd, wearing a grotesque mask over the upper part of his face which leaves his wild red beard visible, arrives in the queen's presence to announce that he has come to sing his passion for her: he has heard tell that the man who does so best during a full moon in March will take the queen for wife. The prophecy also states that the queen will dance, the swineherd will sing and their lips will be pressed together in ecstasy. The queen punishes his insolence by ordering his decapitation, yet, once she holds the severed, bloody head in her hands, she sings and dances out of love and delight. She lays the head upon the throne and, as promised, it begins to sing; she places it on the ground and performs a dance of adoration before it; as climax to the play, the queen lifts up the head, kisses its dead lips, then lays it upon her breast. The attendants accompany the closing of the curtain with their final songs.

As is readily deduced from this short summary of the action, the dance is integral to the story: it expresses all that words could not as it is a symbolic demonstration of both betrothal and sexual union and, thus, it replaces narrative and is elevated to the function of plot itself. In so doing it is redolent of, though not identical to, Japanese Noh, where a celestial being, a 'Tennin', must dance to win her way back to heaven or lovers dance to denote final union between them. While this Queen's dance is reminiscent of those of Salome discussed in the previous chapter, she does not order execution in response to being rebuffed by the object of her desire; rather than one of revenge, her motive is that of pique at the unseemliness of her suitor's reckless wooing. In common with some versions of Salome, however, she reveals herself to be a blend of seductress and castrating woman and she thereby exemplifies the features so feared by contemporary misogyny.

A Full Moon in March is very similar in theme to *The King of the Great Clock Tower* in which the queen wears a 'beautiful impassive mask'[143] and the stroller, like the swineherd of the previous play, a 'wild half-savage mask. It should cover the upper part of his face, the lower part being hidden by his red beard.'[144] The attendants are again musicians with drum and gong who open and close the outer and inner curtains where appropriate and Yeats's stage direction suggests that a semi-circle of one-foot Craig screens (see p. 120 above), could be used for background. Once again the play is performed in a theatre rather than a drawing-room in front of a bare wall as are some of the dance plays, but it is nevertheless indisputably one of Yeats's 'Noh'.

The queen is silent and has remained so for a year after walking into the king's palace and refusing to offer any explanation of her actions or of her past. The king has put her on the throne as his equal and persists, without success, in enquiring for information about her identity and background. (This play was written for the dancer Ninette de Valois who, as a non-actress, was not prepared to speak any lines; hence, for practical reasons, the queen's silence.) A stroller enters the king's house, a poet, who has been singing the beauty of the mysterious queen although he has never seen her; he has sworn an oath that she will dance for him alone and, on the stroke of midnight when the old year dies, she will kiss his mouth. The king, angered and insulted by the man's presumption, orders the poet to be executed and, when this has been performed, sets the dead head as a trophy on the throne. As predicted, the queen dances to it and places it on her shoulder from where it begins to sing. While midnight sounds the queen dances again and presses her lips to the dead mouth of the severed head, thereby fulfilling the prophecies of the wild stroller. Laying the head on her breast, she refuses to be intimidated by the king who first draws his sword in fury, but who then places the weapon at her feet without striking her. The inference is that the king and his sword, representing time and its transience, are overcome by the universality of the archetypes from myth and ritual: beauty and ugliness, male and female, physical love and spiritual hate, silence and eloquence, death and life and sterility and fertility have all been combined in the dance and the kiss. It is thus very evident that the dance is the crux of the play.

Finally, *The Death of Cuchulain* of 1939 demonstrates some characteristics of Japanese Noh, particularly in its climactic complex dance. We are presented with the same rivalry between two women, Eithne Inguba, Cuchulain's mistress and Emer, his wife, as appeared in *The Only Jealousy of Emer* so many years before. While Eithne has brought a letter from Emer begging Cuchulain to delay the pending battle with Maeve until a force of fighting men can join him, Eithne herself urges her lover to fight immediately against impossible odds. The warrior is warned of his imminent death by his mistress's vision of the supernatural powers, here represented by the Morrigu, the crow-headed goddess of war, but he chooses to ignore the omen. Already resolved and prepared for battle before the arrival of Eithne and her conflicting messages, he goes out to fight and is mortally wounded. He drags himself back from the battlefield and ties himself to a pillar that he may remain erect on his feet to face death. Aoife, his old enemy and love, mother of the son he killed in error, searches him out to kill him, but, instead, she winds a veil around the dying man to attach him more securely to the column. Ironically and ignominiously, Cuchulain's head is finally taken, not by an equal, but by the blind man, the scheming, sly beggar, *alter ego* of Conchubar, first encountered in *On Baile's Strand*, who kills the warrior for the twelve pennies he has been promised by Queen Maeve.

The masked Morrigu displays the head of Cuchulain and also exhibits the six heads of the now-dead men who inflicted on him his six mortal wounds. In so doing she sets the scene for the dance of Emer, which is neither one of seduction nor betrothal but of adoration and grief. Emer's pain and sorrow are so intense that she can only express them in dance; in her suffering at the loss of her beloved husband and her rage against those who contributed to it she is compelled to dance to represent the wordless desert where language will not suffice. She prostrates herself to the severed head of her reckless, faithless love and their passion is complete. As in Japanese Noh the dance is here, too, the conclusion of the play; it only remains for the musicians, who are represented as modern ragged street performers, a piper, drummer and singer, to close on the song of both Emer and Aoife:

> But that the flesh my flesh has gripped
> I both adore and loathe.[145]

This short consideration of Yeats's 'Noh' plays raises the question of whether the poet was using the elements of classic Noh – mask, music, chorus, dance – merely as imperfectly understood trappings or whether his plays have the same inner coherence as the Japanese models. We must conclude that they do present an aesthetic entirety, but not that of classic Noh. Doubtlessly Yeats sought the cohesiveness of the Japanese in which the Zen quality of contemplation of *yūgen* is created and the degree of meditation which makes for trance; he stated in 'Certain Noble Plays of Japan' that he was attempting to achieve, particularly through dance, access to the inner 'deeps of the mind'. His 'Noh', however, does not attain the same kind of concentrated spiritual wholeness and the reason for this will be discussed here below; nor does it include the dimension of morality play brought into existence by Buddhist teaching. But instead of dwelling on what Yeats's drama lacks and condemning it for not being authentic Noh, we can focus on its genuine strengths in its very distinctiveness from the Japanese pattern.

The principal difference between the two is in the function and nature of the dance and I have briefly noted the form which it takes in each of the 'Noh' plays. Karen Dorn astutely identifies the essential disparity between Yeats's dance and that of the Noh:

in Yeats's plays even the dance is part of the conflict: ... This is the crucial difference between the view of life represented in the Noh theatre and in Yeats's dance plays – in the one, the creation of *yugen* through brilliant revelation of emotion, in the other, the creation of a quality of energy and lyrical feeling discovered in conflict.[146]

As we have observed, the dance develops through Yeats's plays, growing in centrality, until it becomes the action itself and, in so being, it eschews the induction of trance. In a Noh play such as *Hagoromo* or *Nishikigi*, the dance is less a part of the plot than a celebration of the overcoming of conflict, the resolution of crisis. Rather than occupying the terrain where language ceases to function, it inhabits the area where all has been said. In other types of Noh play like *Kakitsubata* it is the medium through which a spirit can reveal his or her true identity and often nobility: it is the final manifestation of truth in a world of illusion. In the Japanese genre dance is rarely employed in the manner in which it is most commonly used in the West – that of an expression of great emotion and struggle where language has broken down. The Noh dance is, rather, majestic and serene in being the culmination and celebration of peace attained; it is calm and 'elemental', all passion is spent and a new plateau of enlightenment and acceptance has been reached.

Yeats's dances are for a purpose in that they are instrumental to narrative: they either seduce or express sexual passion, adoration or power and victory or they portray passivity and acceptance of violence and they also have another function:

namely to reveal the psychic forces at work behind the forms of the external world.[147]

Thus, their dimension is that of opposition and strife, emotional states which do not readily lend themselves to meditation or trance, but which are capable of penetrating externals to the vital sources of energy and spirit. The Japanese originals gave Yeats models to continue to create what he had first attempted in *The Land of Heart's Desire* in 1894 where he had explored planes of experience, particularly those which are imperceptible from without:

> He grasped with a thoroughness which is astounding in a master of words, that words were not enough for the theatrical task he had set himself, the exploration of the interior. A deep of the mind can only be approached through what is most human, most delicate.[148]

Yeats's dances are less pure than the Japanese in that their purpose is practical as well as aesthetic; they further conflict or constitute action, yet the same *Symboliste* fascination with the dialectical nature of the dancer still applies to Yeats's 'Noh' dances:

> The dance is more perfectly devoid of ideas, less hampered by its means, than poetry, since it has not the strong antipathy of language towards illogic; yet it is not absolutely pure; the dancer is not inhuman.[149]

His introduction to classic Japanese Noh theatre compelled Yeats to advance his meditation on these crucial paradoxes.

We, too, in Britain in the Nineties have similar mysteries to contemplate. The Japan Festival of 1991, designed to celebrate the hundredth anniversary of the founding of the Japan Society, confronted us with a plethora of conflicting impressions, as classic Noh drama (the Umewaka Kennokai troupe at the Queen Elizabeth Hall), reviewed in all shades of press opinion, was presented alongside the highest of hi-tech. The current view was that the 'Japan and Britain: An Aesthetic Dialogue 1850–1930' exhibition at the Barbican continued to foster 'mutual misunderstandings'.[150] The debt of European to Japanese art is evident and unmistakeable, but, in a similar manner to Yeats himself, Occidental painters and poets and dramatists have extracted what they wanted and needed, rather than what they have understood. As for the Japanese artist today, he or she is consciously and somewhat cynically involved in 'specious mimicry'.[151] Alongside the exhibition at the Barbican appeared 'A Cabinet of Signs: Contemporary Art from Post-Modern Japan' at the Tate Gallery, Liverpool. The art critic of *The Independent* summed up contemporary confusion in terms which contained within them familiar echoes from the other writers and 'appreciators' dotted over the preceding century, some of whom have been discussed in this chapter:

> Roland Barthes, a chapter from whose book, *Empire of Signs* provided the Tate's show with its title, thought he had found the essence of Japan in the Zen concept of *satori*, 'the exemption from all meaning'. Maybe, even in post-modern Japanese art, something of the older Japan still survives. Or maybe this is just another fantasy – yet another brief addendum to the volume of occidental misinterpretation of the Orient.[152]

NOTES

1. 'Poet and Dancer', p. 4.
2. RI, p. 92.
3. *Letters*, p. 543.
4. *Ibid.*, p. 610.
5. (i) Gerald William Balfour (1853–1945), British statesman, Chief Secretary for Ireland 1895–96; (ii) John Singer Sargent (1856–1925), painter; (iii) Charles Ricketts (1866–1931), artist, designer and poet; (iv) Thomas Sturge Moore (1870–1944), poet and designer; (v) Augustus John (1878–1961), painter.
6. *Letters*, p. 610.
7. *Ibid.*, p. 608.
8. Ian Fletcher, 'Bedford Park: Aesthete's Elysium?', in *Romantic Mythologies*, ed. Ian Fletcher (London: Routledge and Kegan Paul, 1967), footnote p. 203. Hereafter cited as *Romantic Mythologies*.
9. *Ibid.*, p. 198. A Miss M. Nicolle discussing Japanese artware was quoted in Wilde's *Woman's World*, 1888, p. 94.
10. *Letters*, p. 631: 'September 8, 1917, Hotel Gavarny, Rue Gavarny, Passy. To Lady Gregory: … I expect [to] carry back to London with me part at least of the music to my Noh play *The Dreaming of the Bones.' Letters*, p. 643: 'January 4, 1918, 45, Broad Street, Oxford. To Lady Gregory: I have plans (if we like Oxford) of living here when not in Ireland and making this the centre of my Noh plays which have to be worked out with Dulac.'
11. J. A. Michener, *The Floating World* (London: Secker and Warburg, 1954), pp. 236–8. Hereafter cited as Michener.
12. *Ibid.*, p. 239.
13. Frances Spalding, *Whistler* (Oxford: Phaidon, 1979), pp. 34 and 39. Hereafter cited as *Whistler*.
14. *Ibid.*, p. 38.
15. *Ibid.*, pp. 36–7.

16. *Ibid.*, p. 43.
17. *Ibid.*, pp. 44–5.
18. *Ibid.*, p. 53.
19. Hugh Honour, *Chinoiserie: The Vision of Cathay* (London: John Murray, 1961), p. 219. Hereafter cited as Honour.
20. Christopher Dresser, *Japan: Its Architecture, Art, and Art Manufactures* (London: Longmans, Green, 1882), p. v.
21. *Ibid.*, p. v.
22. *The Times*, 31 May 1887, 8c (i.e. p. 8, column c.).
23. *Ibid.*, 19 October 1896, 6b, 'Japanese Art'; 17 October 12c, atrocities in Formosa.
24. *Ibid.*, 16 June 1889, 15a.
25. *Ibid.*, 15 March 1890, 4a.
26. Honour, p. 209.
27. *A Supplement to the Oxford English Dictionary*, II (Oxford: Clarendon Press, 1976), p. 1222.
28. *The Times*, 16 July 1890, 4a.
29. *Ibid.*, 15 June 1893, 10e.
30. Osman Edwards, *Japanese Plays and Playfellows* (London: Heinemann, 1901), pp. 65–6. Hereafter cited as Osman Edwards.
31. Charles Ricketts, *Self-Portrait Taken from the Letters and Journals of Charles Ricketts, R. A.*, collected and compiled by T. Sturge Moore, ed. Cecil Lewis (London: Peter Davies, 1939) p. 39. Hereafter cited as *Self-Portrait*.
32. *Letters*, p. 346: 6 June 1900.
33. *Self-Portrait*, pp. 39–40.
34. *The Times*, 13 June 1901, 10f.
35. Max Beerbohm, *Around Theatres* (London: Rupert Hart-Davies, 1953), p. 156.
36. *Self-Portrait*, pp. 61–2.
37. *The Times*, 23 August 1901, 8f.
38. *Ibid.*, 10 September 1901, 5c.
39. *Ibid.*, 28 April 1902, 9a.
40. *Ibid.*, 24 July 1902, 11f.
41. *Ibid.*, 2 January 1904, 7e.
42. *Ibid.*, 4 July 1905, 13b.
43. *Ibid.*, 15 July 1905, 8a.
44. *Ibid.*, 15 July 1905, 8a.
45. *Ibid.*, 25 November 1905, 6c.
46. *Ibid.*, 22 January 1906, 4d.
47. *Ibid.*, 9 May 1907, 4c.
48. *Ibid.*, 13 March 1908, 16e.
49. *Ibid.*, 28 April 1910, 10b.
50. *Ibid.*, 16 May 1910, 4c.
51. *Ibid.*, 19 July 1910, 56a.
52. *Ibid.*, 19 July 1910, 56e.
53. *Ibid.*, 19 July 1910, 65c.
54. *Ibid.*, 19 July 1910, 65e.
55. *Ibid.*, 19 July 1910, 66c.

56. *Ibid.*, 16 June 1910, 12f.
57. *Ibid.*, 16 May 1910, 4c.
58. *Ibid.*, 14 July 1910, 13e.
59. *Ibid.*, 19 July 1910, 56e.
60. *Ibid.*, 10 September 1910, 6e.
61. Marie Stopes, *A Journal from Japan* (London: Blackie and Son, 1910), pp. 64–5.
62. *The Mask: A Quarterly Illustrated Journal of the Art of the Theatre*, ed. Edward Gordon Craig, October 1910, first published Florence 1909–29, reissued (New York: Benjamin Blom, n.d.) pp. 76–7 and 90.
63. *The Times*, 14 March 1912, 11b.
64. *Ibid.*, 25 May 1912, 4f.
65. *Ibid.*, 29 August 1912, 3e.
66. Yoné Noguchi, 1875–1947. Wrote extensively on Japanese themes and produced *A Japanese Appreciation of Lafcadio Hearn* in 1910.
67. *The Times*, 15 January 1914, 5e.
68. Yoko Chiba in an article, 'Ezra Pound's Versions of Fenollosa's Noh Manuscripts and Yeats's Unpublished 'Suggestions and Corrections', in Masaru Sekine and Christopher Murray, *Yeats and the Noh: A Comparative Study* (Gerard's Cross: Colin Smythe, 1990) pp. 121–3. Hereafter cited as Sekine and Murray.
69. *The Times*, 11 March 1914, 10d.
70. *Ibid.*, 3 June 1916, 16d.
71. *Ibid.*, 15 July 1916, 9a.
72. *Ibid.*, 2 September 1916, 17a.
73. *Ibid.*, 2 September 1916, 16a.
74. *Ibid.*, 2 September 1916, 10b.
75. *Ibid.*, 2 September 1916, 17c.
76. *Ibid.*, 14 October 1916, 16c.
77. *Ibid.*, 16 December 1916, 20c.
78. *Ibid.*, 1 October 1918, 11d.
79. *Ibid.*, 12 November 1918, 6d.
80. *Ibid.*, 8 December 1919, 12a.
81. *Ibid.*, 15 December 1919, 7a.
82. *Ibid.*, 18 December 1919, 10a.
83. *Ibid.*, 18 December 1919, 8c.
84. *Ibid.*, 2 January 1920, 8a.
85. Earl Miner, *The Japanese Tradition in British and American Literature* (Princeton, NJ: Princeton University Press, 1958; rpt. 1966), p. 237. Hereafter cited as Miner.
86. *Ibid.*, pp. 238–9.
87. Ezra Pound and Ernest Fenollosa, *The Classic Noh Theatre of Japan* (New York: New Directions, 1959), p. 36. Hereafter cited as *The Classic Noh Theatre*. This is a republication of Ernest Fenollosa and Ezra Pound, *'Noh' or Accomplishment: A Study of the Classical Stage of Japan* (London: Macmillan, 1916).
88. Faubion Bowers, *Japanese Theatre* (London: Peter Owen, 1954), p. 17. Hereafter cited as Bowers.
89. Osman Edwards, p. 59.

90. Arthur Waley, *The No Plays of Japan* (London: George Allen and Unwin, 1921; rpt. 1950, 1954), p. 21. It is not clear whom he is quoting.

91. This information on Japanese Noh is severally culled from a reading of Osman Edwards, *Japanese Plays and Playfellows*, 1901; Marie C. Stopes and Professor Joji Sakurai, *Plays of Old Japan: The 'No'* (London: Heinemann, 1913); Arthur Waley, *The No Plays of Japan*, 1954; Faubion Bowers, *Japanese Theatre*, 1954.

92. The pseudonym of the poet William Sharp.

93. *Letters*, p. 280.

94. *Ibid.*, p. 309, To the Editor of the *Daily Chronicle*, 27 January 1899.

95. *Ibid.*, p. 445.

96. Miner, p. 235.

97. *Letters*, p. 366. To the Editor of the *Saturday Review*, 5 May 1902.

98. W. B. Yeats, *Uncollected Prose of W. B. Yeats, II: Reviews, Articles and the Miscellaneous Prose 1897–1939*, collected and edited by John P. Frayne and Colton Johnson (London and Basingstoke: Macmillan, 1975), p. 367, 'W. B. Yeats's speech at the Matinée of the British Association, Friday, September 4th, 1908.' Hereafter cited as *Uncollected Prose II*.

99. W. B. Yeats, *Memoirs*, transcribed and edited by Denis Donoghue (London: Macmillan, 1972), 'Journal begun in December 1908', p. 179.

100. *The Times*, 11 September 1912, 3e.

101. Edward Gordon Craig, *Craig on Theatre*, ed. J. Michael Walton (London: Methuen, 1983), p. 21. Hereafter cited as Craig.

102. *Ibid.*, p. 21.

103. *Letters*, p. 354.

104. Craig, pp. 85 and 87.

105. *Collected Poems*, 'The Circus Animals' Desertion', p. 392.

106. W. B. Yeats, *Essays and Introductions* (London: Macmillan, 1961), 'The Tragic Theatre', pp. 243 and 245. Hereafter cited as 'Tragic Theatre'.

107. James W. Flannery, *W. B. Yeats and the Idea of a Theatre, The Early Abbey Theatre in Theory and Practice* (New Haven and London: Yale University Press, 1976), p. 266.

108. *CP*, p. 171.

109. *RI*, p. 91.

110. *Letters*, p. 293.

111. *The Classic Noh Theatre*, p. 144.

112. Osman Edwards, p. 50.

113. Miner, footnote, p. 59, 'The novel [*Madame Butterfly*] had been written by John Luther Long and published in 1897. ... [David] Belasco finally brought *Madame Butterfly* to the stage of the Herald Square Theatre on March 5, 1900.' It was also produced in London in the same year with Puccini as member of the audience.

114. Worth, p. 60.

115. W. B. Yeats, *Essays and Introductions* (London: Macmillan, 1961), 'Certain Noble Plays of Japan', p. 235. Hereafter cited as 'Certain Noble Plays'.

116. *Ibid.*, p. 221.

117. *The Classic Noh Theatre*, p. 3.

118. 'Certain Noble Plays', p. 221.

119. *Ibid.,* p. 224.
120. *Ibid.,* p. 226.
121. *Ibid.,* pp. 230–1.
122. *Ibid.,* p. 232.
123. *The Classic Noh Theatre,* 'Fenollosa on the Noh', pp. 69–70.
124. *Ibid.,* p. 82.
125. *Ibid.,* p. 87.
126. *Ibid.,* p. 88.
127. *CP,* p. 441.
128. *Ibid.,* p. 442.
129. *Ibid.,* p. 442.
130. *Ibid.,* p. 445.
131. 'Certain Noble Plays', pp. 222–3.
132. Richard Taylor, *The Drama of W. B. Yeats: Irish Myth and the Japanese No* (New Haven and London: Yale University Press, 1976), p. 120. Hereafter cited as Taylor, *No.* Richard Taylor, *A Reader's Guide to the Plays of W. B. Yeats* (London: Macmillan, 1984), p. 62. Hereafter cited as Taylor, *Reader's Guide.*
133. *CP,* p. 214.
134. *Ibid.,* p. 282.
135. *The Classic Noh Theatre,* p. 113.
136. W. B. Yeats, *Explorations* (London: Macmillan, 1962), p. 38. Hereafter cited as *Explorations.*
137. Taylor, *Reader's Guide,* p. 118.
138. *The Classic Noh Theatre,* p. 130.
139. *CP,* p. 461.
140. Taylor, *Reader's Guide,* p. 119.
141. *Ibid.,* p. 145.
142. *CP,* p. 621.
143. *Ibid.,* p. 633.
144. *Ibid.,* p. 633.
145. *Ibid.,* p. 704.
146. Karen Dorn, *Players and Painted Stage* (Sussex: The Harvester Press, 1984), p. 55.
147. Worth, p. 227.
148. *Ibid.,* p. 3.
149. 'Poet and Dancer', p. 24.
150. Andrew Graham-Dixon in *The Independent,* 12 November 1991, p. 16. Hereafter cited as Graham-Dixon. I am grateful to Martin Wright for bringing this article to my attention.
151. *Ibid.,* p. 16, column 3.
152. *Ibid.,* p. 16, column 6.

3

The Dancer in Performance

We can now no more get up a great interest in the Gods of Olympus than we can in the stories told by the showman of a travelling waxwork company. And for the lack of those great typical personages who flung thunderbolts or had serpents in their hair, we have betaken ourselves in a hurry to the poetry of cigarettes and black coffee, of absinthe, and the skirt dance ...[1]

W. B. Yeats penned this condemnation of contemporary effeteness and frivolity in 1893, a year in which some notable dancers were performing as soloists or as principals on the stages of theatres and music halls, among them exponents of the 'skirt dance' mentioned by the poet and of its successor, the 'serpentine'. The most famous draperial dancer of them all, Loïe Fuller,[2] was setting fashions in Paris where women were decking themselves out in Loïe Fuller skirts, hats, ribbons and shoes and even in Loïe Fuller petticoats. Her talents as a dancer were appraised by several newspapers and periodicals; the *Sketch* of 12 April 1893, noted that:

Her dance by turns has been compared to that of the Greek corybantes and to the most graceful up-to-date skirt dancing. Artists have attempted to reproduce the marvellous evolutions of *la danse serpentine* by pen, brush and pencil; but oddly enough, only the sculptor appears to have successfully transferred to plaster, brass or marble an idea of the airiness and witchery of Miss Fuller's drapery effects, and she will be represented by two busts at the forthcoming salon ...[3]

On a darkened stage Loïe Fuller swirled swathed in yards of muslin attached to two batons which, when brandished aloft, allowed the draperies to rise and fall, twist and billow to the accompaniment of music and coloured illumination shed on the fabric from various filters placed over lime- and spotlights. (The Fuller phenomenon could not have been realised without the recent invention of electric stage-lighting.) The effect is widely reported to have been enchanting, although photographs of the dancer in her stage costume show a plump woman with rather a pudgy face and it is difficult to empathise with the contemporary fervour for her and her undoubted skills. Some doubt may, however, be cast on whether she can correctly be designated 'dancer'; she should, perhaps, be more correctly, though pompously, described as an *'animatrice de mise-en-scène'*. The distinction may be petty but it has none the less some justification.

She was very famous and, as we shall note, was approved of by both Yeats and Mallarmé who saw her as emblem of the *Symboliste* dancer. Some months after the *Sketch* report, on 12 July 1893, *The Times* managed to interview Loïe Fuller herself on a fleeting visit to London from Paris and the resulting article summarised her talent as follows:

The serpentine dance has been familiar to Londoners for some time past, and several ladies have performed very gracefully and very skilfully in that particular line: but it has remained for Miss Fuller, who styles herself, and it is believed rightly, *créatrice de la danse serpentine*, to excel all who have gone before. This lady has lately been delighting the audiences at the Folies Bergères, and she is now paying a passing ... visit to London. On Monday night she gave two performances, one at the Gaiety Theatre and the other at the Shaftesbury. This particular form of dance has probably never been made such a distinctive feature in an evening's entertainment before. At the Gaiety the performance was given at the close of the representation of *In Town*, and consequently there was a very full house to greet Miss Fuller. The stage, by means of black hangings, was made perfectly dark, and the dancer went through her graceful and beautiful evolutions amid an iridescent glow from the lime lights. Four times she appeared – the first time in the serpent dance, the second in the violet, and the third in the butterfly dance. The fourth time the audience were left to guess what the dance was. It must not be supposed that the difference here indicated is in the nature of the dance, for that is not so. The term 'serpentine' would apply equally well to the one as to the other. The difference lies in the variation of the traceries of the voluminous skirts, which in the serpent dances are covered with serpents and in the butterfly dance with butterflies. The general effect was very charming, and whether Miss Fuller was the originator or not of this very elegant dance, she is undoubtedly its ablest exponent, and deserved to the full the enthusiastic reception she met with.[4]

Loïe Fuller's own account in her autobiography, *Fifteen Years of a Dancer's Life*,[5] provides perhaps a definitive statement of how she invented the serpentine dance. There she claimed that, when still an actress – her profession before turning dancer – she was called upon in a New York play to take the part of a hypnotised girl. An admirer had presented her with a long Indian skirt, the tissue of which was so flimsy that the whole garment could be packed into a cigar box and she decided to act the role by winding and meandering about the stage, simultaneously agitating her skirt in a kind of dance. Back in her room one afternoon she noticed how the sunlight caught the skirt material and she began to move in a dance measure, wafting it to and fro as she did so. From this chance discovery she went on to develop a career as dancer rather than actress and invented methods of manipulating theatre lights to produce illuminations in the same manner as that which the sun had made on her fragile costume, becoming very expert at lighting techniques in the process.

This personal testimony upholds the theory that the serpentine derived from the skirt dance, the most celebrated exponent of which in London had been Kate Vaughan – who was ballet-trained – in the 1870s, twenty years before Yeats's comment about the genre. I shall examine the Vaughan phenomenon in greater detail below because it is crucial to a discussion of the varieties of dance offered from the glorious explosion of Romantic ballet in the 1840s with London as its Mecca, when Taglioni, Elssler, Cerrito, Grisi and Grahn[6] were to enchant their public frequently as visitors to the English capital and the later Victorian dances such as the Quadrille and the Cellar Flap Dance with which the century closed. The serpentine was thus a development of the skirt dance which, in turn, according to the *Sketch* of 16 October 1895, grew out of something called a 'cloak dance'. In announcing the performance of a master and student (Ernest D'Auban and Coralie Blithe) at the Gaiety and Drury Lane theatres, the periodical reported:

> they will introduce a genuine cloak-dance, a dance which originated with the Spanish bull-fighters, and has since grown into the serpentine and other draperial dances.[7]

The question of the identity of the 'originator' of these dances, however, is one which preoccupied the newspapers and stage journals of the time, partly because the principal exponents of a certain genre had so many imitators. Loïe Fuller often met with disbelief on announcing her arrival to theatre managements because some impostor had already played that theatre under Fuller's name. In 1893, the year in which Yeats revealed his knowledge of the skirt dance, we note briefly that Fuller was also giving a performance as Salome in a version by Armand Silvestre and Gabriel Pierné at the Athenée, while the *Sketch* was interviewing two Fuller clones, the first, on 8 February, being Miss Marie Leyton whom the paper dubbed 'The Electrical Serpentine Dancer' at the Tivoli. Her personal rendering of the dance, as the headline suggests, involved the incorporation of tiny electric lights into her costume which were illuminated when she performed the serpentine on a darkened stage. When Leyton was asked about the originator of this bizarre phenomenon she averred that it had been invented in England:

'The dress came from the comic opera of "The Nautch Girl"[8] here in London. All the girls' dresses were made like that, with very short waists and very full gauzy skirts. And you must know Miss Loïe Fuller, the American actress, was over here at the Gaiety, you remember, and' –
'Miss Fuller was the inventor of the dance, wasn't she?' – 'Well, I'm telling you. She saw "The Nautch Girl", and she got Miss Fisher, the costumier here, to make her a dress like it, to take back to Amurca [sic] for a specialty dance. ... '
'And the dance itself, the movement of the drapery?' – 'That had been done right here in London some years ago by a man dancer, who made a great success with it, only in another form. Loïe Fuller practised in the dress, and found that she could get some striking effects with it, and she got the idea of doing it on a darkened stage with coloured limes, and calling it the "Serpentine."'[9]

And so we are offered yet another variant version of the origin of the dance.

The second *Sketch* report on yet another serpentine dancer appeared on 2 April 1893, the fourteen-year-old Miss Clara Wieland, who was performing at the Empire, and the article is also useful in making very explicit the sheer number of the devotees to this particular Terpsichorean form:

She has a pretty face, an extremely well developed figure, and she manipulates the serpentine skirts with much skill. With the admirable effects of luminous darkness and shifting coloured lights which we get at the Empire, her dance is charming to watch, even for the *blasé* person who has seen all the serpentine dancers – Jennie Joyce, Estrella Sylvia, Marie Leyton, Florrie Hooton, Florence Levey, and, far greater than them all, Legnani. Miss Wieland has succeeded in finding some curves unattempted yet, some new ways of disappearing in the centre of a whirling cloud of colours. In this dance the dancer creates her own scenery, and it is the scenery rather than the dance that counts. The purists complain that it is not a dance at all. It is a development of skirt-dancing, in which the dancer almost entirely disappears in the eclipsing triumph of skirts, with which, by-the-way, Miss Mary E. Fisher, the well-known theatrical costumier, has admirably equipped Miss Wieland. Certainly, there is only one step further, and that is the twirling automaton – Villiers de l'Isle-Adam's 'Eve Future' – in the centre of 80 yards of white surrah. Perhaps that is to be the dancing of the future.[10]

While this reviewer here speculated about the possible developments to emerge out of serpentine dancing, others, as we have seen, preferred to muse about its past and skirt dancing was not yet obsolete in 1893 when, on 2 August, the *Sketch* published an interview with Sylvia Grey whom the paper called 'The High Priestess of Skirt Dancing'. She was appearing at the Gaiety where Kate Vaughan had presented her own version of the dance some twenty years earlier. Yeats was in all probability familiar with the press reports about the exponents of the dance genre which he mentioned above, because, as we shall discover, he had friends who contributed to the *Sketch* in which such articles appeared. Sylvia Grey was asked whether she was responsible for the current skirt dancing craze:

Well, of course, Kate Vaughan danced in long skirts long before my time; but society people only took it up about four years ago, since when I have taught a great many ladies.[11]

Early in the New Year, on 24 January 1894, the *Sketch* noted the success of Miss Alice Lethbridge at the Lyric Theatre in *Little Christopher Columbus*:

her two-minute skirt dance in the second act is received by the audience in a fashion which recalls the ovations accorded in the long ago to Miss Kate Vaughan ...[12]

Once again an investigator is referred to Kate Vaughan and importance clearly attaches to this dancer who had been performing in the 1870s. In an obituary to her on 28 February 1903, the *Era* paid the following tribute:

> She was a skirt dancer in the 1870s and also appeared as an actress in burlesque at the Gaiety in August 1896. She was a pupil of Mrs. Conquest at the Grecian Theatre and played at the music-halls with her sister, Miss Susie Vaughan in the very early 1870s.
>
> Mr. John Hollingshead,[13] writing of this popular member of his old Gaiety company, says that she 'revived, and may almost take the credit of being the founder of a distinct school of dancing. Something like the "skirt dance" was seen upon the Opera stage in the Haymarket about 1750, the dancer being an Italian lady of distinction, whose name I have no means of verifying at this moment. M. Vestris,[14] who married Miss Bartalozzi, the daughter of the great artist-engraver, and made her Madame Vestris, represented this form of choregraphic art, and Madame Vestris was one of Kate Vaughan's predecessors.'[15]

Kate Vaughan was the first performer to make skirt dancing popular and in introducing – or, more correctly, reintroducing – this genre, she represented a bridge in dancing midway between true ballet and the *cancan*, the splits and all the exotica of the Parisian dances of the 1890s. Her grace and modesty along with her undoubted talent as a soloist were refreshing, as Alan Hyman explains in *The Gaiety Years* :

> Kate Vaughan, one of the outstanding dancers of the period, had been discovered by Hollingshead on the music halls. She had a slight figure and a delightful presence and was the first dancer to wear long, graceful skirts instead of the tights and tu-tu ballet skirts of the old burlesque artists. Her black gloves and stockings and her svelte figure fascinated the public for a decade. It was a pleasant change to watch this slim woman on the stage after a succession of girls with full bosoms and enormous thighs.[16]

J. E. Crawford Flitch, looking back from his standpoint in 1912, perceived the skirt dance as a compromise between ballet and step dancing:

> On the one hand was the classical school of the ballet, now in an unfortunate condition of decadence. It lacked all those elements which make of the ballet a living art. The public was sick and tired of it. On the other hand a more or less vulgar type of dancing, which had no relation to art, enjoyed a certain popularity on the music-hall stage. It consisted chiefly of the Clog Dance, believed originally to have come from the cotton mills of Lancashire, and various kinds of acrobatic dancing. In the race for popularity the ugly but energetic Step Dance was first, the classical ballet nowhere. Between the two there was no happy medium.
>
> The Skirt Dance was essentially a compromise between the academical method of the ballet and the grotesque step dancing which appealed to the popular taste of the time. It stood nearer perhaps to the more serious form of dancing, for in its elements, at least, it was modelled upon the method of the ballet. The exchange, the pirouette, the balance, all the first steps necessary to the ballet-dancer, are the same in both. But while retaining the academical steps as a foundation, it permitted the performer greater license in the use of them ... its tendency was towards greater vividness and the play of temperament.[17]

Vaughan was adored for her genuine genius by many admirers, among them Ruskin and Burne-Jones who paid her subtle tribute by naming her 'Miriam Ariadne Salome Vaughan'.[18] Fuller's serpentine, whatever she may claim as its origin, clearly owes something to the skirt dancing phenomenon.

Yeats was also aware of the serpentine and the Loïe Fuller craze, particularly of her Fire Dance which contributed to a wide-ranging repertoire which included a Widow Dance (in black), Rainbow, Flower, Butterfly and Mirror Dances, a Salute to the Sun and, significantly, as we have noted, Salome. The Fire Dance came into being through another happy accident, namely a performance of *Salome* in which Fuller staged a sunset.[19] Yeats did not, however, emulate his friend Arthur Symons[20] in the latter's obsessional attendances of dance performances and courting of particular dancers. The Irish poet probably gleaned his knowledge of the current fervour for dance and solo dancers on both sides of the English Channel from various sources, especially as such voguish phenomena forced themselves upon contemporary consciousness by means of interviews and reports in theatrical journals and even in the columns of *The Times* and he was also sensitive to accounts from those of his friends and acquaintances who frequented music halls and theatres. Arthur Symons, with whom Yeats toured the West of Ireland in 1896, is a key figure to an understanding of the passion for dance and its controversiality in the 1890s. He was a frequent contributor to the *Sketch*, the *Star* and the *St James's Gazette* as a reviewer of new ballets at the Alhambra and the Empire in London and first visited Paris in 1889 where he subsequently became acquainted with the dancers of the Moulin Rouge and Folies Bergère. Before considering his reviews, important though they are for the acute and sometimes surprising *aperçus* into the nature of dance which they contain, insights shared to some degree by both Mallarmé and Yeats, let us first examine some of the poetry written by Symons and others with particular dancers as inspiration. The English poet does not pay tribute to Loïe Fuller in verse and Mallarmé chooses to analyse the effects that her dancing produced in prose notes, 'Crayonné au Théâtre', which were discussed in the first chapter (p. 8), but Yeats himself referred to Fuller years later in the poem entitled 'Nineteen Hundred and Nineteen'. He could have been relying on his memory of her during the early years of the twentieth century or he may have attended a current performance, because in April 1919 her 'Dancing Girls' appeared at the Coliseum and in August she produced in a six-week season at the same venue a 'ballet of light'.[21]

Yeats produced his own tribute:

> When Loïe Fuller's Chinese dancers enwound
> A shining web, a floating ribbon of cloth,
> It seemed that a dragon of air
> Had fallen among dancers, had whirled them round
> Or hurried them off on its own furious path.[22]

We must assume that the poet made an odd error in dubbing Fuller's troupe 'Chinese dancers' as there is no evidence at all that they were; in fact everything points to this being the company headed by Sada Yacco and to their nationality being Japanese. Fuller toured Europe with them in the first years of the century. It is not perhaps surprising that Yeats should have made such a mistake in view of the plethora of dance companies from Asia visiting London and Paris, their performances being reviewed by *The Times* and their enigmatic personalities provoking meditation in the several poets who wrote of Javanese Dancers (who performed in Paris in 1889), Burmese 'yeng' Dancers appearing at the Empire of London Exhibition, Earl's Court, London, on 9 October 1895 and Cambodian Sacred Dancers who presented their art in Paris on 2 July 1906. By 1919 Yeats himself had of course been mesmerised by the skill of the Japanese dancer, Michio Ito, performing in the poet's dance play, *At the Hawk's Well*, in 1916 and later going on to dance in New York, the dancer and poet producing together a rare combination of talents which will be examined later.

Yeats's reference to Fuller, late though it is, acts within the poem as a dating device, a *point de repère* in the poet's memories by means of which to fix events which were contemporaneous with the Fuller phenomenon. Yeats does not here, as does Mallarmé in his prose, analyse Fuller as the *Symboliste* dancer who creates her own context. She is, to use a favourite Yeatsian expression, 'self-begotten': she produces her own being and exploits it to the limits of its possible interpretations. As we observed in Chapter 1 and again above, Mallarmé 'read' the Fuller performance as language: he perceived her as metaphor, as sign, as emblem of identical form and meaning, '*incorporation visuelle de l'idée*'.[23] Yeats's poem, on the other hand, employs Fuller as a historical reference point and relates her to current violent happenings in Ireland by linking her to the Salome/ Herodias tradition – not surprisingly, as for Yeats the figure of the dancer and that of Salome's amoral beauty are never far distant from each other – when he has the dancers 'whirled' and 'hurried' away in the same manner as that of the whirlwinds of the Middle Ages which were known as the dances of the daughters of Herodias, as indeed the poem goes on to make explicit.

But Yeats's account has all the vividness of personal reminiscence and one could be forgiven for assuming that he had witnessed Fuller's performance himself. He perceived her as form invested with meaning, form produced as a result of labour and, above all, as the dancer who is emblematic of unity of being. For Yeats, as for Mallarmé, she represented, more than all other dancers, the fusion of humanity and sterility, the concrete and the abstract; she came near, in all the mechanical artistry of her dance, to approaching pure abstraction as the flesh and blood of the living woman became subsumed into the flowing illuminated draperies.

Symons's own poems to and about dancers were produced with an immediacy which is, in itself, perhaps characteristic of the 1890s, a decade in which experience, however perverse, was rapidly mediated by intellect or imagination into aesthetic form and received with as much enthusiasm as that through which it had been created. A brief appraisal of some of his verse shows the fascination that the music hall and its dancers exerted on Symons. His response is more personal, emotional and intuitive than that of Yeats to Fuller and the English poet does not reveal himself in his verse to be that astute theorist on dance and dancers whom we discover in his articles for reviews and newspapers. The *Sketch* of 4 October 1893, published his poem to the dancer, Minnie Cunningham and this work was one of those collected under the title *London Nights* of 1895 which Yeats reviewed in the August edition of *The Bookman* of that year. The typical 'Symons' note of jaded innocence is in evidence in the two stanzas which I have taken as representative of the whole:

> A rhythmic flower, whose petals pirouette
> In deliberate circles, fain to follow
> The vague aerial minuet,
> The mazy dancing of the swallow; ...
>
> So, in the smoke-polluted place,
> Where bird or flower might never be,
> With glimmering feet, with flower-like face,
> She dances at the Tivoli.[24]

Of *London Nights* Yeats commented: 'the bulk of it is about musical halls', and he identified an unsatisfying lack of robustness in Symons's verse which left both reader and critic disappointed in its absence of definition and distinctness:

At once the charm and defect of the book is that its best moments have no passion stronger than a 'soft joy' and 'pale desire'; and that their pleasure in the life of sensation is not ... the robust pleasure of the man of the world, but the shadowy delight of the artist ... he is at his best when simply contemplative, when expounding not passion, but passion's evanescent beauty, when celebrating not the joys and sorrows of his dancers and light o' loves, but the pathos of their restless days.[25]

It is well-known that Yeats estimated his friend's poem about Jane Avril,[26] one of the solo dancers at the Moulin Rouge, 'La Melanite [sic]: Moulin Rouge', to be 'one of the most perfect lyrics of our time',[27] though even a cursory glance such as that taken in the first chapter (p. 9), would surely suggest that loyalty was impairing his judgement. 'La Mélinite: Moulin Rouge' was written in Paris on 22 May 1892 and does capture the wilful narcissism of Jane Avril, one-time patient of Charcot, who preferred not to be paid for her dancing as the pleasure thus derived from it was greater.[28]

> Alone, apart, one dancer watches
> Her mirrored, morbid grace;
> Before the mirror face to face,
> Alone she watches
> Her morbid, vague, ambiguous grace ...[29]

Only slightly less famous is Symons's 'Prologue' to *London Nights*, written on 17 May 1893:

> My life is like a music hall,
> Where, in the impotence of rage,
> Chained by enchantment to my stall,
> I see myself upon the stage
> Dance to amuse a music-hall ...
>
> 'Tis I that smoke this cigarette,
> Lounge here, and laugh for vacancy,
> And watch the dancers turn; and yet
> It is my very self I see
> Across the cloudy cigarette.[30]

Here again, as in 'La Mélinite', we witness narcissism along with the bitter note of desolation and frustration typical of Symons's music-hall poems.

While 'To a Dancer' of 18 October 1892, illustrates a relationship between poet/onlooker and performer, even here Symons appropriates the other (the dancer with whom he is in love) and draws her into his own egocentricity:

> Intoxicatingly
> Her eyes across the footlights gleam,

(The wine of love, the wine of dream)
Her eyes that gleam for me! ...

Her body's melody,
In silent waves of wandering sound,
Thrills to the sense of all around,
Yet thrills alone for me.[31]

Symons wrote many poems to dancers, both to the Parisian Quadrille stars whom we shall consider below and to his principal loves, ballet dancers:

> Although he refers to Jane Avril, Symons shows little interest in Loïe Fuller (for Yeats the representative dancer of the poetic image); he prefers ballet with its cross-flare of gaslights and foot-lights, its painted figures and its diaphanous but somewhat mechanical order (the dancers of Degas rather than those of Moreau). Ballet's illusion mimics the illusion of life. But the 'free' dancer does not depend on scenery, music, dramatic interest; she depends merely on her own body, and her dance can be readily associated with possession by god or demon. To admire the 'free' dance is to pass from decadent admiration of artifice to symbolist recognition of Mallarmé's 'l'incorporation visuelle de l'idée.' From a frivolous spectacle, the dance was transformed for Symons into something quasi-religious.[32]

Ian Fletcher, in this extract from his article 'Symons, Yeats and the Demonic Dance' (1960), focusses on an essential distinction between the two poets in the perception of dance. The contrast made between the qualities of the ballet dancer and those of the 'free' dancer clarifies admirably Symons's attraction to the tenets of both Symbolism and Decadence and the way in which, while the latter movement stressed a commitment to artifice, the former tended towards an appreciation of ritual and ceremony. Yeats's preference for the 'free' dancer, as we remarked in his enthusiasm for Fuller, mirrors the zeal of Mallarmé in his appreciations of her in prose: she is at once choreographer and performer of her own measures and articulates the expression of her own impulses and emotions.

Symons explored his own fascination analytically in his prose reviews for theatrical periodicals such as the *Sketch* and the *Star* for which he reported mainly on ballet. The statements that he there made were often forceful and insistent: Symons was puzzling over the relationship of dance to reality and illusion. Usually he applauded ballet for its artificiality and thus, as any *Symboliste-Décadent* poet worth his name knew, its truth, but on occasion he slipped into criticising it for aiming at an illusion of reality. A study of these accounts shows that they circle our selected touchstone date of 1893 and the quotation from Yeats recording his awareness of the current vogue for skirt dancing with which this chapter opened. An appraisal of Symons's prose will throw his somewhat manifesto-like accounts into relief and it will also focus on the very interesting conclusions on the nature of dance that the English poet was trying to reach, perceptions with which Yeats himself struggled.

In the *Sketch* of 5 April 1893, Symons interviewed an American dancer, 'Cyrene', at the Alhambra. There he was plotting the progress of the quintessentially French dance, the *cancan*, as it crossed the Channel in its modern form, the *chahut*. Cyrene had been a pupil in Paris of Grille-d'Egout[33] (so named because the shape of her teeth resembled sewer-gratings), one of the dancers grouped around the Moulin Rouge in the 1890s who performed the Naturalist Quadrille, (the *cancan*), with the others who were perhaps even more famous than she, La Goulue[34] and Jane Avril.

> with a sudden kick, done with the greatest ease in the world, Cyrene tapped the palm of her hand, held just above the head, with her instep. The fantastic foot flew into the air, descended almost before one had time to realise it. 'Never did La Goulue, never did Nini Patte-en-l'Air[35] do a kick like that,' I assured her; and we talked of the French high-kickers of the Parisian public balls ... It was indeed a success, this extraordinary acrobatic dance, *cancan* and *cachuha* [sic] in one: a dance which reminds one now of Otero,[36] now of La Goulue; a dance which was joyous and spontaneous and triumphant, which did the incredible with ease, which did the splits and the high kick with modesty, which captivated the eye and distracted the intelligence at once. The extravagance of the thing was never vulgar, its intricate agility was never incorrect; there was genuine grace in the wildest moment of caprice, there was real science in the pointing of the foot in its most fantastic flights above the head.[37]

What obviously fascinated Symons was the mixture of abandon and control, the exploration of the boundaries between vulgarity and grace and, above all, the seeming contradiction which is none the less resolved between gymnastic agility and beauty.

He plotted other paradoxes in his appraising of ballet as when, in an account in the *St James's Gazette* of 16 December 1892, he explained that he had attended a dress rehearsal of the ballet *Aladdin* at the Alhambra as a 'Casual Spectator'. He pondered on the absence in the naked faces and worn rehearsal clothes of the dancers of that artificial quality which he always so admired:

> To the amateur of what is more artificial in the art of illusion there is nothing so interesting as a stage rehearsal, and there is no stage rehearsal as interesting as the rehearsal of a ballet ... Aimless, unintelligible it looked, this tripping, posturing crowd of oddly dressed figures; these bright outdoor faces looked strange in a place where I was so used to see rouged cheeks and lips, powdered chins, painted eye-lashes, yellow wigs. In this fantastic return to nature I found the last charm of the artificial.[38]

In the *Sketch* of 28 June 1893, Symons upbraided the producers of *Fidelia; or the Devil's Violin* at the Alhambra for not creating sufficient beauty when it was the duty of ballet to do so; they had shown an unfortunate and, for this reviewer, an unacceptable tendency to veer towards comic pantomime and mere grandiose spectacle. He berated them for the lack of the artificial:

> A ballet has so many chances of being a thing of beauty that it has no excuse for not being so, or for abandoning beauty in search for humour, variety, the grotesque, or anything whatever. The beauty of dancing is so great, and so entirely in itself, that it requires no outside expedients to give it effect, only due assistance of charming and appropriate scenery and costume.[39]

These sentiments of the English poet were to be echoed years later in 1913 when Yeats discovered the Noh and fashioned his own dance plays after the Japanese model. There, as was described in Chapter 2, an aesthetic was created which, as Symons implies when discussing ballet, was self-referential, hermetic and isolated from the outside world. Within its sphere, all suggestions of realism are obliterated and precedence is accorded to ritual and highly stylised acting and dancing, while the theme of the play is that of a known story of prince, priest or god: the whole is centred on myth and archetype. As early as the 1904 edition of *Samhain* Yeats had expressed his desire for the clearly unrealistic in acting in a manner in which we can decipher, in retrospect, theatrical elements which suggestively anticipate the Noh:

> The larger the actor's audience, the more he must get away, except in trivial passages, from the methods of conversation. Where one requires the full attention of the mind, one must not weary it with any but the most needful changes of pitch and note, or by an irrelevant or obtrusive gesture. As long as drama was full of poetical beauty, full of description, full of philosophy, as long as its words were the very vesture of sorrow and laughter, the players understood that their art was essentially conventional, artificial, ceremonious.[40]

Yeats too commended artifice and called for simple, stylised and symbolic scenery, chorus, musicians and masks. Symons discloses in his reviews and in his essay of 1898, 'The World as Ballet' published in *Studies in Seven Arts* (1906), a dislike of realism which is taken up by his Irish colleague: the latter perceived it as merely presenting the surface of life and he saw in the Naturalism of Ibsen, the movement's most notable exponent, an immense absence:

> The utmost sincerity, the most unbroken logic, give me, at any rate, but an imperfect pleasure if there is not a vivid and beautiful language. Ibsen has sincerity and logic beyond any writer of our time, and we are all seeking to learn them at his hands; but is he not a good deal less than the greatest of all times, because he lacks beautiful and vivid language?[41]

Just as Symons shuns all attempts which endeavour to produce an illusion of reality in ballet, so does his friend eschew it in theatre in all its facets, acting, dancing and scenery included and Yeats's first tentative pronouncements on these subjects date, as do Symons's own, from the 1890s and *The Land of Heart's Desire*, where the pre-occupations with both dance and suggestive rather than mimetic scenery began to be made explicit.

As far as Symons's statements in reviews are concerned, he was again indignant some months later in another *Sketch* article of 1894 when considering *Monkey Island* at the Alhambra. It is in this report that he makes his significant distinction between what he perceives as the dual motivations of devotees to the ballet such as himself, bemusing himself by his own possession of a foot in both camps and, thus, creating a conflict which he never resolved:

> Lovers of the ballet become amateurs for many reasons: from abstract interest in dancing, from concrete interest in dancers, from a general liking for gorgeous spectacle, and from a real taste for the beauty of pictures in motion. But whether they are really guided by the highest aesthetical principles or not, all these very various persons are affected and delighted, invariably, by a good ballet; they are not likely to come twice to see such a performance as 'Monkey Island', the serio-comic *divertissement* which was produced at the Alhambra on Monday, September 24 ... The sight of an Italian *prima ballerina*, dressed as a male monkey, and scratching herself in front of the footlights, is not an agreeable one to those who really care for the dignity of the art of Italian ballet-dancing. Then there is no change of costume throughout the three *tableaux*, and there are practically only two dresses – the white sailor suits and the brown-and-grey monkey arrangements. Neither of them is a graceful dress for a girl, both being quite arbitrary in what they accentuate and what they obscure in the female figure ...[42]

So the presence of mere artifice alone is not enough; it must be pleasant, beautiful artificiality to create a joyful illusion, and girls in monkey suits are simply not sufficiently attractive to be worthy of serious, pleasurable attention.

By scrutinising some further examples of Symons's writings on ballet we may discover more significant links between his articles and those of Yeats on theatre. *The Girl I Left Behind Me* at the Empire, which had been reviewed on 4 October 1893, was more completely in keeping with Symons's demands of ballet. The choreographer and ballet mistress was Madame Katti Lanner,[43] whose reputation proved her incapable of producing shoddy work. Symons remarks, most tellingly:

> The ballet is so entirely and beautifully artificial, so essentially and excellently conventional, that it can gain nothing by trying to become, what it never can and never should be, a picture of real life ... it should be the making of something ... merely beautiful, and nothing more.[44]

And again, some two months later when reporting on *Don Quixote* at the Alhambra,

> One does not go to see a ballet in order to follow a story; one goes to see beautiful dancing, beautiful dancers, and dresses ...[45]

Symons's needs seem to have been simple and easily satisfied and he gave his reasons for being pleased in the *Sketch* for 7 August 1895, when discussing *Titania*, again at the Alhambra:

> It is as fantastic and unreal and impossible as even I could wish for; and I like a ballet to have as much of the fantastic, unreal, and impossible as it can be got to contain. I go to see a ballet in order to get as far as possible from the intolerable reality of the world around me; ... People will go to see 'Titania' because it is a charming pageant of dancing, in which the dresses are quite exceptionally pretty, and the combinations of colours unusually delicate in their shading ... But it is the fairies that I go to see, and these young people, in their gauze and wings, look quite enough like the real thing – the unreal thing, that is; I require no more illusion.[46]

Symons was an amateur whose interest in dance was both, as he outlined it, abstract (an interest in dancing) and concrete (an interest in dancers); he fell in love with a dancer and his book of poems, *Amoris Victima*, charted the end of the affair in 1897 and his friend Yeats also reviewed this work in the *Bookman* of April of that year. As poet, translator, reviewer and man-about-town in both Paris and London, Symons knew English ballerinas and the French music-hall dancers of the 1890s as well as he knew French *Symboliste* poets – he introduced Yeats to Verlaine in 1894 – and, as was noted in Chapter 1 (p. 4), he dedicated his book *The Symbolist Movement in Literature* (1899), to the Irish writer. Symons was the seismograph of movement in dance and poetry (for Mallarmé they approached being the same thing), just as some ten years later another acquaintance of Yeats's, Charles Ricketts, would register and record all the first tremblings stirred by the Russian Ballet and its impact on contemporary London. Yeats benefited enormously from his friendship with both men who also knew and respected each other: through them and their work and leisure pursuits he was *au courant* with many of the facets of the current avidness for dance in its various manifestations and he would later, when composing his own dance plays, draw on this knowledge to reproduce the insistence on artificiality and the stress on the dancer's impersonality as presented by, say, Loïe Fuller, in his dances.

Each of Symons's *aperçus* on ballet and ballet dancers reproduced above finds its parallel in some thought of Yeats's and the main tenor of Symons's argument is, of course, that ballet must focus on fantasy. As we have noted, Yeats wrote on this theme – the responsibility *not* to write realistically – throughout his life, his opinions culminating in delighted recognition at the discovery of the Noh. His articles in *Samhain* of the years spanning 1902 to 1908 analyse the preoccupations with realism and naturalism, view them from many angles, weigh and balance them and return again and again to a plea for artifice. Linked to this and hardly less significant are his views on Ireland and a national drama and whether the spirit of the country lent itself to the current vogue for realism; as he says in *Samhain* of 1904:

> I know that we are at the mere beginning, laboriously learning our craft, trying our hands in little plays for the most part, that we may not venture too boldly in our ignorance; but I never hear the vivid, picturesque, ever-varied language of Mr. Synge's persons without feeling that the great *collaborateur* has his finger in our business. May it not be that the only realistic play that will live as Shakespeare has lived, as Calderon has lived, as the Greeks have lived, will arise out of the common life, where language is as much alive as if it were new come out of Eden? After all, is not the greatest play not the play that gives the sensation of an external reality but the play in which there is the greatest abundance of life itself, of the reality that is in our minds?[47]

Prefiguring the Noh once again is a comment made in 1904 which also anticipates statements which would be voiced years later in the Preface to *Four Plays for Dancers* of 1921:

> That we may throw emphasis on the words in poetical drama, above all where the words are remote from real life as well as in themselves exacting and difficult, the actors must move, for the most part, slowly and quietly, and not very much, and there should be something in their movements decorative and rhythmical as if they were paintings on a frieze.[48]

It is but a small step from this requirement to a belief in the discipline of impersonality as achieved by the wearing of a mask. This is employed in a similar way to that of Symons's ballerinas when they adopt their role symbolically through the artifice of highly stylised costume, make-up and wig. As Yeats was to explain later of *The Only Jealousy of Emer* and the masks fashioned by the Dutchman, Hildo van Krop,

> The masks get much of their power from enclosing the whole head; this makes the head out of proportion to the body, and I found some difference of opinion as to whether this was a disadvantage or not in an art so distant from reality; that it was not a disadvantage in the case of the Woman of the Sidhe all were agreed. She was a strange, noble, unforgettable figure.[49]

In a letter to Olivia Shakespear of 24 August 1929, Yeats excitedly described the London reception of his prose version of *The Only Jealousy of Emer, Fighting the Waves* and he seemed to have devised a new form of theatre influenced, perhaps, by the fusion of elements produced so expertly by the *Ballets Russes*:

> My *Fighting the Waves* has been my greatest success on the stage since *Kathleen-ni-Houlihan*, and the production was a great event here ... Everyone here is as convinced as I am that I have discovered a new form by this consolidation of dance, speech and music. The dancing of the goddess in her abstract almost non-representative mask was extraordinarily exciting. The play begins with a dance which represents Cuchullan [sic] fighting the waves, then after some singing by the chorus comes the play which has for its central incident the dance of the goddess and of the ghost of Cuchullan, and then after more singing is the dance of the goddess mourning among the waves. The waves are of course dancers ...[50]

The distance from realism is so great – as great as even Arthur Symons could have desired – that Yeats was approaching what he had advocated some years earlier in his *Four Plays for Dancers* of 1921:

> The face of the speaker should be as much a work of art as the lines which he speaks or the costume that he wears, that all may

be as artificial as possible. Perhaps in the end one would write plays for certain masks.[51]

Artifice could surely be extended no further.

Yeats valued Symons as unchallenged connoisseur of dance and dancers in the 1890s: as Ian Fletcher explains in his article 'Symons, Yeats and the Demonic Dance',

> In *Autobiographies* Yeats does ... full justice to the dialogue of ideas and personalities between him and Symons in the five years when they were closely associated; ... he appreciated Symons because Symons was, for him, a feminine receptive personality; a conductor of ideas. He never quite treats Symons as a person or a poet in his own right; if he praises anything, it is Symons's translations from the French, which he saw as extensions of Symons's great gift for making immediately current the latest forms in other European literatures.[52]

As has already been suggested, Symons was indispensable to Yeats as a source of information about dance and in particular on the Parisian music hall dancers whom the former had discovered in the French capital in 1892. These were the stars made famous not only by their own talents but also through the sketches and posters of the artist Henri de Toulouse-Lautrec who died in 1901 at the age of thirty-six having documented perfectly in his work a decade of dancers, singers and music-hall artistes such as Yvette Guilbert, whom Yeats saw perform in 1906. These dancers collected at the Moulin Rouge when it opened in 1889 having left the *cafés concerts* and dance halls from the Left Bank's Bal Bullier to the Jardin de Paris in the Champs Elysées. An enquiry into the skills of some of the practitioners of the French mode of dancing, which was translated in turn by English and American exponents of the art in their own music-hall performances, demonstrates the reasons for Symons's captivation and explains Yeats's different response. The latter knew at least of Jane Avril through his friendship with her English devotee and the phenomenon of the *cancan* dancer in which she figures prominently cannot pass unnoticed in a study of the dancer in performance at the turn of the nineteenth century.

Lautrec made studies of Jane Avril and La Goulue and he brought into focus the essential rather prim, priggish solitariness of the one and the greed for life of the other. Jane Avril was always reputed to be genteel, despite her origin as the illegitimate daughter of a Roman gigolo and a French mother. She was, as we may see from Lautrec's posters, pale, thin, with huge eyes, a mop of red hair and stick-like limbs. She established herself when only fifteen as a frequenter of the *bals musettes* of Paris and become notorious in all the dance-halls of the capital. Although she was part of the original team at the Elysée Montmartre, she found it too vulgar for her taste because 'women with a shameless air danced there ... arm in arm with bookmakers who looked like butchers, or worse'.[53] She was obsessed by dancing, but rather than the *chahut*, which she found crude, she improvised her own solo performances and intricately and sinuously interpreted the music of romantic songs: the curvilinear outline impressed many artists when created by such an angular creature and a glance at Lautrec's posters make it clear that the trend of Art Nouveau was being anticipated. Symons saw her later in 1892 when she appeared at the Jardin de Paris and we have already looked at the poem in which he tried to capture the essential privateness of her nature and her dancing in the midst of a life led in public. He also said of her that

> She had about her an air of depraved virginity ... the more provocative because she played as a prude with an assumed modesty, décolleté [sic] nearly to the waist. ... She was a creature of cruel moods, cruel passions ... an absolute passion for her own beauty.[54]

Avril's character as perceived by Symons seems to have contained that ardent and perverse cruelty which was revealed by an investigation of some of the presentations of Salome in the first chapter. In his poem addressed to Avril, Symons attached significance to her narcissism, while here he concentrates on the disturbing nature of her beauty and the manipulatory quality of her sexuality. Her ambiguities – she was reputed to be a lesbian – rendered her endlessly mysterious and exciting.

Louise Weber, nicknamed 'La Goulue', projected a quite different image in her life and dancing. Reviewing her performance in 1890 the journalist Georges Montorgeuil described her as

> pink and blonde, about eighteen years old (she was in fact twenty-five), with a willful, vicious and flushed baby face, a nose with quivering, impatient nostrils, a nose of one sniffing after

love, nostrils dilating with the male odor of chestnut trees and the enervating bouquet of brandy glasses, a mouth gluttonous and sensual, a look shameless and provoking, the milk-white bosom freely escaping from the corsage ... the pretty girl unaware of any modesty or constraint. ... She provokes by the display of bare flesh, or at least that which may be divined amid the turbulent swirl of her underclothes as she deliberately permits a glimpse ... of her naked shin between garter and the first fold of petticoat by lifting her leg. [She is] brutal, blunt, without feminine grace. ... [As a climax] to the salacious meanderings of her sullied imagination, [La Goulue perpetrates] a last audacity when, bending double the better to express her lewd intention, she insolently flings back her petticoats to make a callypygean display of her behind.[55]

Grille-d'Egout and Nini Patte-en-l'Air were co-dancers of Jane Avril and La Goulue, the first being described by Raymond Rudorff in *Belle Epoque* as 'precise, dignified and almost intellectual'. She danced alongside La Goulue but seemed to have condemned her colleague for her coarseness; Grille-d'Egout's own dancing was restrained,

> where La Goulue was frantic and seemed to go into an orgasmic ecstasy at the climax of the *chahut*.[56]

Nini Patte-en-l'Air was older than the others but notable for her wiry, tension-filled but superbly controlled movements. She appeared in London in 1894 when Symons remarked of her:

> Her effects are all conscious, deliberately extravagant for a purpose, and extravagant according to a method; she never loses for an instant that perfect command over herself.[57]

Symons had already demonstrated his admiration for abandonment controlled in his review of Cyrene, the American dancer in April, 1893.

The names of the Parisian performers were as bizarre as the girls denoted: 'Cri-Cri', 'La Sauterelle', 'Le Môme Fromage', 'Cadudja', 'Serpolette', 'Rayon d'Or' were as well known in their epoch as the dancers here briefly discussed. Symons admired them all and conveyed in his writings on them the infectious excitement which they incited in their audience. While Yeats's enthusiasm was reserved for Loïe Fuller, Symons preferred the ballet dancers or the 'free' dancing of the Moulin Rouge stars. He studied the arrival of the *chahut* and *cancan* – their speciality – in England and greeted it with welcoming fervour and a frank astonishment that its exponents should be so accomplished. Symons would not have dreamed of putting the French girls into a separate category from his beloved ballerinas: such snobbery was not in him; they were all united in being a harmonious unity of form and meaning. As he stated of the dancer in his essay 'The World as Ballet' of 1896 already cited in Chapter 1:

> Nothing is stated, there is no intrusion of words used for the irrelevant purpose of describing; a world rises above one, the picture lasts only long enough to have been there: and the dancer, with her gesture, all pure symbol, evokes from her mere beautiful motion, idea, sensation, all that one need ever know of event. There, before you, she exists in harmonious life; and her rhythm reveals to you the soul of her imagined being.[58]

Such a declaration of belief may seem to accord ill with the coarse boisterousness of the *cancan* dancer and yet Symons included her too in his aesthetic in a way that Yeats could not because, I would suggest, her dance did not tend towards abstraction, impersonality and dehumanisation as Loïe Fuller's did. There was detachment in abundance and Symons comments on the matter-of-fact manner in which the French performers made their suggestive steps, but the Quadrille dancers were out to titillate and to shock and such a blatant purpose refused to correspond to the negation of personality and lack of character advocated by both Yeats and Mallarmé. An exception could be made of Jane Avril with her mask-like features, her odd, stick-like movements and monstrous solitariness and Yeats would follow Symons in his admiration for her utter absorption in her own dance which was devised and performed purely instinctively. Unlike Symons, Yeats would perhaps have actively rejected the sexual dancer on the grounds of the insistent and relentless obtrusiveness of her very sexuality because, as Kermode reminds us in *Romantic Image*, Yeats always leant towards impersonality:

> The girl's lack of character, the emptiness of Ariosto's face are the emblems of the tragic art Yeats wants for the theatre. In practical

terms it meant masks; it meant 'rhythm, balance, pattern, images that remind us of vast patterns'. It meant music.[59]

Kermode states of Yeats's desired dancer:

The Image is to be all movement, yet with a kind of stillness. She lacks separable intellectual content, her meanings, as the intellect receives them, must constantly be changing. She has the impassive, characterless face of Salome, so that there is nothing but the dance, and she and the dance are inconceivable apart, indivisible as body and soul, meaning and form, ought to be.[60]

So while Jane Avril would pass Yeats's strictures successfully, the other *cancan* dancers beloved of Symons probably would not, as their acts concentrated too insistently on flesh and extravagant abandon – La Goulue showed her bottom – and insufficiently on the abstract and enigmatic.

As for the choreography of the French dances, the *Sketch* of 1893 announced that Miss May Yohé, who was to appear in *Little Christopher Columbus*, had visited Paris in order to study the Goulue dance:

but an English public would never stand it as it is danced, and I have had to tone it down.[61]

By the following year there is no suggestion in the reviews that Nini Patte-en-l'Air was diluting her *chahut* for a London audience and a long article appeared in the *Sketch* of 24 January which revealed a fascination with this dance that rivalled Symons's own:

For some time past there have been signs of its coming, and those who know have discovered traces of it in some steps of particular dances. There was the Palace Theatre 'Moulin-Rouge' scene, which has a quadrille with a little flavour of the real thing. Now, in some measure, it has arrived, for on Saturday Mdlle. Nini Patte-en-l'Air and her troupe joined the 'Morocco Bounders' at the Trafalgar Theatre. Mdlle. Nini is in the head and front of this offering. 'What is the *chahut*?' you may ask. It is the descendant of the *cancan*, which, some sixty years ago, drove Paris almost mad. For a while it was far more in vogue in the Gay City than the serpentine has been ...

What, then, is the *cancan*, or the *chahut*? Simply a quadrille executed in an extraordinary fashion. This answer, of course, leaves the matter open. It is danced by women and a few men laboriously trained for the purpose, who are able to do almost contortionist feats.

And the report proceeds to analyse the technical names of some of the feats: 'La Série', in which the leg was thrown up until the foot was on a level with the dancer's eye; 'La Guitare', where the performer raised the leg and, catching the ankle with the hand, pretended to play the guitar on the limb; 'Shoulder Arms', in which the line of the shin was parallel with the head; 'Military Salute'; and 'Le Grand Ecart', familiar to English audiences as the 'Splits'.

> These, and other steps equally remarkable, but hard to classify, form the features of the strange performance. Immensely difficult as they are, the stars, such as La Goulue, Grille-d'Egout ... and Nini Patte-en-l'Air, are able to execute them with real grace when they please.
> What is so startling about the performance is the costume. Were these dances performed in tights, as by acrobats, few would be shocked; but in Paris the dancers who dance actually among the audience, come, as a rule, in hats or bonnets and ordinary walking costumes. Their dresses, of course, serve rather to reveal than hide, and the *dessous*, though specially constructed, at first sight seems to be made like the most luxurious of those depicted by the advertisements in ladies' papers. Consequently, the effect is startling even to those who cannot be called prudish ...
> Perhaps I cannot finish my remarks better than by quoting a phrase used by Mdlle. Grille-d'Egout concerning the dance: 'C'est une danse canaille, et en y mettant de la grâce et de la modestie on lui donne et du chien et beaucoup de chic.' I may add that the lady's views of modesty are not so strict as those of my maiden aunts.[62]

Thus, as well as skirt and serpentine dancing, the decade witnessed the arrival of the *cancan* which had probably derived from the circus rather than the ballet; Jane Avril certainly had some circus training in acrobatics. There were also performers of the *danse du ventre*, sand dancing and skipping-rope dancing appearing at the halls and their exponents were, significantly, solo dancers. Whether

Grace Chrystie, an American cancer who to-day enjoys an international reputation, first won Broadway as solo cancer in *What's in a Name?* Later she went to London, where as *première*

danseuse, she appeared in *The League of Notions*. She then went to Paris, where she repeated her great success. This past summer she danced at the European watering-places

The "Peacock Woman." With wide, sweeping gestures the dancer portrays the attitude of the proud, hard, conceited woman, who cares only to display her beauty to the greatest advantage. A dance showing wonderful balance and poise

A highly original interpretation of the Negro spiritual, *Nobody Knows the Trouble I've Seen.* In this dance the artist brings out with flexible movements the meaning of each word, her body rising and falling in marvelous rhythm to the changing mood of the song

The "Flapper Dance," showing the actions of a silly young girl. This dance is filled with a bright humor, comic movement and displays Miss Chrystie's histrionic ability

The dance of the "Lady Who Lived in Herself Alone." A Japanese maiden, who gives nothing to the world and takes very little from it, living entirely within her own being

INTERPRETIVE DANCING

American Artist Wins International Fame in Endless Variety of Classic and Modern Dances

1 'Interpretive Dancing', from *Theatre Magazine*, 19 January 1921

An Episode with Benda Masks (GRACE CRISTIE)

2 'An episode with Benda Masks' (Grace Christie), from *The Play Pictorial, League of Notions*, vol. XXVIII

3   The famous Benda Mask, worn by Grace Christie in *League of Notions*

THE SHADOW OF THE DEVIL! MISS GRACE CRISTIE IN A BENDA MASK.

The Benda Masks in "The League of Notions," at the New Oxford, provide one of the most noteworthy episodes in the production. Our photograph shows Miss Cristie in the Devil Mask, which is one of the most remarkable she wears.

Photograph by Foulsham and Lanfield, Ltd.

4 'The Shadow of the Devil', from *The Sketch*, 23 March 1921

AUTUMN DANCES.
September, 1921.

The Dancing Times

Edited by
PHILIP J. S. RICHARDSON.

1/- NET.

Photo: *Foulsham & Banfield.*

MISS RITA LEE.
A charming dancer who has made a hit in the
Music Box number at the New Oxford Theatre.

5 Rita Lee, New Oxford Theatre, from *The Dancing Times*, September 1921

Exhibition Dancers Use Masks.

A remarkable effect achieved by Frances Mann and Frederick Carpenter by the use of masks in a burlesque number. Some reference to their act will be found in " The Sitter Out."

6   'Exhibition Dancers use Masks', from *The Dancing Times*, March 1930

Ninette de Valois.

Photo: Hana.

Ballet Mistress at the " Old Vic," Choregraphic Director of the
" Festival Theatre," Cambridge, and Principal of the Academy of
Choregraphic Art, has recently opened a School of Dancing attached
to the Abbey Theatre, Dublin. The photograph shows her in a
peacock dance, entitled " Pride," with which she made a big hit in
Cambridge.

7   Ninette de Valois, from *The Dancing Times*, January 1928

"Fighting the Waves"

A ballet on an Irish theme produced by Miss Ninette de Valois at the Abbey Theatre, Dublin. The photograph shows the entry of the Goddess of the Sea.

8 'Fighting the Waves', from *The Dancing Times*, December 1931

Yeats knew of all these divers genres is not certain, but it is clear that he would adopt the figure of the soloist for his own dance plays by concentrating on the impersonality, the essential solitude and dehumanisation of some of these performers which transformed them into artefact, a feat which depended on the body's power

> not to express emotion but to objectify a pattern of sentience. Fuller with her long sticks, her strange optical devices, her burying the human figure in masses of silk, achieved impersonality at a stroke. Her world was discontinuous from nature; and this discontinuity Valéry, speaking of his Symbolist ancestry, described as 'an almost inhuman state'. She withdrew from the work; if to do otherwise is human, said Valéry. 'I must declare myself essentially inhuman'.[63]

The solo female dancers of whom Yeats approved embodied this quality of inhumanity and his later use of the mask to create this attribute for his own dancers produced, as was shown earlier with the figure of Fand (p. 172), one means among many of presenting the fusion of dance and dancer, performer and work. A brief investigation of the historical forbears of the soloist will be made later in this chapter in order to place Yeats's own creations in a context.

The early years of the new century saw the appearance of modifications to familiar dance genres performed in music hall, a development which can be descried by a reading of the theatrical reports in the *Era*, a weekly journal founded in 1837 and originally an organ for licensed victuallers. The paper recorded the talents of several different dancers, most, though not all, of whose names faded into obscurity, yet who indicated the new direction that was being taken. On 21 February 1903, a Mademoiselle Ladora charmed the audience at the Tivoli with a familiar offering followed by an innovation:

> 'La Danse Illumination.' Her diaphanous skirts are enriched by coloured pictures of the rose, the shamrock, and thistle, and patriotic feeling is aroused by portraits of the King and Queen. ... Her most weird effects are to be found in her fire dance – a most realistic picture of lambent flame, produced, too, by means that are entirely devoid of danger.[64]

Props and scenery became highly complex and elaborate as the aim became less that of demonstrating the dancing talents of the central performer than one of creating tableaux. For example, the two following *Era* reports of June 1903, illustrate the lengths to which the production of spectacle would go in these early instances of what would culminate in the huge extravaganza of the Ziegfeld Follies and the Busby Berkeley film musicals of the 1930s. At the Royal the public was presented with a Mademoiselle De Dio,

> in her latest series of allegorical pantomime dances, entitled 'Terpsichore's Dream.' First we have views of the open sea under various aspects; then the bed of the ocean. A diver slowly descends by means of a ladder. As he gropes his way along the shadowy depths he comes across a large shell, which, opening, discloses a nymph of the sea, who goes through some graceful performances. Other charming scenes follow, amidst which flits Mdlle. De Dio, a vision of youthful loveliness. Finally we have presented the wonderful fire effects which generally form an attractive part of Mdlle. De Dio's spectacular entertainment. The flames appear to curl round the lithe figure of the lady as she apparently fans the fire; and then finally a mass of multi-coloured ribbons descend, the whole forming a striking tableau, upon which the eye dwells with delight.[65]

The figure of the dancer seems to have been progressively dwarfed by all the paraphernalia essential in a desperate search for 'novelty'. At the Tivoli a week later we are offered once again the wonders of electricity:

> The guest novelty in Mr. Philip Yorke's most attractive bill is Signorina Margherita in a grand electrical spectacle. When the lady is first seen she is posing in a sort of floral temple, of which the gates gradually open. Every part of her costume – headdress, corsage, skirt, even her stockings – is illuminated by tiny coloured bulbs. Her parasol and fan also become lustrous in the same manner at her own sweet will. Not only she, but the fairy-like dwelling she temporarily inhabits coruscates with brilliant incandescence, and a parterre of flowers is splendidly counterfeited by effulgent property specimens of the kingdom of Flora. Signorina dances in a sober way, and manages to change the whole scheme of coloured radiance as she bows to the plaudits of a well-pleased audience ...[66]

Loïe Fuller had always relied on special technical effects, but she too, ten years after her first appearance in London, had increased her dependence on machinery to absurd proportions. She was performing briefly at the Palace Theatre when the *Era* reviewer appraised her latest 'living artefact':

The description given of the newest development of light and colour is 'Mysterious Dances.' The production is a triumph of graceful movement and mechanical ingenuity. In its evolution no less than sixteen electricians are employed and a large staff have been working night and day putting in cables in connection with the apparatus employed. From a specially constructed box on the balcony tier the light plays, and there are similar contrivances at the wings and beneath the stage. There are four scenes, three of which are variously described as 'In Space,' 'Amongst the Butterflies,' and 'Water.' The fourth is left to the imagination of the spectator. The tableau curtains part and display a scene as dark as Erebus, which rapidly changes to a firmament of twinkling stars. Gradually the light increases, and clouds of grey vapour flit across the scene and these seem to be splashed with streaks of silver. The dancer's voluminous folds are wreathed in an ever-changing scheme of colour. Suddenly we have the effect of a dense fall of snow, in which La Lois [sic] appears as an ice-bound maiden in glistering white. The rigours of winter give way to the warm atmosphere and sunniness of summer, and ever floating upward are gigantic specimens of coleoptera with wings of dazzling hue. In 'Water' the effects of sunlight on the surface and undulations are admirably realised. The suggestion of sub-aquatic vegetation is also very vivid, the fantasy being completed by the graceful form of the dancer gliding about in the manner of one of Wagner's Rhine maidens. In the final scene Miss Fuller becomes a gigantic winged spirit – an ethereal being roaming through richly illuminated groves. Bewildering combinations of orange and red, purple and ochre, turquoise and mauve, flit across the scene in various fantastic forms. It is the Aurora Borealis, and as the tableau curtains slowly descend the dancer lies prone on the stage with her draperies aflame with a reddish yellow glare.[67]

Whether this whole gamut of machinery weighed the dancer down and rendered her insignificant is not clarified by those reviewing the results, but two short comments in the *Era* for 1904 do suggest that the solo performer was in difficulty for some reason and overelaborate productions may have chased off the music hall stage the simple artist with nothing but her skill in dancing to recommend her. (The Empire was actually closed in 1904, ostensibly because of a failure to comply with fire regulations, but more truthfully due to the outcry in certain quarters over the appropriation of its promenade by prostitutes peddling their wares. But in other venues the soloist was in trouble too.) The notice of May Henderson's jig at the Tivoli was introduced with the information:

> Dancing is somewhat neglected on the variety stage at the present time. ...[68]

and, accompanying a complimentary account of the Twin Sisters Andersen at the Hammersmith Palace, came the statement:

> Dancing is rather tabooed by lady artistes on the music hall stage.[69]

Had the French high-kickers of ten years previously rendered it obscene or was the engineering simply taking over? Max Beerbohm had already sounded a warning note of disenchantment in 1900 when he remained firmly unimpressed by Loïe Fuller's panoply of machinery and made some very astute remarks about her pretensions to being a dancer at all:

> At Terry's Theatre Miss Loie Fuller is dancing; also a foreign troupe is performing in dumb show. I saw this dual affair when it was at the Coronet Theatre, a week or two ago. ... Miss Fuller's art had become even more elaborate and startling than it was. But I am no convert to it. If the stage were filled with a hundred Miss Fullers, all working together, all in uniformly whirled and illuminated veils, the effect would please me, no doubt. In a ballet, one forgets the human units. But the solitary dancer on the stage must have personal importance. One wishes her to dance beautifully, to express her soul in movement, to *be* something. Merely mechanical tricks, however skilfully played, will not atone for personal nullity. Miss Fuller seems to me null, and so I can snatch no pleasure from her skill in the art of manipulating layers of gauze, none from the lime-lighter's taste in tinting them. I sit in wonder,

but that is all. Astray from the Lowther Arcade into a kaleido-
scope, a doll would not less enrapture one.[70] [Beerbohm's
emphasis]

Whatever the trend, the *Era* does proceed to review the intrepid
performers who resisted the current tendency by persevering and
presenting merely their dancing talents to music-hall and variety
audiences. An American whose stage name was 'My Fancy' offered
a sand dance at the Paragon in March 1904[71] and a 'musical specialty' act had been discovered at the Bedford in January of that year
called 'Espinosa and Edwards', the former proving herself to be a
gifted dancer:

> her spirited solo, with wonderful double pirouettes and toe danc-
> ing proves a welcome change from the everlasting cake-walk. The
> school of Taglioni, so we are told, is dead in this country. Even if it
> is, which we very much doubt, it is certainly worth reviving, and
> Miss Espinosa knows how to make it attractive.[72]

That the school of Taglioni was dead was much too bleak a prospect to contemplate and one did not need to cling to the skills of
Miss Espinosa alone for consolation. In 1897 Adeline Genée[73] had
left her native Denmark and arrived in London to study with Katti
Lanner at the Empire and she was to remain undisputed queen of
ballet in the English capital for the next ten years until the advent of
the Russian dancers: she would welcome Pavlova and Karsavina[74]
herself in 1910 and Genée and Pavlova would become the subject of
much scrutiny and analysis as their differing styles of dancing were
evaluated by critics. Ballet stars came back into prominence after
some years of the public's attention attaching to music-hall *cancan*
performers. The talents of the ballet dancers adored by Symons
seem not to have been as exceptional as those of Genée and the
Russians since he did not reveal the names of his favoured females
nor mention individually their special qualities as dancers. It was
rather to the entire balletic experience of costume, make-up and flar-
ing lights that Symons responded in the years just preceding the
arrival of Genée. A selection of contemporary reports on the extraordinary skills of the various ballet dancers now appearing from
abroad and of the famous 'free' dancers who rivalled them will
illustrate the aesthetic preoccupations and values of these two versions of the dancer in performance.

The *Era* of the early years of the century charted the career of Genée in a series of complimentary reviews such as that of a Katti Lanner ballet in 1903 called *A Duel in the Snow*:

> In the intervals of the revelry, Mdlle. Adeline Genée, bewitchingly radiant and *riante*, does a bright and clever *pas de deux* with Mons. Sundberg. Clad in the freshest of pink, Mdlle. Genée carries the house with her entirely by her gay *enjouée* and animated expression, and by the finished style of her posing and dancing.[75]

Such energy and luminous gaiety seem to have been characteristic of her style of ballet dancing – they were qualities of the Danish ballet style in which she was trained – and, unlike Pavlova, she was always technically perfect. Her skills as an actress were also reason for praise, as in this brief review of a highly successful ballet at the Empire, *The Milliner Duchess*:

> It is not surprising that the management of the Empire Theatre have so long retained in their programme that dainty divertissement, *The Milliner Duchess*. Much of the success obtained by it is due to the delightful dancing of Mdlle. Adéline [sic] Genée, whose Coquette is a most diverting and clever piece of pantomime. Miss Genée's facial play and gestic expression as the simple country girl are as varied as they are eloquent and amusing; and her dancing is, of course, irreproachably light, active, and graceful. ...[76]

She was equally delightful in *High Jinks* the following year when she played a pierette to Sundberg's Pan in a divertissement called *Pan and Pierette*:

> She gives us of her best in the scene 'The Animation of Pan,' and shows herself to be a perfect pantomimist and a magnificent dancer. The fair prima donna assoluta is evidently pleased to get back to short skirts, and she looks particularly well in a dainty pink costume. M. Paul Sundberg in the part of Pan lends most effective aid to Mdlle. Genée in their combined dance.[77]

Katti Lanner arranged the ballet *The Dancing Doll* around her at the Empire in 1905 and once again Genée triumphed, although we may by now harbour unvoiced suspicions as to the value of the roles that she was finding herself dancing; the ballets in which Genée was involved seem certainly more childish and forgettable, obviously less powerful than those which Diaghilev[78] was to bring with him. In this case,

> The honours of the ballet were as usual carried off by Mdlle. Adeline Genée, whose vitality and versatility were greatly in evidence. As Bébé she danced with her usual grace and agility. As the leader of the toy rabbit soldiers she played the drum smartly; and as a Polichinella in lilac she was full of life and spirit.[79]

A review of her dexterity by Arthur Symons would have been most instructive here; instead we read Max Beerbohm, who examined her performance in *Coppélia* in 1906:

> No monstrous automaton is that young lady. ... Perfect though she is in the *haute école*, ... she has by some miracle preserved her own self. She was born a comedian, and a comedian she remains, light and liberal as foam. A mermaid were not a more surprising creature than she – she of whom one half is as that of an authentic ballerina, whilst the other is that of a most intelligent, most delightfully human actress. A mermaid were indeed, less marvellous in our eyes. She would not be able to diffuse any semblance of humanity into her tail. Madame Genée's intelligence seems to vibrate to her very toes. Her dancing, strictliest classical though it is, is a part of her acting. And her acting, moreover, is of so fine a quality that she makes the old ineloquent conventions of gesture tell their meanings to me, and tell them so exquisitely that I quite forget my craving for words.[80]

The most interesting accolade was accorded four years later by an American critic drawing a comparison between Genée and Pavlova on the occasion of their separate visits to New York, the latter in the spring and the former in the autumn of 1910. The Russian ballerina appeared at the Metropolitan Opera House for a short season with Mordkin as her partner.[81] Alan Dale of the *New York American* perceptively summarised the differing skills of the two ballerinas as follows:

> People wonder ... which is the greater artist – Genée or Pavlova. It is probably the difference between light opera and grand opera.

If one could whistle the classical dancers, one would whistle Genée, and be grandiosely awed by Pavlova. Genée's dance appeals easily to the masses. It is light and pleasant and graceful. Pavlova's is just – long buried joy. It is dark-green pleasure. It is lovely and instructive and deep. So it is a question of mood. If you are gay and happy, you prefer Genée. If you are just good, you select Pavlova. Last night I was glad it was Genée, who is prettier, more attractive to the eye than Pavlova. Also more varied and more adaptable.[82]

So, while some solo dance artistes of music hall were attempting to survive a difficult interlude, Genée seems to have gone from strength to strength and her highly successful career served as a bridge between the draperial dancing and French *cancan* dancers of the 1890s to the coming of the Diaghilev troupe to London in 1911 and after. Genée can justly be said to represent the real British ballet of 1890–1910:

To Adeline Genée England in particular owes a debt greater than to any other dancer. It was she who continued, or rather restored, the tradition of the great dancing of the earlier half of the last century. She aroused enthusiasm for the ballet in an age when that enthusiasm had grown cold. She helped to put an end to a perverted form of dancing. Her example shone out with a clear light in that thick darkness just before the dawn, and for more than a decade she remained true to her ideals through good report or ill.[83]

She intended to retire on many occasions before her eventual final season at the Coliseum in February 1917. She was never supplanted by the *Ballets Russes* (Diaghilev attempted unsuccessfully to recruit her), but they did modify some aspects of her work; for example, she danced once again with a strong, virile male partner instead of the customary *danseuse en travestie* (who, for example, continued to play the role of Franz in *Coppélia* in France until very recently), abhorred by many members of the audience. Diaghilev, coming from a very different tradition in Russia, restored the male dancer to a status equal to that of the ballerina and, thus, the sterility of previous years was attenuated with the advent of Nijinsky[84] and his famous comrades and precursors, such as Pavel Gerdt[85] and Adolph Bolm.[86]

The impact of the Russian dancers was explosive on ballet all over the world – as we shall see, Yeats too derived great pleasure from seeing them perform – but Diaghilev's troupe was itself open to revolutionary influence and this appeared in the form of Isadora Duncan,[87] who had been dancing in Russia from 1905, prior to Diaghilev's setting up his famous company. Before discussing the arrival of the Russians in London in 1910 and 1911, let us first consider the Duncan phenomenon because it was one of which Yeats was aware through his acquaintance with Gordon Craig as well as other sources and because it provides yet another study of a soloist – this time highly controversial and innovative – in dance. We know that Yeats's enthusiasm was not aroused by ballet dancers; he admired rather the expressiveness of the 'free' dance and as Duncan was the most important and celebrated proponent of the genre, a measure of attention will be directed to her here.

Fuller, Genée and Duncan all began performing at approximately the same time and they were also contemporaneous with the French *chahut* dancers from the Moulin Rouge and Folies Bergère, but their respective modes of dancing had otherwise nothing in common; Fuller was a draperial dancer, the French contingent, boisterous and acrobatic, Genée, the supremely classical ballerina and Duncan, the 'Greek' dancer *par excellence*. Isadora first saw Fuller perform in her own miniature theatre in the Rue de Paris of the 1900 Universal Exhibition in the French capital and was enchanted. The serpentine dancer was older than Duncan and took her under her wing for some time, persuading her young compatriot to tour Germany with her late in 1901, but she never received any acknowledgement or gratitude from Isadora, who found being of the Fuller party a stifling and oppressive experience. When Yeats was waxing sardonic over skirt dancing in 1893 and Loïe Fuller was performing in Paris, Duncan was inventing new movements based on the painted and sculpted figures that she found in Greek art, having discarded in disgust her child's ballet shoes in her native San Francisco in the 1880s.

Isadora Duncan, born in 1878, arrived in London in the spring of 1897 where, along with Genée in the same year, she took some lessons in dance from Katti Lanner, the celebrated ballet mistress at the Empire. By 1900 *The Times* was reporting on her performances and it was clear from these early notices that not only was she not a classical ballerina but, moreover, that she was

involved in setting up a form of dance in direct opposition to ballet. Her movements do avow a debt to her Delsarte[88] training. On
17 March 1900, *The Times* commented thus on her first *Dance
Idylls*:

> The entertainment given last night at the New Gallery was
> entirely new to the public, and a pronounced success. Miss Isa-
> dora Duncan is a young dancer of remarkable skill, whose art,
> though it may fail to satisfy the average ballet master, has won-
> derful eloquence of its own. ... Miss Duncan's exceptional beauty
> of face and figure fits her for her self-appointed task of illustrating
> in dance such passages as were chosen from the Homeric *Hymns
> to Demeter* and the idylls of Theocritus: these were read with
> much effect by Miss Jane Harrison [the Cambridge anthropol-
> ogist], and a small orchestra, conducted by Mr. J. E. Barkworth,
> played accompaniments to the dancing ... both in the passages
> requiring the eloquence of gestures and in the more lyrical mea-
> sures of regular dances, such as the mazurka in 'The Triumph of
> Daphnis,' or the rhythmic steps danced to Mendelssohn's 'Fru-
> hlingslied,' [sic] the dancer made a success of no ordinary kind.
> Her powers were exhibited in a most favourable light in 'The
> Water Nymph,' danced to some pretty music by Ethelbert Nevin,
> and from beginning to end the occasion was one of complete
> artistic enjoyment.[89]

By July of the same year she had dispensed with the readings:

> Miss Duncan's evenings: – The second of the charming entertain-
> ments given by Miss Isadora Duncan at the New Gallery took
> place on Tuesday, when the scheme of her programme showed a
> marked improvement on any that she has hitherto given in
> London ... the reading, which has been felt as a wholly
> unnecessary and rather tiresome addition, was left out alto-
> gether. ... Herr Zwintscher played with beautiful finish and
> artistic style three of [Chopin's] preludes, the waltz in C sharp
> minor, and a mazurka in A minor: the third of the preludes, that
> in C minor, was illustrated by an appropriate set of solemn
> gestures, and to the waltz and mazurka Miss Duncan made an
> accompaniment of exquisite grace. Mendelssohn's 'Spring Song'
> and an encore were also danced, as well as the beautiful minuet
> from Gluck's *Orfeo*. ...[90]

These reviews were written by J. Fuller-Maitland who himself advised Isadora to omit the readings and who accompanied her for the July performances on the harpsichord.

All her life Isadora puzzled and theorised about the kind of dance that she wished to create and to teach her pupils (she never ceased to dream of opening a school or to try to raise money for such a project) and, as Victor Seroff's biography, *The Real Isadora*, illustrates, she knew that ballet was not the solution:

> I spent long days and nights in the studio seeking what might be the divine expression of the human spirit through the medium of the body's movement. ...

She explained how her theory differed from that of ballet, but her language seems pretentious and obscure:

> The ballet school taught the pupils that a spring was found in the center of the back at the base of the spine. From this axis, says the ballet master, arms, legs and trunk must move freely, giving the result of an articulated puppet. This method produces an artificial mechanical movement not worthy of the soul. I, on the contrary, sought the source of the spiritual expression to flow into the channels of the body, filling it with vibrating light – the centrifugal force reflecting the spirit's vision.
>
> After many months, when I had learned to concentrate all my force to this one center, I found that thereafter when I listened to music, the rays and vibrations of the music streamed to this one fount of light within me – there they reflected themselves in Spiritual Vision, not the brain's mirror, but the soul's, and from this vision I could express them in dance.[91]

The war waged on ballet was even taken to St Petersburg, the home of the classical dance of Imperial Russia, and when she visited there in January 1905, Isadora condemned most forcibly ballet's deformation of the body:

> The school of ballet today, vainly striving against the natural laws of gravitation of the natural will of the individual, and working in discord in its form and movement with the form and movement of nature, produces a sterile movement which gives no birth to future movements, but dies as it is made.

The expression of the modern school of ballet, wherein each action is an end, and no movement, pose or rhythm is successive or can be made to evolve succeeding action, is an expression of degeneration, of living death.[92]

While on this Russian tour in 1905 Duncan had an enormous effect on the young dancer and future *Ballets Russes* choreographer, Michel Fokine,[93] who created his ballet *Eunice* as a tribute to Duncanism and whose later work was imbued with the influence of her school of thought. She was completely innovatory; even her costume gave rise to scandal in certain quarters and the *Era* correspondent of two years earlier in 1903, when reviewing her current success in Berlin, had commented on her perfectly developed form and the way in which it was revealed:

> Clothed in flesh-coloured tights from neck to foot, and wearing no other covering than a flimsy robe of gauze, Miss Duncan realises the airy grace of Botticelli's 'Spring,' and the severe moods of Florentin De Predi's 'Angel with the Violin,' and other well-known pictures. ...[94]

As Fokine was to state some years later in 1914 in a long letter to the London *Times*:

> The older ballet developed the form of so-called 'classical dancing,' consciously preferring to every other form the artificial form of dancing on the point of the toe, with the foot turned out, in short bodices, with the figure tightly laced in stays, and with a strictly-established system of steps, gestures, and attitudes. Miss Duncan rejected the ballet and established an entirely opposite form of her own. She introduced natural dancing, in which the body of the dancer was liberated not only from stays and satin slippers, but also from the dance-steps of the ballet. She founded her dancing on natural movements and on the most natural of all dance-forms – namely, the dancing of the ancient Greeks.[95]

Isadora Duncan was at the forefront of a movement of thinking which did not restrict itself to dance alone; when in Berlin in 1904 she met the stage designer Gordon Craig and she subsequently had a child by him. Craig was delighted to discover that Duncan, the 'free' dancer, was able to reveal some properties of abstract movement which had remained mysterious to him, full of admiration and joy that she had been travelling down the same artistic path as himself for some time, exasperated and resentful that such genius should reside in the person of a woman. Similarly, when she met Stanislavsky in 1907 in Russia he was amazed to find that in different parts of the world, 'due to conditions unknown to us, various people in various spheres sought in art the same naturally creative principles. ... We understood each other almost before we had said a word to each other.'[96] As we remarked in the previous chapter (p. 121), Yeats was greatly impressed with Craig's work and his own aesthetic beliefs were similar to that of the group of artists who shared Duncan's aims and philosophy, because, as far as dance was concerned, he sympathised with iconoclastic trends and his sentiments too gravitated towards abstract movement and the retreat from naturalism.

Not everyone was so enthusiastic, however: there was a discordant note struck by her use of classical masterpieces as vehicles for her performances and leading musicians objected to her appropriation of such compositions for her own purposes. Nikolai Rimsky-Korsakov voiced his complaints very forcefully and he was not alone in the conception of them:

Concerning Duncan, I shall tell you that I have never seen her. Presumably she is very graceful, a splendid mime, etc; but what repels me in her is that she foists her art upon and tacks it onto musical compositions, which are dear to my heart and whose authors do not at all need her company, and had not reckoned with it. ... works not intended for dancing and miming do not require any mimic interpretations, and, in truth, it is powerless to interpret them. All in all, miming is not an independent kind of art and can merely accompany words or singing, but when it foists itself unbidden upon music, it only harms the latter by diverting attention from it.[97]

Duncan and Yeats shared something of the same dilemma regarding dancing to music, though the latter never intended to employ classical compositions for his accompaniments. Instead he explored the possibilities of music performed on zither, drum, gong or flute specially composed by Arnold Dolmetsch (who built for Yeats the psaltery to which Florence Farr chanted the verse) or

Edmund Dulac who wrote music for *At the Hawk's Well* and Walter Morse Rummell who, in 1917, produced beautiful, difficult music for flute to be played during *The Dreaming of the Bones*. Significantly enough, Yeats stated in the Preface to *Four Plays for Dancers* in June 1920 that,

> I notice that Mr. Rummell has written no music for the dance, and I have some vague memory that when we tackled it over in Paris he felt that he could not *without the dancer's help*[98]   [my emphasis]

and some years earlier, Isadora Duncan as dancer was perplexed by the relationship between her art and the music that she used as impetus to it; she did not emulate Yeats, however, in commissioning her music or in having dancer and composer collaborate. In a letter to Craig from Warsaw late in 1906 Duncan pleaded:

> – I badly need a musician to help me. ... – I would like someone to help me *learn* more about music, and study more *exactly* its different relations to dancing. ... Tell me what you think: does the dance spring from the music, as I think it does, or should the music accompany the dance – or should they both be born together – or How? – Sometimes I think till my poor little head is all muddled – A big library of books – a big studio & a musician – I want.[99]   [Duncan's emphasis]

None the less, apparently undeterred by criticisms such as those of Rimsky-Korsakov, Isadora continued dancing and teaching and preaching. She moved to London to live in 1908 and performed at the Metropolitan Opera House in New York in November of that year; there were tours to France in early January 1909 where Lugné-Poë, director of the Théâtre de l'Oeuvre, offered to manage her performances at the Gaieté-Lyrique Theatre and visits back to pre- and post-revolutionary Russia. In 1921 she was to perform before Lenin at the Bolshoi Theatre to celebrate the fourth anniversary of the Revolution on 7 November: she danced to the music of the *Marche Slav* and the Russian leader stood up to applaud her. But apart from her very real triumphs, the well-known biography of Isadora Duncan is mainly one of tragedy and muddle, constant movement and continual lack of funds, the death of her children and her own early demise in Nice in 1927 in an accident that smacked of the absurd.

Her greatest success had been in Germany where, interestingly enough, Romantic Ballet, though nordic in its mythology, had left little impression and where Classical Ballet had enjoyed scant popularity in the nineteenth century. Isadora arrived there in 1902 and was greeted with wild enthusiasm and it is noteworthy that it was Berlin that witnessed the opening of her only school in 1904.

> Her dionysiac expressionism and earnestness seemed to echo the dreams of Friedrich Nietzsche, a passionate advocate of dance as the symbol of human dynamism. ... Her school did not flourish, but she left behind a rich legacy, the movement which was to become labelled 'modern dance'.[100]

As for the genuineness of her talent and her deeply felt rejection of ballet as a form of dance, it may be instructive to consider Tamara Karsavina's impressions of Duncan in the Russian ballerina's memoirs, *Theatre Street*, first published in 1930:

> I remember that the first time I saw her dance I fell completely under her sway. It never occurred to me that there was the slightest hostility between her art and ours. There seemed room for both, and each had much that it could learn to advantage from the other. Later, in Paris, I viewed her from a more critical angle, because she had developed her now well-known theories and explanations of her art. I could no more see her as an individual artist, but as a militant doctrinaire, and moreover I could feel many discrepancies between her ideals and her actual performances, though her theories were for the most part nebulous, and had little real connection with actual dancing on the stage. ... Duncan's thesis was completely overpowered when Fokine, equipped with all the technique of balletic form, made 'Eunice' as a direct tribute to her, with a far greater range of movements than those at the command of Duncan or her pupils. It was possible for us with our training to have danced as she did, but she, with her very limited vocabulary, could not have emulated us. She had created no new art. Duncanism was but a part of the art to which we had the key. ...
> But when she interpreted the 'Elysian Fields', then her artistic means were not only adequate, but raised to the same level of supreme and absolute beauty as the music of Gluck itself. She moved with those wonderful steps of hers with a simplicity and

detachment that could only come through the intuition of genius itself. She seemed to float, a complete vision of peace and harmony, that very embodiment of the classical spirit that was her ideal.[101]

And so, typically perhaps of the Isadora phenomenon and of the woman herself, she is summed up by a mixture of critical brickbat and frank admiration, tribute from one of the greatest classical ballerinas that the Russian Imperial School could produce. Yeats's father saw her dance in New York in 1908 and he expressed his impressions to his son in two letters; on 11 November he wrote:

She is self-contained and regulates her life according to her own ideas, being, as such women are, free to do so. She said some daring things in a rather captivating way. ...[102]

A second – undated – letter reports on her dancing as well as on her personality, and W. B. Yeats would have been enchanted to be told that she demonstrated, according to his father, that quality of self-possession to which the poet attached such importance:

It seems to me that *great personal charm only belongs to people who are self-contained or when they are so.* They can only say and do the *spontaneous* and the *unsuspected* – everything Miss Duncan says is curiously interesting; it never becomes 'chatter', ... An American lady a few days ago described Miss Duncan as old, at least middle-aged, and 'homely' (American for ugly). I first met her in a restaurant and at once understood her to be the oddest and most unexpected person in the world. She forms her own plans and is quite indifferent to what people think or say, for that reason she is never aggressive just as she makes no effort to conciliate anyone. I met her twice in private and since that I saw her (from her own box) dancing in the biggest theatre, and on the biggest stage in New York – a figure dancing all alone on this immense stage – and there again you felt the charm of the self-contained woman. ... I don't wonder that at first New York rejected her – she stood still, she lay down, she walked about, she danced, she leaped, she disappeared, and re-appeared – all in curious sympathy with a great piece of classical music, and I did not sometimes know which I most enjoyed, her or her music. ...

Quinn[103] says she dances like a cow &c. and has beefy limbs. ...
Genée the rival dancer whom Quinn likes so much has the other
the lesser charm, that she is eager for appreciation and popular
affection, and she is indeed a delightful creature – *you wish her to
succeed*, in the other case you are dominated.[104]   [J. B. Yeats's
emphasis]

As possibly the most celebrated 'free' dancer of them all, it would
have been surprising had not Symons or Ricketts, let alone Yeats
himself, registered her influential presence in the world of dance
from 1900 onwards, especially since there was an identity of ideas
between Duncan and the Irish poet.

He, too, wanted to be free of balletic choreography and to explore
possibilities of movement and gesture which would express certain
emotions whereby the action of his play would be advanced. To do
so necessitated 'free' dance suggestive of passion – seduction, rage,
grief and so on. Duncan liberated herself from the conventional
mimetic gestures of ballet used to tell stories and interpreted her chosen music personally and individually according to what feelings it
inspired in her, but there was no narrative, simply steps and movement of her own devising provoked in the dancer by the music
played. She thus moved away from the representational in dance
and retreated from naturalism into abstract movement. This, of
course, taken to its conclusions, needs no music at all and more
recent choreographers have indeed explored this terrain, but true
abstraction is probably not possible since dancers, whatever their
choreographic creed, are human. The attempt, however, to turn them
into automata or, for Yeats, marionettes, was, as we have discovered
above, a very fashionable one and instigated insistently by Craig in
his theories of the *Ubermarionette*. As Yeats himself stated in a letter
to his father of 14 March 1916, three weeks before *At the Hawk's Well*
was performed for the first time, 'the abstract is incompatible with
life',[105] and stillness, the stasis of death, is what the poet demanded of
his actors so that words would be thrown into relief through their
contrasting vividness. In 1937, in a retrospective appraisal of his
theatrical aims, he wrote in 'An introduction for my plays':

When I follow back my stream to its source I find two dominant
desires: I wanted to get rid of irrelevant movement – the stage
must become still that words might keep all their vividness – and
I wanted vivid words.[106]

As far as his dancers were concerned, Yeats insisted on a version of stylised movement that was not balletic, although he did intimate in the Preface to *Four Plays for Dancers* that he was uncertain of exactly what he wanted of them except that it avoid the contemporary manner of theatrical dancing:

> the dancing will give me most trouble, for I know but vaguely what I want. I do not want any existing form of stage dancing, but something with a smaller gamut of expression, something more reserved, more self-controlled, as befits performers within arm's reach of their audience.[107]

Both Yeats and Duncan also asserted the autonomy of dance and dancer into an indivisible unit of form and signification and, in this belief, were linked to other experimenters of the time including Loïe Fuller, whom the former always and the latter initially admired.

Duncan had her imitators and rivals and when she arrived in London in 1908 it was to be confronted with the fact that a Canadian dancer brought up in America, Maud Allan,[108] had supplanted her in the public's affections and had most strenuously denied accusations – many of them from the press – that her dancing was directly derived from Isadora's own. The rivalry gave rise to bitter wranglings in the newspapers over the supremacy of one or the other dancer:

> She [Maud Allan] had only one advantage over Isadora – she had introduced herself to the London public long before Isadora's return to England. ... Allan's programs were designed to appeal to music hall audiences rather then to the kind of public that had applauded Isadora on the continent and at the Duke of York Theater.[109]

The public made a choice between the two dancers and Duncan had reason to be satisfied with the outcome because supremacy of technique and originality was accorded to her.

Allan was completely undaunted by any adverse comment, however and proceeded to commission no less a figure than Claude Debussy to compose music for her based on a scenario by W. L. Courtney. Allan's most famous dance, *The Vision of Salome*, was one of her triumphs and at the same time a source of great controversy. It was already an established part of her repertoire when *The Times* heralded her debut at the Palace Theatre on 10 March 1908:

Last night Miss Allan performed two dances; the first was a dramatic comment, so to speak, on Rubinstein's *Valse Caprice*; the second a realization of the dance of Salome, inspired, no doubt, by Wilde's play and Strauss's opera, but danced to the music of a modern French composer. ...The dance was good, but hardly prepared us for the dramatic force and finished beauty of the Salome dance – a dance of many passions, the mere intoxication of movement to music, allurement, exultation, rage, fear, despair, even exhaustion. Her mere steps were of less account than in the valse; every limb and muscle of the dancer was called upon to take its part, and every movement was beautiful. There is no extravagance or sensationalism about Miss Allan's dancing; even when crouching over the head of her victim, caressing it or shrinking from it in horror, she subordinated every gesture and attitude to the conditions of her art. It will, perhaps, be fair to the public to say that her dress as Salome is daring; it would be very unfair to Miss Allan not to add that, like her performance, it is absolutely free of offence.[110]

A later account on 23 July explained:

Fundamentally there is something childish and untutored about Miss Allan's performances, which seems to generate their spontaneity. The music speaks through a new and lovely instrument; there appear to be no rules, no science to come between the music and its expression in music and gesture.[111]

This impression of unschooled naiveté is certainly reinforced by Allan's autobiography *My Life and Dancing*,[112] in which she elaborates upon her theories of the Greeks as natural dancers, performing in the fresh air with movements that were an unconscious reflection of their surroundings and reproducing the harmony of nature in gesture. According to her, the Greek dance became deformed, profaned and unrecognisable the moment that it was transferred to the confines of the theatre and it is through similar reasoning that Allan, along with Fuller and Duncan, detested ballet for all of its unnatural constrictions.

Allan had made her debut as Salome in Vienna as early as 1903 using music by Marcel Remy and she danced the role again in London from about 1908 onwards, as *The Times* article cited above indicates. In her version of the Salome dance she held the severed head and kissed its lips. Years later, in 1934, Yeats may have been remembering hearing of Allan's performance when he had his Queen in *The King of the Great Clock Tower* dance with the head in her hands and caress it. In a letter to Olivia Shakespear of 7 August of that year he mentioned the originality of his own play in differing from Oscar Wilde's in which Salome was not portrayed as dancing while cradling the head.[113]

The Times was complimentary about Allan's Salome but its opinion was not universally shared and a Member of Parliament, Noel Pemberton-Billing, made an unprecedently zealous attack on the dancer in April 1918 in the legal case discussed briefly in the first chapter (p. 51). Allan was to take the part of Salome in a private production of Oscar Wilde's play and, in so proposing, brought the wrath of Pemberton-Billing about her head; 'Salome' as character in the production was deemed a sadist and her current interpreter proclaimed a lesbian. As we noted previously, Allan and J. T. Grein, the Manager of the Independent Theatre and would-be producer of Wilde's play, lost their libel action against Pemberton-Billing.

Yeats would have known of Maud Allan not only through the columns of *The Times* but also through his acquaintance with Charles Ricketts, who certainly was familiar with her Salome. Ricketts received a letter from Robert Ross on 13 June 1918, commenting on the legal action against the dancer where Ross stated his belief that Pemberton-Billing would be acquitted,[114] and Ricketts went on to mention in August 1919 in a letter to Mrs Muriel Lee Mathews that he was reconstructing the play *Salome* for a proposed production by the Shochiku Theatrical Company, Tokyo. He described the Japanese actress who would take the celebrated role as wearing 'Maud Allan pearls in her hair'.[115] The stage designer had already created a set for Wilde's *Salomé* in about 1896 and another sketch for the play in 1906 in which he dressed Salome, Herod and John and took rehearsals himself. He was gratified when the audience insisted on four calls at the end, but then had to face a boycott by the press, the return of his ticket by *The Times* reviewer and a refusal by all the illustrated papers to publish the photographs. After this failure there is an absence of work on this theme by Ricketts until the designs for this 1919 Japanese production, but, through his friendship with the designer, Yeats would have benefited from Ricketts's familiarity with the various performers of the Salome role, among whose number figured Allan herself.

Ricketts was at his most fervid, however, when admiring Russian dancers and they had been appearing in London sporadically since the 1890s. He reserved his most enthusiastic praise for Diaghilev's company which first appeared in Paris in 1909 and in London two years later – they were due to appear in the English capital in 1910 but refrained out of respect for the death of Edward VII on 6 May of that year. At the beginning the outriders were not ballet dancers trained at the Imperial School and performing at the Maryinsky Theatre, but troupes of singers and dancers who appeared in music hall and were acclaimed for their virtuosity. In March 1903 the *Era* had reported on an act at the Alhambra:

> The Wolkowsky Troupe of vocalists and dancers give an exhilarating exposition of Russian song and dance, the animation and spirit of their movements proving intensely exciting. Their pretty and quaint costumes add much to the success of their entertainment[116]

and again the same journal commented on a visit to the Empire by another company in May of that year:

> The Tartakoff Troupe have the vivacity and strength necessary for the vigorous movements of the Russian dance; and exhilarate beholders by the activity and spirit with which they join in their national measures.[117]

These performers shared the bill with Adeline Genée who was appearing in *The Milliner Duchess.*
In 1907 Lydia Kyasht[118] arrived in London partnered by Adolph Bolm and she was already at the Empire in 1908 when Genée left for America on 1 January. Tamara Karsavina elected to perform in London because of her love for Dickens and 1909 saw her at the Coliseum immediately after dancing for Diaghilev's first Paris season at the Théâtre du Châtelet; Pavlova appeared with her partner Mordkin in the summer of 1909 at a private party given by Lord and Lady Londesborough and attended by the King and Queen of England when the dancers presented *Russian Dances*. But

Pavlova's performance at the Londesborough party on July 19, 1909, was her second appearance in London. Her first, hitherto generally unknown, took place a week earlier, on July 12, at a private party in the home of Mrs. Potter Palmer at Carlton House Terrace.[119]

Mathilde Kschessinskaya,[120] the Tsar's mistress, led a Russian company which was presenting *Swan Lake* at the Hippodrome in 1910 and in April of that year Pavlova and Mordkin made their debut at the Palace Theatre; before the month was out Lydia Kyasht and Adolph Bolm were drawing big audiences at the Empire and Olga Preobrajenskaya,[121] with a company of twenty including Ludmilla Schollar[122] and George Kiaksht,[123] appeared at the Hippodrome in a condensed version of *Swan Lake* in a bill which included the celebrated French *diseuse*, Yvette Guilbert. 16 May 1910 witnessed the return of Karsavina to the Coliseum with a troupe of thirteen, of whom Baldina[124] was one, to perform in *Giselle ou les Wilis*. Another St Petersburg ballerina, Ekaterina Geltzer,[125] was dancing with her partner Tikhomirov[126] at the Alhambra in 1911 and Karsavina's old class-mate, Lydia Kyasht, was at the Empire in a short version of Delibes' *Sylvia* with Phyllis Bedells[127] in 1911 when the full impact of Russian ballet was registered – Diaghilev's *Ballets Russes* appeared in London for the Coronation Gala at Covent Garden. It could be expected that the English capital had been admirably primed for its arrival by the pioneers and outriders of the previous years, yet nothing in the world of dance, music and art would ever be the same again.

Reference has already been made to Kermode's essay 'Poet and Dancer before Diaghilev' in which he explains that the Diaghilev phenomenon, when it presented itself in Paris in 1909, 'arrived not a moment too soon in response to prayers from both sides of the Channel'.[128] Mallarmé's dream of a confluence of arts which yet remained theatre was actualised as it had not quite been by the *Symbolistes'* idol, Wagner:

> The Ballets Russes demonstrated the correspondence of the arts so wonderfully that in comparison Wagner's effort was, said Camille Mauclair, *'une gaucherie barbare'*.[129]

A glance at Diaghilev's history reveals why he attached such importance to a combining of the arts – such a blending was the salient feature of his professional pedigree. A letter of 1928 written by Diaghilev shows in retrospect what he had been attempting to create with his ballet and it is evident that the proposal came from a man who had trained when young as a musician, possibly – it is not quite clear – under Rimsky-Korsakov and who had already enjoyed great success in staging art exhibitions: his first one of English and German watercolourists in 1897, followed by the production of *Mir Iskusstva*, a magazine the first edition of which appeared on 10 November 1898 and which proceeded over the next two years to contain articles from a plethora of foreign writers and painters, Maeterlinck, Grieg, Nietzsche, Huysmans and John Ruskin among them. However, Diaghilev's thoughts soon turned to dance:

> je me demandai s'il ne serait pas possible de créer un certain nombre de ballets nouveaux qui, tout en étant pourvus de valeur artistique, établiraient un lien plus étroit que jusqu'alors entre les trois facteurs principaux qui devaient les composer: la musique, le dessin décoratif, et la chorégraphie.[130]

For Diaghilev this fusing of the arts entailed employing celebrated artists as scene painters and costume designers such as Benois[131] and Bakst[132] and later, Picasso, Rouault, Matisse, Braque and Utrillo and commissioning music from Rimsky-Korsakov, Stravinsky, De Falla, Debussy, Ravel and Prokofiev as well as using the existing work of great composers like Tchaikovsky, Moussorgsky, Borodin, Glinka and others.

As far as the dancers were concerned, Diaghilev had the flower of the St Petersburg Imperial Theatre School performing for him along with a scattering of non-Russians who were recruited in Paris, London or Monte Carlo as time went by and the need arose and they were placed in remarkable settings which, as Lifar[133] explains quoting Benois, were much more than simply 'decor':

> Cette fois c'est Benois qui corrobore mes dires au sujet du degré de l'influence exercée sur Fokine par Diaghilev et son groupe de peintres. Le rôle joué par les peintres a été de la plus grande importance, et ce serait le minimiser que de dire que Bakst, Benois, Serov, Korovin, et Golovine ont simplement créé un cadre dans lequel Fokine, Nijinsky, Pavlova, Karsavina ... et d'autres exécutaient et combinaient leurs danses, alors qu'en réalité ces peintres inspiraient toutes les idées dirigeant les évolutions chorégraphiques. Ce ne furent pas des brosseurs de décors professionnels, mais nous, peintres véritables fort attirés par le théâtre, qui contribuâmes à *rénover l'art de la danse*. Notre

influence non-officielle, non-professionnelle, communiqua un caractère spécial à toutes nos productions, et nous pouvons lui attribuer, sans présomption aucune, la plus grande partie de leur immense succès.[134] [Benois' emphasis]

Paris was overwhelmed by the spectacle, and accolades on every side, to painters, dancers and musicians, were published in the press:

Un coup mortel avait été porté par ces peintres aux principes vénérables de la perspective scénique. Elle devait être désormais remplacée par cette agie de couleurs, ce festin des sens que le spectateur cherche au théâtre, ne pouvant le trouver dans la vie. 'C'était presque de la stupéfaction qui s'empara des spectateurs,' écrit André Warnod, et même avant que commençât la danse, le dessin du rideau, les premières mesures de la musique, avaient déjà créé l'atmosphère propice.[135]

A letter from Yeats to Lady Gregory informs us that Ricketts took the poet to see the Diaghilev ballet on 7 March 1913, at the Royal Opera, Covent Garden. It was evidently not Yeats's first visit: he and Lady Gregory had seen a previous performance. Perhaps he was referring to a date in 1911, just after the company's arrival in London: he explains that he has written a new version of a lyric for the second act of *The Countess Cathleen* and concludes, most interestingly, 'I made the little dance poem after seeing the Moscow Dancers.'[136] In the letter of 1913 his enjoyment and excitement are unmistakeable:

Ricketts brought me last night to the Russian Ballet last night [sic]. This time I was well in front & could see the whole picture (do you remember our box high up at one side) & thought it most exquisite, most simple & strangely profound. The one beautiful thing I have seen on the stage of recent years.[137]

Yeats's joy and approval are heartening since he can be very dismissive of ballet on other occasions. At the Royal Opera House, Covent Garden, he would have seen a ballet in one act, *Le Dieu Bleu*, by Jean Cocteau and F. Madrazo, choreographed by Fokine and with decor and costumes by Bakst. Nijinsky's *L'Après-Midi d'un Faune* was performed the previous week. In *Le Dieu Bleu* Nijinsky performed along with Karsavina, Nijinska,[138] Rambert[139] and Bolm.

1913 saw all three of Nijinsky's ballets appearing in London and in February, a month before Yeats's visit, there was wide reportage in the press, interviews with the choreographer and general speculation engendered by *Faune*. July brought the brilliant *Sacre du Printemps*.[140] Yeats's delight is obviously not misplaced.

His essay 'A People's Theatre – a letter to Lady Gregory', published in the *Irish Statesman* somewhat later in the autumn of 1919, makes it quite evident that Yeats was very aware of the innovations of the *Ballets Russes* and of their impact, both through his personal experience and the reports of Symons and Ricketts. He exclaimed somewhat jaundicedly:

> What alarms me most is how a new art needing so elaborate a technique can make its first experiments before those who, as Molière said of the courtiers of his day, have seen so much. How shall our singers and dancers be welcomed by those who have heard Chaliapin in all his parts and who know all the dances of the Russians?[141]

And indeed, from the very first, in Paris, the programme was a positive cornucopia of different styles of dance, opera and superlative graphic and artistic talent. A citation of the 1909 programme will demonstrate the typical richness of the offering.

(i)   *Cléopâtre* – mimodrama in one act. Music by Arensky, Rimsky-Korsakov, Glinka, Moussorgsky and Glazounov. Choreography by Michel Fokine. Decor and costumes by Bakst. Principal dancers: Pavlova, Ida Rubinstein, Karsavina, Fokine, Nijinsky and Bulgakov.

(ii) *Le Festin* – suite de danses. Music by Rimsky-Korsakov, Tchaikovsky, Moussorgsky, Glinka and Glazounov. Choreography by Petipa, Gorsky and Fokine. Decor by Korovine. Costumes by Bakst, Benois, Bilibine and Korovine.

(iii) *Ivan the Terrible* – opera in three acts and five tableaux. Music by Rimsky-Korsakov. Decor and costumes by Roerich, Golovine and Steletsky. Principal dancers: Smirnova, Fedorova and Bolm.

(iv) *Judith* – two acts of the opera by Alexander Serov. Decor by Valentin Serov and costumes by Bakst.

(v)   *Le Pavillon d'Armide* – ballet in one act. Music by Tcherepnine. Choreography by Fokine. Decor and costumes by Benois. Principal dancers: Pavlova, Fokine, Nijinsky and Bulgakov.

(vi)   *Le Prince Igor* – one act of the opera. Music by Borodin. Choreography by Fokine (*'Danses polovtsiennes'*). Curtain, decor and costumes by Roerich. Principal dancers: Smirnova, Fedorova and Bolm.

(vii)   *Rousslan et Ludmilla* – first act of the opera. Music by Glinka. Decor and costumes by Korovine.

(viii)   *Les Sylphides* – Romantic reverie in one act. Music by Chopin. Choreography by Fokine. Decor and costumes by Benois. Principal dancers: Pavlova, Karsavina, Baldina and Nijinsky.[142]

Diaghilev had negotiated a contract with the management of the Covent Garden Opera House from 21 June to 31 July in 1911, an auspicious and resplendent setting with which to begin a relationship between the ballet and the city which would sometimes involve playing in music halls and variety theatres as well. The London repertoire included *Le Pavillon d'Armide*, the exciting *'Polovtsian Dances'* from *Prince Igor*, *Le Spectre de la Rose*, *Les Sylphides* and the company counted Karsavina, Vera Fokina,[143] Ludmilla Schollar, Nijinska, Bolm and Maestro Enrico Cecchetti[144] among its number, along with a *corps de ballet*. The *régisseur* was Serge Grigoriev and the conductors were Nicholas Tcherepnine and Thomas Beecham. When the company returned to Covent Garden for a second season spanning 16 October to 9 December 1911, the troupe consisted of even greater names than before now that they had been joined by the distinguished Mathilde Kschessinskaya.[145]

Diaghilev's aesthetic aims can be clearly deduced from such an examination of the repertoires which he presented and from his selection of only the greatest talents to perform and produce them. His influence on dance was immeasurable: his juxtaposing of well-known ballets with most-recent experimental pieces such as *Faune* or *Jeux* demonstrates that his constant practice was to discover and encourage new dancers and innovative choreographers and composers and perpetually to extend the limits of what was acceptable in dance. He himself was receptive to all fresh ideas and artistry whether derived from contemporary music or movements in sculpture and painting. His ideology which supported all the various interests, however, was indeed that of a confluence of the arts, one mingling with and contrapuntal to another.

The characteristic opulence of Diaghilev's creations was not to the taste of Anna Pavlova who did not remain long with the company: she, on the other hand, felt overwhelmed by the repertoire, complaining that in Paris 'they served up Russian art like Russian food – too luxuriously and too copiously'.[146] Her few appearances with Nijinsky, however, were outstandingly beautiful and exercised a magical effect on the audience. In *Les Sylphides*,

> She was the very essence of the romantic, ethereal and unearthly, a sylphide incarnate; and if Nijinsky was compared to Vestris, Pavlova in the opinion of all who saw her was a second Taglioni. ... Nijinsky created an unforgettable image as the youthful poet. His dancing was faultless, and the renderings of the valse by him and Pavlova truly incomparable.[147]

The Times of July 1910 had already praised Pavlova's dancing before she joined the *Ballets Russes* in a famous article, 'If Pavlova had Never Danced',[148] in which her work was judged to be the most artistically important event of the past season. This newspaper was joined by the *Daily Mail* and the *Daily News* in appraising her great gift. In their *pas de deux* from *L'Oiseau d'Or* (the Blue Bird *pas de deux* from *Sleeping Beauty*, called *L'Oiseau de Feu* in 1909), *The Times* critic of 4 November 1911, extolled both the ballerina and her partner Nijinsky:

> Taken by itself it is little more than a display of the virtuosity of the two dancers, Mme. Pavlova and M. Nijinsky, but that is enough to make it memorable, for it includes feats of arms (and still more of legs) which take one's breath away because of the extraordinary control of muscle and limb which they entail.
> Here the pointed toe step, which Mme. Pavlova does with an entrancing grace which no one else can quite attain, is used in a new way, with little clawing movements as though only a small thread held her to the ground and she were trying to free herself and sail away in mid-air. As in her famous 'Papillon' dance, so in 'L'Oiseau d'Or' her art is more suggestive than imitative. She does not copy a bird, but she seems for a moment to partake of its nature ... M. Nijinsky has long succeeded in setting the law of gravitation at defiance, and he makes one exit here which rivals

his final one in 'Le Spectre de la Rose'.[149] His dancing, too, has new elements in it, wonderful rhythmic patterns of the body which he has not shown elsewhere.[150]

As for the *pas de deux* being 'little more than a display of ... virtuosity', it must be pointed out that the male dancer begins the coda with a *diagonale* of twenty-four *brisés volés* executed alternately to front and back – a feat comparable with Legnani's famous thirty-two *fouettés*.[151] Pavlova's artistic decision to suggest rather than to imitate, however, would have delighted Yeats.

Pavlova's seventh performance on 11 November 1911, was the last she ever gave with the Diaghilev company and she danced in *Le Pavillon d'Armide*, *Les Sylphides* and *L'Oiseau d'Or* with Nijinsky. Of the great stars, Nijinsky and Karsavina remained and the latter was still being counted on to perform by Diaghilev just before his death in 1929. The English press continued fervid in its praise of the sumptuousness and magnificence of the Russian achievement and the conspicuous success of the dancers. Of the first ballet, *Le Pavillon d'Armide*, to the original choreography of which was added Nijinsky's role, the *Daily News* critic announced:

> M. Nijinsky has come here with a great reputation ... In the part of the slave of Armida, he showed that the praise bestowed upon him has not been extravagant. His feats in dancing border on the miraculous, he hardly seems to touch the stage ... One would think he were supported by invisible wings.
>
> Charmingly pretty and a miracle of imponderability, Mme. Tamara Karsavina was a delightful vision. She was a pathetic fairy rather than a guileful enchantress.[152]

The most breath-taking and exotic item in that early repertoire was that of the *'Polovtsian Dances'* from *Prince Igor*; they were so new and alien that the London public was initially unsure how to react. It took but a little time to decide, however and the *Daily News* correspondent chronicled the frenzy of astonishment and admiration with which these exotica were received:

> The scene, all red, with a background of radiant yellow sky, was curious, but beautiful, with the beauty of some strange impressionist sunset, and the barbaric dances performed by a crowd of richly-dressed figures were nothing short of amazing.

Purists in Russia criticised this ballet very severely as being too great a departure from the traditional style of ballet dancing. It was keenly appreciated by the general public, and the reception it met with last night was a foregone conclusion. Judging from the behaviour of the audience at Covent Garden, the Russian term for enthusiasts for the ballet, BALLETOMANIACS, will have to be incorporated into the language.[153]

Charles Ricketts would have wholeheartedly concurred: he came under the spell of the Russians in the winter of 1911, their second season in London when the company still included Kschessinskaya (the dancer to whom the Tsar had given diamonds), Pavlova, Karsavina, Nijinska, Schollar and Nijinsky, Bolm and Maestro Cecchetti among other less famous names. Early in 1912 Ricketts wrote to Mrs Muriel Lee Mathews:

the Russians have left us! … On the last night they danced as they dance only in Paradise – Karsavina destroyed utterly all the diamonds which the Tsar had given to the rival lady! (I forget her name), and Nijinsky never once touched the ground, but laughed at our sorrows and passions in mid-air. It was I who got the encore for Chopin's ironical and immortal valse. In *Schéhérazade* they put such beauty into their deaths that we became amorous of death and a Jew behind me cried out, 'Oh! My God!' The audience was cowed, and applauded silently, one faded round of sound, whereupon that pimple of a French conductor struck up 'God save the King,' which of course suggests to the Britisher coats, hats, and trains to the suburbs. I was white with rage and, the moment he ceased, I yelled 'Karsavina' twice at the top of my voice; there was a boom of a distant sea, and the house applauded for twenty minutes.[154]

We may note in passing that Karsavina tells in her *Theatre Street* how she once heard Nijinsky asked if it was indeed difficult to leap and stay in the air in the way that Ricketts here described:

he did not understand at first, and then very obligingly: No! No! not difficult. You have to just go up and then pause a little up there.[155]

Ricketts continued in his praise for Nijinsky when he wrote to his friend, the poet Gordon Bottomley, of his anticipation of the Russian arrival again in London for a season lasting from 12 June to 1 August in which they would once more perform at Covent Garden and offer some works new to England: *Thamar* with decor and stage design by Bakst, *L'Oiseau de Feu* with music by Stravinsky and *Narcisse* with decor by Bakst and with Fokine as choreographer of all three.

> We both look forward to the Russian dancers, they have been something like a passion during past seasons; with them the lambent sense of beauty and desire for perfection is so great that one watches the dancing of Schumann's *Carnaval*, in crinolines and toppers, before a purple curtain, with authentic tears in one's eyes, and with crumpled gloves which are split to ribbons at the end. The Chopin Valse Opus 64 No. 2, passes into an indescribable twilight world of beauty and tender irony; the rapid portions are played *a la sordina*, to soundless dancing so rapid that it seems disembodied. All that the antique world thought and said about the famous male dancers who were seduced by Empresses, etc., is quite true. Nijinsky outclasses in passion, beauty, and magnetism all that Karsavina can do, and she is a Muse, or several Muses in one, the Muse of Melancholy and of Caprice, capable of expressing tragedy and even voluptuous innocence; the wildness of chastity, and the sting of desire; she is the perfect instrument upon which all emotion can be rendered. Nijinsky is a living flame, the son of Hermes, or Logi perhaps. One cannot imagine his mother – probably some ancient ballerina was answerable; but I prefer to believe in some sort of spontaneous nativity, at the most a passing cloud may have attracted some fantastic and capricious god.[156]

Ricketts's appreciation of and enthusiasm for the dancers arise in response to qualities which would not have been esteemed laudable by Yeats's own dance aesthetic. Karsavina and Nijinsky were considered by Ricketts to be superlative in their expression of emotion and their art on this occasion was passionate, yet superlatively and realistically mimetic. In admiring them as instruments 'upon which all emotion can be rendered', Ricketts parts company with Yeats who called, rather, for a degree of stylisation and distantiation as the desired feature of his own dances. The Irish playwright demanded artifice – masks which were abstract and non-representative – so that the dancer appeared to be as alien as possible – a faery child, a goddess, a hawk or ghosts. Only when he has Emer dance 'as if' in 'adoration' or 'triumph' does Yeats approach the presentation of an expressive dancer on whom demands are made similar to those on Karsavina and Nijinsky in his friend's account.

With *L'Oiseau de Feu* Stravinsky's music was heard in London for the first time and, although the composer's later work would become the subject of fearful controversy, this ballet was met with almost unanimous approval. *The Sunday Times* carried its own version of the Stravinsky story as well as a tribute to Karsavina's prowess in this new repertoire which was particularly demanding on her. Stravinsky was described as

> a young Russian composer who was originally a pupil of Rimsky-Korsakov, but has settled down in Paris, and is very much in the modern 'movement' of that capital. His music is impressionistic in character, very advanced in its idiom, free and varied in its rhythm, and elaborately scored. Its new and subtle harmonies, its delicate broidery, and its unfailing *esprit* give it a charm of its own, and though it is hardly the sort of music that one would expect in alliance with the choreographic art, it fits the action of 'L'Oiseau de Feu' like the proverbial glove, and seems to be very congenial to the dancers. ...
>
> Mme. Karsavina – whose staying power and variety were alike exhausted this evening, for she had earlier appeared in *Thamar* and *Les Sylphides* – took the name-part, and quite unforgettable was her bird-like grace and fleetness of movement, and the suggestion of palpitating fear and violated purity with which she shrank from the arms of her captor.[157]

Closely following every movement and aspect of the *Ballets Russes*, Ricketts discussed the work of Bakst in a letter in the summer of 1912 and, since one of the Englishman's principal talents (among many) was that of stage and costume designer, it is not astonishing that he met Bakst in person and invited him to the home he shared with Charles Shannon in the autumn of 1913:

> his work enchants me, whether I think it really good or not, I met him and found him, as an art lover, superior to his work, sane on difficult points, where I would have thought him out of sympathy – the English School, for instance – and quite passionate over the noblest art. He discovered Rossetti in our home, adores Piero della Francesca and Michelangelo in the National Gallery. He has

all the quickness of the Jew but seems free from the Jew's lack of the sense of proportion. I feel I have reached the stage in life when I only care to talk to women and Jews.[158]

Vaslav Nijinsky had been encouraged by Diaghilev to develop as choreographer as well as dancer and the 1913 season presented all three of Nijinsky's ballets, including that which had scandalised Paris the previous year, *L'Après-Midi d'un Faune*. The uproar that had ensued there after the first performance is well-known and well-documented: Paris considered obscene Nijinsky's frankly erotic final pose as he gently lowered himself down onto the veil shed by the fleeing nymph, placed his hand under his body, covering his genitals and quivered. The French were also shocked by this new style of ballet, a composition of plastic poses and heavy steps. The piece was rechoreographed before arriving in London, so the English capital was not given the opportunity to witness the controversial gesture and, thus, it not only took *Faune* in its stride but accepted the innovations with enthusiasm. The critics of both *The Times* and the *Daily Mail* (Richard Capell, for years a loyal friend to the *Ballets Russes*) were fulsome in their praise:

> The critic of *The Times* considered the work seriously and at some length, deemed Nijinsky's 'stiff poses and particularly his last action when he lies down to dream beside the scarf ... extraordinarily expressive' and paid the budding choreographer a fine compliment in his concluding words: 'We realized again how apparently inexhaustible are the resources of the ballet, for we had been given a new phase of its art which appealed through quite different channels from those with which anything else in the repertory has been concerned.'[159]

Capell is still more energetic in his compliments:

> The miracle of the thing lies with Nijinsky – the fabulous Nijinsky, the peerless dancer, who as the faun does no dancing. The two inspirations of his subtle and unapproached miming in this piece would appear to have been the Greek pottery at the British Museum and a study of the gambols of chamois or goat. He wears a mottled or rather piebald skin – rather like the coat of a young calf; it is admirable. His movements are at once abrupt and stealthy. He jumps once. This one leap is a surprise and an illum-

ination. It is a full evocation of a being half-brute, consummate and also uncanny.[160]

It is very curious that Ricketts made no mention of this ballet in his journal or letters, but the great Austrian poet and librettist Hugo von Hoffmansthal did. He also, along with Yeats, had been experimenting with ballet and dance plays such as his *Furcht* in 1907:

with the severe inward strength of Nijinsky's short scene, Debussy's music seems to fade away gradually till it becomes merely the accompanying element – a something in the atmosphere, but not the atmosphere itself. And again, the famous poem of Mallarmé, from which the music takes its title, is not the key; rather do we tend to find this in the verse of Horace: *Faune nympharum fugientum amator* '(Faun, you have a passion for fleeing nymphs!) (Odes; Book III, No. 18.)' which concentrates a bas-relief into few words. This bas-relief is what one finds in the work of Nijinsky – a vision of the antique, which is quite our own, nurtured by the great statues of the fifth century – the Delphic charioteers – the archaic statues of youths in the museum of the Acropolis, with a touch of fate and tragedy in them far removed from the antiquity of Winkelmann, of Ingres, of Titian.[161]

We are irresistably reminded once again of Yeats's earlier wish to train actors who 'must move, for the most part, slowly and quietly, and not very much, and there should be something in their movements decorative and rhythmical *as if they were paintings on a frieze.* [my emphasis]'.[162] Hoffmansthal's comment on Nijinsky's choreography of his dancers as forming a bas-relief had, by now in 1913, become a cliché. The notion of figures poised in two-dimensionality in a classical frieze had already been employed in Todhunter's *Helena in Troas* as early as May 1886, but the Austrian writer discerns a new characteristic in the Nijinsky version, one which is also to be found in the Acropolis models but absent from the work of imitators such as Winkelman, that of 'a touch of fate and tragedy'. It is as if Nijinsky had added a human element of personal destiny to the majesty of his dancer statues, thereby partially eliminating the most significant feature of the earlier arrangements of the figures – their very impersonality.

Ricketts's silence seems all the more odd when we realise that, with his interest in costume design, he would probably have been aware of the way in which contemporary fashion was mimicking this ballet: the Parisiennes were so enthusiastic over Bakst's classic draperies worn by the nymphs in *Faune* that they reproduced for their own apparel the Greek softness of outline in chiffon and muslin.

Le Sacre du Printemps – *Tableau de la Russie Païenne* by Nijinsky with music by Stravinsky was also considered to be revolutionary when first performed in Paris in May 1913 and then at Drury Lane in July. It was severely attacked in the press and even the tolerant Ricketts who usually loved experiment and innovation was moved to remark in the postscript of a letter to Mrs Lee Mathews that summer:

> The music of 'Le Sacre du Printemps' made me want to howl like a dog. I thought of doing so, but realized that I should not be heard[163]

and yet he was totally conscious that this new work, with its bold Stravinsky score, was heralding a new era in the history of music and dance. Nijinsky was fighting against conventional academic rules and, in his search for the movements which he desired, retrained dancers who had performed classical ballet steps since their initiation in the art:

> For months, dancers who had schooled themselves to give the public the impression of weightlessness had to learn to 'weight' their bones; instead of rising on point, they had to learn to turn around on their heels, their feet toed inward.[164]

Nijinsky was assisted in his mammoth task by Marie Rambert, then a student at the Dalcroze School of Eurhythmics.[165] The leading parts of *Le Sacre* were danced by Karsavina, Schollar, Nijinska, Bolm and Maestro Enrico Cecchetti, all usually admired by Ricketts, but he nowhere comments on their aptitude and skill in this thoroughly new work. Nor does he mention Nijinsky's third ballet of that year, *Jeux, poème dansé*, with music by Debussy and decor by Bakst. This too met with criticism for the demands made on dancers and audience alike; it was so new and unfamiliar in approach that Diaghilev decided to date it 1930 and called it 'an attempt to forge a synthesis of the trends of the twentieth century'.

But Nijinsky's period of genius and *éblouissement* was to end in a monstrously unjust manner; shortly after his marriage to Romola de

Pulszky – for which temerity Diaghilev severed all connection with his former protegé – he was to be diagnosed insane and to spend from 1919, when he gave his final performance in a hotel in Switzerland, to his death in England in 1950 in a series of mental hospitals. Modern explanations of his illness give less extreme and disturbing physiological reasons for his very real suffering. He and Diaghilev, however, had changed the world's perception of the male dancer: since the Romantic Ballet adulation had been devoted to the woman who was Muse and diva and the part of the male dancer, as we have remarked, had often been performed by a woman *en travestie*. What was new and slightly scandalous about Nijinsky and the other Russian men was that they were admired for their grace and beauty and to do this was, in some circles, inconceivable. Théophile Gautier,[166] poet, balletomane and fanatical writer on dance, had complained bitterly in 1838 about the nasty muscular male dancer of his period who introduced his obvious masculinity into the ballet that Gautier loved. For the French poet, ballet should always present fragility, ephemerality and enchantment – a world of graceful women all contributing and subscribing to the mystique of the ballerina:

for nothing is more abominable than a man who displays his red neck, his great muscular arms, his legs with calves like church beadles', this whole heavy masculine frame, shaken with leaps and pirouettes.[167]

Richard Buckle admirably sums up Nijinsky's quirky brilliance; the dancer always found it difficult to think himself into the role of Albrecht in *Giselle* because

Princes, cavaliers, manly straightforward lovers – these were the stock heroes of the old ballets, and he was not at home in such conventional roles, in which all that was needed, besides firm support for the ballerina, were a proud bearing and good manners. To become a ghost, a puppet, a half-animal creature, a faun, a character from the Commedia dell'Arte or even a Greek boy in love with himself was much easier for him. He needed a mask.[168]

He also, significantly, played a slave with great success in *Le Pavillon d'Armide* and *Schéhérazade*. Ricketts would have shared Buckle's evaluation because he esteemed Nijinsky very highly as a dancer and he may well have communicated his enthusiasm to Yeats who would have known of the Nijinsky phenomenon from his own acquaintance with the *Ballets Russes*. The Irish poet himself was delighted to employ male dancers when they had 'Mr. Ito's genius of movement'[169] and Ito revealed his artistry when taking the role of the Hawk Woman in *At the Hawk's Well* in April 1916. Yeats had no qualms about casting a man to perform a woman's role as he had invented a part which called for a power independent of gender. Through his interest in the company and its repertoire he would register Karsavina's appearance in a version of *Salome* in Paris and in London in 1913, the very year in which Yeats saw Diaghilev's dancers and expressed such joy in them.

La Tragédie de Salomé, after the poem by Robert d'Humières with music by Florent Schmitt and choreography by Romanov, did not meet with success either in Paris or in London where it arrived on 30 June 1913. Actually Loïe Fuller had commissioned it in 1907 and she presented it at the Théâtre des Arts in Paris, using it to display her lighting techniques. Karsavina, however, always believed that it had been intended as a platform for her own balletic gifts and that Diaghilev had given Schmitt the task of composing the music especially for her. It is likely that Diaghilev saw the Loïe Fuller production and decided that Schmitt's music could be used by his company for some future ballet. The stage and costume designer Soudeikine personally painted a rose on Karsavina's thigh before every performance: his decor, heavily influenced by Aubrey Beardsley, may have been over-elaborate. Richard Capell reviewed it in the *Daily Mail* and made it sound a perfectly plausible – though innovatively different – attempt at yet another *Salome*, but the audience did not share his admiration:

> The person of the Russian Salomé, as we first see her, when a curtain of tropical foliage parts and she stands in relief against the star-strewn blueness of no terrestrial night, her garb and hood and a prodigiously-trained cloak, comes indeed from one of the pictures of Beardsley, and so do her monstrous Court of ostrich-plumed negroes and the suite of negro executioners. But rather more extravagant than the nature of Beardsley's decoration is the Russian artist's efflorescence of giant vegetation that shadows this scene of Salomé's death-dance round the martyred saint's head. (But last night there was no head on the pillar in the middle of the stage that should have borne it.)

Mme. Karsavina is by nature a fairy, who condescends to be human at times, and at times, as in the erotic torment of the Queen in 'Scheherazade', subhuman. But what is her Salome? A witch, a Lilith, from an oriental poet's inferno. Merely in the way of endurance, her atrocious dance is probably the most amazing feat in all the annals of Ballet.[170]

Yet again Ricketts made no mention of this ballet although he was usually devoted to Karsavina and everything that she created. We have observed that he had personal and professional interests in the staging of the versions of *Salome* having designed for some productions himself, so his silence on this point is strange and especially so when no comment is recorded from Yeats either.

The early months of 1914 saw Ricketts working closely with Yeats and Lady Gregory, as he was devising costumes for *The King's Threshold*. He received a letter on 11 June from the poet expressing gratitude for the designer's astoundingly good creations just a few days before Ricketts made a diary entry noting a performance by the Russians of Rimsky-Korsakov's opera-ballet, *Le Coq d'Or*.[171] Yeats would have considered it a noteworthy production because the singers were ranged on each side of the stage in oratorio fashion, while the action was mimed and danced in the centre. His own 1907 production of *Deirdre* had included a chorus who performed in a similar way to these singers and later in the *Four Plays for Dancers* begun in 1916, the musicians would be present on stage in a fashion suggestive of Diaghilev's singers in this case. As Ricketts commented:

It is a most picturesque interpretation of the principle which obtained at the birth of Greek tragedy, and which still obtains in the Japanese No Dances. The interpretation was magnificent. Karsavina looked like a bewitching Hindu idol, her dancing and miming were incomparable.[172]

The reference to the Noh at this point is of interest, as Yeats had been studying Japanese Noh plays since Ezra Pound's introduction to them the previous year.

Diaghilev's repertoire for the June–July season at the Theatre Royal, Drury Lane, consisted of *Daphnis and Chloe, Papillons, Le Coq d'Or, Le Rossignol, Midas, La Légende de Joseph, La Nuit de Mai, Le Carnaval, Cléopâtre, Le Lac des Cygnes, Narcisse, L'Oiseau de Feu, Petrouchka, Prince Igor, Schéhérazade, Le Spectre de la Rose, Les Sylphides* and *Thamar*. Ricketts went to see the ballet twenty times that season and observed that, while Fokine danced admirably as a replacement for Nijinsky, he lacked his 'spontaneity and flame'.[173] A newcomer had joined the company who would go on to dance the parts that were associated with Nijinsky and in later years would rechoreograph his *Le Sacre du Printemps*: his name was Léonide Massine.[174]

Ricketts related his impressions of *La Légende de Joseph* for his friend Bottomley in a letter of March 1915 from his memory of the production of the previous summer. During the war years the Russians went on tour to America and did not perform again in London until 1918. In the United States in 1915 Nijinsky directed the company through some seasons fraught with difficulty, not least that of his own impending illness. Ricketts was therefore forced to depend on remembered impressions and his retrospective portrait of this Richard Strauss ballet, with libretto by Count Harry von Kessler and Hugo von Hoffmansthal, scenery by José Maria Sert[175] and costumes by Bakst, was eulogistic about the dancers but not won over by the music. *Joseph* illustrated the Bible story of the wife of Potiphar through 'an exaggeratedly sumptuous, non-realistic Renaissance setting with Potiphar robed like a Doge and Joseph dressed – or undressed – in skins of ermine'.[176] Potiphar's wife was played by Karsavina, who,

> from the first sight of Joseph becomes attentive. She watches his first movements, becomes more and more absorbed, more and more intent, till she looks like a cat watching a mouse, and her eyes and head turn and follow, fascinated and absorbed, the every motion of the dancer. ...
>
> If the Russians had not been the inspired interpreters of the thing, it would have been intolerable and fatuous. Karsavina as Potiphar's Wife was superb. A creature of gold and marble at the start, her sinister repelling of the begging dancer was evil and passionless; it suggested the avoidance of something unclean. When she strangled herself with her pearl necklace, the act was spontaneous and spasmodic like a moth meeting a flame.[177]

During the war Ricketts was in constant contact with Yeats and Lady Gregory and shared their grief when the *Lusitania* was torpedoed on 8 May 1915, with her nephew Hugh Lane on board. When Yeats visited Ricketts and Shannon in April 1916 he was noticeably affected by current events and anguished about the Irish situation.

He was also concerned about the fate of Hugh Lane's collection of French art which Yeats wished to be conserved in Dublin rather than London; Ricketts promised his support for this project. Out of the distress, as we know, came poetry.

There were no *Ballets Russes* to lift the spirits and chase away dull care and, in place of reviews, *Self-Portrait* lists a series of bombing raids on London for most of the years 1914–1918, but in October 1917 Diaghilev regained the English capital and was welcomed at the Ricketts–Shannon home. He was endeavouring to persuade Beecham to accept and conduct his recent productions and was negotiating a theatre in which his company could perform. None of the stars would be present – they were dispersed and dotted severally over the maps of Europe and the United States – but a new name, that of Pablo Picasso, would draw interest as he had staged one of the new ballets, *Parade*, in Paris in 1917 and would go on to paint the decor and curtain and design the costumes of *Le Tricorne* in London in 1918. Ricketts and Diaghilev

> quarelled over German music, which Diaghilev wants to persecute and suppress; he means to scrap *Carnaval, Papillons* and *Spectre of the Rose*.[178]

The Russian troupe finally reassembled in London at the end of 1918 for a season at the Coliseum spanning September 1918 to March 1919. They performed new works largely choreographed by Massine: *The Good-Humoured Ladies* with music by Scarlatti and stage design by Bakst, *Sadko, Midnight Sun* with music by Rimsky-Korsakov and *Contes Russes*. Although Karsavina was still absent, her parts were danced brilliantly by Lydia Lopokova.[179] Ricketts attended the new production of *Cléopâtre* and found the setting hideous; he also saw fit to comment, as did the press, on the Diaghilev company's appearing in music hall rather than theatre, however sumptuous Oswald Stoll's creation might be:

> [The setting of *Cléopâtre*] is by the post-Impressionist round the corner, pink and purple columns, a pea-green Hathor cow, and yellow Pyramid with a green shadow and red spot; curiously enough, like many efforts at intensive colour, the effect is not coloured. ... Massine dances well, but he is uninspired; he has huge square legs. ... He is stark naked save for some rather nice bathing-drawers, with a huge black spot on his belly. ...

Will the masses turn Bolshevist or suffer in silence this intrusion of art in their national Shrine? Will the snobs, like myself, pip it?[180]

The 'post-Impressionist round the corner' was Robert Delaunay whose task in reworking a decor that had originally been conceived by the brilliant Bakst was invidious in the extreme.

Ricketts's last comment on the *Ballets Russes* – he ceased his long series of eulogies and occasional complaints in 1919 – was in a letter to Gordon Bottomley on 29 January when reminiscing about a production of *Le Coq d'Or*: 'Karsavina's miming of the songs was an event in my life. I shall never forget it.'[181] The Diaghilev ballet continued to visit London for two seasons a year until and after the death of its creator in Venice in 1929, but there is no further evidence that Ricketts and through him, Yeats, was receptive to its glories. Ricketts, as he suggests above, may have been dissuaded from attending by the fact that the dancers were appearing as part of a music hall bill, although two years later in 1921 they performed a complete ballet at the Coliseum, *La Princesse Enchantée,* and so could not be considered merely as a 'turn' and their venue was certainly not the vulgar, seedy 'dive' of popular stereotype. The April–July season of 1919 saw them dancing at the Alhambra and the return of Karsavina, but even her reappearance does not seem to have tempted Ricketts to venture again into the celebrated magnificence of the *Ballets Russes* which was still bursting with energy, experiment and innovation for another ten years.

By the time that Ricketts had concluded his enthusiastic and informative appraisals of the Russian Ballet and switched his affiliation to opera, Yeats had already begun work on his *Plays for Dancers,* first published in 1921, in which he introduced characters who perform a dance which is integral to the plot and action of the play. Yeats knew of Diaghilev's achievements and surely they were of assistance to him – he was so fulsome in his praise – in developing his own aesthetics of dance. For a working playwright, Yeats did not himself attend theatre often and he was less than fond of music hall and yet an unpublished letter of 1915 to Lady Gregory shows that he was obliged to go to a matinée with Lady Cunard. The outing was certainly a duty and a chore:

I give my lecture in the first week of December at the Duchess of Marborogh's [sic] who kindly lends me a great room of hers. I owe this to Lady Cunard & so far it has only burdened me with three tea parties & two hours at a music hall matinee. ...[182]

During the First World War the Abbey Theatre survived only by producing plays at the music hall, a strategy which Yeats detested, as the following selection of unpublished letters will demonstrate:

If you get a good American offer for the spring of 1914 I think it would be well to make no Music Hall engagements for next autumn and winter. They do not help our work which is after all to educate Ireland. ... I feel that the Dublin public will have a real cause of complaint if we neglect them for music halls where we have no educational or artistic mission. As it is I do not like the four weeks at the music halls in the autumn & the winter at Liverpool for the whole company now they will be away again in spring. I think too that the appetite of the players for money will grow with what it feeds on. Then too so far as I know everybody is agreed to the evil effect of large halls & music hall audiences on any fine & sincere dramatic art. It would be a poor thing if Home Rule should find us not able to take advantage of the new life in the country but with our art made cheap and with our plays, With [sic] what sense of Ireland remains to them gone. In a little we will have players, who can go to the Music Halls if necessary without weakening or coarsening our chief company but we have not got them now. It is not a cause in which we should run any risks because it has nothing to do with our main purpose.[183]

As we can see, Yeats's pragmatism is reluctant and a source of genuine concern that he is betraying what both he and Lady Gregory perceive as the moral duty of the Abbey Theatre to Ireland:

I am afraid you may think I have done wrong about bringing them [the Abbey Company] back to Dublin, but I only did it after getting a strong impression that it was necessary if we are to hold our Dublin audience. I also felt that it was an ignoble way of coming to grief, playing duties at the music-halls all the winter and that it was better even to increase the danger of coming to grief by insuring its dignity. ... They were pelted with onions by some indignant Irishman in the gallery at some provincial music-hall, and I believe he had the sympathy of all the players including [Arthur] Sinclair. Sinclair said rather an interesting thing about

Music-halls on Sunday. He said they don't listen to us – they only overhear us.[184]

In a letter to his father in 1916 the poet makes the following distinction between poetry and what is served up in music halls as 'verses'. The bitterness of his scorn is quite apparent and acute:

> I separate the rhythmical & the abstract. They are brothers but one is Abel & one is Cain. In poetry they are not confused for we know that poetry is rhythm but in music hall verses we find an abstract cadence, which is vulgar because it is a part from imitation. The cadence is a mechanism, it never suggests a voice shaken with joy or sorrow as poetical rhythm does. It is but the noise of a machine & not the coming & the going of the breath.[185]

After damning music hall so totally it is with some surprise that we discover, documented in a published letter, a voluntary visit. The letter to Olivia Shakespear of 17 May 1921, testifies that Yeats did attend a performance at

> the new Oxford music hall where I spent 19/- to see a woman dance in masks in imitation of Ito. She danced beautifully and looked very beautiful masked. ... The rest of the performance, or what I saw of it, was dull and mechanical. I knew that a grotesque mask was enormously effective, but was not sure of the effectiveness of a beautiful one till I saw her.[186]

He does not identify the dancer by name and he somewhat grudgingly, though tellingly, informs us that his seat cost him 19 shillings. He was, as just remarked, usually snobbish about music hall, but the very price of his ticket leads us to discover that the New Oxford was indeed no dubious venue but a recently refurbished palace of art, certainly on a par in terms of luxury with the most exclusive of theatres. But Yeats retained his prejudices. Even during the heady 1890s when his friend, Arthur Symons, revealed himself to be such a devotee of both music hall dance and ballet, Yeats chose not to follow suit and fashion by accompanying him on his outings, although he did, from the sanctity and safety of his study, review the poems which Symons addressed to the dancers of whom the English man-about-town was so enamoured.

The show which Yeats saw that evening in 1921 was produced by Charles Cochran[187] and was called *The League of Notions*.[188] Cochran was himself responsible for the magnificent renovation of the New Oxford at a cost of £80,000; the Prince of Wales and Prince George had attended the first night performance on 17 January 1921. The programme[189] demonstrates that Yeats enjoyed the charms of the masked female dancer, Grace Christie,[190] an American whose performances were strongly influenced by the exotica of the Canadian dancer of the early years of the century, Ruth St Denis.[191] Christie was part of a current vogue for masked dancing and when Yeats chooses to identify Michio Ito as her precursor he is being conservative in his estimation of influence, but also, as we shall see, extraordinarily insightful.

Oriental and exotic dance was at a premium and found its roots in the fashion for *Japonisme* of the previous century. But Ruth St Denis had indeed been the first to present more or less authentic Eastern dances to the West when she came on her much acclaimed initial European tour in July 1906 (and even she, it can be surmised with a degree of justification, owed something of the manipulation of the scarves and drapery of her exquisite costumes to Fuller and Isadora Duncan, both of whom she had seen dance). Her tour lasted for three years. She performed an Indian dance, *Radha, the Dance of the Five Senses*, to the music of Delibes' *Lakmé* and, most significantly, mounted her first Japanese ballet, *O-Mika*, to a spoken text in 1913.[192] This was based on Lafcadio Hearn's story 'A Legend of *Fugen-Bosatzu*', and told of a celebrated courtesan who became an incarnation of Fugen-Bosatzu, a goddess of old Japan.[193] Early in January of the previous year Diaghilev had recruited Mata Hari[194] as a performer of exotic dance in *Le Dieu Bleu* which Yeats saw in 1913. She did seven recitals and followed in the footsteps of Ida Rubinstein[195] whom Diaghilev had employed in his earlier exotic ballets.[196] The demand for such genres was fervid in all quarters of the dance world.

It is important to note that the bill included not only Grace Christie in her Benda masks[197] but also Rita Lee, a pupil of Pavlova's.[198] The Russian ballerina had given many a performance in music hall herself and, as she was completely aware of current trends in dancing, she was to insist a year later in August 1922 when her company first went to Japan that an Englishman baptised *à la Russe* by Victor Dandré, Pavlova's life-partner, learn dances from Japanese masters who were Kabuki- and Noh-trained. 'Algeranoff',[199] originally

'Harcourt Essex', was the first English dancer to take instruction from one of the most famous teachers in the country, Matsumoto Koshiro VII.[200]

We may harbour unvoiced suspicions that an educational transaction of such a nature should have occurred long before, especially considering that the Japanese ballet, *Yolande*, by Alfred Thompson was produced at the Alhambra as early as 1860,[201] but in fact teachers from London, Miss Mix and Mr and Mrs G. V. Rosi, went to train Japanese ballet dancers in Western academic dance at the Imperial Theatre Opera Department only in 1910 and 1912, respectively. Pavlova's 1922 visit had been preceded by Yelena Smirnova and Boris Romanov in June 1916 and this had been the first opportunity for Japanese audiences to see world famous dancers from the West. Ruth St Denis added her talent in the cultural exchange by taking the Denishawn Dancers[202] to Japan in 1925, twelve years after her own Japan-inspired performances had reached Western stages.[203]

As for Algy, his lessons continued even when in other countries. In San Francisco in 1923 another member of another famous Kabuki dynasty taught him, Madame Yasao Kineya:

> Pavlova was very keen for me to be taught the masked dance she had seen in Tokyo, for she had never forgotten it and she still insisted that it was my dance.[204]

Diligent in his studies and insatiably curious, Algeranoff gained insight into the spirit of Japanese dancing and became very proficient (between classes Algy was reading Wilde's *Salomé*!):

> I unlearnt my fancy-dress ball notions of Japan and gradually I understood what it was all about. I learnt that a fan, according to the way it is moved or held, can indicate the rising moon, falling rain or blossom, a bird, opening a sliding door and innumerable other things. The music began to have a meaning of its own and gradually I felt that the angle of my knees, feet and hands was bearable to Japanese eyes.[205]

His technique in acting and gesture echoes those explained by the masters of Noh discussed in Chapter 2.

Pavlova, too, demonstrated her own fascination with styles oriental by making Indian dance a notable part of her repertoire: she

would, in Paris in 1930, dance Radha to Algeranoff's Krishna.[206] As
for the diva herself (or her pupils) performing in music hall rather
than 'legitimate' theatre, it would be misleading to insist on a distinction between socially acceptable ballet, on the one hand and
rather *roué* exotica being performed in music hall or variety on the
other. The ballerina, along with dancers of all genres, found employment where she could, and the summer of 1921 saw Karsavina and
Maud Allan sharing a bill: there was a considerable amount of
blurring of the overlapping edges of dance forms:

> In the summer of 1921 all the traditional London theatres for
> dance seemed to be either closed or already booked. Diaghilev
> was in the midst of a season at the Prince's Theatre, with its
> unsuitable stage, while both Karsavina and Maud Allan were part
> of the mixed bill at the Coliseum. Now that the Palace had
> succumbed to moving pictures, and Alfred Butt's other franchise,
> Drury Lane, was temporarily closed, Pavlova took her chances
> under the management of Edmund Russen at the Queen's Hall.
> This was really a small concert hall, hopelessly ill-suited to dance.
> Pavlova opened there on June 27.[207]

A stage was a stage.

Yeats seems not to have stayed for the complete programme
offered at the New Oxford and, thus, would not, perhaps, have
seen Pavlova's pupil, Rita Lee, because, as he states in his letter,
'The rest of the performance, or what I saw of it, was dull and
mechanical.' Yet once again what is significant at this venue, as
elsewhere, is that a classically trained ballerina shares a bill alongside other very diverse performers in what Cochran described as
'An Inconsequential Process of Music, Dance, and Dramatic Interlude',[208] that the Dolly Sisters contributed a Persian Dance as well
as a Clog Dance and that Grace Christie danced in masks. This particular entertainment may be taken as supremely typical of its time.
Cochran, the impresario and consummate showman, would not
have fashioned it so exotically had the demand not existed. After
all, he financed boxing matches as well as classical ballet when the
need arose.

Rita Lee danced as Columbine and 'The Dancer' in the fifth part
of an entertainment called 'Patches' (see Plate 5): the whole show
was built around the versatility of the Dolly Sisters. But Yeats's
enthusiasm for Christie was evidently not misplaced, as a glance at

the illustrations from the current theatrical journals will testify. Yeats would naturally, if perhaps mistakenly, draw the parallel with Ito because 1921, the year of this excursion, also saw the publication of his *Plays for Dancers* and in crafting them he had become receptive to the possibilities of mask, dance and chorus himself. And there is, perhaps, another interesting connection. It is less than clear why Yeats should have chosen to go to see *The League of Notions* at all. As we shall see, the masked dancing was reviewed enthusiastically in the press and the poet may have become aware of the revue through its notices. But also, very significantly, Grace Christie had performed the previous year on Broadway in a two-act revue called *What's in a Name?*, which had been choreographed by none other than Michio Ito himself. It had opened on 19 March 1920, at the Maxine Elliott theatre in New York.[209] There too the Benda masks had been employed. Christie had then crossed the Atlantic to appear, again masked, in the Cochran revue which Yeats saw. Was it indeed the Ito-connection that attracted Yeats to the New Oxford?

The famous masks had been discovered in Benda's New York workshop by John Murray Anderson.[210] *The Daily Express* of 19 January 1921 reported his brilliant find under the headline 'Polish Artist's Creations in a London Theatre':

The masks are the work of a Polish artist, Mr. W. J. Benda, whose magazine illustrations are prominent in America. They were discovered by chance in the artist's studio by Mr. Murray Anderson, the producer of the new revue.

'I went one day to have tea in Mr. Benda's studio, and saw the masks worn by one of his models,' said Mr. Anderson to a 'Daily Express' representative yesterday. 'I was struck immediately with the stage value. ...' [He first used the masks for *Greenwich Village Follies* of 1919, another production in which Ito danced.]

'The success of the masks, I am convinced, is due not to their grotesqueness as to their life-likeness.'

The Daily Graphic of the previous day reported that the 'Episode with Benda Masks' in *The League of Notions* 'stopped the show', but the fullest account, however and one which, along with the Ito-Christie connection, may have lured Yeats into making his inhabitual expedition to the New Oxford, was carried by *The Irish Times* on 24 January 1921:

One is the mask of a beautiful Oriental girl. Another, very grotesque, was suggested by a Japanese doll. The third is purely fantastic, with an enormous head-dress of pheasant's feathers; and the fourth is the face of a flapper with rose-bud mouth and surprised 'glad eyes.' ... The masks are made, not from casts, but from adhesive paper, and then moulded. Compared with ordinary masks, they are very thin, consisting of no more than three or four layers of paper. But they are marvellously finished, and cover not only the face of the artist, but almost the whole of the head. 'The extraordinary thing about the masks,' Mr. Anderson said 'is that they really possess a living quality. ... These masks have, besides, many possibilities. With their aid one artist could play in one piece many parts.'[211]

Anderson produced *What's in a Name?* and devised and staged *The League of Notions* for Cochran. Wherever we discover the guiding presence of Anderson we also find the use of Benda masks and they became such a popular feature that society ladies took to wearing them or their imitations for chic parties (see Plates 1–4). The press loved them. Some years later in March 1930 the *Dancing Times* reviewed two exhibition dancers performing at Ciro's, Frances Mann and Frederick Carpenter, who also performed in masks. Their most acclaimed number was that entitled 'The Prom' in which they satirised the 'flapper' and the 'collegiate' (see Plate 6). Once again it is revealed that they had come from a John Murray Anderson production in New York and, to continue to demonstrate the interrelation of dance genres of the period, we notice that Miss Mann was a pupil of no less a personage than Fokine himself, while Mr Carpenter was trained by another classical dancer, Mikhail Mordkin.[212]

The last solo dancer to whom importance will be attached in this chapter on the dancer in performance will naturally be the widely acclaimed Michio Ito,[213] the magnificent interpreter of Yeats, admired also by many classically-trained dancers including Pavlova.[214] Although he was Dalcroze- (not Noh-) trained, many of his dances were based on Noh pieces. His gestures in particular were influenced by Dalcroze, and Ito attended the former's school at Hellerau from 1912 to 1914 having been inspired in 1911 by seeing Nijinsky at the Châtelet in Paris where Ito had gone with the intention of studying singing. In Berlin, also in 1911, he had attended a performance by Isadora Duncan and had conceived the notion of going to Paris to study with her sister, Elizabeth, so impressed had he been by the American dancer. This project never materialised, however and instead he continued to study German at Leipzig and then moved to Hellerau. He was obviously galvanised into such action by having witnessed the work of both classical and 'free' dancers. Using his Dalcroze instruction as foundation, he too devised his own system of ten arm gestures with which to compose his dances, with the stipulation that no dance was to end on the gesture with which it began.

When war broke out Ito was obliged to move to London where, at the Café Royal (which he frequented because the waiters there spoke French and German and he had as yet no command of English), he met Augustus John, Jacob Epstein and Ezra Pound. He went on to be introduced to W. B. Yeats, Sturge Moore, George Bernard Shaw and, most usefully, Lady Emerald Cunard at that haven for artists, Lady Ottoline Morrell's home, to which he had been escorted by a Café Royal acquaintance. Lady Cunard invited him to dance in her famous drawing-room.

Before leaving Japan at the age of eighteen Ito had undergone early training in Kabuki and this, in conjunction with his Dalcroze studies, his own natural genius for movement and his perfectionism, led him to devise a style of dance which Yeats found so entirely fitting to his purposes and which was fervidly admired among audiences of lay enthusiasts and classical ballet dancers alike. It was quite appropriate that Ito should have joined Adolph Bolm and the 'Ballet Intime' company in early summer 1917, in a tour of American East Coast cities on behalf of war charities. It was equally understandable that in 1928 he took part in a performance with Martha Graham.[215] His versatility and cross-cultural background were both much missed when he left Britain for New York in 1916.

In order to play Yeats's Hawk Guardian so brilliantly, Ito spent hours outside the hawk aviary at London zoo meditating on the movements of the birds as preparation for his solo dance. Yeats accompanied him on these study forays and was thus endorsing and participating in an act of pure mimesis; this was the kind of exercise of which the poet totally approved in the invention of a dance. When Ito had devised his famous masked 'Fox Dance' the previous year in 1915 he had tackled the task with the same thoroughness and sensitivity:

My fox dance is furtive and independent and cunning and staccato. I studied a fox and his ways with a biscuit long before I worked out my dance. Then I went to a great hill in Hampstead and I made my soul into the soul of a fox, and so I evolved my fox dance.[216]

As for his relationship with classic Noh dancing, he had purported to find the genre tedious when a young man at home in Japan, but he both used and developed its principles magnificently when dancing Yeats:

> The dance performed by the hawklike Guardian, as composed by Michio Ito, was, in fact, a modified Noh dance – tense, continuous movement with subtle variations on its monotony, inducing a trancelike state in both personages and audience – but its increase in tempo was more rapid than in genuine Noh and the arm movement was broad and smoothly dramatic, recalling Egyptian representations of the hawk with spread wings and giving a feeling of a great bird's gliding and wheeling.[217]

Just how much the poet depended on his soloists to be able to invent and choreograph their own individual dances is evident when Yeats's stage directions are scrutinised: they contain no indications as to dance steps at all, simply clues to the function and emotion of the dance – 'She moves as if in adoration or triumph'[218] – and so on. Otherwise, as already examined in Chapter 2, it is the plot of the play which suggests the nature of the dance to be presented, one of rage or seduction or grief. How did Michio Ito fulfil the terrifying responsibility – how did he dance?

> Artistic dances, like great lyrics, are objective. Ito, for example, never 'expressed himself' in his dances. Rather, they bring to life ideas and emotions common to all men, even though as perceived or felt by the artist. To quote Yeats again: 'All that is personal soon rots; it must be packed in ice and salt,' and, he added, 'ancient salt (i.e., traditional form, traditional idea, traditional fable) is best.'[219]

Ito was also allied to Yeats in his enormous interest in Greek and Egyptian dancing and he too, experimented with choreography based on sculpted friezes or on figures on ancient Greek amphorae. Yeats had found a soul mate.

The dramatist took the line of those who rebelled against the constrictions of ballet and sought a mode of expression somewhere other than the fixed mimetic language which it has employed for centuries. Later, in the 1920s, Ninette de Valois[220] would take Ito's role and even wear his original hawk costume and, thus, a classically-trained ballerina would mould her talent so as to appear in a 'free' dance. To do so would have been inconceivable without the Duncan phenomenon and the iconoclasm of Diaghilev's *Ballets Russes* as precedents and trail-blazers.

Like many of the dancers discussed earlier – Duncan and Allan among them – Yeats abhorred classical ballet: he had his Old Man say as prologue to the last play, *The Death of Cuchulain* in 1939, that

> I spit upon the dancers painted by Degas. I spit upon their short bodices, their stiff stays, their toes whereon they spin like peg-tops, above all upon that chambermaid face. They might have looked timeless, Rameses the Great, but not the chambermaid, that old maid history. I spit! I spit! I spit![221]

and it may be assumed with a degree of security that this too was the poet's own opinion, even though in 1927 he was determined to have a small school of dance at the Abbey Theatre with de Valois to direct it and to produce and perform in his *Plays for Dancers* herself. She had already in the previous year arranged some choreography for an Abbey production of *On Baile's Strand* and Yeats rewrote *The King of the Great Clock Tower* and *The Only Jealousy of Emer* so that de Valois could interpret the Queen of the former and the Woman of the Sidhe of the latter in dance mime wearing masks.[222] This dancer also appeared with the Massine-Lopokova company in 1922 and for Diaghilev from 1923 until his May–August season of 1925 at the Coliseum, so she might have communicated to Yeats the direction that the company was taking in the middle and late 1920s, thus filling the void left by Ricketts's dereliction of this pleasant duty. Yeats may well have detested ballet but he was obviously ambivalent about its performers' capacity for understanding his own requirements because, late in 1934, he invited Frederick Ashton[223] to take over the Abbey, but the dancer–choreographer declined. It was, however, clear that Ashton in that year could not have been considered as a 'pure' ballet product. He had been trained by Marie Rambert who was herself Duncan-inspired and influenced before moving on to Dalcroze and from him to Diaghilev. Frederick Ashton was, rather, a consummately versatile man-of-the-theatre and dancer in many genres. It comes as no surprise to discover that he had danced with Ida Rubinstein.

Again in 1934 Ninette de Valois choreographed a ballet called *Bar aux Folies Bergère* in which dancers interpreted the Quadrille stars of the 1890s, Grille-d'Egout, Jane Avril and her comrades, thus providing Yeats with an opportunity to refamiliarise himself once more with Arthur Symons's idols.[224] But, as Kermode points out, for Yeats's dancer-as-Image:

> The language of the freely-moving dancer is more like the Image than the virtuosity of the ballerina's more limited range of movement; … the freely-moving dancer is in less danger of seeming mechanical, her dance is more likely to have form, the ballerina's often only shape.[225]

When Yeats introduced a child dancer into *The Land of Heart's Desire* as early as 1894 he had been impressed by the theatrical experiments of Todhunter but also influenced perhaps by Symons's accounts of particular dancers in the 1890s as well as his own knowledge of how Loïe Fuller was transforming herself into a living icon. As is customary, the stage direction for the young actress is simply 'She dances'.[226] And yet, despite the paucity of explanation, Yeats well knew what he wanted and what he did not want of his theatrical dancers and such certainty was gleaned from familiarity with what was then being performed on the stages of London and Paris. Added to this awareness was also the conviction that he shared with Mallarmé that the figure of the dancer was one which resolved the old antinomies of blood and marble, concrete and abstract, face and mask, all of the teasing contradictions which so obsessed him at those frontiers where art and life and death meet and the soul becomes the body – a beautiful woman's body, that of the Fifteenth phase in his system researched in *A Vision*.[227]

Yeats never seems to have thought of using a pure ballet ensemble, but always prefers the 'free' dancer who is also a soloist and in order to place Yeats's own versions of this figure in terms of his or her historical context, we have discussed several of the proponents of the art from the 1890s onwards in this chapter. In his choice the poet establishes his part in a long sequence which leads up to such performers as Duncan, Allan and Fuller, each one interpreting music according to her mood and skill. The soloist has an interesting history in that he or she may be traced back to the origins of ballet on the one hand and, I suggest, to the circus on the other: the gulf between the two milieux is not as wide as might be imagined today and Marian Hannah Winter makes the point in *The Pre-Romantic Ballet* that

> [Pre-Romantic ballet] was primarily – just as the *ballet de cour* had been – a Franco-Italian hybrid, yet nurtured to an even greater degree than its predecessor in London, Stuttgart, Berlin and Vienna. In fact its major text was English. Essentially it was as international as its performers and choreographers, who moved from country to country with the mobility of strolling fairground dynasties, with which they often had family ties.[228]

In ballet the soloist dates back to the first productions of the *Ballet du Roi* in France of the 1580s in which the King and Queen would themselves sometimes perform. At this point in ballet history there was no convention of a raised stage partitioned off by proscenium arch and curtain to divide dancers and spectators: all present were potential dancers and individuals gave solo performances at will.

The most famous, most passionate dancer at court was indeed Louis XIV who had participated in *ballets de cour* since the age of eight. He most frequently took the part of a god or, later, in his most famous role, as the sun. When he finally retired in 1670 because, it is widely believed, he was too fat, the day of the amateur was over.

> Why did Louis XIV stop dancing when he did? Was it just that he got too fat? ... The question has often been discussed (since the ballet had been an instrument of policy throughout his reign) and has more than anecdotal interest. When Louis withdrew (his last appearance was in *Les Amants magnifiques* in 1670), many other nobles withdrew also. It was this withdrawal that gave Lully[229] his opportunity to take over Perrin's[230] abortive Academy of 1669 and transform the ballet into a fully professional organization. It is this transformation that marks the end of ballet as a socially pivotal institution in Europe (... but the granting of the privilege to open Perrin's academy in 1669 presumably shows that the King already planned to phase himself out).[231]

Thus, in the reign of Louis XIV the ballet changed its locus from court to theatre. Originally the performers had all been men, with graceful boys taking the parts of nymphs and goddesses, aided in illusion by the use of masks. (The convention of the mask was taken into the theatre and the half-mask continued at the Paris ballet until 1772.) In 1681, however, in a ballet given at Saint-Germain entitled *Le Triomphe de l'Amour*, Lully, the composer, broke with tradition by introducing female dancers:

The fashion became immediately popular. The part of the male dancer grew continually less important until in the ballets of the latter part of the nineteenth century it became altogether negligible, to be revived again in the Russian ballet of our own day.[232]

An equally great innovation was also to be found in costume, as we shall go on to discuss. The magnificent Camargo[233] in the first half of the eighteenth century took upon herself the notion of shortening her skirts so that she was thus enabled to execute the light and airy steps which had proved impossible when burdened down with paniers and other bulk. Ballet became technically difficult, the realm of the professional who underwent gruelling training in order to perform the *pirouettes, entrechats, jetés-battus* and *ballons* which were then introduced. An amateur would-be dancer, albeit a king and portly, no longer had a place in the ballet.

Playbills of the 1790s show that then ballet was an adjunct to some other form of entertainment, either a short play or an acrobatic or equestrian act; dance *divertissements* were commonly inserted into opera programmes and, in later years, ballet was offered side-by-side with music-hall turns. Continuing this tradition, Pavlova even consented to appear in an abridged version of *The Sleeping Beauty* in the United States in Charles Dillingham's *The Big Show* at the New York Hippodrome on 13 August 1916, her dancing flanked by vaudeville acts of spectacular proportions – with West Point cadets and 400 minstrels – and an Ice Ballet. One contemporary reviewer perceived her as 'a jewel in a garish setting'.[234]

As for the 'free' dancer, she was probably an extension of the more acrobatic routines of the circus performer. It is typical of the period that the soloist who graces the programmes for Sadler's Wells during the months of 1793 should be mysterious. She appears alongside names of ballet soloists such as Signora Bossi del Caro, an established and celebrated principal ballerina; but the playbill simply announces

The pleasing exertions of La Belle Espagnole.[235]

She could have been any one of a number of genres of performer –
acrobat, contortionist, equestrienne or dancer. There is no further
indication to be gleaned from the announcement, but we may
indeed deduce that she came from a circus background. She can be
identified, however, as Madame Paulo Redigé who was also known
as 'Signora Spagniola', and her chosen metier was rope dancing. She
had made a very successful debut in Paris in 1785 and her special
versatility involved dancing with two swords on her feet. It is also
of interest to note that she was performing at Sadler's Wells in 1793
and had previously appeared there in January 1785, but, in August
and September of the same year, her venue had been Astley's
Amphitheatre. She is certainly not alone in defying modern popular
prejudices and stereotypes about genres of theatre and the type of
performance which might be expected from each.[236]

Ballet dancers originally shared the same status with circus and
fairground stars and the division between the two genres of performance is a modern concept. One phenomenon which occurred on the
second, deviant track which leads to the 'free' dancer is possibly that
of the celebrated 'poses from the antique' of Emma Hart, later Lady
Hamilton, at a private reception in Naples in 1787. Wearing the simple muslin dresses that Isadora Duncan and Maud Allan would
adopt out of their antipathy to ballet costumes and standing stock
still, Emma demonstrated her curvilinear form to her public. She was
very famous and influential in the spheres of theatre and outside:

> Emma's poses influenced not only drawingroom theatricals but
> neo-classic costuming in the professional theatre and professional
> actresses in their search for new plastic effects. The great German
> exponent of mimo-drama, Henrietta Hendel Schutz, still only an
> actress who had received some dance and pantomime training, is
> known to have studied the Rehberg sketches of Emma, and her
> vocation was certainly clarified thereby.[237]

While the ability to strike attitudes is of course a lesser talent than
that of dancing, Emma's popularity was very real and, as Winter
indicates, her choice of dress was significant as it would coincide
with the fashion that followed the French Revolution of two years
later in 1789: she affected the neo-classical look which was subsequently to be called 'Directoire' or 'Empire'.

History seems to run in cycles on this important issue; after all,
fashion is also a manifestation of current values and philosophy and

a rebellion against tightly laced bodices, lambrequins, stays and paniers has happened more than once. As Ivor Guest informs us in his *Romantic Ballet in England*, the ballerina Marie Sallé danced at Drury Lane as early as 14 February 1734, in a simple muslin dress, her long hair flowing.[238] We may glean from advertisements in the newspapers of the 1790s that gauzes and muslins and French lawns were the fabrics fashionable at the time,[239] and the dresses of the various Countesses attending the King's birthday celebrations in June 1793 were all of gauze and crape ornamented with foil:

> Countess of Lisburne – A crape petticoat, richly embroidered in bouquets of fancy lilac foil flowers, green leaves and silver spangles, drawn up in festoons, trimmed with silver fringe; train, a lilac and silver gauze.[240]

The flowing lines of classical Greek dress seem to reappear at moments of the expression of newly won liberties for women, the attainment of a new image and place in society, a rebellion against old values and such change manifests itself through garments worn both within and without the theatre. The 'free' dancer is one who has rebelled against everything fixed and rigid and he or she belongs to this tradition of revolt. It is in this latter context rather than that of the classical ballet that Yeats's Ito belonged.

And yet the phenomenon of Nijinsky, whose own reaction against classical ballet was indicated in his choreography, cannot be discounted in a discussion of the derivation of Yeats's dancers. The Russian's innovations were very real: *The Times* of July 1913 spoke of 'The Old Ballet and the New: M. Nijinski's Revolution':

> the effort to get beyond the mere gracefulness of the traditional ballet has led M. Nijinski to 'Post-Impressionism' and the sacrifice of beauty to expressiveness, while the effort to infuse into dancing a genuinely barbaric quality of emotion has led him to follow the 'Cubists' in their return to the sculptural ideals of ages which were too rude to appreciate the languorous charm of curves.[241]

This description of 'sculptural ideals' interpreted by and through a dance invented by Nijinsky has something in common with a dance invented by Yeats, that of the Woman of the Sidhe in *The Only Jealousy of Emer* (1919):

Her mask and clothes must suggest gold or bronze or brass or silver, so that she seems more an idol than a human being. This suggestion may be repeated in her movements. Her hair, too, must keep the metallic suggestion.[242]

Yeats too gets 'beyond ... mere gracefulness' and imbues a 'barbaric quality of emotion' in the dances that he suggested for the two Salomes/Queens in *A Full Moon in March* (1935) and *The King of the Great Clock Tower* (1935), both of whom have been considered in previous chapters. All of his dances owe something to mime in that dancers' feelings in response to their part in the action of the play are being expressed: as we observed, dances in Yeats's work are vehicles of significance; they are never, as they sometimes are in ballet, mere *divertissement*. In this quality they may also be indebted to the mimed interpretations of classical music by Isadora Duncan and Maud Allan, both celebrated 'free' dancers.

If we may refer to Max Beerbohm's criticism of Loïe Fuller in 1900 (p. 182), there we rediscover the opinion:

In a ballet, one forgets the human units. But the solitary dancer on the stage must have personal importance. One wishes her to dance beautifully, to express her soul in movement, to *be* something   [Beerbohm's emphasis]

and he proceeds to berate Fuller for her 'nullity' in these respects. It is startling to realise that Beerbohm considered absent in Fuller the very qualities which Yeats admired in her: her lack of realism, the absence of the personal and, hence, the fusion of Being with Image. Where Beerbohm stresses the individuality of the woman and wishes to see interpreted in dance the peregrinations of her soul and the essence of her humanity, he was combating the contemporary vogue among solo female dancers. Many of the soloists, as we remarked earlier (p. 181), became increasingly the subject of and submissive to their machinery, their stage engineering, in order to create tableaux in which their principal role consisted less of dancing than that of manipulating the gadgets which threatened to dwarf them by transforming them into mechanics or, as Beerbohm goes on to intimate, mere dolls. (Courageous exceptions to the automata-mode must, of course, be made of Duncan, St Denis and Allan.)

And yet Yeats thoroughly approved of such dehumanisation; in the Preface to *Four Plays for Dancers* he invokes his actors to

move a little stiffly and gravely like marionettes and, I think, to
the accompaniment of drum taps.[243]

His fascination for the mask as a means of eschewing vulgar personality has already been touched on, but he adds another dimension
when he mentions, in the 'Note on the First Performance of "At the
Hawk's Well"', the source from which expressiveness must derive:

> It would be a stirring adventure for a poet and an artist, working
> together, to create once more heroic or grotesque types that, keep-
> ing always an appropriate distance from life, would seem images
> of those profound emotions that exist only in solitude and in
> silence. Nor has any one told me after a performance that they
> have missed a changing facial expression, for the mask seems to
> change with the light that falls upon it, and besides in poetical
> and tragic art, as every 'producer' knows, expression is mainly in
> those movements that are of the entire body.[244]

His suggestion, advanced in 1916, is redolent of the credo of Isadora
Duncan who also insisted on the dance being interpreted by the
whole body and there is an echo of the aims of Diaghilev too, where
a collaboration of poet, artist and, by implication, dancer, is envis-
aged. Yeats makes the last connection even more solid when he
returns to the viability of a mingling of art forms in the essay called
'A People's Theatre – a Letter to Lady Gregory' published in the
Irish Statesman in the Autumn of 1919:

> The two great energies of the world that in Shakespeare's day
> penetrated each other have fallen apart as speech and music fell
> apart at the Renaissance, and that has brought each to greater
> freedom, and we have to prepare a stage for the whole wealth of
> modern lyricism, for an art that is close to pure music, for those
> energies that would free the arts from imitation, that would ally
> acting to decoration and to the dance.[245]

This last perception is almost identical to the statement of Diaghilev
cited previously when he charted the aesthetic goals of his ballet in
its early years.

Yeats had much to say about stage decoration; it was a subject to
which he constantly returned in his writing on theatre throughout
his life and some of his thoughts have already been examined in

relation to Noh drama in Chapter 2. It is also clear, however, from a reading of Symons's views of the 1890s and his stress on the importance of artifice that the Irish poet had his mind made up early on the issue of scenery and his opinions may have been further endorsed by the later experimentations of the _Ballets Russes_, Craig and his abstract screens and Isadora Duncan with the famous blue curtains that accompanied her all over the world. In _Deirdre_ Yeats employed a pattern of forest trees: in _At the Hawk's Well_, a cloth background painted with a hawk symbol and a second piece of blue fabric to represent the well; in _The Dreaming of the Bones_, a screen or curtain with a design of mountain and sky covered the back wall, 'but the pattern must only symbolise or suggest'.[246] His constant emphasis in his writings on scenery is that it must be suggestive rather than mimetic because, as he stated as early as in _Samhain_, 1904:

> Illusion ... is impossible and should not be attempted. We should be content to suggest a scene upon a canvas, whose vertical flatness we accept and use, as the decorator of pottery accepts the roundness of a bowl or a jug. ... We can only find out the right decoration for the different types of play by experiment, but it will probably range between, on the one hand, woodlands made out of recurring pattern, or painted like old religious pictures upon a gold background, and upon the other the comparative realism of a Japanese print.[247]

Yeats not only always insisted on these attributes of his ideal stage decor but also paid an equal amount of attention to the costumes of the players, which, he declared, should harmonise with the set behind them and complete it:

> The poet cannot evoke a picture to the mind's eye if a second-rate painter has set his imagination of it before the bodily eye; ... The actor and the words put into his mouth are always the one thing that matters, and the scene should never be complete of itself until the actor is in front of it.[248]

As Serge Lifar pointed out in writing of Diaghilev and his claims of stage decoration discussed above (p. 201), the dancers were not simply framed by the brilliant decor of Bakst, Benois and later, Picasso: the stage painting entered actively, as it were, into the totality of the production and, echoing Yeats's maxim, flared into life as the dancers appeared before it. It is of course noteworthy that the poet's plea for such scenery and design appeared in the very early years of the twentieth century, some time before the Russians exploded on the scene.

All of Yeats's demands of his theatre circle around the central tenet which he shared with Arthur Symons, that of the primacy of artifice in every aspect of the play to be staged. His actors had to move stiffly like marionettes when they moved at all and to be able to chant their words in the beautiful manner in which Florence Farr spoke to a psaltery and his dancers had to be masked and to embody the qualities of archetype, myth and ritual in their stylised steps with metallic precision. In *Samhain*, (1905), Yeats stated his belief in a dimension which was greatly distantiated from that of the real:

> It is only by extravagance, by an emphasis far greater than that of life as we observe it, that we can crowd into a few minutes the knowledge of years. ... If you wish to represent character or passion upon the stage, as it is known to the friends, let us say, of your principal persons, you must be excessive, extravagant, fantastic even, in expression; and you must be this more extravagantly, more excessively, more fantastically than ever, if you wish to show character and passion as they would be known to the principal person of your play in the depths of his own mind. The greatest art symbolises not those things that we have observed so much as those things that we have experienced, and when the imaginary saint or lover or hero moves us most deeply, it is the moment when he awakens within us for an instant our own heroism, our own sanctity, our own desire.[249]

In this wish for a plane of dramatic consciousness which surpassed in its extravagance the limits of the every day, Yeats, as has been indicated by an examination of the forms of dance and the dancers who were his contemporaries, was firmly of his time. He was not so much influenced by current conceptions as already familiar with the ideas involved and, as was evidenced by his introduction to the Noh, delighted to recognise theories related to his own aesthetic beliefs born of individual strivings and personal experimentation. He began to construct his theatrical creed in the 1890s and pursued his insights long after they were fashionable in the late 1930s with his last dance plays, but the application of the 'new' ideas about drama and dance reached its culmination probably around 1912 when Huntly Carter, a prolific writer on theatre and cinema up to the 1930s, published his review of the arts, *The New Spirit in Drama and Art*. His introductory statement reflects the preoccupations not only of Yeats but of Diaghilev, of Craig and of such dancers as Loïe Fuller:

> My own idea of the first form of national drama which this country will see adopted comprises a rhythmic conception of play, player, decoration and music. This drama will be represented in a rhythmic form of theatre. Everything henceforth is to be orchestrated to produce a single but infinitely varied total effect.[250]

Of course we perceive here the echoes of the dreams of the *Symbolistes* for total theatre brought up-to-date, as they constantly were by Diaghilev until 1929 and continually promulgated by Yeats until the 1930s.

Emphasis has been placed in this chapter on music hall specialty dancers and 'free' dancers as well as on those of the ballet and such stress may be justified by an opinion of Huntly Carter of 1912 that:

> there is the added stimulus to the cultural movement in the big music-halls – the Palace, Palladium, Hippodrome, Coliseum, Alhambra and Empire. Here it is shown in the improvement in scenery and stage effects ... Besides this, the entertainments are growing more and more refined in tone; while the old chaotic scenes are being replaced by others having unity of scheme and decoration. In fact, the improvement in the music-hall is so great that the artist in search of materials for the study of stage-craft cannot afford to neglect the place any longer. Of course, he has never had a reason to neglect it, seeing there was always more art to be found in the music-hall than in the theatre.[251]

The several strands of Yeats's own personal weaving of dance, mask, music, decoration and verse into his dance plays derive too, perhaps surprisingly, from a variety of sources such as music hall, ballet, theatre and circus and from a plethora of different dance genres. This chapter has attempted an identification of some of them and of the manner in which they contributed to that particular fabric which was none the less original and individual to Yeats himself as craftsman.

NOTES

1. W. B. Yeats, *Uncollected Prose by W. B. Yeats, I: First Reviews and Articles, 1886–1896*, collected and edited by John P. Frayne (London: Macmillan, 1970). From *Speaker*, issue of 19 August 1893, pp. 284–5. Hereafter cited as *Uncollected Prose, I*.
2. Loïe Fuller, 1862–1928.
3. *Sketch*, 12 April 1893, pp. 642–3
4. *The Times*, 12 July 1893, 4e.
5. Loïe Fuller, *Fifteen Years of a Dancer's Life with Some Account of her Distinguished Friends* (London: Herbert Jenkins, 1913), originally published in French, 1908. Hereafter cited as Fuller, *Fifteen Years*.
6. The great Romantic ballerinas: Marie Taglioni (1804–84), Fanny Elssler (1810–84), Fanny Cerrito (1817–1909), Carlotta Grisi (1819–99), Lucille Grahn (1819–1907).
7. *Sketch*, 16 October 1895, p. 659.
8. *The Nautch Girl or the Rajah of Chutneypore*, Savoy, 30/6/1891–16/1/1892. Libretto by George Dance, music by Edward Solomon, costumes by Miss Fisher, Auguste, Alias, director, Charles Harris.
9. *Sketch*, 8 February 1893, p. 86.
10. *Ibid.*, 2 April 1893, p. 40.
11. *Ibid.*, 2 August 1893, p. 38.
12. *Ibid.*, 24 January 1894, p. 688.
13. John Hollingshead, manager of the Alhambra, then the Gaiety (1827–1904).
14. Armand Vestris (1786–1825), French dancer and choreographer, son of Auguste Vestris, worked mainly in London 1809–16.
15. *Era*, 28 February 1903, p. 17.
16. Alan Hyman, *The Gaiety Years* (London: Cassell, 1975), p. 13.
17. J. E. Crawford Flitch, *Modern Dancing & Dancers* (London: Grant Richards, 1912), p. 85. Hereafter cited as Crawford Flitch.
18. Ibid., pp. 71–2.
19. Ibid., p. 73.
20. Arthur Symons (1865–1945).
21. *The Times*, 29 April 1919, 9a, and 25 August 1919, 8d.
22. *Collected Poems*, p. 234.
23. Mallarmé, *Oeuvres Complètes*, 'Crayonné au théâtre', p. 306.
24. A. Symons, 'The Primrose Dance', *Sketch*, 4 October 1893, p. 516.
25. *Uncollected Prose, I*, 'That Subtle Shade' – a review of Symons' *London Nights*, p. 374.
26. Jane Avril (1868–1943).
27. *Uncollected Prose, II*, p. 40.
28. C.f. 'There is less pleasure in it if you get paid.' Peter Leslie, *A Hard Act to Follow: A Music Hall Review* (New York & London: Paddington Press, 1978), p. 93. Hereafter cited as Leslie.
29. Arthur Symons, *Poems*, vol. I: *London Nights* (London: Martin Secker, 1924), p. 190. Hereafter cited as *London Nights*.
30. *Ibid.*, 'Prologue', p. 170.
31. *Ibid.*, 'To a Dancer', p. 171.

32. Fletcher, p. 54.
33. Grille-d'Egout (fl. 1893).
34. La Goulue, stage name of Louise Weber (1865–1929).
35. Nini Patte-en-l'Air (fl. 1893).
36. Caroline, La Belle Otero, Spanish dancer and singer, debut 1889 (1868–n.d.)
37. *Sketch*, 5 April 1893, pp. 608–10.
38. *St James's Gazette*, 16 December 1892, p. 5.
39. *Sketch*, 28 June 1893, p. 461.
40. *Explorations*, p. 192.
41. *Ibid.*, p. 166.
42. *Sketch*, 3 October 1894, p. 557.
43. Katti Lanner (1829–1908). Dancer, choreographer and ballet mistress at the Empire, 1887–1897, with occasional returns afterwards. Austrian by birth, daughter of composer Joseph Lanner.
44. *Sketch*, 4 October 1893, p. 488. I am indebted to John Stokes for directing my attention to these reviews of Symons's for 1892–1895.
45. *Sketch*, 20 December 1893.
46. *Ibid.*, 7 August 1895.
47. *Explorations*, p. 167.
48. *Ibid.*, pp. 176–7.
49. *Ibid.*, p. 370: 'Fighting the Waves', Introduction.
50. *Letters*, p. 767.
51. W. B. Yeats, *Four Plays for Dancers* (London: Macmillan, 1921), p. vi. Hereafter cited as *Four Plays*.
52. Fletcher, p. 47.
53. Leslie, p. 92.
54. Symons, quoted by Leslie, p. 94.
55. Montorgeuil, quoted by Leslie, p. 91.
56. Raymond Rudorff, *Belle Epoque* (London: Hamish Hamilton, 1972), quoted by Leslie, p. 92 and note p. 248.
57. *Star*, 22 January 1894, 'A Famous Dancer'.
58. Symons, *Seven Arts*, 'The World as Ballet', p. 246.
59. *RI*, p. 92.
60. *Ibid.*, p. 99.
61. *Sketch*, 4 October 1893, p. 484.
62. *Ibid.*, 24 January 1894, p. 726.
63. 'Poet and Dancer', p. 27.
64. *Era*, 21 February 1903, p. 23.
65. *Ibid.*, 13 June 1903, p. 19.
66. *Ibid.*, 20 June 1903, p. 19.
67. *Ibid.*, 3 October 1903, p. 21.
68. *Ibid.*, 6 August 1904, p. 21.
69. *Ibid.*, 6 August 1904, p. 21.
70. *Saturday Review*, 17 November 1900, p. 616.
71. *Era*, 26 March 1904, p. 21.
72. *Ibid.*, 2 January 1904, p. 27.
73. Adeline Genée (1878–1970).
74. Anna Pavlova (1881–1931), Tamara Karsavina (1885–1978).

75. *Era*, 28 March 1903, p. 21.
76. *Ibid.*, 23 May 1903, p. 21.
77. *Ibid.*, 10 September 1904, p. 21.
78. Sergei Diaghilev (1872–1929).
79. *Era*, 7 January 1905, p. 21.
80. Max Beerbohm, 'A Note on the Ballet', *Saturday Review*, 19 May 1906, quoted in Ivor Guest, *Adeline Genée*. *A Lifetime of Ballet under Six Reigns* (London: Alan & Charles Black, 1958), p. 79. Hereafter cited as Genée.
81. Mikhail Mordkin (1880–1944).
82. Genée, p. 121.
83. Crawford Flitch, pp. 181–2.
84. Vaslav Nijinsky (1888–1950).
85. Pavel Gerdt (1844–1917).
86. Adolph Bolm (1884–1951).
87. Isadora Duncan (1878–1927).
88. François Delsarte (1811–1871). Having analysed the gestures and expressions of the human body, he formulated his system of teaching the control of body movements. Pioneer of modern dance who influenced Dalcroze and Ted Shawn among others. Taken from *The Concise Oxford Dictionary of Ballet*, Horst Koegler (London: Oxford University Press,1977), p. 152. Hereafter cited as Koegler.
89. *The Times*, 17 March 1900, llf.
90. *Ibid.*, 6 July 1900.
91. Victor Seroff, *The Real Isadora* (New York: The Dial Press, 1971), pp. 44–5. Hereafter cited as Seroff.
92. *Ibid.*, p. 86.
93. Michel Fokine (1880–1942).
94. *Era*, 14 February 1903, p. 24.
95. *The Times*, 6 July 1914, 6a/b.
96. Stanislavsky quoted in Seroff, p. 109.
97. Rimsky-Korsakov quoted in Seroff, p. 118.
98. *Four Plays*, p. vi.
99. Francis Steegmuller, *Your Isadora: The Love Story of Isadora Duncan and Gordon Craig* (New York: Macmillan, 1974), p. 175. Hereafter cited as Steegmuller.
100. Alexander Bland, *A History of Ballet and Dance in the Western World* (London: Barrie & Jenkins, 1976), p. 114.
101. Tamara Karsavina, *Theatre Street: The Reminiscences of Tamara Karsavina* (1930; rpt. London: Dance Books, 1981), pp. 197–202. Hereafter cited as Karsavina.
102. Steegmuller, p. 395.
103. John Quinn, close friend of the Yeats family; New York lawyer and collector of modern art (1870–1924).
104. Steegmuller, p. 396.
105. *Letters*, p. 608.
106. W. B. Yeats, *Essays and Introductions* (London: Macmillan, 1961), p. 527. Hereafter cited as *Essays and Introductions*.
107. *Four Plays*, p. v.
108. Maud Allan (1883–1956).

109. Quoted in Seroff, p. 125.
110. *The Times*, 10 March 1908, 5e.
111. *Ibid.*, 23 July 1908, 13e.
112. Maud Allan, *My Life and Dancing* (London: Everett, 1908).
113. *Letters*, 7 August 1934, pp. 826–7.
114. *Self-Portrait*, p. 297.
115. *Ibid.*, 4 August 1919, p. 319.
116. *Era*, 28 March 1903, p. 21.
117. *Ibid.*, 23 May 1903, p. 21.
118. Lydia Kyasht (1885–1959).
119. John and Roberta Lazzarini, *Pavlova: Repertoire of a Legend* (London: Collier Macmillan, 1980), footnote, p. 211. Hereafter cited as Lazzarini.
120. Mathilde Kschessinskaya (1872–1971).
121. Olga Preobrajenskaya (1870–1962).
122. Ludmilla Schollar (1888–1978).
123. George Kiaksht (1873–1936).
124. Alexandra Baldina (1885–n.d.).
125. Ekaterina Geltzer (1876–1962).
126. Vassili Tikhomirov (1876–1956).
127. Phyllis Bedells (1893–1985).
128. 'Poet and Dancer', p. 1.
129. *Ibid.*, p. 1.
130. Serge Lifar, *Serge de Diaghilev* (Monaco: Editions du Rocher, 1954), p. 152. Hereafter cited as Lifar.
131. Alexander Benois (1870–1960).
132. Leon Bakst, originally Lev Semuilovich Rosenberg (1866–1924).
133. Serge Lifar (1905–1986).
134. Lifar, p. 167.
135. Lifar, p. 198.
136. To Lady Gregory, 30 May 1911. I am deeply indebted to John Kelly for this and the following information from his collection of Yeats's unpublished letters.
137. To Lady Gregory, 8 March 1913.
138. Bronislava Nijinska, sister of Vaslav Nijinsky (1891–1972).
139. Marie Rambert, originally Cyvia then Miriam Ramberg (1888–1982). Her father had his name changed to Ramberg from Rambam by his father.
140. Nesta Macdonald (ed.), *Diaghilev Observed by Critics in England and the United States 1911–1929* (New York: Dance Horizons, 1975), p. 74. Hereafter cited as Macdonald.
141. *Explorations*, p. 256.
142. Information gleaned severally from Lifar, p. 313 and S. L. Grigoriev, *The Diaghilev Ballet, 1909–1929*, translated and edited by Vera Bowen (1953; rpt. Harmondsworth: Penguin, 1960), p. 268. Hereafter cited as Grigoriev.
143. Vera Fokina (1886–1958).
144. Enrico Cecchetti, celebrated ballet teacher (1850–1928).
145. Cyril Beaumont, *The Diaghilev Ballet in London: A Personal Record* (London: Putnam, 1940), p. 329.

146. Lazzarini, p. 13.
147. Grigoriev, p. 33.
148. *The Times*, 18 July 1910, 12d.
149. The ballet in which Nijinsky made his exit by a giant leap through the window.
150. *The Times*, 4 November 1911, quoted in Macdonald, p. 52.
151. I am indebted to Martin Wright for this observation.
152. *Daily News*, 22 June 1911, quoted in Macdonald, p. 32.
153. *Ibid.*, 22 June 1911, quoted by Macdonald, p. 34.
154. *Self-Portrait*, pp. 174–5.
155. Karsavina, p. 198.
156. *Self-Portrait*, 12 May 1912, pp. 176–7.
157. *Sunday Times*, 23 June 1912, quoted by Macdonald, pp. 67 and 69.
158. *Self-Portrait*, letter to R.N.R. Holst, Autumn 1913, p. 184.
159. *The Times*, 18 February 1913, quoted in Richard Buckle, *Nijinsky* (London: Weidenfeld and Nicolson, 1971; rpt. 1974), p. 275. Hereafter cited as Buckle.
160. *Daily Mail*, 18 February 1913, quoted in Buckle, p. 275.
161. *The Standard*, 15 February 1913, quoted by Macdonald, p. 80.
162. *Explorations*, pp. 176–7.
163. *Self-Portrait*, p. 183.
164. Boris Kochno, *Diaghilev and the Ballet Russes*, translated from the French by Adrienne Foulke (New York: Harper & Row, 1970), p. 88.
165. Emile Jaques-Dalcroze, born Jakob Dalkes (1865–1950). Swiss music teacher and theoretician who developed a system of training musical sensibility through the translation of rhythm into bodily movements – Eurhythmics. This continued the work of Delsarte in the evolution of modern dance. Insistence was placed on self-expression and imagination in the creation of movements. The Institute for Applied Rhythm was established in Hellerau in 1911 and there were trained many of the dancers who later became prominent in the German modern dance movement, including Wigman and Holm. Rambert also studied with him. The London based school opened in 1914. (Taken from Koegler, p. 279.)
166. Théophile Gautier (1811–1872). One of the leading figures of the French Romantic movement, he exerted enormous influence on the course of ballet in the Paris of the late 1830s and 1840s as the critic of *La Presse*.
167. Deirdre Priddin, *The Art of the Dance in French Literature, from Théophile Gautier to Paul Valéry* (London: Adam & Charles Black, 1952), p. 41.
168. Buckle, p. 217.
169. 'Certain Noble Plays', p. 236.
170. *Daily Mail*, 1 July 1913, quoted in Macdonald, p. 95.
171. *Letters*, p. 587; *Self-Portrait*, pp. 196–7 and 199.
172. *Self-Portrait*, 15 June 1914, p. 199.
173. *Ibid.*, 21 July 1914, p. 204.
174. Léonide Massine, originally Leonid Fedorovitch Miassine (1895–1979).
175. José Maria Sert (1876–1945), Spanish painter and designer.
176. *Self-Portrait*, 25 March 1915, p. 233.

177. *Ibid.*, pp. 234 and 237.
178. *Ibid.*, October 1917, p. 283.
179. Lydia Lopokova (1891–1981).
180. *Self-Portrait*, August 1918, pp. 301–2.
181. *Ibid.*, p. 312.
182. To Lady Gregory, 4 November 1915.
183. To Lady Gregory, 7 February 1913.
184. To Lady Gregory, 13 October 1915.
185. To J. B. Yeats, 14 March 1916.
186. *Letters*, p. 669.
187. Charles B. Cochran (1872–1951).
188. Charles B. Cochran, *The Secrets of a Showman* (London: Heinemann, 1925), pp. 326 and 345. Hereafter cited as *Showman*.
189. I am indebted to Melanie Christoudia of the Theatre Museum, Covent Garden, for discovering the programme of *The League of Notions*.
190. Grace Christie, active during the 1920s.
191. Ruth St Denis (1877 or 1878 or 1880–1968).
192. Koegler, p. 459 and Suzanne Shelton, *Divine Dancer: A Biography of Ruth St Denis* (New York: Doubleday, 1986), pp. 106 and 110.
193. *The Dancing Times & Social Review*, founded 1894, December 1934, p. 257. Hereafter cited as *DancingTimes*.
194. Mata Hari (1877–1917).
195. Ida Rubinstein (ca.1885–1960). Studied recitation and mime and inspired by Duncan. Fokine choreographed *Salome* for her. Member of Diaghilev's company 1909–1911 and much admired for her exceptional beauty as Fokine's Cléopâtre and Zobeide. Not a classically trained ballet dancer. (Taken from Koegler, p. 456.)
196. Buckle, p. 224.
197. Benda. 'Mr. Benda, the Polish–American painter (not the French artist who has designed costumes for Charlot) lent me his wonderful masks, which were so effectively used by Miss Grace Christie' (Cochran in *Showman*, p. 347).
198. Rita Lee: 'Miss Rita Lee … is one of the most brilliant of our dancers. When she toured North and South America with Mme. Pavlova she was so successful that she was acclaimed as La Pavlovita … Miss Lee, by the way, was discovered by Mr. Charles B. Cochran during his visit to the States, and she is the only English girl of the company he gathered there' (*Daily Mirror*, 1 January 1921; taken from the Cochran Scrapbooks).
199. Harcourt Algeranoff (1903–67).
200. Harcourt Algeranoff, *My Years with Pavlova* (London: Heinemann, 1957), p. 70. Hereafter cited as Algeranoff.
201. I am indebted to Martin Wright for this information which he discovered in Reginald St Johnston, *A History of Dancing* (London: Simpkin, Marshall, Hamilton, Kent, 1906), p. 112.
202. Denishawn dance company formed by Ruth St Denis and Ted Shawn (1891–1972) in 1915. Disbanded in 1932. Shawn's All-Male Dancers' Group established in 1935. (Koegler, p. 480.)

203. Shigeo Ogura, 'Ballet in Japan. A history of fifty years', in *Ballet Today*, March–April, 1970, p. 18. English version by Don Kenny.
204. Algeranoff, p. 110.
205. *Ibid.*, p. 77.
206. *Ibid.*, p. 111.
207. Keith Money, *Anna Pavlova: Her Life and Art* (London: Collins, 1982), p. 292.
208. *The Play Pictorial*, Vol. XXXVIII. January 1921, p. 76.
209. Helen Caldwell, *Michio Ito: The Dancer and His Dances* (Berkeley: University of California Press, 1977), pp. 70 and 73. Hereafter cited as Caldwell.
210. John Murray Anderson (1886–1954).
211. The Cochran Scrapbooks, Theatre Museum, Covent Garden.
212. *Dancing Times*, March 1930, p. 678.
213. Michio Ito (1893–1961).
214. *New York Tribune*, 7 December 1916, cited in Caldwell, p. 167, note 11.
215. Caldwell, p. 86.
216. Quoted by Caldwell, p. 42.
217. Caldwell, p. 45.
218. *CP*, p. 703.
219. Caldwell, pp. 10–11, quoting Yeats, *Essays and Introductions*, pp. 522 and 509; 'cf. Works of art are always begotten by previous works of art'.
220. Ninette de Valois, originally Edris Stannus (1898–), *Come Dance with Me: A Memoir 1898–1956* (London: Hamish Hamilton, 1959), p. 86. Hereafter cited as de Valois.
221. *CP*, p. 694.
222. de Valois, p. 86.
223. Frederick Ashton (1904–88).
224. I am indebted to Martin Wright for this information.
225. *RI*, p. 82.
226. *CP*, p. 66.
227. *A Vision*, p. 135.
228. Marian Hannah Winter, *The Pre-Romantic Ballet* (London: Pitman, 1974), p. 1. Hereafter cited as Winter.
229. Jean Baptiste Lully, originally Gambattista Lulli (1632–1687). Italian–French dancer, composer, conductor and supervisor in the Court of Louis XIV. Appeared as a dancer with the King in several ballets. Supervisor of royal music in 1661 and director of the Académie Royal de Musique in 1672. Collaborated with Racine and Molière. (From Koegler, pp. 336–7.)
230. Pierre, Abbé Perrin (1620–1675).
231. Francis Sparshott, *Off the Ground: First Steps to a Philosophical Consideration of the Dance* (New Jersey: Princeton University Press, 1988), p. 48, note 33. Hereafter cited as Sparshott.
232. Crawford Flitch, p. 29.
233. Marie-Anne de Cupis de Camargo (1710–1770).
234. Buckle, p. 367.
235. La Belle Espagnole (fl. 1785–1796). *Star*, 20 June 1793.

236. Martin Wright kindly provided this information from Philip H. Highfill, Jr, Kalman A. Burnim & Edward A. Langhans, *A Biographical Dictionary of Actors, Actresses, Musicians, Dancers, Managers, and Other Stage Personnel in London, 1660–1800* (Southern Illinois: Carbondale & Edwardsville, 1978), pp. 290–1.
237. Winter, p. 175.
238. Ivor Guest, *The Romantic Ballet in England: Its Development, Fulfilment and Decline* (London: Phoenix, 1954; rpt. with new introduction, Pitman, 1972), p. 14.
239. *Star*, 3 July 1793.
240. *Ibid.*, 5 June 1793.
241. *The Times*, 5 July 1913, 11d.
242. *CP*, p. 291.
243. *Four Plays*, p. v.
244. *Ibid.*, p. 87.
245. *Explorations*, p. 258.
246. *Four Plays*, p. 53.
247. *Explorations*, p. 178.
248. *Ibid.*, p. 179.
249. *Ibid.*, pp. 195–6.
250. Huntly Carter, *The New Spirit in Drama and Art* (London: Frank Palmer, 1912), p. vi. Hereafter cited as Carter. (He also produced *A Sketch Plan for a Cine Museum for London*, 1908; he edited *Women's Suffrage & Militancy*, 1912; he wrote on: *The Theatre of Max Reinhardt*, 1914; *The New Theatre and Cinema of Soviet Russia*, 1924; *The New Spirit in the European Theatre 1914–1924: A Comparative Study of the Changes Effected by the War and Revolution*, 1925; *The New Spirit in the Russian Theatre, 1917–28: And a Sketch of the Russian Kinema and Radio 1914–28*, 1929; *The New Spirit of the Cinema*, 1930, as well as numerous other publications.)
251. Carter, p. 27.

4

Dialogue into Dance: The Plays of Yeats

Since motion and not language is truthful, we have accordingly perverted our powers of comprehension.[1]

It must ... be conceded that there are moments in great drama for which words prove an inadequate medium for the expression of emotion. ... At such moments ... the character should dance. ... Where words become artificial and unnatural, movement does not, because it can never be so. ...[2]

In a letter to Carl Burckhardt of 1928 Hofmannsthal outlined the plan of a comedy never completed in which one character, a notorious liar, decides to become a dancer and 'says he has chosen this profession because he adores the truth, and dancing is the only profession in which there is nothing but truth'.[3]

I promise a dance. I wanted a dance because where there are no words there is less to spoil.[4]

The earliest of the above pronouncements on the respective advantages of dance over words in the expression or articulation of 'truth' is the first one and it dates from 1908 and the initial French publication of Loïe Fuller's autobiography from which it derives. But the debate is older than that and, at the same time, more recent, because, as I shall endeavour to demonstrate, it persists today among those who meditate upon dance and language – critics, philosophers and dancers themselves. The belief in the primacy and purity of movement over the corruptness and only approximate adequacy of language for conveying meanings of a certain order is a legacy in its most immediate form both of *Symbolisme* and its enquiry into theories of the relationship between words and the realities that they attempt to express in poetry and of

Nietzsche. The latter, in *Also sprach Zarathustra* of 1884, stated in 'Das Grablied' that 'Nur im Tanze weiß ich der höchsten Dinge Gleichniß zu reden',[5] and Mallarmé is concerned to 'Donner un sens plus pur aux mots de la tribu'[6] (1887) and discovers that, as we noted in Chapter 1, dance could be spoken of in the same way as poetry. But Mallarmé's attraction to dance rested on the early belief – he later subtly changed his thinking on this – that it was not a receptacle or purveyor of meaning. As A. G. Lehmann points out:

> Mallarmé thinks that ballet can be innocent of meaning, simply gesture, and pins his faith in it:
>
> 'La Danse seule capable, par son écriture sommaire, de traduire le fugace et le soudain jusqu'à l'Idée – pareille vision comprend tout, absolument tout le spectacle future' –
>
> but fails to see that if this gesture embodies 'un état-d'âme', as by his admission it does, then it cannot be but that it has meaning, if only in quite embryonic form.[7]

This question – as to whether or not dance has meaning – is a crucial one and is obviously raised as a result of the very old debate: can dance be considered as a language? From the beginnings of philosophy, thinkers have likened dance to language, but they have not stipulated what those cited above argue, that dance was a *preferable* form of language to words. Yet indeed it is a well-established contention that dance may be a language in its own right because, despite Mallarmé's fondly cherished belief (and that of Yeats discussed below), dance may be a purveyor of meaning.

Plato, in Book 7 of *The Laws* in which he meditates on dance, draws a similar parallel between it and language and states quite clearly, brooking no objection:

> the more composed the man's temperament, and the tougher he has been trained to be, the more deliberate are his movements; on the other hand, if he's a coward and has not been trained to show restraint, his actions are wilder and his postures change more violently. And in general, when a man uses his voice to talk or sing, he finds it very difficult to keep his body still. This is the origin of the whole art of dancing: *the gestures that express what one is saying*.[8]   [my emphasis]

Aristotle, in his *Poetics*, also intimated that dance referred to life outside itself which it imitated and interpreted:

> Rhythm alone without tune is employed by dancers in their representation, for by means of rhythmical gestures they represent both character and experiences and actions.[9]

André Levinson, in an article of 1927, examines theories of dance from Aristotle onwards and discovers that the latter's dictum here quoted was a 'fatal text'[10] which

> assigns to the dance an aim *outside of itself* and creates confusion between saltatory motion and expressive or descriptive gesture, using the dance as a substitute for words. The dance ceases to be a thing in itself. Aristotle declares that it interprets and imitates life. Lucian repeats his dictum. For the soaring of the dancer through space, for the inherent beauty of this divine sport, the philosophers substitute the concrete excellencies of the sign language. From Plutarch to Cassiodorus, there is little mention of anything but 'speaking hands' and 'eloquent fingers'.[11]   [Levinson's emphasis]

We may suspect that Levinson in discussing Aristotle is making a fuss over a relationship which is simply metaphorical – 'dance is language' – but when we proceed to read in the dance theories of the sixteenth century, the *Orchesography* of Canon Thoinot Arbeau, that dance is 'a speech in dumbshow' which the dancer executes with 'her own feet'[12] (1588) and that Arbeau states quite openly, much to Levinson's chagrin: 'but first and foremost, all experts agree that the dance is a sort of silent rhetoric',[13] we discover a continuum in the modes of thinking about dance that reaches up to the theoreticians of today. Its force appears to be both stronger than and distinct from the merely metaphorical.

In 1760 one of the most celebrated writers on dance, Jean-Georges Noverre,[14] used similar terms with which to consider ballet:

> Il faut conclure de cette comparaison que la Danse renferme en elle tout ce qui est nécessaire au beau langage, & qu'il ne suffit pas d'en connôitre l'Alphabet. Qu'un homme de génie arrange les lettres, forme & lie les mots, elle cessera d'être muette, elle *parlera* avec autant de force que d'energie. (Lettre II)[15]   [my emphasis]

He employs the same term in Lettre IX:

> je demande plus de variété & d'expression dans les bras; je
> voudrais les voir *parler* avec plus d'energie.[16]   [my emphasis]

In notional terms it is not a far jump from these concepts to recent
work by Ann Hutchinson on Labanotation,[17] although the leap in
time is considerable:

> Movement means change and to produce change an action of
> some sort must occur. In the grammar of movement, these actions
> are the verbs. The parts of the body that move are the nouns. How
> the action is done, the degree of change or the manner of perform-
> ance, is described by the adverbs.[18]

This exercise of equating dance movement to grammatical labels
seems to me to be a highly dubious one, but I cite the work simply to
reinforce and emphasise the manner in which dance has for centuries
not only been linked to language through metaphor but also viewed
as a language in its own right. Thus Fuller and Gray, Hofmannsthal
and Yeats, in their preference for dance to words, were perhaps only
substituting one linguistic system for another. This claim may not be
too fanciful if we take Chomsky's definition of language:

> To determine whether music, or mathematics, or the communica-
> tion system of bees, or the system of ape calls, is a *language*, we
> must first be told what counts as a language. If by language is
> meant *human language*, the answer will be trivially negative in all
> of these cases. If by language we mean *symbolic system*, or *system of
> communication*, then all of these examples will be languages, as
> will numerous other systems.[19]   [Chomsky's emphasis]

Dance is certainly a 'symbolic system', the unit of which is gesture,
but if we refer to some characteristics of language, such as synonym-
ity or translatability, then it is clear that such conditions are not fulfilled by dance. The situation is that, while certain of the most salient
features of language are upheld by dance, others are not. For example:

1. A language is a system of communicating information between
   ourselves and others. The information may be about the social
   or physical environment, or it may be about ourselves.

2. Language serves other purposes of communication. It is used in non-informational and not purely informational social interactions: to greet, question, command, joke, offend, abuse, intimidate and so on.

3. ...

4. Implicitly, the above talk of language has been restricted to the 'natural' languages of humans; for example, English or Swahili. Such languages are not our only communication systems; think of flag signals or 'body language', for example.[20]

These demands devised to answer a definition of 'language' can arguably be met by dance, while other stipulations cannot. But, I would suggest, the most essential characteristic of all is one already touched upon and which is still pondered over by numerous theoreticians of dance today, namely whether or not dance has a semantic content. If, as we have established, dance can communicate, then the thing communicated is surely 'meaning'? Such a statement forces the consideration of two possible responses: firstly, that dance meanings are somehow different in kind and quality from those derived from language – the very position taken by the writers quoted at the outset and, secondly, that, speaking purely linguistically of meaning, the claim may be simplistic. While it is accepted that pantomimic dance relates a narrative and that expressive dance can transmit emotion, it is perhaps less appropriate to talk of a dance's 'meaning' than of its 'function'. Thus, the communication of pride or anger by means of dance could be seen as its purpose or outcome rather than its signification. The question is a vexed one, though none the less as closely scrutinised today as throughout dance history. Because it is so, this chapter will now consider three strands of thought: whether dance indeed conveys meaning, whether dance is a language and, thirdly, in reference to Yeats's plays, how dialogue is there replaced by dance and the interrelationship between the two. It will then conclude on a discussion of a dimension so far scantly treated in this study, that of the plays in performance.

Mallarmé, as previously observed on page (p. 6), yoked dance and poetry together in his manner of discussing them:

A savoir que la danseuse *n'est pas une femme qui danse*, pour ces motifs juxtaposés qu'elle *n'est pas une femme*, mais une métaphore résumant un des aspects élémentaires de notre forme, glaive, coupe, fleur etc., et *qu'elle ne danse pas*, suggérant par le prodige de raccourcis ou d'élans, avec une écriture corporelle ce qu'il faudrait des paragraphes en prose dialoguée autant que descriptive, pour exprimer, dans la rédaction: poème dégagé de tout appareil du scribe.[21] [Mallarmé's emphasis]

The dancer is thus perceived in terms of language: she is a symbol, a metaphor, whose body 'writes', and yet she may easily be the unconscious revealer of something which she symbolises without understanding what it is. She must be deciphered by the onlooker. Carol Barko in an article on Mallarmé called 'The Dancer and the Becoming of Language' takes up this point:

The whole value of the dancer's presence as an active sign is that she joyously confirms the operations of poetry as an act of self-creation and self-reading – 'preuve de nos tresors' (296). For the only meaning of the process that she transmits is to be found in 'le regard' of the spectator who, like the reader, recognizes in this illusion the movement of his own reverie and desire. The power to reveal, and conceal, that Mallarmé accords to the dancer as sign is summed up in the lyrical passage concluding 'Ballets' where the poet counsels the fictitious spectator/reader (ourselves) who asks what the *meaning* of the dancer's gestures can be, to read her movement as a Sign.
     ... alors, par un commerce tout paraît son sourire verser le secret, sans tarder elle te livre à travers le voîle dernier qui toujours reste, la nudité de tes concepts et silencieusement écrira ta vision à la façon d'un Signe, qu'elle est.[22] [Barko's emphasis]

From the viewer's perspective the dancer must be decoded by a 'reading' of her gestures, but whence do those gestures derive? Mary Sirridge and Adina Armelagos writing in the same year as Carol Barko, 1977, in *The Journal of Aesthetics and Art Criticism* correct a common misconception in their article 'The In's [sic] and Out's [sic] of Dance: Expression as an Aspect of Style':

The dancer's movements are learned as movements – not as gestures for articulating emotion. The head follows the backward extended arm, not because that pose does or can express regret, but because any other combination would violate line or sequence constraints. ... There are ideals of position and ideals of consonance, but none of them, from the dancer's point of view, has anything to do with the expression of feeling or emotion.[23]

These writers thus put paid to the prevalent and accepted notion that the dancer learns gesture in order to convey or express feelings: rather, Sirridge and Armelagos argue, similarly to Mallarmé, that those watching invest the movement with meaning. Thus, the dance audience 'reads' the dancer and the alphabet employed is that of gesture, of the potency of which the performer of it may very well be unaware. Sirridge and Armelagos draw attention to the fact that even in the Martha Graham system, 'the gesture functions to point to a particular emotion only in context'[24] and they quote Leroy Leatherman in his book on Graham, *Portrait of the Lady as an Artist* (1966), where the same method was used by both the American dancer and classical ballet:

The technique is taught devoid of verbal content; no movement or series of movements has meaning. Communication occurs when the technique once mastered is put to use in the dramatic situation and there every movement must be meaningful.[25]

So the many among us who believed that gesture was learnt as code, a means of expressing emotion, are shown to be suffering under a misconception and yet we may be forgiven as we find ourselves in very good company. Suzanne Langer, one of the first philosophers of this century to address the phenomenon of dance, figures briefly in a discussion of aesthetic theory in Kermode's *Romantic Image*. There her definition of the Symbol in art is examined and the manner in which she claims that it starts from music and from thence moves towards poetic discourse.[26] Langer stated in her study of aesthetics, *Feeling and Form* (1953):

The most widely accepted view is that the essence of dance is musical: the dancer expresses in gesture what he feels as the emotional content of the music which is the efficient and supportive cause of his dance. He reacts as we all would if we were not inhibited; his dance is self-expression, and is beautiful because the stimulus is beautiful. He may really be said to be 'dancing with music'.[27]

She goes on to elucidate the function and nature of gesture:

> *Gesture* is the basic abstraction whereby the dance illusion is made and organized.
>   Gesture is vital movement: to the one who performs it, it is known very precisely as a kinetic experience, i.e. as action, and somewhat more vaguely by sight, as an effect. To others it appears as a visible motion, but not a motion of things, sliding or waving or rolling around – it is *seen and understood* as vital movement. So it is always at once suggestive and objective, personal and public, willed (or evoked) and perceived.
>   In actual life gestures function as signals or symptoms of our desires, intentions, expectations, demands, and feelings. Because they can be consciously controlled, they may also be elaborated, just like vocal sounds, into a system of assigned and combinable *symbols*, a genuine discursive language. ... But whether a gesture has linguistic meaning or not, it is always spontaneously express-ive too, by virtue of its form: it is free and big, or nervous and tight, quick or leisurely, etc., according to the psychological condi-tion of the person who makes it. This self-expressive aspect is akin to the tone of voice in speech.[28]   [Langer's emphasis]

I should like here to pursue this debate by theoreticians on dance a little more closely because the link between gesture and language is common and will, I believe, lead us back to that most important concept of whether dance has meaning. Again, at this point, the views of Fuller, Gray, Hofmannsthal and Yeats himself come into focus because, if dance is somehow a 'truer' purveyor of meaning than mere words, then we should be able to pinpoint from whence that meaning derives. To do so we must obviously consider gesture further.

Langer remarks astutely that gesture in dance does not spring from real emotion, as many theorists and audiences believe, but from imagined feeling. This is an important distinction to draw:

> It is *imagined feeling* that governs the dance, not real emotional conditions. If one passes over the spontaneous emotion theory with which almost every book on the dance begins, one quickly comes to the evidence for this contention. Dance gesture is not real gesture, but virtual. The bodily movement, of course, is real enough; but *what makes it emotive gesture*, i.e. its spontaneous

origin in what Laban calls a 'feeing-thought-motion,' is illusory, so the movement is 'gestic'only within the dance. It is *actual movement*, but *virtual self-expression*.[29]   [Langer's emphasis]

We may note that Rudolf von Laban constantly insisted, however, that gesture sprang from *actual* feeling: 'Suddenly, from some single point, the germ of sorrow or joy unfolds in a person. Conception is everything. All things evolve from the power of gesture, and find their resolution in it.'[30] But Langer's distinction still stands:

In the dance, the actual and virtual aspects of gesture are mingled in complex ways. The movements, of course, are actual; they spring from an intention, and are in this sense actual gestures; but they are not the gestures they seem to be, because they seem to spring from feeling, as indeed they do not. The dancer's actual gestures are used to create a semblance of self-expression, and are thereby transformed into virtual spontaneous movement, or virtual gesture. The emotion in which such gesture begins is virtual, a dance element that turns the whole movement into dance-gesture.[31]

A fellow-American, Marshall Cohen of the Philosophy Department at the City University of New York, has in more recent years taken Suzanne Langer to task for her charting of gestic expressiveness in dance in the manner just examined. In a paper given in the summer of 1979 at the American Dance Festival on the campus of Duke University, Durham, North Carolina and entitled 'Primitivism, Modernism, & Dance Theory', Cohen criticises Langer's view of 'virtual' gesture in the following way:

Langer supposes that real gestures are expressions of emotion. She thinks, correctly, that dance theorists (especially theorists of modern dance) have often falsely supposed dances are really expressions of the dancer's (or of the choreographer's) emotions. But she wrongly supposes the proper way to correct this mistake is to declare these expressions of emotion only apparent or illusory. No doubt, this solution appeals to her because, in her view, dance like every other art must present some illusion or other. Why not suppose, then, that dance creates, if not the reality, then the illusion that emotion is being expressed? Mrs. Langer is undoubtedly correct in thinking dancers do not always express emotions, but it is important to insist that they do not always give the impression of expressing them either. Mrs. Langer has merely sophisticated and attenuated the expression theory of dance. She ought to have rejected it outright.[32]

She should also, according to her compatriots at that conference in 1979, have discarded the theory to which, as we have seen, she was certainly not the only subscriber, that of dance as language. They will go so far as to concede that dance is a language in Chomsky's sense, in that it is a symbolic system and that gesture is its unit of meaning, and they all agree that this concept of meaning in dance is a very problematical one. But they no longer, as did their eminent predecessors, speak in terms of the 'language of dance' except when they slip inadvertently into the metaphorical mention of dance 'vocabulary'. Of course, it is easy to apprehend meaning if the dance is narrative, but the story-line alone is not responsible for the conveying of meaning:

> While it is true that some dances have meaning in the sense that they employ dramatic situations, many dances do not employ such narrative technique. And even more important, it seems such narrative elements do not form the crucial vehicle by means of which dance communicates. ... One thing upon which critics and dancers seem to agree is that dance, while it does manage to communicate with its audience, does so in a non-linguistic or non-discursive manner. It is the sense of movement, rather than words, that is the primary mode of dance signification. Like music and abstract art, dance employs as elements of its 'language' items that in themselves are not usually thought of as having meaning. A movement of the arm is no more tied to a specific meaning than a C-sharp or the color yellow, although all of these can acquire a type of meaning in a specific context such as that provided by works of art.[33]

Thomas Wartenberg, here presenting a conference paper called 'Is Dance Elitist?', emphasises his point that dance is neither a language nor a system of symbolic representation analogous to a language since such a view, as we noted above, would only be true of dance drama and not of the more abstract forms of dance. Instead he explores dance's conveyal of meaning in the following terms:

I wish to claim that dance selects a certain range of motions as its basic vocabulary of movement and that this very selection process is the basis of dance's conveyal of meaning. For by its selection, dance presents us with an idealized version of human movement. We see, in dance, a human body or human bodies moving in certain specific ways. These manners of movement are ideal in that they are abstraction from real life motion, an adaptation of recognizable motion to the specified syntax of a dance. But they are also ideal in the sense that they are held up as ideals, that is, they present us with a version of the human being as a moving, active creature that is to serve as a grounds for our evaluation of human life.

It is this latter feature of dance, its presentation of an ideal of human life by means of a special syntax of movement, that I see as the central means whereby dance conveys meaning.[34]

For Wartenberg it is therefore in the discrepancy between normal movement and dance movement that meaning is engendered.

The semioticians as well as the philosophers have recently addressed themselves to the questions of meaning in dance and dance as language. Jacob Zelinger, in an article on 'Semiotics and Theatre Dance', extends the above argument while reiterating the relationship drawn by Wartenberg between dance movement and everyday movement:

One must not forget that theatre dance is a cultural convention where access is only possible if the spectator knows the difference between this idiom of dancing and everyday actions. It is for this reason that one of the primary signals in theatre dance concerns its differentiation from everyday movement. This is achieved through 'poetic' devices such as rhythm, stylization, the use of particular posture, etc. These characteristics constitute part of the code of dance. The theatre code (lighting, stage and costume design, music, acting, etc.) offers additional 'clarification' of the context. Of course, all aspects of the dance-theatre code work at both the denotative and connotative levels. As dance becomes more lyrical, as a dependence on traditional narrative themes diminishes, so do the denotative modes of signification. Then connotation dominates the spectator's interpretation.[35]

In her book *Next Week, Swan Lake: Reflections on Dance and Dancers* (1982), Selma Jeanne Cohen continues an enquiry begun in an article of twenty years before, 'A Prolegomenon to an Aesthetics of Dance', by asking 'What does the "Dance of the Sugar Plum Fairy" *Mean?*' She is modest in her claims for meaning in dance, stating conservatively,

> But dance is always about something, something that it displays, draws to our attention, not as a means to something else, but as an end in itself. It creates a world that exists apart from our real world, yet resembles it enough that perceiving the dance world can illuminate the real one[36]

and comes to the conclusion that the Sugar Plum Fairy expresses graciousness, kindness, generosity and hospitality to those visiting her kingdom, but that this expressiveness is perhaps not quite synonymous with meaning. In her article of 1962 she wrestled with the same problem:

> We watch the great adagio in *Swan Lake* for several minutes, and all we can say in the end is that the boy and girl are in love. We would find it difficult to pinpoint the 'meaning' of any one of the ballerina's many pirouettes. The dance as a whole has an expressive quality, but this quality does not account for all its parts. It cannot, because its movements are designed for a purpose beyond expressiveness. Dancing may be thought of as movement framed to be seen for its own sake and interest seen above its interest of meaning.[37]

Selma Jeanne Cohen analyses the nature of the meaning of which dance may be capable and concludes that,

> Neither factual relations nor ideas are promising choreographic material. The area of dance is not that of concepts, which are grasped by the mind by way of words, but of percepts, which are grasped by the eye, by way of movement. ...
>
> Taking gesture, the natural sign of character or emotion, as his base, the choreographer builds from it a movement that has both a visual and an aural design. ... He may extend or elaborate [the gesture's] configuration, so that the angry stamp is preceded by a kick high in the air. ...
>
> Such manipulations ... do not obliterate the significance of the gesture, but rather they enhance it. Prolongation may emphasize

a movement; quickening of tempo may create excitement. Choreographic enhancement, or stylization, extends the emotional expressiveness of the gesture. The dance has not merely added form to the movement; it has intensified the meaning of the movement.[38]

She also explores the possibilities of dances devoid of meaning and appraises recent experiments by choreographers to devise such phenomena by creating dance that depends entirely on interest of movement for its own sake. To do this, she indicates, they have attempted to divorce gesture and emotion by isolating the former from the context in which it is usually apprehended and by employing artificial or even random relationships between movements:

But meaning in dance, as we have seen, need not refer to a specific dramatic character or situation, or even to a personal emotion. The choreographer may comment on depersonalized quality of behavior. Even chance continuity, if it is carried out consistently, makes a comment. It may be: 'What wonderfully strange and beautiful things the human body can do when it is not trying to say something.'[39]

A more recent theoretician on dance, David Carr (1987), summarises the thoughts on dance, gesture and meaning presented above by stressing these very roles of context and intentionality:

Precisely what a physical movement of a particular human agent might be said to mean on any particular occasion, then, depends on various considerations including an appreciation of the context in which it is performed and some grasp of the purpose for which it is performed in that context; but merely construed as a bare physical event, a human movement can mean *nothing*.[40] [Carr's emphasis]

A pirouette, outside of some wider context and choreographic purpose, is meaningless: it may be used, however, to express a variety of ideas which contribute to an understanding of the meaning of a dance. Carr proceeds to elucidate:

For the purposes and intentions whereby the physical performance is invested with meaning are related not causally or productively to the movement but *logically* or *internally*; the purposes are *inherent* in the movement rather than *antecedent* to it. ... It is the dance performance itself, then, not the thoughts of the choreographer about it that expresses the meaning of the dance; the dance performance is not a mere causal product of artistic purposes but that which embodies or expresses artistic purposes which can have no genuine logically separate existence apart from the dance which expresses them.

The purposes that give meaning to a given dance have no independent existence apart from the dance in question.[41] [Carr's emphasis]

It is manifest that neither Selma Jeanne Cohen nor Carr has doubts that a meaning can indeed be conveyed and yet what is its nature? Maxine Sheets-Johnstone, an American dance critic, writing in the summer of 1981, reminds us: 'to have meaning is not necessarily to refer and neither is it necessarily to have a label',[42] and Nelson Goodman in his influential study, *Languages of Art: An Approach to a Theory of Symbols* of 1969, appositely calls to mind the very old debate between dance and language and whether this order of meaning can be expressed linguistically. He concludes that it cannot, and in so stating refers us back to the intuitions and instincts of Fuller, Gray, Hofmannsthal and Yeats. Goodman is alluding to modern dance which, he argues, exemplifies, rather than to classical dance, which denotes:

To regard these movements [i.e. of modern dance], as illustrating verbal descriptions would of course be absurd; seldom can the just wording be found. Rather, the label a movement exemplifies may be itself; such a movement, having no antecedent denotation, takes on the duties of a label denoting certain actions including itself. Here, as often elsewhere in the arts, the vocabulary evolves along with what it is used to convey.[43]

So, in our turn, to employ the term metaphorically, dance does have a 'vocabulary', albeit one idiosyncratically its own and peculiar to whatever it is seeking to impart. Nevertheless, Valéry's Socrates insisted on asking in *L'Ame et la Danse*, a dialogue of 1923 – a time when Yeats had his *Plays for Dancers* recently behind him –

SOCRATE: Mais qu'est-ce donc la danse, et que *peuvent dire* des pas?[44]   [My emphasis]

and when his pupil Phèdre demands of his teacher

PHEDRE ...   Crois tu qu'elle represente quelque chose?

Socrates answers:

SOCRATE: Nulle chose, cher Phèdre. Mais toute chose, Eryximaque. Aussi bien l'amour comme la mer, et la vie elle-meme, et les pensées ... Ne sentez-vous pas qu'elle est l'acte pur des métamorphoses?[45]

André Levinson takes these words responding to Phèdre's demand as being supremely revelatory:

Marvellous words! In dismissing, summarily, this common misapprehension, they go straight to the foundation, to the scheme of the dance and its meaning, which is neither expression nor imitation but pure function.[46]

We may round off this section of the discussion by letting two contemporaries of our own, both American Professors of Philosophy, Paul Ziff from the University of North Carolina and Francis Sparshott in his recent book, *Off the Ground: First Steps to a Philosophical Consideration of the Dance* (1988), have the penultimate word on this still disputed issue of dance and language, dance and meaning:

Speaking precisely then the reason dance cannot be a language is that it lacks the appropriate syntactic and semantic stuctures requisite for a language. It has syntactic and semantic structures adequate for a symbolic system, but not for a language. ...
The meaning of complex movements the significance of complex movements in dance is not a simple function of the meaning of its constituents. It doesn't build up recursively in the way linguistic elements build up.[47]

This statement was made in 1979 and Sparshott alludes to it and adds his own view on the dance-language debate:

The general question of the analogies and disanalogies between linguistic and dance systems is complex. (Paul Ziff makes a start in his contribution to Fancher and Myers 1981, 69–83.) But we can perhaps see already that the parallel can hardly go through, just because dance is inseparable from the actual flow of body movement in a way that has no linguistic analogue. Linguistic structures are equally exemplified in written and vocal discourse and hence are abstractable. That is to say, what is linguistically significant in the vocal sign can be identified as what it shares with the equivalent inscription, and vice versa. By contrast, there is no reason for dance systems to be comparably abstractable. Whatever the range of meanings they can bear, they do not perform the function of comprehensive conceptual formulation and communication that determines the kind of grammatical structure languages have to have. All human cultures have dances. But all human cultures also have languages. It is absurd to suppose that the two systems do the same job.[48]

Sparshott's summing up of the strands of the debate in 1988 may be followed by one of a contemporary of Yeats's own, Virginia Stewart, and will bring us to the next part of this chapter, that in which those opinions cited initially about whether dance could express and convey greater and more significant truth than could language will be appraised by reference to specific plays by the Irish playwright. The claims derive from a discussion of modern dance first published in 1935, the year in which Yeats produced his 'Salome' dance plays and they treat of such celebrated practitioners as Mary Wigman and Doris Humphrey[49] – the generation of innovators in dance to follow Isadora Duncan and Loïe Fuller:

> Whether in Germany or America, the modern dance is an expression through an irrational medium of bodily movement of the grasped but inarticulate emotional and intellectual experiences which Man, in the whole history of his culture, has never been able to convert into words. If the spiritual content, the meaning of a dance, could be converted into words it could be better written than danced. It is the high purpose of the dance to convert these intangible mental urges, these deeply felt but inexplicable emotions, into movement. ...

Movement, the substance of the dance, reveals that 'inexpressible residue of emotion' (GILBERT MURRAY) which cannot be conveyed through words or pantomime.[50]

We may assume with a certain degree of security, given Yeats's own sometimes meagre pronouncements on the subject in his stage directions and through the mouthpieces of his protagonists themselves, that the poet was quite aware of the discussion in his time of dance as aesthetic medium and of the debate over whether or not it lacked meaning. To me, Yeats's principal concern about dance lay in his belief – one shared with others, as we have observed – that the significances which it conveyed were of a non-linguistic and non-discursive order. It is both curious and sobering to see in such a master of words the total recognition and acceptance of the limitations and shortcomings of the very medium in which he excelled, that of language and he reveals a painful consciousness even in his very earliest poems in 1889 that, in his own measured, conservative estimate, 'Words alone are certain good'.[51] In common with many of his contemporaries, when words failed, he turned to dance and gesture. I do not wish, however, to isolate Yeats's relationship with dance as a simple-minded *faute de mieux* solution of a dilemma posed by language. The images of the dancer which recur constantly in his poetry illustrate copiously that the poet had an intellectual as well as emotional interest in her as 'Sign', the emblem of which Mallarmé wrote so insistently, the timeless figure who, while being subject to the mortal and temporal, simultaneously transcends both through the abstraction of her performance which also transfigures all merely human elements into artefact. As we have discovered in previous chapters, in subscribing to this belief Yeats was very clearly attuned to the obsessions of French *Symboliste* poets, to Valéry and to English admirers like Arthur Symons. In his study on Yeats, Denis Donoghue relates the images crafted by the *Symboliste* poets to the poetic truths of a Yeatsian dance play:

the images, since they live by action rather than by knowledge, refuse to be translated. This gives them their esoteric aura. The climax of a dance-play does not disclose a meaning separable from the aura of this action; it is exactly the form which subjective intensity takes and apart from that form it is nothing. As for the words, it would be better if we received them as 'vocables' than as counters to be construed from a dictionary.[52]

His dance plays are given special status by Yeats and, while there are a number of salient features in common, as we shall discover below, he tended to tackle the problems raised by each particular dance individually. As for the theorising in which we have been indulging, Yeats, given his predilection for non-discursive image, would probably wish to agree with André Levinson that, in contradiction to Aristotle's remarks about dance imitating and representing life outside it, choreographic movement is rather 'self-begotten' and self-referring. While Yeats will have a witness comment on a dance and indeed interpret it, as in *The Dreaming of the Bones*, he nowhere attempts to translate gestures into a set of words which 'explain' them. Thus, the narrative outcome of the Hawk Woman's trance-like gestures is to decoy Cuchulain from the well, to condemn him to a life of restless searching and strife and so on, but the gestures themselves, the movement of arms and head, do not reduce to an explanation of such actions as 'meanings'. The Guardian of the Well is not performing a mime but a dance. Yeats's testimony on the subject would, I believe, have accorded with that branch of thinking culminating today in the opinions of such theoreticians as David Carr when the latter claims, as cited above (pp. 259–60), that

the purposes and intentions whereby the physical performance is invested with meaning are related not causally or productively to the movement but *logically* or *internally*; the purposes are *inherent* in the movement rather than *antecedent* to it. ... The purposes that give meaning to a given dance have no independent existence apart from the dance in question.   [Carr's emphasis]

This is the conclusion that Valéry's Socrates attains in his dialogue *L'Ame et la Danse* of 1923 with which Yeats was probably familiar since he took a similar line himself. Dance steps are emotionally neutral although, by the time that they have been built into a movement such as a balletic *enchaînement*, they have begun to possess expressive force. While Langer claims that gestures are 'virtual' because they do not spring genuinely from the feelings from which they purport to derive, Yeats avoids this whole discussion of actuality or illusion by having his dialogue lead up to a transfiguration of language into passionate moment and thence into dance; he thus proved himself more akin to Laban's belief in the sincerity of gesture rather than to those opinions framed by Langer some years later. In his dance plays Yeats's dances always occur at a point where emotion runs so high that language teeters on the verge of the chaotic. Dance metamorphoses that anarchy by both portraying and revealing it and, at the same time, controlling it by its very nature. Another contemporary theorist on dance, Marshall Cohen, would reject the still prevalent hypothesis which Yeats seems to advance, that of dance as an expression of emotion, while his colleague, Thomas Wartenberg, would agree with the poet that dance communicates in a non-linguistic manner. Yeats found himself, fifty years ago, very much at a crucial point in the 'Dance Debate' and the dilemmas with which he wrestled are clearly still being faced today.

It is evident from the above discussion on theory that Yeats was far from alone in his beliefs in and preoccupations about the potentiality of dance in drama and it is important to analyse the significance within the play of his dances. As we have discovered, a consideration of 'meaning' in dance may be a thorny and delicate procedure and it is perhaps useful to adopt Levinson's term, 'function' or else the word which I have just myself employed, 'significance'. For a dance can be decoded even if it is simply *divertissement* and an onlooker performs the act of deciphering with different degrees of consciousness. Yeats himself, when meditating upon Salome as the figure of the dancer, followed Mallarmé in wanting the dance to be an emblem devoid of meaning:

> Yeats's actors would have the blank, inward faces of the wooden Japanese masks; they would not necessarily even speak their own lines. Musicians would frame the action, and comment in song. All would be inexplicit, suggestive, but faultless in design; and often the climax of the play would be a dance like Salome's. There would be no separable meaning; the verses would be spoken as the dance was danced, and would dispense with that kind of expression that points 'meaning'.[53]

And yet, despite Kermode's overall and synthesising view, very few generalisations can be made about Yeats's dances even in the light of all the above theories and philosophies of dance, because Yeats was supremely a pragmatist. When theories – even his own –

are set against practice we must conclude that his approach remained pluralistic: he utilised and was inspired by all the many sources from the *Zeitgeist*, his own research, to the influences of friends, but he crafted his work according to subject matter and choreographed his dances according to the idiosyncratic needs of each individual play. It is here, therefore, that close attention to the plays themselves must be paid in order to glean from them the manners in which dance and verse complement each other, whether there are extractable significances from the dances, however contrary they might be to Yeats's avowed intent and why dialogue moves to dance at the point that it does.

But first an important issue must be tackled: what constitutes a dance play? It is not sufficient for a play to contain a dance to be recognised as a dance play. While dance is employed in *The Land of Heart's Desire* (1894) and in the late play *The Player Queen* (1922), these plays do not share the unity from within of *Four Plays for Dancers* (1921). One of the last plays, *The Herne's Egg* (1938), presents a report of the priestess's dance-like movements, but, as I hope to demonstrate, it can hardly be considered a dance play. And yet *The Resurrection* (1931), is quite arguably a dance play while containing no dance at all. As we discovered in the discussion of the dance plays and Japanese Noh at the end of Chapter 2, Yeats's dances, unlike their Japanese models, serve to further narrative and embody the conflict which is endemic to the plot. They take over where language leaves off, where dialogue is transformed into dance and, hence, they are not detachable from the plot as a whole. In fact, they become increasingly central to the play, as was remarked from a consideration of the last plays, *A Full Moon in March* and *The King of the Great Clock Tower* of 1935. The dance plays, I would argue, display an organic unity and this should be demonstrable.

We can perhaps at this point attempt to infer by contrast with the plays which fail to be dance plays, because they do not correspond to an admittedly tentative set of criteria, the salient features of the genuine dance play itself. The latter all demonstrate a tightly unified structure, the revelation of one intense episode which is effected by the interrelation of several media, that of narrative, verse, song and dance. As an examination of the individual dance plays will attempt to show, one medium prefigures another which, in its turn, provides comment on what went before. Thus, dialogue will give way to song which is then transfigured into dance. This highly charged and controlled use of counterpoint is the most striking characteristic of the dance play, but it is also usually accompanied by the employment of mask, a chorus which comments on the action and mediates between audience and main plot and music. The climax of the Yeatsian dance play is usually that of the executing of the dance itself which is never merely decorative and it occurs at the point where the necessary dramatic function can only be served by the movement which it provides. As we have previously proposed, the most significant attribute of the dance in these plays is that it represents a point in the narrative where language itself is ineffectual in the communication of great passion. While the *function* of the dance may be interpreted through words, as has been illustrated by a brief consideration of the Hawk Woman's dance, and will play a crucial part in narrative significance, the *meaning* may be grasped as the logic of choreography alone. An attempt to sum up Emer's dance in Yeats's last play results only in an insubstantial and unsatisfactory approximation in language of the real power of her movements.

This unity and cohesion of different media makes for an impression of inexorability: a machine has been wound up that is unstoppable. The fusion of aesthetic forms adds to this sensation by creating a tight construction containing a plot which moves relentlessly towards a combination of all forces to produce a passionate episode. The plays contain in visible measure the attributes of ritual and ceremony.

The stage setting of the dance play is often simply a corner of a domestic drawing-room and 'theatre' is suggested by the Musicians' unfolding and folding of a cloth in order to signify the beginning and end of the play. His last dance plays, however, are staged in a conventional theatre, but Yeats none the less remained true to his conception of a chorus of musicians whose function is to open and conclude the action and to comment on the narrative or indeed to speak on behalf of some of the characters. Thus, the song of the severed head, for example, in *A Full Moon in March* or *The King of the Great Clock Tower* is performed by a musician, as is the speaking part of the Queen in the latter play. Yeats also retained his enthusiasm, which dates from 1910, for putting certain of his players into mask.

The above sketch delineates the most significant features which go to define the genre. Let us now consider some plays which might at first glance appear to conform with the classification of dance plays, but which, I suggest, do not quite qualify for that title.

In *The Land of Heart's Desire* the Faery Child's dance is conceivably the climax of the play and yet, somewhat paradoxically, it could well be omitted without any ill being done to the entirety of the piece. At this early point in Yeats's writing the dance represents the forces and pleasures of Faery or the Land of the Blessed. His poetry of this period abounds with images of faeries dancing amid a dancing landscape, just such visual pictures as we now discover the Child depicting in this play:

> THE CHILD: The reeds are dancing by Coolaney lake,
> And I would like to dance until the reeds
> And the white waves have danced themselves asleep.[54]

She repeats Mary's own words when the young wife begged: 'Come, faeries, take me out of this dull house!'[55] and when the Faery lures her victim into her magic, she promises dancing:

> THE CHILD: You love that young man there,
> Yet I could make you ride upon the winds,
> Run on the top of the dishevelled tide,
> And dance upon the mountains like a flame.[56]

The Child sings and dances to exert her power over Mary, the newly married bride, and both of these actions serve to shatter what is left of Mary's resolve to stay among human beings. The Faery Child represents spontaneity and freedom and anarchic loss of control and in so doing emblematises certain of the essential qualities of dance itself. And yet, from a narrative point-of-view, the dance here could be omitted and its function expressed in words. Why, then, was its power not indeed conveyed through the medium of language? Partly, and somewhat prosaically, because Yeats had been very impressed by Todhunter's Bedford Park production of his own play *A Sicilian Idyll* in 1890 which contained a dance, and he wanted to try his hand at emulating the English playwright by incorporating a dance into his own drama. There is another more trivial reason: Florence Farr had asked Yeats for a part to be written for her nine-year-old niece, Dorothy Paget.

Let us consider how *The Land of Heart's Desire* possesses certain of the characteristics of the dance plays, so that indeed it is almost a dance play *avant la lettre*. This dance, one exerting power, is arguably celebrating movement for itself merely decoratively; in this it is unlike the dance plays. But, in common with them, bodily movement has subverted language for a moment, just as the function of an aria in opera is to stop the recitative and so pause at the height of passion. We discover in this very early experiment the first intimations of Yeats's method of relating dialogue to dance which the genuine dance plays exhibit and which will be examined below.

In *The Land of Heart's Desire* the dance is preceded by the snatch of a song which recurs as *Leitmotiv* throughout

> THE CHILD: Here is level ground for dancing; I will dance.
> (*Sings*) The wind blows out of the gates of the day,
> The wind blows over the lonely of heart,
> And the lonely of heart is withered away.
> (*She dances*)[57]

It is an essential part of her Faery nature that the Child should insist on dancing. (Interestingly, Cuchulain is allied to her later in *On Baile's Strand* (1904), when Conchubar attempts ineffectively to rein him in. The young warrior defiantly proposes to look for a 'level place among the woods' for dancing.[58]) This song is a fragment of that which the Faery Child sang outside in Faeryland before she was brought into the home by Maurteen, father-in-law to Mary Bruin. And it recurs again at the end of the play when a multitude of Faery singers takes it up in chorus and as conclusion. The song, unlike the blank verse pentameters which form the basis of the dialogue, is in tetrameters, thus signalling a rupture in the metre and rhythm used for narrative purposes. It is in rhyme, abab, but the snatch of it that is performed leading up to the dance leaves one rhyme unmatched in the air:'day heart away'. 'Heart' is left dangling alone, rhymeless and it is the dance that will serve to complete the song by expressing the moods and vicissitudes of the human heart, that of Mary Bruin. Thus, the dialogue is transfigured and movement is proposed as its answer. But the dance finds its own response in the reaction of Mary who claims to have heard a swarm of faeries dancing in the house. She is alone in her perception; her husband insists:

> SHAWN: I heard no steps but hers[59]

and in so doing creates yet another breach between himself and his young, beloved bride, thus increasingly isolating her and making it clear that 'the lonely of heart' of which the song spoke and the dance reiterated is undeniably Mary herself. A threat hangs over her, for the song promises that, the lonely of heart is withered away[60]

and the play progresses from the climax of this dance towards the death of Mary in the fight for control over her heart by the priest, Father Hart, and the toils of Faery represented as the call of freedom, eternal youth and spontaneity. As opposed to what the young wife so fears – domesticity, mediocrity and bitterness at the non-realisation of dreams

> THE CHILD: you grow like the rest;
>   Bear children, cook and bend above the churn,
>   And wrangle over butter, fowl, and eggs,
>   Until at last, grown old and bitter of tongue,
>   You're crouching there and shivering at the grave[61]

the Faery proposes an escape from what is, in effect, captivity, however lovingly intended:

> THE CHILD: But I can lead you, newly-married bride,
>   Where nobody gets old and crafty and wise,
>   Where nobody gets old and godly and grave,
>   Where nobody gets old and bitter of tongue,
>   And where kind tongues bring no captivity;
>   For we are but obedient to the thoughts
>   That drift into the mind at a wink of the eye.[62]

And the Child most insinuatingly takes up the echo of 'heart' from her song and appeals to Mary by challenging Father Hart, whose name, rather troublingly, seems to incorporate both notions of 'heart' and 'hard':

> FATHER HART: By the dear Name of the One crucified,
>   I bid you, Mary Bruin, come to me.
> THE CHILD: I keep you in the name of your own heart.[63]

The Faery is astute and potent in her method of waging war upon the forces of Christianity.

As was remarked above, this play is almost a dance play in its manner of connecting dialogue and dance. But the introduction of the dance is crude and arbitrary: 'Here is level ground for dancing; I will dance', and it is on this point that *The Land of Heart's Desire* shows an immature clumsiness which by the time of the genuine dance plays has been rectified. The problem partly consists in the fact that, for Yeats and Irish legend, a Faery must dance – this is the very nature of Faery – and any play or poem dealing with a Faery demands it. In later plays, however, the character who performs a dance is not expected or required to do so because of her essential identity. There she dances in response to pressure of emotion or to exert mysterious power, not simply to fulfil the needs imposed by stereotype. Here the dance has arisen as a function of the character who performs it: in the dance plays the dance provides response to the demands of the plot. From a narrative point-of-view both Faery song and dance as a given conflation could be omitted, while in the later dramas the dance cannot be removed without destroying the entirety, as we shall see.

This statement of the difference is largely true, but caution must still nevertheless be advocated, as the striking element when the plays are analysed in the above terms is not that there exists a theory which will include them all, but that they are supremely individual in their handling of the dance. They therefore demand to be treated separately as units. Let us first consider the plays that are akin to *The Land of Heart's Desire* in that they contain dances but are arguably not dance plays and use them as yardsticks with which to compare the acknowledged versions of this genre.

While *The Unicorn from the Stars* (1908), written in collaboration with Lady Gregory, does not present a dance, the play on which it is based, *Where There is Nothing* (1902), does. The dance is a very curious performance, a ritualistic weaving of Friars around the unconscious body of Paul Ruttledge and it is scripted in stage direction rather than anticipated by dialogue. This, the most Nietzschean of Yeats's plays, deals with a rich country gentleman who turns tinker, marries a tinker wife and takes to the roads. He uses his wealth to subvert and disrupt and wishes to destroy the mediocre institutions of society as he perceives it, but he is forced to abandon travelling, cock-fighting and revolution when sickness obliges him to be cared for at a monastery. The opening to Act iv Scene 2 is as follows:

(The crypt under the Monastery church. A small barred window high up in the wall, through which the cold dawn is breaking. Altar in a niche at the back of stage; there are seven unlighted candles on the altar. A little hanging lamp near the altar. Paul Ruttledge is lying on the altar steps. Friars are dancing slowly

before him in the dim light. Father Aloysius is leaning against a
pillar. Some Friars come in carrying lanterns.)[64]

Paul entered the monastery as a lay brother and in five years has
risen to friar. He has been subject to fits of death-like unconscious-
ness and has asked his brothers to dance around him should he
suffer falling into a trance again:

> THIRD FRIAR ...   He told them it was a kind of prayer and would
> bring joy down out of heaven, and make it easier for him to
> preach.[65]

The dancing friars chant the twenty-second psalm in Latin as their
own accompaniment, but are chastised by their Superior for blasphemy. Paul is also punished for the preaching which springs from
his trance meditations for he announces that:

> We must destroy the World; we must destroy everything that has
> Law and Number, for where there is nothing, there is God.[66]

His Superior judges him a heretic and expels him, but several friars
wish to follow him and he dies among them, an outcast and vaga-
bond, still contending that all must be torn down in order to find
God.

The dance is a curious one and could easily be omitted from both
narrative and choreographic points of view. No claim could
seriously be made for *Where There is Nothing* as a dance play. The
whole work, both in this early form and in its later version, *The
Unicorn from the Stars*, is very experimental with a long and loosely
constructed plot admitting of many episodes. It is totally lacking in
Yeats's characteristic tightness and intensity of grasp. Of the two
differing accounts, my personal feeling is that the former is the less
unsuccessful, but the dance which it includes could hardly be perceived as the climax as it is on other occasions: it is not introduced
by song or dialogue and it does not either effect a transformation of
events which preceded it or exert any influence on those which
ensue. One can imagine it being very effective when staged, however and we take the point, derived from Nietzsche whom Yeats
started to read in 1902, the very year in which this play was written,
that dance was seen by the hero to be a form of prayer. But we cannot pretend that this fascinating dance is integral to the action.

While the climax is more arguably the mock trial scene in which the tinkers try the notables of the town for their pomposity, greed and materialism, this dance of prayer remains a haunting possibility to be remembered and perhaps recrafted as the dance of the Roman soldiers in *Calvary* of so many years later or transformed into the chorus of *Deirdre* of 1907. It is a seductive notion, but the play which provides it is not a dance play.

The Player Queen in its much revised and rewritten final version of 1922 also contains a dance. It does not resemble a dance play, however, although Yeats had been creating true examples of this genre since 1916. Some of the more superficial elements of the *Plays for Dancers*, such as mask, are present, but no display of tight and organic unity is in evidence. On the contrary it is, in common with *Where There is Nothing*, sprawling and episodic and played on a conventional stage.

There are two dances, both performed at the whim of Decima: the purpose of the second is to provide a conclusion to the drama and to separate her from her former companions as she has elected to tread a different path – rather than act a Queen, she will be one. This final dance is preceded by a minor one in which the actors, disguised as animals for a projected performance of *Noah's Flood*, move around the central figure of Decima. She, having been freed of her drunken poet-husband Septimus, expresses the need for someone with whom to dance in order to celebrate her new-found liberty and opportunity to choose his successor:

> DECIMA: Dance, Turkey-cock, dance – no stop. I cannot have you, for my man must be lively on his feet and have a quick eye. I will not have that round eye fixed upon me now that I have sent my mind asleep. Yet what do I care who it is, so that I choose and get done with it ? Dance, all dance, and I will choose the best dancer among you. Quick, quick, begin to dance. (*All dance round Decima.*)[67]

As in the dance plays, the dance here is accompanied by a song, but a more neatly-drawn parallel could be traced with the dance in *The Land of Heart's Desire* because *The Player Queen* does not display tight construction, it does not provide musicians or a chorus and the dance is eminently detachable in that it does not transfigure or respond to language but is simply a performance executed in answer to Decima's request:

I'm too happy now that I am free. I must find somebody who will
dance with me for a while. Come, we must have music. (*She picks
up a lute which has been laid down amongst some properties*.) You can't
all be claws and hoofs.[68]

The dance here resembles a *divertissement*, and its accompanying
song,

> DECIMA: Shall I fancy beast or fowl?
>   Queen Pasiphae chose a bull,
>   While a passion for a swan
>   Made Queen Leda stretch and yawn,
>   Wherefore spin ye, whirl ye, dance ye,
>   Till Queen Decima's found her fancy[69]

in which Decima dons the title 'Queen' well before there is a risk of
her so becoming, adds to the impression of a set piece and this effect
is further upheld when we perceive that the performers are pro-
fessionals, actors ever-ready and willing to do a turn. Thus, the
dances are passionless party-pieces and the dancers always-primed.
Once she has indeed replaced the genuine queen, Decima uses her
power to demand of her comrades the performance of a dance of
farewell in which they sever connection. This too, although a satisfying conclusion to the play, is introduced rather arbitrarily: we cannot suggest that language has broken down, nor that great emotion
has been transfigured into a different medium. Instead, in both
cases, the dance is rather a parody of the climax in a dance play,
since the final performance which closes *The Player Queen* provides a
mundane and prosaically convenient image of order and reconciliation won only by Decima's banishing of her former fellow-actors
from her kingdom in order to prevent any future disclosure of her
real identity.

The last play to include a dance while not itself being a dance play
is a late creation of 1938, *The Herne's Egg*. In it a battle is stylised and
presented in dance form and a solo dance is reported by onlookers.

Attracta is priestess to her god, the Great Herne, and is moved to
dance out of homage and adoration and to woo him to marriage.
Agnes, one of her young friends, asks whether the bird will 'Do all
that a man does?'[70] and Attracta responds with the eulogy that introduces her dance:

ATTRACTA: Strong sinew and soft flesh
   Are foliage round the shaft
   Before the arrowsmith
   Has stripped it, and I pray
   That I, all foliage gone,
   May shoot into my joy –[71]

An answering melody on the flute, an air called 'The Great Herne's Feather', suggests that Attracta's god is summoning her and also accompanies her dance. Instead of stage directions, Yeats provides the words of the three girl-witnesses to comment on Attracta's movements:

MARY: Her eyes grow glassy, she moves
   According to the notes of the flute.
AGNES: Her limbs grow rigid, she seems
   A doll upon a wire.[72]

She intersperses her puppet-like steps with 'long leaps' which the girls describe as

KATE: Travelling fast asleep
   In long loops like a dancer.
MARY: Like a dancer, like a hare.[73]

Attracta's dance, performed in a trance-like state, is both one of obedience and joy, the pleasure that she anticipates from her imminent coupling with her god and, unlike the trance of the Hawk Woman in the earlier *At the Hawk's Well*, it is executed by a disciple, even a minion, whereas the Woman of the Sidhe is invested with divine power. Instead of intercourse with the godhead, however, Attracta is supposedly raped by seven soldiers of Connacht led by Congal, their king, whom we witnessed in a battle dance in the scene with which the play opened. While predicting the ecstasy that she will experience when she loses her virginity to the Great Herne:

ATTRACTA: ... I pray
   That I, all foliage gone
   May shoot into my joy –[74]

(and we may note in passing how the metaphor is interestingly that of male sexuality, the image of an arrow which shoots and penetrates; a curious view of Attracta, so far so docile, as initiator of sexual union), the priestess's words are answered by flute music which moves her to dance. Here Yeats is frankly employing his technique in earlier dance plays: language, poetry, gives way to movement. And her dance is also necessary to the narrative because, while in her trance, she replaces the prized Herne's egg with that of a mundane hen. In so doing, she brings about the battle between Congal, insulted by his simple supper and his enemy, Aedh, who is privileged in enjoying the greater delicacy and this fight results in the latter's death after fifty equally matched skirmishes between them:

> JAMES: By changing one egg for another
> She has brought bloodshed on us all.[75]

In revenge, as we have observed, the seven men of Connacht resolve to possess Attracta in order to transform her into a 'sensible woman'[76] from a 'snow image',[77] but they are too much in awe of the god to make good their threats. She, on the other hand, firmly believes herself to have coupled with the Herne and to have put on his might with the thunderbolts which he bestowed upon her as symbol of his power.

The play is not a dance play: there are no choruses or masks; it is set in a conventional theatre with scene decor and backdrop and the construction is episodic. The dance, however, is functional in the action, as in the dance plays and does ensue from dialogue by means of which it is anticipated, but this play, which combines realism and surrealism, resists presentation of one intense episode. Nevertheless, in common with the *Plays for Dancers*, Attracta's dance is not capable of being detached from the play since it summarises previous and furthers ensuing action. The dance, though not the play in which it is encapsulated, could be placed with security in a dance play: it is not in this aspect (as was the case with *Where There is Nothing* and *The Player Queen*), that the play fails to be included in that genre, but in its overall structure.

A fine curiosity should now be examined. An early play, *On Baile's Strand* (1904), represents an experiment that succeeded and which constitutes a dance play in embryonic form. While it contains no dance, it provides ample motive and opportunity for one, and the theatrical ideas revealed here in draft act as precursor to Yeats's balletic *Fighting the Waves*, a prose version of *The Only Jealousy of Emer*, which appeared much later in 1929. There the waves of the sea with which Cuchulain does battle in his mad frenzy are represented by dancers (see Plate 8).

On Baile's Strand charts clearly dramatic techniques and aspects of stylisation which surface again in *Four Plays for Dancers* and in later dance plays. A subplot involving two masked figures, a Blind Man and a Fool, frames the main action in a manner which would subsequently be transformed by employing a chorus or musicians whose songs both encapsulate and comment upon the events of the principal narrative strand. *Deirdre*, published three years later in 1907, already manifests a confident use of chorus, but the experiment was first attempted here where we discover a song accompanying the swearing of an oath between Conchobar and Cuchulain performed by a group of women and where another assembly, this time of kings, speaks as a body to incite Cuchulain to engage in combat the stranger to whom the middle-aged warrior has unconsciously warmed, not yet aware that he is his own son. The tragic climax to the play is reported by the Fool and the Blind Man: having vanquished the young champion, Cuchulain learns his identity and, in his grief, fights the sea. The last words are vouchsafed to the Fool and the Blind Man and Yeats elects to conclude by permitting subplot to take precedence. In a dance play their roles would obviously be accomplished by chorus or musicians.

The elements of the dance play are clear – Cuchulain's insane battle could be represented as a dance – but the whole would need to be transformed from a series of mutually mirroring narrative episodes into a tighter unity in order to create a dance play proper. Even here, however, the varying media presented, song and dialogue, do show signs of interreacting contrapuntally, one picking up the threads of the dramaturgy where the other left off. Such a concord and harmony can be clearly demonstrated in the dance plays; it is indeed one of the qualities which allow us to label them thus.

Strikingly conspicuous in *On Baile's Strand* is the notion of inexorability. Tragedy will result from cruel endeavours to rein in Cuchulain, to tame his valour, and we are prepared for something dreadful by the Blind Man's knowing hints to his crony in the first section of the play. This helplessness with which we witness the inevitable unfolding, step by step, of the narrative adds to the creation of dramatic unity which is poetically produced. There is a similar air of finality about Yeats's last play, also on the Cuchulain theme, *The Death of Cuchulain*, thirty-five years later and all of the dance plays portray, to a greater or lesser degree, the relentless movement towards a climax which is sometimes, as in the case of *Calvary* or *The Resurrection*, already known to us. I would suggest that Yeats reinforced an already existing embryonic talent for crafting such a dimension from his discovery of ritual in Noh drama in 1913. The base elements of such a ceremonious, weighty disclosing of events are already manifest, however, as early as this play of 1904 and both song and chorus act alongside a subplot in contribution to it. We are shown heroism in its many different forms; that open-handed valour of Cuchulain which contrasts with the wily self-interest of Conchobar, that of Aoife's impetuous young son, the true heroism of his father's refusal to fight and the tragic mockery of it when Cuchulain vents his despair upon the sea waves.

The songs, too, discuss various facets of the heroic impulse and prefigure the action to come, just as in the dance plays, where they are answered by and transfigured into dance. Thus, in this case the Fool's song foreshadows the ultimate tragedy because,

> FOOL: Cuchulain has killed kings,
>   Kings and sons of kings,
>   Dragons out of the water,
>   And witches out of the air. ...[78]

The first rendering of this song is heard only by the Blind Man who is anxious to disclose the true identity of the young warrior come from Aoife's country to kill Cuchulain, but the Fool repeats the same chant again as Cuchulain and Conchobar enter quarelling and the song is then met by Cuchulain's own personal version of its reality:

> CUCHULAIN: Because I have killed men without your bidding
>   And have rewarded others at my own pleasure, ...
>   You'd lay this oath upon me. ...[79]

The Fool's final song:

> FOOL: When you were an acorn on the tree-top,
>   Then was I an eagle-cock;
>   Now that you are a withered old block,
>   Still am I an eagle-cock[80]

is performed before both the Blind Man and Cuchulain himself and it emphasises the Fool's consistency of character across time, while the fighting man has been ravaged by the passing of the years. This culminates in his loss of integrity in swearing the High King's oath. The Fool may be recklessly risking Cuchulain's anger, but he will continue to blurt out home truths: it is through his innocent garrulousness that Cuchulain will glean the information that he seeks – that the young champion just killed was son of Aoife and himself.

The song of the chorus of women accompanies the swearing of the oath and tells of figures with whom we, as students of Yeats, are familiar – those of truly heroic women and their predatory counterparts:

THE WOMEN: Names whereby a man has known
The threshold and the hearthstone,
Gather on the wind and drive
The women none can kiss and thrive,
For they are but whirling wind,
Out of memory and mind.[81]

Cuchulain himself has pursued the Shape-Changers and will continue to do so, as later plays make evident. While he is reluctantly making his pledge to Conchubar, Aoife's son demands entry and a chance to pit his courage against that of Cuchulain. The boy represents the flowering issue of domestic bliss – the two lovers housed on the cold hillside, the nearest that Cuchulain and Aoife approached to 'threshold' and 'hearthstone' – and he also embodies the presence of his warrior-mother herself whom her now middle-aged lover remembers as valiant and majestic:

CUCHULAIN: Ah! Conchubar, had you seen her
With that high, laughing, turbulent head of hers
Thrown backward, ...
although she had no child,
None other had all beauty, queen or lover,
Or was so fitted to give birth to kings.[82]

Such tribute is eloquent riposte to the spurious joys offered by the Shape-Changing creatures of whom the chorus of women sing. While Aoife's power is genuine, that of the supernatural temptresses is insidious and ultimately emasculating. The contrast between the portrait depicted in the chorus's song and Cuchulain's previous eulogy of Aoife's splendour is most telling. In a letter of 16 February 1906, to Florence Farr Yeats remarked of the women's incantation:

> The hero has been praising an indomitable kind of woman and the chorus sing of her evil shadow.[83]

The first chorus also anticipates that of the kings which disastrously convinces Cuchulain that the physical resemblance which he detects between his youthful challenger and Aoife is a chimera resulting from witchcraft. The most obvious explanation is never deduced until it is too late.

In both cases the employment of chorus is slightly different from that in later plays. They do not here comment on the action: they are indeed instrumental to it. As has been described, the knowledge about the mysteries of the main plot are granted to the Blind Man who, in divulging the secrets to which he is privy to the Fool, also informs the audience. These two characters were not originally masked: this addition was mooted only in 1910 after Yeats's work with Craig:

> If the masks work right I would put the fool and the blind man in *Baile's Strand* into masks. It would give a wildness and extravagance that would be fine. I should also like the Abbey to be the first modern theatre to use the mask.[84]

Our consideration of Noh drama revealed that Yeats had been experimenting with mask some years before writing his dance plays in which mask plays a prominent part.

Despite the absence of a dance, *On Baile's Strand* presents itself perhaps as a truer precursor to the *Plays for Dancers* than either *The Land of Heart's Desire* or *Where There is Nothing* in which a dance is indeed performed, but where the plot and narrative technique veer towards realism rather than to the tight integrity of artefact and inexorability illustrated by the dance plays.

And so to the avowed and acknowledged dance plays proper: *Four Plays for Dancers* (1921), *The Cat and the Moon* written in 1917 but published in 1926, *The Resurrection* (1931), *A Full Moon in March* (1935), *The King of the Great Clock Tower* (1935) and *The Death of Cuchulain* (1939). Their dances were considered briefly as contribution to the action in Chapter 2. In *At the Hawk's Well* (1916), the first of the dance plays, the dance is that of the Hawk Woman, Guardian of the Well, and it is one of gesture, not of story. The dancer's brief is to embody the attributes of the hawk, which the Woman of the Sidhe represents and incarnates and the Old Man himself summarises the bird's characteristics:

> OLD MAN: She is always flitting upon this mountain-side,
>   To allure or to destroy.[85]

The woman's dance embodies the expression of these two ominous purposes although, as Taylor proposes, it 'suggests rather than defines meaning'.[86] While 'alluring' may be performed by means of words, though it is a difficult act for language to undertake without sounding ludicrously overwrought, 'destroying' is even more complex and, thus, dance takes over. In other plays it has been possible, to a greater or lesser degree of persuasiveness, to discern how the poetry anticipates dance. In this case the dance echoes and answers the Young Man's vainglorious challenge:

> YOUNG MAN: Why do you fix those eyes of a hawk upon me?
>   I am not afraid of you, bird, woman, or witch.
>   (*He goes to the side of the well, which the Guardian of the Well has left.*)
>   Do what you will, I shall not leave this place
>   Till I have grown immortal like yourself[87]

and it is at precisely this moment that the Guardian of the Well begins to move like the hawk, her model and perhaps avatar. While she does so the Musicians take over the commentary, meditating in song on the very magic that Old and Young Man seek – immortality: for this chorus, however, such deathlessness is something to be eschewed at all costs,

> FIRST MUSICIAN: O God, protect me
>   From a horrible deathless body
>   Sliding through the veins of a sudden[88]

and as the dance continues the Young Man does indeed break his rash promise by leaving the place by the well which he vowed he would keep. The Musician's words that accompany his movement not only depict it clearly but explain his state of consciousness and motivation for acting thus:

> FIRST MUSICIAN: The madness has laid hold upon him now,
> For he grows pale and staggers to his feet.[89]

Language is complementing action.

The Hawk Woman's performance draws Cuchulain on to still further bravado:

> YOUNG MAN: Run where you will,
> Grey bird, you shall be perched upon my wrist.
> Some were called queens and yet have been perched there.
> (*The dance goes on*).[90]

And the blank verse in which the young impetuous fighter makes his rash claims is interestingly weighted. The first four monosyllables, 'Run where you will', constitute threat and inexorability and the short line which they construct is portentous in its brevity. The apostrophe, 'Grey bird', bridges the gap between the first condition and its inevitable outcome: 'you shall be perched upon my wrist', the only word of more than one syllable being 'upon' with all its significances of dependency and ownership. The interplay of 'will' and 'shall' is noticeable, the first denoting the wishes of the bird/dancer and the second, the resolve of the hunter to break that will. This determination is also emphasised by the passive construction, 'you shall be perched', which obliterates all notion of a voluntary acceptance of the fate mapped out by the warrior. His boast, 'Some were called queens and yet have been perched there', is also monosyllabic and this contributes to the statement's matter-of-fact simplicity. The line is longer than the customary pentameter, just as the initial line was too short, and the whole speech breaks the rhythm of the blank verse with its awesome warnings, and yet the dance shows all this verbosity to be hubristic, as it nevertheless proceeds without the slightest hesitation. It renders Cuchulain's boastful pronouncements hollow and void. Ironically, it is Cuchulain himself, not the Hawk Woman, who will be made victim because her dance takes sway over his words, impressive though they may be. Despite everything that he has said, he follows her and deliberately turns his back on the splashing water which he came to seek. The song of the chorus of Musicians sums up both the outcome of the dance and its further ramification:

MUSICIANS: He has lost what may not be found
   Till men heap his burial-mound
   And all the history ends.
   He might have lived at his ease,
   An old dog's head on his knees,
   Among his children and friends.[91]

All the rhymes are true and the only one not in a couplet, 'ends'/ 'friends', emphasises what Cuchulain has chosen to reject and, thus, lose. The final four lines which contain these rhymes are a beat short – they are trimeters following tetrameters – and convey a fitting sense of loss. The young warrior has fallen under the curse of the Woman of the Sidhe and is now doomed to wander and fight and never find satisfaction in love. He is also destined to father a child on Aoife whom he will later kill unknowingly. This song prefigures the verses of the Musicians which conclude the play and which imply that Cuchulain has been stupid in his reckless preference of risk, power and danger over the comforts and pleasures of domesticity:

MUSICIANS: 'The man that I praise',
   Cries out the leafless tree,
   Has married and stays
   By an old hearth, and he
   On naught has set store
   But children and dogs on the floor.
   Who but an idiot would praise
   A withered tree?'[92]

It is a harsh and intransigent final estimate.

The force of the episode derives in the interplay between language and dance and our realisation that, although Cuchulain speaks of power, his is illusory, warrior though he is, and genuine authority resides in the dance of the Hawk Woman. Her transition into movement renders more clearly than would words the struggle of conflicting forces, man/woman, youth/age, natural/supernatural, mortal/ immortal, action/contemplation and adventure/caution which battle to take precedence in the encounter of the three protagonists, Old and Young Man and Guardian of the Well. It is a dance of strength and authority which is not celebrating movement for its own sake but imitative, in Aristotelian terms and expressive of abstract qualities. Through it we are presented with an intensification of what has gone before into a different medium, the transfiguration into dance of language.

In the second of *Four Plays for Dancers*, *The Dreaming of the Bones* (1919), the dance is not one of seduction but of pleading. It is not choreographed in stage directions; instead it is described by an onlooker who thereby provides its commentary. In this case the dance is more pantomimic than that examined above: it narrates a story, that of lovers, traitors to their country, who do centuries of penance yet who remain doomed to frustration since their eyes may meet but never their lips. Here dialogue and dance occur together; they are married in a manner not demonstrated by the previous dance play in which the one is a prelude to the other.

The dance occurs as a climax to the lovers' laments that they can find no forgiveness for their treachery and, thus, the expression of their love for each other is destined to disappointment:

YOUNG GIRL: If some one of that race forgive at last
  Lip would be pressed on lip.
YOUNG MAN: O, never, never
  Shall Diarmuid and Devorgilla be forgiven.[93]

The words of the young soldier act as refrain and response to the girl's supplications. She summarises the plight of the lovers in simple and effective terms, made more desperate by the enjambement leading up to the forlornly desired outcome: 'Lip would be pressed on lip'. The repetition but separation of 'Lip' from 'lip' stresses the gulf between the two and the line is met – after the caesura which brings a short respite to the suffering – by the rebel's unforgiving 'O, never, never'. He counters the Girl's poetry by a barrier of uncompromising negatives in just the same manner as that in which their dance collides only with refusal.

In response to his intransigence a balletic movement ensues which is interpreted through language:

YOUNG MAN: Why do you dance?
  Why do you gaze, and with so passionate eyes,

One on the other; and then turn away,
Covering your eyes, and weave it in a dance?
Who are you? what are you? you are not natural.[94]

The poetry, 'weave it in a dance', is delicate and sensitive as the young rebel warms, against his will, to their account of their plight as demonstrated through both words and movement. His introductory harsh pronouncements are slightly convoluted, thereby putting precedence on his principal concern, that of Ireland:

YOUNG MAN: Our country, if that crime were uncommitted,
Had been most beautiful.[95]

The tone of the sentence in parentheses, 'if that crime were uncommitted', is savage and bitter and contrasts sharply with the lyricism of the phrases which contain it. The Young Man has the gift of eloquence in words: he is as capable of conjuring landscape as of presenting the dance descriptively:

YOUNG MAN: That town had lain,
But for the pair that you would have me pardon,
Amid its gables and its battlements
Like any old admired Italian town[96]

while the ghosts are eloquent in movement.

It is interesting to wonder at Yeats's decision to dispense with stage directions and employ an onlooker as interpreter. Perhaps he did so because this dance is pantomimic; its gestures express both emotion and relate narrative. The dance of the Hawk Woman does not convey a story, nor does that of the Faery Child in *The Land of Heart's Desire*. The technique employed here prefigures the dance of Attracta in *The Herne's Egg* which is construed in words by the three young girls. In this case the poetry admirably conveys what the movement in its turn and form expresses without, however, scripting it:

YOUNG MAN: They cannot hear,
Being folded up and hidden in their dance.
The dance is changing now. They have dropped their eyes,
They have covered up their eyes as though their hearts
Had suddenly been broken – never, never

>   Shall Diarmuid and Devorgilla be forgiven.
>   They have drifted in the dance from rock to rock.
>   They have raised their hands as though to snatch the sleep
>   That lingers always in the abyss of the sky
>   Though they can never reach it.[97]

His accuracy of perception and lyricism recalls that of the chorus of
Musicians who set the scene with which the play opened:

>   MUSICIANS: and all about the hills
>   Are like a circle of agate or of jade.
>   Somewhere among great rocks on the scarce grass
>   Birds cry, they cry their loneliness.[98]

In both cases a great degree of realism, 'Somewhere among great
rocks on the scarce grass / Birds cry', is combined with an elegiac
decoding of it, 'they cry their loneliness'. Matching this is the Young
Man's interpretation in language of the action before him: 'as
though their hearts / Had suddenly been broken'; 'as though to
snatch the sleep ... Though they can never reach it'.[99]

This dance is similar to Attracta's also in furthering the play's
action. The Young Man is abandoned by the lovers because he has
insisted that their pleas are hopeless; he will not yield. In the event,
their dance is thus one of desolation, but it has encapsulated in a
different medium the longing and desperation contained in their
words which led up to it:

>   YOUNG GIRL: ... I spoke
>   Of that most miserable, most accursed pair
>   Who sold their country into slavery; and yet
>   They were not wholly miserable and accursed
>   If somebody of their race at last would say,
>   'I have forgiven them'.[100]

The self-disgust and remorse of the two ghosts is evident in the
repetition of 'miserable' and 'accursed' and in the manner in which
the Girl must speak of herself and her lover in the third person in an
attempt to distance herself from that unnatural 'pair'. Her self-
accusation is most harsh and flagrant because, it is intimated, the
ghosts may experience a love of country as acute and elevated as the
rebel's own. The 'and yet' acts as a pivot between two perfectly

balanced statements while at the same time suggesting that there is still a strand of hope. But when the spectres finally perceive that their mission is fruitless, they move into the dance described above as a more telling method of recounting their history and subsequent failure. This dance is most poised and delicate and the words which provide its commentary match it in their fragility. The pentameters are linked by enjambement emphasising the inexorability of the situation – they must accept their fate as no mercy is forthcoming – and alliteration adds to the almost incantatory quality of the poetry: 'They have drifted in the dance from rock to rock', 'to snatch the sleep', which is violent in its despair. The image of that sleep 'That lingers always in the abyss of the sky' is touching in its frailty and poignancy.

The Dreaming of the Bones is most effective and achieved in its marriage of words and dance. The intimation that the pain of language is too acute for the suffering ghosts resolves itself by their transfiguration of it into movement. The Musicians provide a rollicking, boisterous image of treachery as response to the keen complaint of the lovers and thereby debunk the fears and hopes of the night:

MUSICIANS: My heart ran wild when it heard
    The curlew cry before dawn
    And the eddying cat-headed bird;
    But now the night is gone.
    I have heard from far below
    The strong March birds a-crow.
    Stretch neck and clap the wing,
    Red cocks and crow![101]

It is in such muscular sanity that the spectral dance finds its perhaps callous reply.

In the next of the *Four Plays for Dancers*, *The Only Jealousy of Emer*, also of 1919, a Woman of the Sidhe again dances in order to lure the Ghost of Cuchulain to her kingdom Under-the-Waves and away from his loyal wife, Emer. He recognises her as a different incarnation of the Hawk Woman whom he tried to tame, as related in *At the Hawk's Well*: there he pursued her as his prey, while in this case Fand is courting him so that, by their union, the supernatural forces of which she is one may realise themselves in the temporal world. In this play the manner in which dialogue is transfigured into dance is very clear to trace.

Emer is unable to perceive the Ghost of Cuchulain crouching in foetal position at the front of the stage until Bricriu, usurping and posing as the Figure of Cuchulain, has touched her eyes with his left hand. She in turn cannot be seen by the spectre of her husband. When Fand enters, having hurried from her element to woo Cuchulain or rather to 'fish for men / With dreams upon the hook',[102] Emer reacts instantly and violently against the rival trying to supplant her:

EMER: I know her sort.
    They find our men asleep, weary with war,
    Lap them in cloudy hair or kiss their lips;
    Our men awake in ignorance of it all,
    But when we take them in our arms at night
    We cannot break their solitude.[103]

Her astutely delineated portrait, as we noticed in Chapter 1, is worthy of that of Salome. The description is lyrical and pays tribute to the beauty of the enemies of the good wives: the reiteration of the possessive 'our men' is powerless when confronted with the dreamy delicacy of 'Lap them in cloudy hair'. The trenchant and bitter colloquialism, 'I know her sort' – it is the scorn of the virtuous wife for those women less decent than herself – is in contradistinction to the poignancy and empathy of 'weary with war'. The resigned inevitability of the enjambement of the last two lines emphasises the tragic impotence of those attempting to win back bewitched husbands:

But when we take them in our arms at night
We cannot break their solitude[104]

and the final line is a tetrameter, shorter than the pentameters which precede it and trenchant in its air of conclusiveness, loss and defeat. As if Emer realises that words alone, albeit poetry of some value, will not be sufficiently potent to vanquish her foe, she draws a knife from her girdle. It is a brave gesture, but vain, because Bricriu scoffs that 'No knife / Can wound that body of air'.[105] Neither weapons nor words can make even a dint on the metallic idol which is Fand and Emer is ineffectual against the witchcraft of the goddess. She is forced to witness just in what Fand's strength consists; it may not manifest itself in language, for Emer has already proved herself mistress of that. It is, of course, in dance.

The Hawk Woman's seduction consisted in luring Cuchulain away from the well, withdrawing into hiding and, thus, frustrating his eager pursuit. Here Fand is aggressive in her courtship of the now middle-aged warrior:

> (*The Woman of the Sidhe moves round the crouching Ghost of Cuchulain at front of stage in a dance that grows gradually quicker, as he slowly awakes. At moments she may drop her hair upon his head, but she does not kiss him. ...*)[106]

On reading this direction or on seeing the dance performed on stage it is difficult to resist Mallarmé's dictum that the dancer is a sign: the function of this dance is to seduce, while at the same time its signification, its presentation of an ideogram to be decoded, interprets as sexual tyranny. Yeats insists:

> (*Her mask and clothes must suggest gold or bronze or brass or silver, so that she seems more an idol than a human being. This suggestion may be repeated in her movements. Her hair, too, must keep the metallic suggestion.*)[107]

In common with the Hawk Woman and the ghosts, it is the distantiation brought about by the lack of humanity of the dancer as well as by the mysterious rites of the dance itself that is so memorable and significant.

Fand's dance, before which poetry yielded, is met with poetry. This time, however, it is not the achieved loveliness and fragility of Emer's verse, but the somewhat mechanical rhymes of the Ghost of Cuchulain:

> GHOST OF CUCHULAIN: Who is it stands before me there
> Shedding such light from limb and hair
> As when the moon complete at last
> With every labouring crescent past,
> And lovely with extreme delight,
> Flings out upon the fifteenth night?[108]

As students of Yeats are aware, Phase Fifteen of the moon in Yeats's 'System' is that of complete beauty and unity of being. Apart from the energy and emphasis of 'Flings out', the couplets do not impress by their lyricism and the whole of the encounter with

Fand is expressed in such jangling rhymes. We are meant, I think, to note that, while the quality of this poetic intercourse is less elevated than that with Emer, it is one with which Cuchulain feels at ease. He may profess himself to be paralysed by memories of his wife whom he has humiliated, but the weight of his being matches more closely that of the temptress, Fand. Emer is too noble for Cuchulain and has greater integrity. For all her appearance as an idol to be worshipped, Fand never achieves the dignity which is naturally Emer's and her dance is staccato and frenzied since she is desperate for a consort. Ironically enough, while the dance demonstrates that he is a passive recipient of her favours, perhaps victim, the language which follows illustrates that the two, Fand and Cuchulain, would be well mated: they seek no further than sexual passion. When Fand's influence wanes and she is cheated of her prize through Emer's loyal courage, Cuchulain awakens to the arms of his young mistress, Eithne Inguba, a mortal version of the defeated goddess from the sea, not to the selfless love of his wife to which he had just been alluding so insistently and with such remorse.

As in *At the Hawk's Well* the dance is crucial to *The Only Jealousy of Emer* and comprises the climax of the play. Once again it is anticipated by dialogue – Emer's battle through poetry with the would-be usurper, Fand, a challenge which can only be taken up through dance. And movement is met in its turn by language: the verse of the Ghost of Cuchulain which explains and comments on what has just been danced and the nature of the dancer:

GHOST OF CUCHULAIN: Who is it stands before me there
    Shedding such light from limb and hair …[109]

but cannot capture the ephemerality of the dance. We discover in this play an organic unity between dialogue and dance in which both media attain a level of skill which is mirrored, echoed and sometimes surpassed by other instances of Yeats's dance plays.

The last of *Four Plays for Dancers* of 1921 is *Calvary*, written in 1920. This play too demands to be taken individually on its own merits. Although its dance may seem to present features in common with others, I shall attempt to demonstrate that it is more genuinely and usefully considered as unique.

As in *The Land of Heart's Desire*, the dance here is announced beforehand by those who will perform it, but whereas the Faery

Child simply proclaimed that she would dance, in this play the whole narrative which the dance will express and summarise is anticipated by the Roman Soldiers and the only possible outcome that is left to chance – all others are foreseen – is that of who among them will win Christ's cloak according to a dice throw. As Katharine Worth astutely remarks:

> In *Calvary* for the first time, indeed, [Yeats] exploits to the full the opportunities the dance convention gives for self-conscious play with the theatrical illusion. ... In our role as audience we are drawn deep into [the] paradox ... on which the dance convention rests: the play pretends to be an improvisation, yet seems to deny that improvisation is possible; the plot is fixed, variations must always lead back into the main event. The characteristic impression the dance plays make of a machine that has been wound up and cannot stop is particularly strong and painful in *Calvary*.[110]

Thus, because of Yeats's working of the Christ story in which all events are already known, suspense is waived and, however much the details of the narrative are modified or indeed innovatory, the consequent outcome is quite familiar and unchangeable. Even so it is surprising to encounter a Lazarus who hates the miracle which deprived him of death and a Judas, anticipating existential drama, who, by complicated sophistry, endeavours to wriggle out of the fact that his decision to betray was preordained and not an act of free will. In this play it is tempting to regard the entire final section as a dance in which poetry acts contrapuntally in a crescendo culminating in the plain, homespun actual shift into movement of the Roman Soldiers:

SECOND ROMAN SOLDIER: Come now; let us dance
   The dance of the dice-throwers, for it may be
   He cannot live much longer and has not seen it.[111]

Calvary presents living creatures, including human beings, living so fully to the extremes of their own natures and personalities that they encroach on the exhibition of their own archetypes. The birds, to whom God has not appeared – they are not saved by Christ's love – exult in their own fullness and self-possession; thus a sea-bird performs the mysterious rites of its species:

FIRST MUSICIAN: Lonely the sea-bird lies at her rest,
  Blown like a dawn-blenched parcel of spray
  Upon the wind, or follows her prey
  Under a great wave's hollowing crest[112]

while the ger-eagle

THIRD MUSICIAN: … has chosen his part
  In blue deep of the upper air
  Where one-eyed day can meet his stare;
  He is content with his savage heart.[113]

Randomness, free will and determinism are not distinguishable one from another, as Judas, too, has cause to realise and the bird has 'chosen his part' in exactly the role and environment which is naturally and biologically his. Similarly the swan follows the demands of its own intimate nature as it joyfully flings out its white wings, for,

FIRST MUSICIAN: What can a swan need but a swan?[114]

And in the same manner the heron, bemused by its own reflection in the water, a *Leitmotiv* running through the play, is

[JUDAS]:   So full of itself that it seemed terrified.[115]

So also are the characters dancing out their part in the casual comedy of the Easter story: Lazarus and Judas are so superlatively themselves in performing their respective rebellions that they are moved to chuckle in glee when they erroneously believe that they have escaped Christ's influence and asserted their own will. And like the heron, Christ is Himself 'so full' of Himself that He seems terrified. He is subjected to the mockery of the crowd, the ministrations of Martha and the three Marys, the gibes of Lazarus and Judas and the matter-of-fact calmness of the Roman Soldiers and His terror culminates in the shout of despair which responds to the Soldiers' dance:

CHRIST: My Father, why hast Thou forsaken Me?[116]

Unlike the Roman Soldiers, however, none of these living things is aware that he is a fusion of both Self and Image, face and mask.

The Soldiers are supremely self-conscious and know and accept to the full that they are simply performing the required motions of somebody else's script. Such cynicism and a sense of the absurd are the very components which constitute their natures and, thus, they too, for all their astuteness, are allied to the rest by being wholly 'full of themselves', such as those selves are.

From their entrance until the end of the play Yeats achieves a dance of both language and movement. Their initial words override Christ's order that Judas should leave Him because Judas, they say, 'has been chosen to hold up the cross'.[117] It seems that the unlucky Judas has stumbled upon yet another script in which he must take a shabby part and we cannot resist calling to mind the gallic cynicism of the proverb, 'Christ a eu le beau rôle'. The Soldiers expect and get no rebellion because they only obey orders themselves and antici-pate no less in others. They do show compassion:

THIRD ROMAN SOLDIER: Die in peace.
    There's no one here but Judas and ourselves[118]

and when interrogated by the dying Christ as to their identity they announce that they are indeed the element which has so far been missing from the story which demands it, that of 'the gamblers'. As Worth remarks above, there is scant room for improvisation.

THIRD ROMAN SOLDIER: We are the gamblers, and when you are
    dead
    We'll settle who is to have that cloak of yours
    By throwing dice[119]

but the familiar account, keeping. as it must, to the stock themes, exhibits a certain elasticity. Thus, each known and expected element is countered by a stroke of Yeats's invention. So the detail that the dice were carved 'Out of an old sheep's thigh at Ephesus',[120] pre-sumably from the pagan Temple of Diana, introduces a note of panic and absurdity for who, in this extremity of suffering, cares? We immediately remember, however, that the gamblers' dance is that of chance and choice and the origin of their dice is of genuine import-ance to them as gamesters. Yeats contributes to the horror by invest-ing the trivial with grotesque significance.

The poetry of this final episode is very poised and charts a contrapuntal curve between seeming callousness and kindness:

thus the transformation of 'What does it matter?'[121] by the first Soldier into,

> FIRST ROMAN SOLDIER: They say you're good and that you made
>   the world,
> But it's no matter[122]

is balanced by

> THIRD ROMAN SOLDIER: Had you sent
>   A crier through the world you had not found
>   More comfortable companions for a death-bed
>   Than three old gamblers that have asked for nothing.[123]

And, for all their weary cynicism, they do recognise Christ as a god, if not as the only one:

> THIRD ROMAN SOLDIER: If he were but the god of dice he'd
>   know it,
> But he is not that God.[124]

This marriage of concern with its opposite, a lack of care or involvement, culminates in the Soldiers' own mapping of their script for the dance. They may explain and interpret what they are about to perform out of charity and a desire to be of comfort to the dying figure on the cross, but the effect is that of blunt want of feeling:

> SECOND ROMAN SOLDIER: In the dance
>   We quarrel for a while, but settle it
>   By throwing dice, and after that, being friends,
>   Join hand to hand and wheel about the cross.
>   (*They dance.*)[125]

It is not astonishing that Christ responds to their action by crying out in anguish the words expected of Him. What could be more terrifying than witnessing three figures, whose prosaic detachment amounts almost to lunacy, wheeling about in a dance? Ultimately, for all their bonhomie, the Roman Soldiers are horrifying. The echoes of their originals, the Torturers in medieval cycle plays, are inescapable.

The dance forms the climax of the preceding poetry and the latter underlines the Soldiers' unquestioning acceptance of all. Typically the speech, in blank verse, of one soldier will fade away only to be taken up by another. They are not readily distinguishable one from the next:

SECOND ROMAN SOLDIER: They are always wanting something.
THIRD ROMAN SOLDIER: Die in peace.[126]

THIRD ROMAN SOLDIER: ... By throwing dice.
SECOND ROMAN SOLDIER: Our dice were carved ...[127]

FIRST ROMAN SOLDIER: But it's no matter.
SECOND ROMAN SOLDIER: Come now, let us dance.[128]

THIRD ROMAN SOLDIER: But he is not that God.
FIRST ROMAN SOLDIER: One thing is plain.[129]

Even the gamblers, emblems of chance and the random, are confined by their script to act in a prescribed manner and the to-and-fro of their conversation has an air of ritual and ceremony about it from which, at intervals, they step aside in order to comment on the very rites which they are performing. As was the treachery of Judas, all this too has been foreseen.

The final episode of *Calvary*, then, presents a dance of voices which find their incarnation in the actual performance of choreographed measures. Dialogue and dance complement each other in ways with which we are now familiar from a consideration of previous plays, but what is unique to *Calvary* is an impression of plenitude of being verging on the achievement of archetypal stature: every living creature, bird or man, while living to the fullness of his own nature, at the same time expresses that nature in terms of a fixed script. The dance of the Roman Soldiers is first mapped out in words in order to illustrate the strictures being imposed on the dancers by the story in which they find themselves as instrumental, and then performed in movement to show the transcendence of those very limitations. Dance is the most effective way of reconciling the polarities of chance and choice, the mutable and the static, life and death because, as Denis Donoghue claims:

In gesture there is no distinction between content and form: gesture is the dance of attitude.[130]

The Cat and the Moon, written in 1917 at the same time as certain of the *Four Plays for Dancers* but published much later in 1926, is Yeats's version of a *kyogen* – a farce performed between two Noh dramas – and it is principally in prose, a lilting, merry reproduction of Irish speech, encapsulated by the polished poetry of the 'Minnaloushe' songs. The two dances – the first to represent a beating given the Lame Beggar by his companion, the Blind Beggar, for stealing the latter's sheepskin and the second, the Lame Man's dance celebrating his being blessed by the Holy Man – are pantomimic and expressive, respectively. Their function is clearly integral to the action of the play and they are both incorporated naturally into the script.

The first dance, the Lame Man's drubbing, prefigures the initial battle scene in *The Herne's Egg* which is also represented as a stylised dance: in this case it is quite simply to mime the punishment of a thief, albeit harmless and 'flighty'. It appears as a culmination of verbal threats over the stolen sheepskin which intensify in terms of language in the cured Blind Beggar's blasphemy:

> BLIND BEGGAR: I have been saying to myself, I shall know where to hit and how to hit and who to hit.
> LAME BEGGAR: Do you not know that I am blessed? Would you be as bad as Caesar and Herod and Nero and the other wicked emperors of antiquity?
> BLIND BEGGAR: Where'll I hit him, for the love of God,where'll I him?[131]

For all his restored sight, he is unable to see the Holy Man even though his comrade claims that the Saint is standing before him, laughing. The formerly Blind Beggar, who represents corporeal man and materialism, never aspires to spiritual grace; he leaves the stage, presumably to embark on one of his many raids of kitchens and gardens but, for the first time in forty years, unaccompanied by his alter ego, the Lame Beggar. The latter, once having been blessed, carries the Holy Man on his back and observes, to his great delight, that a miracle has enabled him to dance. This joyful discovery is prepared by a renunciation of words as inappropriate:

> LAME BEGGAR: Let us be going, Holy man.
> FIRST MUSICIAN: But you must bless the road.
> LAME BEGGAR: I haven't the right words.

FIRST MUSICIAN: What do you want words for? Bow to what is before you, bow to what is behind you, bow to what is to the left of you, bow to what is to the right of you.

(*The Lame Beggar begins to bow.*)

FIRST MUSICIAN: That's no good.

LAME BEGGAR: No good, Holy Man?

FIRST MUSICIAN: No good at all. You must dance.

LAME BEGGAR: But how can I dance? Ain't I a lame man?

FIRST MUSICIAN: Aren't you blessed?

LAME BEGGAR: Maybe so.

FIRST MUSICIAN: Aren't you a miracle?

LAME BEGGAR: I am, Holy Man.

FIRST MUSICIAN: Then dance, and that'll be a miracle.[132]

The gentle comedy of the last line does not conceal the fact that here, through an undulating dialogue that recalls the confessional with the simple and credulous questioner and the loving representative of God, the Lame Beggar slowly comes to comprehend in full what it means to be blessed and it does not consist simply in having his name written in the Saint's big book. The dialogue is very poignant because the Lame Beggar is touching in his faith in the Holy Man on his back; the knowing and sophisticated Blind Beggar would be incapable of such confidence, but then he was never 'flighty'. This is a tender story of a saintly Fool who is much wiser than he knows and, significantly enough, Yeats has him shed words and transfigure emotion into dance. Yeats said of *The Cat and the Moon*:

> I wrote this play with the intention of including it in 'Four Plays for Dancers', but did not do so as it was in a different mood[133]

and the link with the first four dance plays is certainly very evident from this second dance of disbelief turning to joy, since language is once again rejected in favour of movement:

> (*The Lame Beggar begins to dance, at first clumsily, moving about with his stick, then he throws away the stick and dances more and more quickly. Whenever he strikes the ground strongly with his lame foot the cymbals clash. He goes out dancing ...*)[134]

The Musicians' songs about the cat and the moon also culminate in a depiction of a dance. It is not, perhaps, too far-fetched to suggest that the relationship between Minnaloushe and the moon is a reflection of that between the Lame Beggar and spiritual enlightenment. Yeats informs us that cat and moon are kindred spirits; the cat is contemplating its own antithesis and, at the same time, its desired mask:

> FIRST MUSICIAN: Black Minnaloushe stared at the moon,
>   For, wander and wail as he would,
>   The pure cold light in the sky
>   Troubled his animal blood.[135]

The next song accompanies the beggars' hobbling journey to St Colman's Well. Minnaloushe responds to being troubled by expressing his lack of ease through dancing, as it is the most fitting manner of resolving the antinomies of warmth and cold, mortality and immortality, flesh and spirit:

> FIRST MUSICIAN: Do you dance Minnaloushe, do you dance?
>   When two close kindred meet
>   What better than call a dance?[136]

and the moon may itself learn a new choreography from the prancing patterns traced by the black cat. This song about a dance prefigures the actual performance of one, that of the Lame Beggar with the Saint on his back: here also two close kindred meet – the Lame Man has chosen his next of kin by electing to be blessed – and celebrate their encounter in dance. It is a fitting and satisfying culmination of the play, leaving only the third and last of the Musicians' songs to provide conclusion and comment.

Minnaloushe creeps from place to place bathed in the moonlight which he adores: but the planet's phase has changed, so the cat's eyes transform themselves in accordance with the new shape of the moon overhead. The two complement each other's essential nature by the one's dancing and the other's shedding light, just as Blind Beggar and Lame Beggar completed each other before the former was cured and his crony blessed. Now, however, in a subsequent phase of the moon, the poles of attraction have shifted and the Lame Beggar is appropriately allied to the Holy Man.

The Minnaloushe songs are beautifully balanced in their structure and measured rhythm and so reflect the equilibrium established between cat and moon. The poetry is polished and highly achieved with a noticeable rhyme scheme which supports the equations charted:

FIRST MUSICIAN: The cat went here and there
  And the moon spun round like a top,
  And the nearest kin of the moon,
  The creeping cat, looked up.[137]

Both moon and cat are casual, informal, the one stepping out 'here and there' while the other, in colloquial terms, 'spun like a top', but the weight of the verse suggests that the two are co-ordinates on the same graph, opposite and equal. The pattern is reversed in the third and fourth lines in which the moon is introduced before the cat: the rhyme, 'top' and 'up', is not a true one and the sense of dislocation which it induces is ample introduction to the poet's claim that the moon 'troubled' the animal. The two elements are as yet out of harmony and their reconciliation is achieved through their dance illustrated in the second song:

FIRST MUSICIAN: Maybe the moon may learn,
  Tired of that courtly fashion,
  A new dance turn.[138]

In this central and mediating song the rhymes are all true; the dancers are well-matched.

The last song acts as response to the Lame Beggar's dance while also demonstrating a transcendence of separation and opposition, for the cat, instead of randomly moving 'here and there', now creeps from 'moonlight place to place'[139] – its environment is satisfactory to its longings, just as the dancing Lame Beggar has too found his rightful element. Once again the rhymes jar; 'place' is partnered by 'phase', but this discordant note will be honed and polished into harmony by the rest of the song which presents a resolution of the forces which were previously at odds in the main body of the play as well as in the verses. The images are of strengths linked contrapuntally:

FIRST MUSICIAN: Does Minnaloushe know that his pupils
  Will pass from change to change,
  And that from round to crescent,
  From crescent to round they range ?
  Minnaloushe creeps through the grass

Alone, important and wise,
And lifts to the changing moon
His changing eyes.[140]

The regular trimeters are undercut by the final short line which
succinctly and trenchantly focusses on what is most important in
the poem, 'His changing eyes'. The enjambement following 'the
changing moon' stresses that the two elements are now indeed
unified in an equation of equal forces. This song acts as echo to the
Lame Beggar's own miraculous dance: those in search of spiritual
enlightenment have attained it.

The Resurrection (1931), is a dance play without a dance and is
thus in obvious contradistinction to those plays considered above
which contain dances but are not themselves dance plays. It was
written to be performed either as one of the dance plays with the
typical folding and unfolding of the cloth, or at the Peacock Theatre,
a small conventional theatre in Dublin which shares a roof with the
Abbey.

The play plumbs the nature of mystery, the fact of Christ's resurrection. The Syrian has been to the tomb and brought back to his
fellow-followers of Christ, the Hebrew and the Greek, the heady
information that it is empty: the stone has been moved and Christ
has been seen alive by the women who love Him. The very nature
of the miracle, Christ's rising from the dead, is not negotiable by
language and the climax of this play, in common with all the dance
plays, is the movement that the risen Messiah makes to cross the
stage from the door of the room in which the Hebrew, Greek and
Syrian exchange creeds and interpretations to the inner chamber,
where the eleven apostles break bread and await both news and
persecution. This crossing of the stage replaces a dance and it is
anticipated by dialogue in a like manner to that of earlier and later
dance plays, as I have been attempting to demonstrate. In ironic
contrast to the revelation of a living Christ is the worldly turmoil of
the rabble outside in the street dancing their worship of Dionysus,
also a god, killed by Titans but reborn yearly. The songs of the
Musicians relate his history: his murder and subsequent rebeget-
ting by his father, Zeus, on Semele. Dionysus, in common with
Christ, was born of mortal woman. The anarchic horror of the
procession of the mob of Dionysian worshippers outside is charted
by the commentary of the three young men inside the house. They
recount the excesses to which the crowd goes, the gashing of

themselves with knives in order to represent the killing by the Titans, the coupling of a man and woman in the street, but, above all, the frenzied dances which culminate in an awesome calm as the revellers approach the house which shelters the apostles and the Hebrew, Greek and Syrian. The mob falls quiet when it perceives something which two of the young men will have difficulty in admitting, the entry of the supposedly dead Christ into the room harbouring His followers.

While the songs seem to be extolling the massacre and resurrection of Dionysus and are reportedly celebrated and actualised in dance, they in fact prefigure Christ's manifestation of Himself after His death to those who loved Him and His crossing of the stage – His dance. The first song anticipates the Syrian's reaction; he is the only one of the three to realise that a new dispensation has insisted on being recognised in which it is necessary to accept the irrational – that a deity may be born a mortal man and die a mortal death, but, as a god, can overcome it and return in the guise of a human being without, however, losing any part of his godhead:

MUSICIANS: Another Troy must rise and set,
Another lineage feed the crow,
Another Argo's painted prow
Drive to a flashier bauble yet.
The Roman Empire stood appalled:
It dropped the reins of peace and war
When that fierce virgin and her Star
Out of the fabulous darkness called.[141]

The songs are in flagrant contrast to the dialogue of the play, a prose particularly suited for argument and discourse. As if to emphasise the degree of shock and the reorientation necessary to comprehend and cope with the pending events, Yeats has introduced the quirky rhyme 'crow' and 'prow', 'war' and 'Star' into the set order of the surrounding true rhymes. So too are the organised patterns of life and convenient beliefs of Christ's followers shaken up and rendered tumultuous by the happenings in which they find themselves implicated.

The second song, in very tight trimeters, presents a bridge between pagan and Christian worship. The singer, a boy from the theatre dressed and wigged as a girl, calls on the holy virgin Astrea to succour those mourning the Titans' slaughter of Dionysus. The women attempted to lure the god away and save him, but were impotent against his persecutors: they then sing and pray for his resurrection:

MUSICIAN: On virgin Astrea
That can succour all
Wandering women call;
Call out to Astrea
That the moon stood at the full.[142]

It is quite evident that the song also includes the notion of that other virgin, Mary, mother of Christ and she is thus invoked to play her part in interceding for her dead son. This anticipates what we are about to learn on the Syrian's return from the empty tomb, the report that Mary has witnessed Jesus's resurrection.

Christ, when he reveals Himself in the outer room, does not speak because the event is too great and too impressive. And we have been prepared for a climax which is not rooted in language by the narration of the antics of the worshippers of Dionysus and their metamorphosis of song into silent dancing. So, too, here, the Hebrew falls into terrified taciturnity as the curtain before a blank wall begins to move as if a man is behind it; the Syrian has been speechless for some moments; the Greek, the logician, greets the figure of Christ which enters 'wearing a recognisable but stylistic mask' with his conviction that 'it is the phantom of our master'.[143] He is destined to discover differently, however, and his scream on discerning a human, beating heart gives way to Christ's wordless crossing of the stage. Yeats has presented a moment of epiphany in theatrical terms.

Once Christ has performed His movement, language, dialogue, takes up the thread of narration once more, having been vanquished by its inappropriateness and lack of required subtlety; but the Hebrew, understandably, perhaps, as he had been so certain that Christ was not the Messiah, remains silent until the end of the play. The Syrian depicts for his fellows and the audience the events that he can see occurring in the inner room as Christ joins the apostles:

THE SYRIAN: ... He shows them his side. There is a great wound there. Thomas has put his hand into the wound. He has put his hand where the heart is.[144]

He is the astute and precise witness and commentator and can bear mystery. The Greek continues to deal in the abstractions which he enjoys and with which he can cope: his universe has been overturned and thereby he has gained enlightenment into something which he had never understood before because of the blinkers imposed by his previous faith:

> THE GREEK: O Athens, Alexandria, Rome, something has come to destroy you. The heart of a phantom is beating. Man has begun to die. Your words are clear at last, O Heraclitus. God and man die each other's life, live each other's death.[145]

In common with the other dance plays, *The Resurrection* closes with the Musicians' song which, in this case, serves to elucidate and summarise the action of the play. Thus Christ's crossing the room is portrayed as 'Galilean turbulence'.[146] All Babylonian mastery of astronomy and calculation is rendered null by the 'fabulous, formless darkness'[147] which has accompanied the resurrection and the assertion of Christ's immortality, just as Greek skill, science and artistry have been annulled by His human attributes:

> MUSICIANS: Odour of blood when Christ was slain
> Made all Platonic tolerance vain
> And vain all Doric discipline.[148]

The last stanza of the final song dwells firmly on the transience and mutability of everything attributed to the human:

> MUSICIANS: Everything that man esteems
> Endures a moment or a day.[149]

The deliberate presence of pain is stressed by the choice of 'Endures' over 'lasts' or any other synonym and in a world of mortals, the text insists, everything is temporary and contains within itself its own end and oblivion:

> MUSICIANS: The painter's brush consumes his dreams.[150]

Man is left with his 'own resinous heart'[151] which burns up itself, his passions and creations.

The setting is austere and the stage bare: most of the actions – the dances of the Dionysiacs in the street; the encounter between Christ and His apostles; and the view of Calvary and the meeting of Christ and the women – are conveyed through the report of a character on stage. Apart from His crossing of the acting area, the arrival of the Syrian and the recoil of the Hebrew closely followed by the Greek's scream, the play is built entirely of discussion, argument and song. It is therefore, in this mass of debate and verbosity, so moving and eloquent when words prove themselves to be inadequate because they are confronted by miracle.

A Full Moon in March of 1935 is the first of a group of late dance plays which also includes *The King of the Great Clock Tower* (1935) and *The Death of Cuchulain* (1939), Yeats's last play. They were all designed to be acted upon a conventional stage with a proscenium and outer and inner curtain, unlike the folded cloth tradition of the *Four Plays for Dancers* and yet they are unequivocally dance plays; nowhere else is it more apparent how dialogue is transfigured into dance.

In *A Full Moon in March* two Attendants represent the customary Musicians and we have already demonstrated in Chapter 2 the Pirandellian manner in which they destroy theatrical illusion by discussing their own roles and what they have been instructed to do. One informs the other that they can act in whatever manner they fancy, sing whatever they choose, since nothing could disturb or destroy the inevitability of what is to follow. Therefore they sing of that love which exchanges and reconciles 'Crown of gold' and 'dung of swine'[152] and their verses serve as preamble to the wooing of the Queen by the Swineherd. The initial reaction that the union is unequal and inappropriate is reinforced by the clumsiness of the song: there is no satisfactory rhyme for 'love'; it is either matched by 'enough' in the first couplet portraying the 'loutish lad' or, in the second stanza, it is rhymed with 'thereof'. Similarly, 'foolishness' is echoed by the maladroit 'sweetness is'. The final stanza of this opening song, however, serves to demonstrate, as will the play as a whole, that the union of the Swineherd and Queen is quite apposite: they complement each other because, opening wide 'those gleaming eyes' 'can make the loutish wise'.[153] According to Yeats's schema, completion of the self and unity of being are achieved only by the reconciliation of opposites.

This play is based on song and dance: either one prefigures the other or, in the case of the final magnificent song, the dance finds its achievement in verse. It is not a mere extra-literary device since it absorbs into its gestures the issues of most significance in the play in which its weight and centrality are undisputed. The three dances are anticipated by language which they then in turn transfigure. The second song delivered by the First Attendant, the elderly woman, deals with:

FIRST ATTENDANT: An ancient Queen
    That stuck a head upon a stake.
SECOND ATTENDANT: Her lover's head[154]

and is performed while the decapitation of the Swineherd takes place off-stage. The Queen claims the head as desired trophy and nurses it between bloodstained hands. In the song the woman denies responsibility for the decollation discharged out of 'mere woman's cruelty'.[155] The verse summarises the preceding dialogue in which the Swineherd had 'famished in a wilderness / Braved lions for my sake'[156] and

FIRST ATTENDANT: He swore to sing my beauty
    Though death itself forbade.[157]

At the same time it also serves to anticipate what is to come – the song from the dead head – and puts forward the premise that just as empresses have been created out of innkeepers' daughters (such as the one who married the Emperor Romanus), so women of great prestige and power have chosen to bed

FIRST ATTENDANT: … with their fancy-man
    Whether a king or clown.[158]

But however capricious and extravagant they were in love, they will never witness what falls to this Queen:

FIRST ATTENDANT: O they had their fling,
    But never stood before a stake
    And heard the dead lips sing.[159]

When the inner curtain is drawn open the Queen is revealed holding the severed head and this attitude is the preliminary to her dances. She sings a loving cradle song which will be matched by the nursery-rhyme ditty to be performed by the head of the Swineherd. The Queen's version is tender and maternal:

> FIRST ATTENDANT (*singing as Queen*):   Child and darling, hear my
>   song,
>   Never cry I did you wrong;
>   Cry that wrong came not from me,
>   But my virgin cruelty.[160]

The rhymes are true and the verse polished and the perfection of the stanzas is taken up by dance in order to demonstrate, as the song cannot, the reconciliation of forces: that of 'virgin cruelty' which demands severed heads and that of a genuine tenderness for the victim who made himself her equal, which the Queen in her arrogance would prefer to deny experiencing. She pays him homage by placing his head upon the throne as she dances to drum-taps. When the dead lips reply they do so by means of the parody of the child's verse 'Jack and Jill', only in this case, instead of fetching water:

> SECOND ATTENDANT (*singing as Head*):   Jill had murdered Jack,[161]

and

> Had hung his heart on high.[162]

As is the Queen's lullaby, this too is a version of the treatment of the power relationship between men and women and, in both cases, the man is simultaneously victim and beloved of the woman. The Queen's response to the dead head's song is once more to dance in a manner which Yeats stipulates is both 'alluring and refusing'.[163] The ditty has prepared for this by expressing in macabre terms the woman's ferocity: it is in tetrameters interchanged with trimeters and the rhymes are pat and facile; 'Jill'/'Jack', 'hill'/'back'. In her song the Queen tried to deflect accusation from herself. Here she remains firmly accused, nay, guilty and her sole reaction to the charge is a laughter which is echoed by that of the Swineherd. Both lovers thus express the mutuality of their delight at their discovery of each other and their reciprocated passion. The two opposing forces, 'alluring and refusing', are neatly captured by dance movement and can intimately portray the Queen's teasing sexual play.

Finally, the conflict is resolved and brought to a close by the Queen's dancing in adoration and kissing the lips of the severed head. It is not astonishing that spontaneous laughter should culminate in a dance of ecstasy when we realise that it expresses recognition of a worthy partner and gratitude for such a find. But the First Attendant may also voice another truth:

FIRST ATTENDANT: She is crazy. That is why she is laughing.[164]

The modernity and colloquial quality of 'crazy' contrasts sharply with the imposing nature of the concepts that have been discussed by the play and we irresistibly remember the series of Yeats's Crazy Jane poems which dealt so perceptively and truly with the complexities of physical love. One thing is certain; if the Queen is indeed crazy then it is a form of lunacy which the Swineherd shares and she would never have contracted it had it not been for his impudence and temerity in claiming her love for his own. The concluding dance stresses that the irrational has conquered over the more polite and decorous virtues of human intercourse and that all propriety has been sacrificed to passion.

And the final song emphasises such a reading of this dance. By closing the inner curtain and thereby concealing the Queen cradling her lover's head, the Attendants are transformed back into a chorus commenting on the action, rather than as Musicians implicated therein by their respective roles in singing on behalf of the protagonists. The Second Attendant, a young boy, who was so knowledgeable and confident at the opening of the play, now is in search of answers to the mysteries which he has witnessed. The elderly woman, the First Attendant, can throw some light on his perplexity because the second song was entrusted to her, that in which she explained that great ladies would follow their inclinations in love, even if the object of their passion were a clown or a Swineherd. The boy's question is posed thus:

SECOND ATTENDANT: Why must those holy, haughty feet descend
    From emblematic niches, and what hand
    Ran that delicate raddle through their white?[165]

He wonders, not unnaturally, why the pure, aristocratic spirit of artifice should seek to enter the human world of the flesh and be contaminated by the blood and mire of which it is composed. And in response, the elderly, maternal, woman provides the riddle of sexual longing:

FIRST ATTENDANT: For desecration and the lover's night[166]

before which both high nobility and proud disdain succumb. As did the Queen and the Swineherd, the frozen creations of art also seek their opposites in order to be fulfilled.

The play itself has provided the replies to the boy's enquiries: he has been spectator to the solutions of the puzzles posed as they were acted and danced out before him. But he, being human and obstinate, with what he calls a 'savage, sunlit heart',[167] insists that the lady whose 'emblem is the moon'[168] can, being so perfect and complete, lack nothing. The First Attendant simply reiterates that such a woman seeks to be enmeshed in the toils of 'desecration and the lover's night'.[169] The boy makes one last attempt at accepting her explanation and invokes his instructor and mentor to contemplate the imagined mosaic again and note 'the pitchers that [the figures] carry; tight / Therein all time's completed treasure is'.[170] The mention of the incongruous, homely 'pitchers' may hark back to the 'Jack and Jill' rhyme of the severed head. Even the carriers of these vessels – vessels which I take to be amphorae containing the liquids or unguents of regeneration – experience the same sexual longings and the boy's confidante concludes the discussion by finally insisting on what has become a refrain: 'desecration and the lover's night'.

The interrelationship of song and dance is a subtle one in this late play and it affects that between narrative and dance. While the songs both prepare the action and comment upon it, that action becomes expressed and epitomised in terms of choreography. Thus, the first dance is prefigured by the Queen's song which stressed that 'virgin cruelty' which we witness in her interview with the peremptory Swineherd, but which is actualised through movement as she dances with the severed head and, paying tribute to it, places it upon the throne. The combination of fascination and love that she felt for the grotesque clown and his bravery has wakened her nascent sexuality, and such temerity must be punished by death in order to negate and obliterate the genuine power that he exercises over her, a tyranny which she at the same time acknowledges and is delighted by. In her dance we can perceive the unification of these mixed motives and conflicting sentiments.

The next song, introduced by the head's 'Jack and Jill' rhyme, gives way to a different dance, that of flirtation and sexual teasing. The Queen is as wayward and provoking as a young woman in love who is sure of her power over her chosen partner: the 'virgin cruelty' is replaced by skittishness and playfulness which the nursery rhyme, however insistent its accusation of murder, anticipates. The final dance is the most impressive and achieved although introduced by the dialogue which precedes it as 'crazy'. It emblematises for the audience or reader in just what this craziness consists. We have seen how Yeats, in his stage direction, interpreted this dance as one of 'adoration': the Queen has attained a maturity of self-expression in which she can convey a degree of passion which is both unmixed and unmediated. The head in her hands, she dances as sexual equal to the Swineherd, kisses his dead lips in a gesture of love and longing and her body expresses orgasmic climax in her shivers. In the lull that follows this ballet of the wedding night, which the Swineherd anticipated in his unseemly manner, the Queen's last attitude is one of maternal instinct as she holds the head to her breast. Dance has indeed metamorphosed dialogue and furnished a different degree of intensity, but Yeats then has the singers close by interpreting through language the gestures which they have witnessed and to which they provided the preamble.

The King of the Great Clock Tower, also of 1935 in its verse version although it appeared initially the previous year in prose, has much in common with *A Full Moon in March*. While the plots are very similar, in this case the King mediates between the masked Queen and the Stroller: it is the King who demands the latter's execution and who subsequently enthrones his head. Yeats's own notes on this play illustrate that he first wrote the prose version of *The King of the Great Clock Tower* and later revised it into a form which became *A Full Moon in March* because:

> In *The King of the Great Clock Tower* there are three characters, King, Queen and Stroller, and that is a character too many; reduced to the essentials, to Queen and Stroller, the fable should have greater intensity. I started afresh and called the new version *A Full Moon in March*.[171]

The version of *The King of the Great Clock Tower* which is today published in *The Collected Plays* and which is now under consideration was actually written after *A Full Moon in March* and in verse.

The first words of the play sung by the two attendants relate to dancing and indeed the inner curtain, according to Yeats's directions, should represent 'perhaps a stencilled pattern of dancers'.[172] Such hesitation and seeming self-doubt are typically found in Yeats's stage directions; not only was he always experimenting but was also ever open to new suggestions and ideas. The chorus sings of a country similar to the land of Faery depicted in *The Land of Heart's Desire* where dance is a magical medium which replaces words and in which the trammels wrought by the passing of time are non-existent because time itself has been annihilated:

> SECOND ATTENDANT: They dance all day that dance in Tir-nan-oge.
> FIRST ATTENDANT: There every lover is a happy rogue;
>   And should he speak, it is the speech of birds.
>   No thought has he, and therefore has no words,
>   No thought because no clock, no clock because
>   If I consider deeply, lad and lass,
>   Nerve touching nerve upon that happy ground,
>   Are bobbins where all time is bound and wound.[173]

A picture of the Land of the Blessed also includes that of sexual desire and union. This is clearly conveyed through the First Attendant's description of the pursuit of the hound for the hornless deer which follows the above lines; the chase is an image for Yeats from Celtic mythology of sexual conquest. The paradise world of Tir-nan-oge is marred by the presence of a woman who refuses to give up the apple that she is clasping to a man who is clamouring for it. As in *A Full Moon in March*, the woman is again cruel, but here an echo is introduced not present in the previous play, that of an Eden in which Eve refuses indulgence with Adam however 'famished'[174] he may be. The dancing land is exempt from words and, thus, of thought and reason and, consequently, 'every lover is a happy rogue'.[175]

The ensuing dialogue and action of the play prove the opening songs to be prescient, for while the King directs his diatribe against the silent and mysterious Queen, the only response of which she is capable is framed by dance. The King may interrogate her brutally but she refuses to accommodate his demands and remains speechless. It is only the impudent Stroller who can draw any passion from the masked Queen and, to him, she is a disappointment in not being as beautiful as he had anticipated in his dreams and in the poetry which he penned in her honour:

THE STROLLER: Neither so red, nor white, nor full in the breast
　As I had thought. What matter for all that
　So long as I proclaim her everywhere
　Most beautiful![176]

As did the Swineherd in the earlier play, the Stroller insists that the Queen shall dance, that he will sing in gratitude and, at the stroke of midnight 'when the old year dies',[177] she will kiss his mouth. He is executed for his boldness and the King orders his head to be brought in order to provoke some reaction from the inert Queen whom the Stroller insulted. She begins to sing and the King greets her verses as a song of euphoria that the upstart has been killed. But he is mistaken in his interpretation: the Queen's song is actually one of apprehension and submission anticipating her dance. Rather than a celebration of sexual union, it expresses dread of such intercourse:

SECOND ATTENDANT (*singing as the Queen in a low voice*):   He longs
　to kill
　My body, until
　That sudden shudder
　And limbs lie still.[178]

While she allows the Stroller's desire for her, she is anxious about its consequences:

SECOND ATTENDANT: O, what may come
　Into my womb,
　What caterpillar
　My beauty consume?[179]

The echoes of Blake's 'The Sick Rose' must surely be intentional. They are certainly insistent and Yeats furnishes a similar continuum of the heaven and hell that characterise sexual congress. The Queen perceives the act as murder: 'He longs to kill / My body'.[180] In this stanza the use of rhyme and enjambement is striking: the rhymes are true and frame the focal word, 'shudder', while the enjambement throughout indicates that the act portrayed is relentless. The following stanza, on the other hand, is characterised by a series of echoes rather than rhymes: 'come', 'womb', 'consume', leaving 'caterpillar' to stand clumsily alone. The whole is awkward and expressive of anxiety, since the final clause, 'What caterpillar / My

beauty consume?' is disordered in such a way as to throw emphasis
upon 'My beauty' and, hence, suggests that the Queen views the
proposed union as a rape rather than reciprocated pleasure and her
concern is for the preservation of her own integrity.

The King, brandishing the severed head which he places mockingly on a throne, demands the promised song from its lips, but, as
predicted, the Queen must first dance. Just as the King misinter-
preted her song, so he does her dance:

> THE KING: Dance, turn him into mockery with a dance!
>   No woman ever had a better thought. ...
>   Dance, give him scorn for scorn,
>   Display your beauty, spread your peacock tail.[181]

Her dance is not one of contempt and derision, however, but is
instead engendered out of her desire to resist the fear and threat of
the 'caterpillar' of sex as destruction and to convey a preparedness
to play her part in the ritual instigated by the Stroller's arrival at
court. The year is dying and the Queen, in her placing of the severed
head upon her shoulder, participates in a ceremony of regeneration
which is best expressed by dance. Her actions were predicted by the
Stroller who was informed of them by the Irish god of love, Aengus,
in a vision and so, as foreseen, the Queen's dance is met by the
severed head's song of gratitude. It now has arcane knowledge, that
of death, and from this beyond-the-grave perspective can compare
immortal and mortal beings:

> FIRST ATTENDANT (*singing as Head*):   Clip and lip and long for
>   more,
>   Mortal men our abstracts are.[182]

The argument of the song suggests that all human endeavour is null
to the joys of the supernatural world where:

> FIRST ATTENDANT: Crossed fingers ... in pleasure can
>   Exceed the nuptial bed of man.[183]

While the song choreographs the Queen's next movement:

> FIRST ATTENDANT: What marvel is
>   Where the dead and living kiss ?[184]

its chorus predicts its timing, 'A moment more and it tolls midnight'.[185] The Stroller's song depicts the wonders of the sphere of the dead, but can only succeed in a limited way in communicating with the temporal world which is no longer his own: 'But there's a stone upon my tongue'.[186] His reduction to silence effects a transfiguration of the medium of expression, from words into dance, for, as hinted by the song, the Queen embarks on a new movement and, as the last stroke of midnight sounds from the clock, she presses her lips to the lips of the head. Then, despite the King's threatened assault on her with the sword that he has drawn in jealous anger, she places the head upon her breast. In *A Full Moon in March* these actions were tokens of adoration as the Queen there expressed her delight at having found a worthy partner who pleased her; there was finally reciprocity of affection. Here, although the dance is almost completely identical, the force of it is slightly different. Firstly, the Queen is reluctant to play her role in that regeneration ritual suggested by the realisation that the court is that of the King of Time and that the year is almost over. Secondly, there is in this case less motive for a dance of triumph because it is the King who is insulted by the Stroller's rashness and he mediates between the Queen's reaction and the audience. This Queen is a much less independent figure for all her mysterious and obstinate silence.

As in the other dance plays, the climactic dance, in which the Queen vanquishes the King by her outfacing him and braving his intention to strike, gives way to song. And just as in the first one considered above, 'They dance all day that dance in Tir-nan-oge', so this concluding song, too, treats of dancing:

FIRST ATTENDANT: O but I saw a solemn sight;
  Said the rambling, shambling travelling-man;
  Castle Dargan's ruin all lit,
  Lovely ladies dancing in it.[187]   [Yeats's emphasis]

These figures are the dancing dead; the faeries and blessed ones of Tir-nan-oge have been supplanted by a set of ghosts:

SECOND ATTENDANT: Lovely lady, or gallant man
  Are blown cold dust or a bit of bone.[188]

The image of the dance is eternal, representing concord and unity, fixed order and yet passionate spontaneity, art and yet the flux of life. The song is not perfect and polished, however; its tetrameters are uneven and shambling and its rhymes are rarely true. Alliteration, 'O, but I saw a solemn sight' and 'a bit of bone', emphasises weight and balance in the first instance which gives way to deliberate triteness and triviality in the second. These verses, a meditation on death and immortality, are fitting response to the Queen's dance with the severed head and the consequent conquering of time as represented by the King and Yeats obviously intended them to provide counterpoint in such a manner, since he has the Queen come downstage just before the final stanza and stand 'framed in the half-closed curtains'.[189] Her presence there is also encapsulated between the two last stanzas of the song:

SECOND ATTENDANT: Nobody knows what may befall,
  Said the wicked, crooked, hawthorn tree.
  I have stood so long by a gap in the wall
  Maybe I shall not die at all.[190]   [Yeats's emphasis]

This is an account of another approach to the secret of immortality, that of extreme longevity and the knowingness that it bestows. The final impression is none the less one of the challenge of time to the timeless. While the hawthorn tree is ancient and 'wicked' and 'crooked', the Queen is self-possessed and still wearing her beautiful, impassive mask. As she stands between the curtains, her presence throws down the gauntlet to those who would possess or tame her: unlike her counterpart in *A Full Moon in March*, this woman is hardly touched by events; she remains aloof and intact despite her passionate dancing and proves herself more than a match for both King and Stroller.

An attempt has been made to demonstrate how dialogue, song and dance are intimately linked in this play. In all the dance plays the dance takes precedence and has a precise function in the narrative and action; it is never merely decorative. The interconnections between the different media of the plays makes for a unity created from within and is thus arguably inherent and organic as opposed to mechanistic and imposed.

Yeats's last foray into writing for the stage was also a dance play, *The Death of Cuchulain* (1939). The Musicians or Attendants whom we have come to expect are replaced in this case by an irascible old man, whose views and opinions parody Yeats's own and a Singer, Piper and Drummer with whose contemporary rollicking street music the play closes. Emer's dance provides the climax and is anticipated in the Old Man's preface:

OLD MAN: I promise a dance. I wanted a dance because where there are no words there is less to spoil. Emer must dance, there must be severed heads – I am old, I belong to mythology – severed heads for her to dance before.[191]

He goes on to voice Yeats's own preoccupation with the kind of dancer which he was always seeking: Salome with her impassive face and virgin cruelty as in *A Full Moon in March* and *The King of the Great Clock Tower*; a dance, as Kermode stated above (p. 9) which would be innocent of meaning. Instead of the performances of the reviled ballerinas painted by Degas, the Old Man demands a facial expression devoid of emotion but emblematic of 'love and loathing, life and death',[192] the cursed antinomies: 'They might have looked timeless, Rameses the Great'.[193] And yet, when the moment comes for Emer's dance, the stage directions suggest an interpretation of its function which collides firmly with narrative and, perhaps, 'meaning'.

The dance is thus foreshadowed by the prose preface and it is directly introduced by the Morrigu, goddess of war, who recounts Cuchulain's final battle in blank verse. Her account is a full balance-sheet of wounds received and she illustrates the identity of the dead by reference to the black parallelogram of wood representing Cuchulain's head just taken, absurdly, by the Blind Man and to another six parallelograms – the severed heads of those of his enemies who contributed to the warrior's death. She characterises in a thumb-nail sketch the nature of each fighting man:

THE MORRIGU: This man came first;
Youth lingered though the years ran on, that season
A woman loves the best.[194]

The inventory proceeds from listing those who showed valour in braving the courage and might of the unhurt Cuchulain down to the craven cowardice of those who delivered the fifth and sixth wound:

THE MORRIGU: These other men were men of no account.
They saw that he was weakening and crept in.[195]

We are quite aware that Cuchulain went out to fight Maeve against enormous odds and knew himself that a death was imminent that he unflinchingly sought. His recklessness, however, deserved better than a beheading by a Blind Man's sharp kitchen knife for twelve pennies. Because Cuchulain refused to act on the advice of Emer telling him not to engage in battle until the morrow when reinforcements would arrive, there is already a tinge of inevitability about the action of the play with death as its expected outcome. The Morrigu's tribute has the same air of inexorability about it; its verse is based on enjambement and caesura and, thus, is irregular; it is given its cohesion only by the listing of the six warriors:

> THE MORRIGU: This head is great Cuchulain's, those other six
> Gave him six mortal wounds.[196]

The final information disclosed by the Morrigu is stated in a plain, matter-of-fact manner which contrasts with the preceding tributes to 'great' Cuchulain or to 'Two valiant men' and to the lyricism of some of the poetry: 'youth lingered' and 'crept in'. Her account also opened on a note of unadorned statement of fact:

> THE MORRIGU: The dead can hear me, and to the dead I speak [197]

and, thus, it also closes:

> Conall avenged him. I arranged the dance.[198]

These two conclusive actions are necessitated as fitting ceremonies for a great fighting man: nothing has been left undone and the dance of death is as essential as Cuchulain's revenge.

Emer's dance in response is both expressive and pantomimic: she conveys both the grief and anger of the deserted wife in mourning. While her movements are a vehicle for her emotions, they also further the narrative towards its close:

> *(She so moves that she seems to rage against the heads of those that had wounded Cuchulain, perhaps makes movements as though to strike them, going three times round the circle of the heads. She then moves towards the head of Cuchulain; it may, if need be, be raised above the others on a pedestal. She moves as if in adoration or triumph. She is about to prostrate herself before it, perhaps does so, then rises, looking up as if*

listening; she seems to hesitate between the head and what she hears. Then she stands motionless. There is silence, and in the silence a few faint bird notes.)[199]

It is noteworthy and appropriate that Yeats refrains from having Emer dance holding the severed head of the dead man in the fashion of the two more obviously 'Salome' plays which precede this one. Emer has not been responsible for or instigator of his death; hers is not a virgin cruelty. In Chapter 1 we observed that she is a curious Salome figure in not having desired her husband's demise, instead in doing everything in her power to prevent it, even to sending his young mistress to woo him into not doing battle. Nor does she, in a maternal gesture, place the head upon her breast and cradle it. Her instinct is rather quite other; she is moved to prostrate herself before it in tribute and recognition of the reverence in which she held Cuchulain despite his many failings. Curiously, this mark of respect only serves to emphasise the equality between them: she had always been a fitting helpmeet to the great warrior. Her dance is a very impressive one manifesting, as it does, the powerful yet conflicting emotions with which Cuchulain and Emer had conducted their love match, for so it was despite all evidence to the contrary. This dance is possibly the most achieved in Yeats's theatre; it carries much significance and draws to a natural close in stillness: 'Then she stands motionless',[200] listening to the few faint bird notes which indicate that Cuchulain's soul has begun its spiritual journey.

The play could have ended here quite satisfyingly, but Yeats makes language take over once again from dance as he does in the songs of the Musicians which terminate his earlier dance plays. Three ragged modern street musicians at an Irish fair adopt the Cuchulain legend for their own ends and place it in a contemporary context. Cuchulain was 'thought'[201] by the Irish soldiers participating in the 1916 Easter Rebellion at the Dublin Post Office and today a statue stands there,

> SINGER: to mark the place,
>   By Oliver Sheppard done[202]

an ironical note which serves by its jokiness to distance the audience out of the events portrayed on stage and back into an anti-illusionistic world.

The song is that which the harlot sang to the beggar-man, from
one victim and social outsider to another, with its arcane yet worldly
wisdom. She lists the beautiful, brave heroes and women of the
ancient race of Irish warriors and praises their physical loveliness:

> SINGER: I adore those clever eyes,
>   Those muscular bodies, but can get
>   No grip upon their thighs.
>   I meet those long pale faces,
>   Hear their great horses, then
>   Recall what centuries have passed
>   Since they were living men.[203]

The rebels of the Easter Rising, Pearse, Connolly and the others to
whom Yeats pays tribute in his poem 'Easter 1916' are the modern-
day equivalents of the legendary heroes, but they lack the physical
perfection of their predecessors:

> SINGER: No body like his body
>   Has modern woman borne.[204]

Yet they are indeed the legacy of those ancient warriors and again,
ironically, their lament is being celebrated by their opposites, a
harlot and a beggar-man.

The song is in alternating tetrameters and trimeters, the shorter
lines producing emphatic statements: 'I meet them face to face', 'I
adore those clever eyes', 'I both adore and loathe'[205] and also carrying the rhymes, which in the first stanza are all true, but which
become slightly distorted in the next: 'reality/Connolly', 'blood/
stood', 'done/man'. The song is written in ballad metre with, however, a boisterous rhythm which is jogged along from rhyme to
rhyme thereby creating a 'tune' redolent of a jig. There is certainly a
tripping, dance-like impulse behind the words: Emer's silent mime
has been met by a frolic of language.

The tale treats of dead but glorious heroes yet it is sung by two on
the edges of society who have difficulty in surviving. They cannot
afford illusions or romantic aspirations, but they none the less have
the last word over the lords and ladies of epic and legend. Just so,
the play has proved to us, does the Blind Beggar strike the final
mortal blow against the magnificence of Cuchulain for twelve
pennies reward. The anarchic truths of the jig outweigh the passions

and nobility of Emer's dance and Yeats seems to intend reckless modern energy to sound the final note.

An examination of the plays has surely revealed that Yeats was forever perfecting a model, replicating elements of it elsewhere, adjusting and, thus, innovating and moving on. Even plays as superficially similar as *A Full Moon in March* and *The King of the Great Clock Tower* possess subtleties of difference from each other along with those features which they manifestly hold in common and *The Death of Cuchulain*, dance play *par excellence* though it is, threatens, in its employment of several commentators to replace the customary chorus and its boisterous modern envoy, to shatter its own mould. This very template is itself receptive to amendment and novelty: it is not mere coincidence that so many of Yeats's stage directions contain questions, tentative hesitations and honest bemusement. The playwright was ceaselessly experimenting and inventing anew.

His presentation of dance in his dance plays is vital in serving many narrative and theatrical purposes, not least that of the manifestation and expression of internal conflict, as is demonstrated in the preceding discussion. In his belief in the capacities of dance to convey significances which were inachievable through language, Yeats was firmly of his time, yet the echoes of the debate also continue to resound in the minds of those who know the issues involved today. If a number of dramatists were crafting plays which included dance, mask and chorus, with Gordon Bottomley and Terence Gray among them, why were the versions created by Yeats so obviously superior? Mainly, I would argue, for the reasons suggested in the above consideration of the plays; Yeats had achieved an integrity from the interplay of several aesthetic forms and had forged a unity of medium which responds to both emotional and intellectual demands of an audience. The dance plays end in a trance-like stillness attained by working through song, verse and dance – a culmination which convinces an onlooker or reader of the justice of the bleak inevitability of the outcome of the play, however bitterly he or she resents and combats it during the action.

Although his modest hesitancy on the subject is telling, Yeats fully understood the nature of theatrical dance and his understanding matured and deepened through time. The dance of a Faery Child gives way to the profound complexities of Roman Soldiers wheeling about a cross; the seductive measures of a Goddess from the sea are granted enormous poignancy and power when imitated, then exploded, by a mourning wife attempting to obliterate memories of her beloved husband's infidelities. Yeats too imitates, explodes and transcends his own dramaturgy. I have endeavoured to propose a set of characteristic features of his dance plays and while the suggested schema still stands and is, I believe, of a certain usefulness, I am well aware that the criteria invoked will not always suit. None the less, the very drawing up of such yardsticks serves to expose the nature of the points in debate and the investigation has enabled a probing into Yeats's dance plays which must always prove fascinating and rewarding, provoking, as it does, all sorts of questioning into the very nature of dance itself.

If the lengthy discussion on dance-as-language and dance and meaning with which this chapter opened is indicative of anything, it is certainly to prove that Yeats was grappling with essential issues, the significance of which continues to incite speculation and further theorising in our own time. This is one of the reasons for the seeming modernity of Yeats's dance plays: we may say of them what Valéry's Eryximaque claimed for the dance:

L'instant engendre la forme, et la forme fait voir l'instant.[206]

And so we come to that 'instant' of performance – the energy which is indeed made visible by the form of the movement and reflects back upon that form – the mysterious dialectic of the dance and its controlled lack-of-control. I have discussed the manner in which the dance plays exhibit a poised integrity between language and its transubstantiation into movement from an examination of the plays as texts. To grasp the way in which they were played when first produced and how they play now is an elusive affair, but one which must be attempted in order to illustrate, in a fashion that literary analysis does not, Yeats's genius as a playwright. Many of his contemporaries, including Joseph Holloway (1861–1944), the inveterate Dublin playgoer and chronicler of theatre in Dublin, said of Yeats that he was not a practical man of the stage,[207] that his notions on the chanting of verse were cranky, that his ideas of staging, particularly in his collaboration with E. Gordon Craig, were innovative but not pleasing and press reviews of the plays as they were mounted in Ireland or England reveal bewilderment, sometimes mockery, but also a grudging or guarded tribute in their realisation that Yeats was indeed a visionary and revolutionary whose ideas were in advance of his time.

It is interesting to perceive where newspaper reviews, such as those in *The Irish Times*, coincide in their account with the personal testimony of Holloway, the man-on-the-spot, in his *Journal* which is now housed in The National Library of Ireland. I shall consider some of these contemporary opinions before bringing the discussion of performance into our own period by an appraisal of the Yeats Festival staged from 27 August to 21 September 1991, at the Peacock Theatre in Dublin, when *Deirdre, A Full Moon in March* and *The Shadowy Waters* were presented under the direction of Professor James Flannery.

Joseph Holloway was of course present at the opening of the Abbey Theatre on Tuesday, 27 December 1904, when the bill comprised Yeats's *On Baile's Strand* with the Fay brothers, *Cathleen ni Houlihan* and Lady Gregory's farce *Spreading the News*. Holloway, an architect by training and profession, had been responsible for transforming a morgue attached to a Mechanics' Institute in Abbey Street into the new theatre. He had the following to say about *On Baile's Strand* in his *Impressions of a Dublin Playgoer*:

At the opening of the pretty little Abbey Theatre, the Messrs. Fay covered themselves with glory, both as the guiding spirits of the new theatre and as actors. The night was a memorable one, and the house was thronged and genuinely enthusiastic. ...

Two pieces were presented for the first time on any stage, and both proved successes. W. B. Yeats's legendary play, *On Baile's Strand*, ... was most excellently played.The novel staging proved most effective – the figures of the play as standing well out in relief against the multi coloured-draperies of which the boxed-in scene was composed. ... .A really fine poetic impersonation of Cuchullain was that of Frank J. Fay, the music of whose speech and the beauty of whose diction, together with the natural dramatic effectiveness of his acting excited all to admiration. It was a performance any actor ought be proud of and I shall long remember. F. Walker also made quite a hit as his son. His entry was very picturesque and his acting generally forcible, yet commendably restrained. This was the first real chance this earnest young actor has ever got to distinguish himself and he took it. His will shortly be a name to conjure with as 'juvenile lead' in this wonderful little company. George Roberts was impressive though somewhat [handwriting illegible] as King Concobar. ... Arthur Sinclair's speech was thick and hard to follow as the

drunken King Daire. The young and old Kings were all cabably
[sic] filled while the crafty blind-man, Fintain, and his dupe, the
fool, Borach, were happily characterised by [illegible] – Shemus
O'Sullivan and W. P. Fay – the latter was inimitable in some of his
'business' and remarks. This actor is a fellow of infinite jest, and
knows how to be as solemn as a judge when occasion demands
it. He rarely if ever plays the fool at the wrong moment! Tact is
his key note, and art his goal. Loud applause followed the fall of
the curtain on this dramatic poem-play, and the author on being
called, after the players had bowed their acknowledgement
spoke a few words of thanks and publically acknowledged the
debt of gratitude due to Miss Horniman for her gift of the theatre
to the Society.[208]

Holloway did have reservations, however, about Yeats's portrayal
of women – Irish women – and he expressed them most forcefully.
His displeasure was obviously shared by many in the Abbey's
audience, as they demonstrated three years later in the fiasco over
Synge's *Playboy of the Western World*:

I noticed with regret a tendency on the part of the poet to use
imagery of degraded womankind at every turn that was not
agreeable to hear, and could very well be done without. This
eternal harping on the one string about letcherous [sic] women
and amorous, animal-loving goddesses grates on the ear, and
surely is not the way to purify the stage as the object (or one of
them) of the I.N.T.S.[209] purports to be. Constant reference to loose
women (Goddesses or other wise) no matter what poetic clothing
you envelope the reference in is scarcely edifying or good to hear.
At least such is my sentiment on the point.[210]

A revealing comment made by Yeats in a conversation with
Holloway some six months later on Wednesday, 26 April 1905,
discloses that the poet was more aware of matters political than
sexual when creating On *Baile's Strand*, although the latter had
redounded on the former in the manner in which Synge and Joyce
and O'Casey too would find typical of Irish consciousness:

[W. B. Yeats] said he had Charles Stewart Parnell in his mind
when he wrote On *Baile's Strand*. 'people who do aught for Ireland
… ever and always have to fight the waves in the end.'[211]

Saturday, 24 November 1906 saw the opening night of Yeats's *Deirdre* which was greeted with a plethora of reviews and accounts. Holloway's initial lavish praise gave way some five days later to disapproval on, by now, customary grounds:

> Another great night at the Abbey. ... The curtains were drawn aside on Yeats's new one-act play of *Deirdre*. The setting ... [sic] was very effective, and the costumes beautifully harmonized in the colour scheme designed by Robert Gregory. The play is a thing of beauty, ending in tragedy, and for a one-act piece unusually long. ... Yeats's play was followed with rare attention and was keenly appreciated to judge by the applause ... [sic] Miss Darragh's 'Deirdre' was consistent and beautiful, with an undercurrent of intense subdued emotionalism underlying her outwardly seeming calm. Her acting was always skillful [sic], artistic, and dramatically effective (she is an artist to her fingertips). ... Miss Darragh's realisation of the part had too much of the flesh and too little of the *spirituelle* in its composition. Some of her movements were delicious – her description of how she would set out the body of her dead lover I thought particularly so. Here her gestures were exquisitely appropriate. The way she extended her two hands in front of her with entwined thumbs to express the laying out of her lover's feet was perfectly lovely in conception. ...
>
> F. J. Fay's 'Naisi' was vigorous in the dramatic moments and impressively subdued when occasion required. He spoke his lines with due reverence to the metre, and were it not for his lack of inches ... he would have filled the eye as well as the mind. ... He sings his words too much on occasion. ...
>
> Arthur Sinclair as 'Fergus' struck twelve o'clock too quickly in his acting and began to rant and fume almost from the first, instead of gently and gradually leading up to ... his rage at the King's treachery.
>
> J. M. Kerrigan made a most promising debut as the love-tormented 'King Concobar', and spoke his lines well and musically, if in a trifle too measured and monotonous voice. For a baffled lover, he struck me as too calm in manner and statuesque in deportment. A really beautiful impersonation was the 'First Musician' of Miss Sara Allgood; her beautiful voice was a joy to the ear, and her singing of the various snatches of songs was thrilling in its purity of tone and pathetic significance.[212]

By Thursday, 29 November 1906, Holloway's ambivalent attitude to Miss Darragh's performance had certainly resolved itself and his opinion of the play as a whole had been violently transformed:

> I saw Yeats's *Deirdre* played for the second time to-night and must confess that I thought it tame and lifeless. ... Sensuality is over the entire play, and nightly-decreasing audiences testify to the lack of interest taken in such-like work. Miss Darragh's 'Deirdre' does not improve on acquaintance; it lacks sincerity and charm.[213]

Such *volte-faces* are not at all uncommon in Holloway's chronicles and seem not to embarrass him one whit.

The review which appeared in *The Leader* for 1 December 1906, questions the fundamental base of Yeats's stagecraft:

> We do not think that Mr Yeats's 'Deirdre' could be called a play. There was little or no action in it, as we understand action in plays. Action on the stage ought to convey much, and to dispense with a great deal that, were the printed book the medium, should have to be set out at length. To be sure, some of Mr Yeats's characters waved their hands and walked up and down the stage as they were orating – in excellent prose, we have no doubt – but that is not what we understand by dramatic action. Fine phrasing and polished language is more or less out of place in an acting play; you cannot follow it. These sort of things are for the study and not for the other side of the footlights. The stage, even the scenery, has to be highly artificial in order that it may appear natural. ...
>
> The elocution of Mr F. J. Fay was very good, the music was good, and so also the elocution and staging of Miss Allgood. But candidly we did not think very much of Miss Darragh. Perhaps, she having been boomed too much, we expected too much. We certainly think that Miss Allgood would have put more life into the part of 'Deirdre'; the 'Deirdre' of Miss Darragh belonged rather to the 'atmosphere' of Mr Pinero's plays, than to that of Pagan Ireland. ...
>
> If the Abbey goes in for too much of this 'Deirdre' sort of performance it may find that it is giving too little sugar and too much pill, and that the public will make a wry face at the fare.

W. B. is a thing apart – from life![214]

And yet, within two years, Yeats's 'curiosity', this verse-play, *Deirdre*, which aroused such hostility and resentment, had become so firmly part of an established bill that Mrs Patrick Campbell herself would play the title-role in a programme which also included Hoffmansthal's dance play *Electra*, translated by Arthur Symons. Holloway saw it on Tuesday, 10 November 1908 and was finally won over:

> At first her mannered style of delivery and somewhat stooping form did not attract me much, but as the piece progressed one forgot her strongly marked mannerisms, and only saw the baffled woman's fight for death by the side of her loved one, slain by the order of the treacherous king who coveted her body. Her cajoling 'Concobar' into allowing her to attend to the dead body of her beloved 'Naisi' was a supreme piece of dramatic art, full of subtlety and intense emotionalism. Her savage outburst on his refusing her first request was superb in its tigerish savagery; the baffled woman let loose the floodgates of her wrath on the loveless old man who waded through crime to attain her, and annihilated him into submission. ...
>
> Mrs Campbell's 'Deirdre' grew on one until it quite captured by its sheer intensity. When the actress is moved by emotion or passion, her whole body moves in jerk-like wriggles that punctuate her every word.[215]

The Peasant carried a review on Mrs Campbell's performances of 'Deirdre' and 'Electra' at the New Theatre in London in its issue of Saturday, 26 December 1908. The theatre critic, who signed himself 'D.O'D', at last makes it very clear that Yeats's unconventional theatrical experiments were finding the acceptance and respectability that they undoubtedly deserved:

> I came away from the New Theatre with the realisation that all my theories require re-casting. For 'Deirdre' is a not unworthy successor to 'Kathleen ni Houlihan'. The effect was altogether delightful, and it is long since I have derived such genuine pleasure from the theatre. An atmosphere is created and sustained, and the story moves naturally in its poetic setting. The characters, too, get infused with life – a want that one misses in many of Mr. Yeats's plays. Of the quality of the verse I am not in a position to speak – I have not read the play – but at least once it

made a most moving impression upon me. And Mr. Yeats has, I think, the theory that the value of all verse is in the effect produced by the speaking of it aloud.

I do not speak of Mrs. Patrick Campbell's acting in the part of Deirdre. Always she has individuality and arresting force, but personally I think the part of Electra better suited to her very great powers. They are perhaps so great because they are limited, and she shows to much greater advantage in the brooding intensity of the girl who brings events to pass than in the part of the woman we have come to know as Deirdre –half-fawn, half-seer – but wholly lover, who is entangled in the meshes of fate, and falls back baffled from every effort to extricate the man she loves.[216]

The Times had noted that Clytemnestra had been movingly played by Florence Farr in Hoffmansthal's *Electra* and that the unusual and beautiful scenery and dresses for both plays had been due to suggestions by Mr Charles Ricketts.[217]

Holloway was venomous about the Abbey's first attempt to stage Yeats's very early play *The Land of Heart's Desire* on Thursday, 16 February 1911. He claimed that it

failed completely to convince. Were it not for the beautiful playing of Sara Allgood as the bewitched, newly-made bride, 'Maire Bruin,' the piece would be hopeless as a stage play.[218]

And the *Irish Times* printed a letter two days later in which the scenery for the same play was criticised by 'An Abbeyite':

Sir – Many of those who saw for the first time that beautiful little play, 'The Land of Heart's Desire' must have been astonished at the ugliness and carelessness of the setting. Simplicity is not dinginess, and the very cool and brief applause that the play received is, in some measure, explained by the setting.

The Abbey excels in realism, but this particular play is not on the realistic plane. Why, then did the Bruins live in a cottage so hopelessly dingy and ugly? The value of the figures is entirely lost against the drab walls. Then the light is a hard bright glare that effectually dispels any mystery or sense of the faery.

Why should the stage be so light? It is evening. How different the effect would have been had the light only been thrown from the fire and from the unshuttered window. Moonlight and firelight might have met and symbolised the two forces that are at war over the heart of Maire Bruin. One candle would have been enough for the supper table, and if the draught from the open door had blown this out, the figures would have moved between the moonlight and firelight.

In the staging last night there was no mystery and no atmosphere. The power of that magical night world that calls Maire Bruin finds no suggestion, for there is no window, and one cannot see the sky, or mountains, or trees, through the open door. Why should there not be a glimpse of sky and trees seen through an unshuttered window and through the open door?

The excellent acting of the play lost its value in this ugliness of production. Had it even been acted before a green curtain in a half light one would have realised more the value of the poetry.[219]

A play by Yeats could still incite extremes of passionate reaction and Holloway needed to use all of his meagre portion of diplomatic power a few years later on Tuesday, 9 December 1919, when the Abbey staged *The Player Queen*:

At the Abbey all the highbrows congregated in great force. ... Yeats's play was looked forward to with interest and modified excitement owing to rumours of its nature. Its strange story baffles me, while its unfolding is set in so picturesque an environment that it charmed the eye if it didn't wholly satisfy the mind.

... There is a lot of talk in Act I about the chastity of a unicorn, and in Act II marriage is made very light of, indeed. Willmore thought the play 'gorgeous,' but neither Starkey nor Higgins had a good word to say of it. It baffled all, but its beauty of setting pleased most, and the acting of May Craig as 'Nona' was really fine dramatically; she can get right into the heart of a character and be the person she creates for the time being. ... Arthur Shields in fantastic character, in out of the way periods and costumes, invariably is quite good. His muddled poet-player, 'Septimus,' proved to be one of his happiest efforts ... Though its purport is wrapt in mystery, its beauty won home.[220]

Yeats made a speech at the Abbey before the performance of two of his 'Noh' plays, those for Dancers, *The Only Jealousy of Emer* and *The Cat and the Moon* on Sunday, 9 May 1926 and Holloway recorded his impressions of this new departure in theatre:

[The three Musicians'] getup was weirdly Japanese. Two carried in the bier on which the figure of 'Cuchulain' lay, and the three drew a dark cloth with a strange device on gold across the stage, and when it was withdrawn the figures of 'Emer' and the ghost of 'Cuchulain' were discovered, and 'The First Musician' told their story up to a certain point, and then the players took it up. ... The two figures of 'Cuchulain' wore masks, also 'The Woman', whose hands, arms and legs and mask were gold. ...

Immediately after, *The Cat and the Moon* began by the three 'Musicians' returning to the stage, Lennox Robinson replacing E. Leeming. ... I liked Eileen Crowe's 'Emer' in the opening play. Norah McGuinness, who designed the costumes and masks, as well as playing 'The Woman of the Sidhe,' gave an interesting performance of a strange, uncanny character. The masking of the 'Ghost' and the 'Figure of Cuchulain' was not effective, and Shelah Richards's getup as 'Eithna' [sic] Inguba was to my eye ugly.

All literary and artistic Dublin were present, and great stillness prevailed during the enactment of both pieces. The audience was all on the ground floor to get the proper effect intended on the stage. ...[221]

Yeats was yet again breaking new ground and challenging the deep-dyed conservatism, not only of staunch Dubliners such as Holloway, but of Theatre itself.

In 1927 the Abbey School of Ballet was set up under the auspices of Ninette de Valois and two years later *Fighting the Waves* resulted from the collaboration of Yeats and the dancer. Holloway was not alone in his adverse reaction to this very avant-garde piece and his account of the performance at the Abbey of Thursday, 13 August conveys gratingly the shock and discomforture that he felt:

I met F. J. McCormick and Eileen Crowe as I came out of the Abbey at 11 o'clock after the ballet, *Fighting the Waves*, and Mac said to me, 'I see you have survived it. Oh, what noise!'

It is the first time I ever heard Stephenson sing that I didn't enjoy his lovely, clear, carrying voice. Oh, the harsh, discordant notes he had to sing. I said when I heard that Yeats liked the music that was enough for me – as he has no ear for sound!. ... The principles [sic] wore masks and also some of the dancers. It was a pity to waste such talent on such strange materials. In the balcony, people started to leave shortly after the ballet started. It was worse than the talkies. The steam whistle organ or a merry-go-round discourses heavenly music by comparison with the music shook out of a bag of notes anyhow by the American concoctor of this riot of discords ...

Well, of all the noisy noise I ever heard George Antheil's music to *Fighting the Waves* capped it all, and, oh, to hear poor J. Stephenson as 'singer' try to get music out of the discordant notes he had to vocalize, and also to convey the poet's words he sang, was to hear a sweet clear voiced singer at times howl out notes that seemed out of tune. It was only when he was let declaim his lines unaccompanied that his words rang out with clarion clearness ...

I had seen the play – part of the Ballet – before at an At-Home held by the Drama League. The masked figures seemed strange to the eye, but there was a certain weirdness in that worn by the demon of the sea who replaces 'Cuchulain' in the bed. This part was well played by Michael J. Dolan. Meriel Moore's beautiful voice gave clearness to the text as 'Emer,' though spoken through a mask. Shelah Richards as 'Eithne Inguba', one of 'Cuchulain's' many lovers was as effective as her mask would allow. Those masks suggested the big-head of my early pantomime days, and conveyed nothing to me save a more or less obstruction to the spoken words. Ninette de Valois was 'Fand,' and Hedley Briggs (a dancer from London) was the 'Ghost of Cuchulain,' and six of the Abbey Ballet Class were the waves. The opening ballet of 'Cuchulain' fighting the waves was decorative and beautiful to the eye, but the music that accompanied it was like the falling of a tin tray on the flags.

It took as many to concoct this ballet as go to make a musical comedy ... Fancy having to engage a full orchestra of musicians to try to play such stuff that could be as well interpreted by children on tin cans! ... It was a really typical Abbey first night.[222]

Incidentally, Ninette de Valois was proving herself to be a superb practitioner and performer of her art and high praise was granted to the dancer by *The Independent* on the occasion of her performance in Dublin on 14 January of the following year:

The greatest thing of the night in ballet delineation was the presentation of 'Pride,' from Scriabin, by Ninette de Valois, who did most things splendidly, and this best of all.[223]

It is enormously cheering to find Holloway, usually so disgruntled and irritated by Yeatsian experiments, according tribute to a performance of what is perhaps the finest of *The Plays for Dancers, At the Hawk's Well*, on Tuesday, 8 November 1930:

> I saw Dolan pass in to make up for the 'Old Man' in *At the Hawk's Well*, and also Sara Patrick go in to see this piece. The music and costumes were by Edmund Dulac, and they were very rich. I like this Irish 'Noh' play ... Michael J. Dolan was quite excellent and impressive as 'The Old Man' ... This play for dancers by W. B. Yeats gave me much pleasure.[224]

And from this point onwards Holloway seems to have been almost quite won over by Yeats's dance plays at the Abbey and was not alone in so being. By the time of his review of *The Dreaming of the Bones* on Sunday, 6 December 1931, it is clear that his apprenticeship in Yeatsian curiosities is complete and we can be pleased and relieved for Yeats himself who was now approaching the end of his life of courageous poetic and theatrical innovation:

> The first production of the imitation Japanese 'Noh' play, *The Dreaming of the Bones*, by W. B. Yeats was a complete success; it worked out quite simply and beautifully. ... Yeats was called at the end of the piece and spoke a few words about the ballet and such-like plays as suited the ballet treatment. ...
> J. Stephenson's diction as 'Stranger' was clear and beautiful ... W. O'Gorman was quite good as 'Young Man,' but Dr. Gogarty afterwards in the vestibule said, 'He was made too common to represent those who occupied the G.P.O. in Easter Week.'[225]

While the production of *The Resurrection* on Monday, 9 July 1934, met with a rather mixed reception, *The King of the Great Clock Tower*, with which it shared a bill, was more pleasing and seemed to be more accessible to an audience now schooled in Yeats's ways. As usual, however, Holloway took exception to the overt sexuality of the Queen's dance with the severed head:

> *The Resurrection* is a short play which is supposed to take place in an antechamber in a house near Jerusalem some days after the crucifixion of Our Lord, and we find 'The Hebrew' (A. J. Leventhal), 'The Greek' (Denis Carey), and 'The Syrian' (J. Winter) speaking

about the death of Our Lord and of the strange happenings that were taking place when into the room in which they all three are walks 'Christ' and then passes out leaving them astonished. 'Christ' wears a mask which gave too large an appearance to his head, I thought. The whole piece was not impressive, and Leventhal made an ugly slip in the text, and when Denis Carey tried to get him out of it, he went back in the text and aggravated the slip. Michael J. Dolan and Robert Irwin took the role of 'Musicians' and pulled back the curtains and then seated themselves with fine elocutionary effectiveness and distinction ... I didn't like the way the programme announced 'The Christ' in the cast. Liam Gaffney made his first stage appearance in the Abbey in the part. He had no words to speak. I thought Robert Irwin's singing a little too strong and jarred somewhat on the spoken word.

I liked better *The King of the Great Clock Tower*, in which F. J. McCormick filled the role of 'The King' and Ninette de Valois that of 'The Queen.' Yeats has used the symbol suggested by Wilde in his *Salome* [sic]. ...

The two 'Musicians' have a lot to sing, but the air to which their words are set made it difficult to catch the words sung. Robert Irwin and Joseph O'Neill were the 'Musicians.' 'The Queen's' dance with 'The Stranger's' head by Ninette de Valois did not impress me very much. McCormick spoke with dignity and diction as 'The King'. Arthur Duff composed the music. Both 'Queen' and 'The Stranger' wore masks designed by George Atkinson, and D. Travers Smith (Mrs Lennox Robinson) designed the costumes. ...[226]

As a very old man Yeats attended a performance of *Deirdre* on Monday, 10 August 1936, in which Jean Forbes-Robertson played the lead and Micheal MacLiammoir took the part of Naoise. According to Holloway it was enthusiastically received, but some sacrifices to Yeats's original intention for the acting of his play had been made in the production:

Miss Jean Forbes-Robertson as 'Deirdre' looked the part and acted and spoke the ever-varying emotions she was called on to portray with telling dramatic emotionalism. Her voice was ever agreeable to listen to, and if the poetic diction of the poet suffered a little, the gain to its dramatic effectiveness was palpable.

This shift in emphasis gives rise to another of the many sly digs that Holloway can never resist directing at Yeats, this time from both a personal and an aesthetic point of view:

> W. B. Y. left after *Deirdre*, as he can't stand anyone else's plays but his own, and therefore couldn't sit out the other two.
>   The present interpretations of *Deirdre* emphasised its worth as drama at the sacrifice of its verse.[227]

Yeats was thus destined to be an unhappy man as far as his ideas for the performance of his drama was concerned. He was disappointed by this version of *Deirdre* even though we can now see how seriously his 'curiosities' were being taken and how firmly they were accepted as part of an established repertoire after years of frustration and incomprehension or downright bloody-mindedness on the part of his audiences. Yet his objection remained:

> Yeats missed the poetic diction and intoning of the earlier performances. He thinks in poetry rather than drama ...[228]

The overall impression gleaned from these reviews and eyewitness accounts of performance is that Yeats won through to the respect which was rightly his despite his being characterised as a poet-in-the-theatre rather than a playwright. He was very demanding of his actors and dancers as well as his audiences. When interviewed by Sam McCready in 1975 Dame Ninette de Valois said:

> A strict classical dancer could not have satisfied Yeats ... it was necessary also to be an actress[229]

and we do suspect that, except on very rare occasions, Yeats never saw realised in performance quite what he had visualised for his play in his mind's eye. Part of his genuine genius, however, certainly lay in his integrity of vision and the incessant effort to make that vision and the performance of it correspond. The other part lay in his constant readiness to adapt, to suggest, to experiment, as a consideration of some of his stage directions has shown. Theatre people found him quirky and difficult, but they responded in various ways to the challenges set, even though he himself may not have approved of their manner of meeting his demands. Some of them, like Holloway, poked fun at him and his theatrical innocence, but nevertheless the plays were put on. He remains difficult but still very immediate: contemporary stagings of his plays in no sense expose him as outmoded, as the 1991 Dublin Yeats Festival demonstrated.

At the Peacock Theatre the audience sat in steeply raked tiers on three sides of the acting area making it into something like a cockpit. Thus, we were above the action, god-like, but also so close to the actors below that we were implicated, almost victims of that action as well as spectators of it. We were to witness the struggle between the two fighting animals which the plays presented as antagonists, Love and Death, at the same time as being acutely aware of the presence of the rest of the audience in the tiers on the side and opposite and of their anguish which matched our own. The acting area was closed on the fourth side by an awesome wall with niches housing skeletons and skulls; one central door led inside Conchobar's palace. Already the images of death were prominent along with a pervading mysticism, as the recesses in the wall were suggestive of settings for statues of saints and religious icons, rather than for the bones with which they were inhabited. Along with the allusions to Celtic Neolithic longbarrows and grim burial chambers, the echoes of Mayan walls of skulls were insistent and the references to the two cultures added an element of ritual which was essentially pagan and bloodthirsty. The sight of this enclosing wall also struck terror because nobody could see beyond these emblems of death except into a further dark.

For the first play, *Deirdre*, the place was obviously the territory of Conchubar, an alien barrenness which, in its turn, constructed the lonely and desolate niche for the High King of Ireland in which to brood and conspire during all the empty years spent among the macabre relics while Deirdre and her lover Naoise remained out of his jealous clutches in their Scottish exile. The only vital impulse left to Conchubar was focussed on his obsession with revenge and the winning back of Deirdre as his bride.

The acting space before the wall displaying its grotesque trophies was at first in darkness. Little by little the audience was allotted sufficient light to glimpse an unbroken circle of shapes, then revealed to be black-clad male figures crouching in a ring, themselves enclosed by the huge nets for snaring prey which each man bore on his back. They were frightening and anonymous – the hunters/henchmen of Conchubar, out to entangle and entrap their prey, Deirdre and Naoise, the fleeing, desperate victims of the

High King's wrath. As the stage-lighting increased in power, they broke the fearsome completeness of their circle and disappeared from view through the door in the gruesome wall into the 'palace' off-stage.

Their places were taken by three very individualised Musicians, three women of different ages, who contrasted in their idiosyncratic variety of figure, voice and demeanour with the automata of the circle of hunters. The women were dressed in complicated and disturbing costumes. They suggested both Victorian mourning garments as well as the gear for riding to hounds: black top hats and habits to which bizarre tulle bustles were attached. Their chief, convincingly played by Joan O'Hara, intoned the measures of the story, of Deirdre's childhood, her wooing by the High King, subsequent rejection of his overtures, her genuine love for Naoise and elopement and exile with him. The First Musician was bewildered and scared by her witnessing of preparations for lavish hospitality at the palace; she could not decipher the motivation for such celebration and was afraid of her own intuitions. It was only when Fergus, played by Derek Chapman as a delightful busybody aspiring to the position of Master of Ceremonies, interrupted the tremulous musings of the First Musician with his organising energies and naïve good humour that we were told that the expected guests were indeed Deirdre and Naoise, returned from Scotland and intending to make their peace with Conchubar. Through the bonhomie of Fergus, the simple and perturbing comment of the First Musician injected a note of terror. Joan O'Hara rendered good-natured platitudes null when she demanded to know: 'Are Deirdre and Naoise tired of life ?' The audience was desperate to ignore, to cancel her clear-sighted perception and be wooed by Fergus's bland confidence. While we elected to be bludgeoned by the old man's faith in his own power as peacemaker, the harsh melodies and truths of the women haunted us as testimony and echo until they were rendered real by the entrance of Deirdre and Naoise themselves from out of the surrounding forest into the space defined by the wall of skulls.

Mary McGuchian's Deirdre was young and vibrant and sensual. Dressed in green leotard and leggings and barefoot, she entwined her legs around her lover's waist and encircled his upper body with her arms. The two were linked, intertwined with one another as if they were one character. Sean Rocks presented an impressive Naoise in his combination of genuinely soldierly physical power and sensuality as he carried the woman he doted upon to the centre of the stage to where the red and white chess pieces on the board waited to be moved. The physical attraction between the two lovers was suggested by the delight they took in each other's words and gestures and as the two interlocked limbs with an agility tinged with despair, the audience perceived a unity which the High King of Ireland would only sever with brute force. Fergus could be trusted to have the words for it as he addressed audience and assembled company on stage:

> Shake all your cockscombs, children; these are lovers,

and the three Musicians, recognising their own impotence as mere commentators, added:

> What is all our praise to them
> That have one another's eyes?

And yet, despite their reciprocity of passion, we saw that Deirdre had surrendered to Naoise's wish to return and to his faith in Conchubar's pardon. As she decked herself with rich jewels she constantly stressed the word 'husband', for she, in terror for her own life and his, was here doing Naoise's will against all her native instincts and judgement. The unity between them was not as solid as it seemed and from this rift stemmed the despair-filled clinging witnessed at their entrance. As the women put raddle on Deirdre's cheeks to cover the whiteness, fear was masked by bravado and the very slightness of figure of Mary McGuchian won the sympathy of the audience as we saw her do battle with herself to attain genuine courage and the status and self-control of a Queen. Sean Rocks too portrayed Naoise as a man in conflict with himself. At first he showed indulgence to his lover's terror-filled predictions, but then surprised himself by his own alarm at catching sight of the chess-board at which the doomed Lugaidh Redstripe and his wife played before their execution. The same board was now set up for Deirdre and himself to while away their last hours. He chased away such horrors from his mind, however, by allying himself with the deluded Fergus. While Naoise reassured himself that all was well, Deirdre, more realistically, questioned the First Musician and forced her to disclose Conchubar's plans in their regard. The woman protested that her words were essentially random and any ominous significance was projected by Deirdre herself. The Musicians thus endeavoured to extricate themselves from responsibility in the event which they witnessed but in which they shied from participating and at this point their weird garments accorded strangely, mockingly, in their arch self-consciousness with the dress of the two lovers which was one of camouflage, a blending of woodland and mountain. And it was this beauty, that of harmony with nature, that Deirdre would not be able to destroy for all her threats that she would render herself ugly and, thus, no longer be the object of Conchubar's passion. Mary McGuchian's desperation was expressed most movingly as she realised the futility of her words in the very act of voicing them:

> I'll spoil this beauty that brought misery
> And houseless wandering on the man I loved.
> These wanderers will show me how to do it;
> To clip this hair to baldness, blacken my skin
> With walnut juice and tear my face with briars.

What she came to recognise was that the magnitude of being Deirdre overwhelmed whatever transformations she could make in her mere face, because fate in tales such as hers was implacable. The story of Deirdre and Naoise was the stuff of legend and she had to live up to its demands in full consciousness and acceptance of her heroic role, which was also and at the same time her very being.

> Whatever were to happen to my face
> I'd be myself, and there's not any way
> But this to bring all trouble to an end.

Deirdre's 'self' is not seen in her face, which can lie, but in her body, which cannot. We thus discover anew the belief in the integrity of gesture, physical expression and being in the safeguarding of 'truth' and in movement as its revelation.

James Flannery directed the three plays which he linked as 'Sacred Mysteries' as a study in Love and Death, male and female sexual energies and clearly his fascination for each play lay in the decision made by the heroine which is crucial both to the relationship of which she is part and to the outcome of the drama. Thus, he had Deirdre steel herself against her own intuition and love for Naoise and adopt the qualities of Conchubar himself – his ruthlessness and wiliness and cold will to win. In her death she countered the King's murder of her lover by learning to combine their two sets of characteristics, the cunning of Conchubar and the bravery of Naoise.

Sean Rocks's Naoise vied with Deirdre in nobility when he realised that he was trapped, the victim of treachery. Yeats's stage direction indicates Naoise's courage:

Naoise (who is calm, like a man who has passed beyond life).

It was a courage that would lead him to give chase to Conchubar who basely came to spy on the chess-playing lovers. While her lover was outside their shelter in pursuit of his enemy, Deirdre prepared for her own battle by snatching a knife from the First Musician and concealing it in some folds of flimsy stuff about her waist. In atonement for the theft, she vouchsafed her bracelet to the First Musician as undeniable proof of authenticity when the women took the tale of Deirdre and Naoise and the High King 'about the world'. As do all the characters of Yeats's legends, Deirdre too knew that she would leave a name 'upon the harp' of posterity and her awareness was significantly expressed seconds before Conchubar – a High King but a shabby enemy – chose finally to enter and display his victim Naoise bound and ensnared in a net like any wild creature. In similarly craven manner, he used Deirdre's plea for pardon, made on her knees, to mask the gagging of Naoise and leading him to execution through the door in the terrible wall. Stanley Townsend's Conchubar was indeed opportunistic and pragmatic and too old to bargain or equivocate. The speech in which he numbered his activities during Deirdre's seven-year escape from him emphasised that this had become a pursuit almost for its own sake, an obsession with a logic of its own which finally had little to do with Deirdre as beloved. The overriding emotion had become dotage rather than love and, as he fully knew that his passion was not reciprocated, he had resorted to love charms and magic stones to try to excite loving response in Deirdre:

> Do you think that I
> Shall let you go again, after seven years
> Of longing and planning here and there,
> And trafficking with merchants for the stones
> That make all sure, and watching my own face
> That none might read it?

Hurt pride and humiliation had joined with real authority to engender the banality of superstition and the mediocrity of cunning.

Flannery's direction thus became a meditation on varying orders of power and in *Deirdre*, as in all the plays selected for this Festival, the palm was bestowed on the woman, since by cajoling and trickery and sheer bravery Deirdre persuaded Conchubar to permit her to see her dead lover. She retreated through the opening in the wall of skulls. She was last seen standing on the threshold next to Naoise whom she had willingly joined in death. So the two lovers had also been allotted their niche among the skeletons; they stood side-by-side, framed in the doorway, ready for their portrayal in the legend that was theirs – a fitting resolution, for their vibrant energy was transmuted into dignity, stasis and artefact. Against the powerful mystery of the two now-magical emblems of loyal passion, the conjuring tricks of the High King appeared ludicrous, as he did himself in his regal but impotent loneliness.

The play ended on this final triumphant tableau with the two new inhabitants of Bronwen Casson's perplexing set finding their appropriate, impressive places. James Flannery and Casson between them explored in this production Yeats's own tentative belief that Being may only be possessed by the Dead.

The same stage design was employed for a very provocative and disturbing rendition of the late play, *A Full Moon in March*. In this case the Queen, with mask-like white face and white billowy overgarment, was first distinguished when the light playing over the wall of skulls revealed her crouching in a niche high up from the ground. Unlike the bones around her, she was bursting with life, but death would be the price for her initiation in the mysteries that fascinated her and in plumbing the secrets of sexuality and virgin cruelty, she would ally herself with its very tyranny and the powers of non-being.

The two Attendants who introduced the play were dressed in rich scarlet satin, gold and black variations on a kimono with padded-out trousers like a sort of oriental clown. Their make-up suggested Japanese Noh in the starkness of its black and white lines and their movements were staccato and stylised. This stiff jerkiness carried over to their manner of reciting their lines – they were reminiscent of marionettes as they ritualistically engaged in an interplay of question and answer as preamble to some arcane ceremony which nevertheless, Yeats says, celebrated spontaneity and freedom in their choice of what they would sing and the lines they would speak. The individuality of the two was stressed, paradoxically, through the very sameness of their costumes: we perceived their human intelligence and difference beneath the outer casing of the automaton and they were arrestingly powerful.

Sara-Jane Scaife's Queen yawned and stretched in her recess in the wall of skulls, then swung to the stage by scrambling hand-over-hand down a conveniently-placed knotted rope-ladder. While framed in her symbolic niche, she was still out of her element. Through wooing and dancing and cruelty she would find it.

As movement director at the Peacock Sara-Jane Scaife was also responsible for choreographing Jack Walsh's dance as the Swineherd. While the Queen was disturbingly overdressed, buttressed from the world and her own impulses by yards of white cotton, the Swineherd was naked except for a ragged loin cloth. He was made-up to appear scratched and torn and bleeding, but not, as Yeats wished, masked. Neither was the Queen and, consequently, attention was directed away from the head of the actors to the mus-cular, acrobatic movements of the whole body in dance.

The question-and-answer technique of the first Attendants was taken up echo-like by Queen and Swineherd with a notable equality of weight and balance between them. Jack Walsh's temerity and per-sistence were engaging and the Queen was attracted. Because she was won over, she had to force herself, in an attempt at preservation of her self, to dub his brave playfulness 'insolence' and sentence him to death on its account. Once the Swineherd had gone to his – monstrously unjust – execution, the Queen stripped herself of her white garment to reveal a scarlet red ('blood-stained') dancing dress and to disclose a miniature symbolic severed head in her embrace. Scaife's dance with this trophy in her hands was disturbingly powerful as she lay on the ground and applied its dead lips to her feet, calves, knees, thighs and finally to her groin. She cradled it on her belly, lifted it level to her face and kissed it. Scaife and Flannery decided to focus on a mistress–paramour dance, that of Salome, rather than display the element of maternal tenderness suggested by Yeats in his own stage directions. Thus, the Queen's dance was violent, almost brutal and the dimension that it actualised was rather one of fascinated horror along with personal resentment that she had permitted herself to be so vulnerable to wooing and, indeed, love.

The dance disturbed us. One male member of the audience, visibly embarrassed by the naked eroticism, was heard to say that

Yeats was a man who 'liked his joke' and it is quite understandable that even those who were familiar with Yeats's plays and knew what to expect should still today risk being shocked. Students of Yeats may tend to forget that his dramatic works, particularly his dance plays such as *A Full Moon in March*, have not lost their power as avant-garde innovation and the relentless demands that they make on their audiences have not weakened through time. James Flannery's direction reminded us. Yeats's proposed solution of the actress–dancer dilemma was to have a dancer replace a veiled Queen for the last part of the play. Neither switch nor veil was needed in Sara-Jane Scaife's interpretation of the role because of her gifts in both capacities. Flannery chose to stress the Queen's erotic cruelty and, with the constant unforgettable presence of the wall of skulls dominating the set, he left it to the Second Attendant, Stephen Holland, in his puzzled innocence, to place the wilful Queen back where she belonged in the eternity of artifice, now that she had plumbed the mysteries of her own being:

> Why must those holy, haughty feet descend
> From emblematic niches, and what hand
> Ran that delicate raddle through their white.
> My heart is broken, yet must understand.
> What do they seek for? Why must they descend?

The dancing, bloodthirsty Queen did indeed descend from her niche, dip her hands in the raddle and fulfil that gory quest summed up by the First Attendant who knew why she was compelled to do so:

> For desecration and the lover's night.

After her sally into the 'red' world, that of lust and passion and death as bloodshed, the Queen can embrace again death as white purity and nullness and stasis. The play stressed most insistently the clash and interplay between these two colours, the two forces battling out their struggle below the audience in the cock-pit theatre and in so doing echoed the chessboard symbol of *Deirdre*, the previous play.

Flannery linked the very early *The Shadowy Waters* (1911) to *Deirdre* and *A Full Moon in March* by the element common to all three of the growth of selfhood on the part of the heroine. I do not propose to discuss at length the performance of the last of his trilogy at the Peacock in September 1991, because this play, fascinating though it is, lies outside my dance play concerns. Suffice it to say that the production was dynamic and exciting in its employment of a double for each principal actor who also carried a puppet representing himself or herself as artefact. Full and impressive use was made of lighting, incense, perfume and jewellery in the sacking of Dectora's treasure ship. It will always remain a difficult play to stage, but the puppets added a dimension of overt theatricality from which this symbolic drama drew energy. And Professor Flannery's selection and direction of these three plays provided a persuasive meditation upon energy, both aesthetic and erotic. He thus allied himself admirably with Yeats's own concerns, for the Irish poet always followed Blake in finding energy 'Eternal Delight' and struggled to harness its mysteries when transubstantiating his plays-as-poetry into performances vitalised on the stage.

An accepted view of at least one of these very mysteries on a stage – even, perhaps especially, one in the corner of a drawing-room – is that the actor combines 'being' with 'representing'.[230] The audience deciphers the code presented by the actor and his/her role by our awareness that the actor is at one and the same time both Hamlet and X-playing-Hamlet and, thus, not-Hamlet at all. Yeats, however, used masks and peopled his theatre with figures from myth and legend and was not able, nor did he wish, to distinguish the dancer from the dance. As Deirdre so poignantly becomes aware through the experience of the play in which she (literally) finds herself and as the Roman Soldiers in *Calvary* know from the outset, what the theorist terms 'being' and 'representing' become the same thing. They must all dance to measures that are already implacably scripted and any possible discovery of Self means full acceptance of and, thus, magically, transcendence of the role assigned to them. In Yeats, as in most tragedy, this transcendence usually finds its process through death and its articulation in the name that will be celebrated in the harp song of the bards and story-tellers who will narrate the hero's story after his death.

While heroes and heroines come to consciousness of Self through the play, so too is Yeats's theatre eminently self-conscious. We come to realise that we are in the realm of metatheatre where Musicians or Attendants or Chorus comment on their own roles in interpreting the action which they witness and 'read' and the masks of course never permit the audience to forget that Yeats is dealing in his personal vocabulary of emblems. The dancer too marries spontaneity of gesture and emotion with the fixity and control of an icon. So, when we reconsider the 'being'/'representing' distinction we need to refashion it subtly when we apply it to the complexities of Yeatsian theatre. When employing our consciousness of the actor's 'being', we are concerned with talking theatre, with the face, the mouth which is shaping speech and defining the character through what he or she says. (Beckett of course takes this notion to its poetically obvious conclusion in his 'talking mouth' in *Not I*.) We measure the authenticity of the 'being' of Ophelia by the criteria of verisimilitude within the play, of the aptness to the narrative, and we ourselves have carried the personal and cultural yardsticks of reference used into the theatre as we took our seats and played our own parts in participating in the total experience of the play. As far as 'representing' goes, however, this involves the performance dimension and we are assessing not Ophelia, but Judi Dench's Ophelia – the actor's performance in terms of the character played and his or her interpretation of that character and whether it tallies with our own preconceptions, expectations, reading of that role.

We have examined how, in the dance plays, speech is transformed into another medium, the movement of the dancer: in the dance the first criterion, 'being', becomes subsumed by 'representing' and instead of concentrating on the face, the mouth, as agent of words delivered, we focus on the body which, as Deirdre discovers and as Yeats, Hoffmansthal and those quoted at the outset of this chapter believe, cannot lie. Were we indeed to conceive of a dance which embodied 'Deceit' as an abstract concept, rather as Ninette de Valois danced 'Pride', that delineation of lies would contain a truth – the essence of deceitful emotion taken to its extreme, distilled emblematic form: its truth would be that of the purity of its falsehood, the truth of its lies. Any consideration of the dance of a ballet's wicked stepmother or Demon King will bear this out.

The dancer expresses the abstract concept (for Yeats's Emer, 'adoration and triumph') and the concept in turn defines the movements of the dance. And the circularity of this interdependence makes for the completeness, self-referentiality and authenticity which Yeats demanded of it. The mask too invites identification of the actor with the role emblematised; 'being' is subsumed into 'representing' as the fluidity of the actor's humanity merges with and is defined by all that is suggested by the stasis and fixity of the mask. Yeatsian characters such as Judas or Lazarus may equivocate and attempt to wriggle out of their assigned realities, only to discover that all improvisation has been allowed for by the script. Katharine Worth has argued persuasively that Yeats was a European, that his theatre found its precursor in Maeterlinck and its successor in the French plays of Samuel Beckett.[231] She does not mention, however, the mythic theatre of Jean Anouilh or Giraudoux, in plays by both of whom a young girl realises and accepts how she must act, nay be, because her *name* is Judith or Antigone. These writers echo Yeats in their definition of Self through recognition of the legend in which people are agent and instrument. But they do not dance and in Yeats's canon that would be a weakness, for his dances are revelatory of his dancers' essential Selves and the purity of the emotions and energies which fuel those Selves.

As is demonstrated by reference to reviews and appreciation of the performances of Yeats's plays, his drama is always demanding of audiences and despite all developments in theatre in the intervening years, still retains an element of strangeness. Audiences have not become blasé, although they may be dismissive, just as some were in Yeats's own time. The challenges posed are real and some play-goers respectfully decline the invitation. Today's reviews show that audiences in Britain are responding in similar fashion to the demands of what has come to be known as 'live art' – they too are walking out of theatres.[232] This is arguably no coincidence. 'Live art' has been defined by Andy Lavender in a *Times* article on the Belgian director, Jan Fabre, on 27 July 1992, as 'the theatre of the future' and there is surely a visible continuum to be drawn from Yeats's forays into dramatic experiment to this dance- or performance-oriented, rather than text-based, theatre. At the moment the British hate it, but it is well-received in Europe.

And we cannot help but bear Yeats in mind when Fabre says of his show *Sweet Temptations* at the Queen Elizabeth Hall in London: 'There are meanings in it, but not one-dimensional meaning. There's an empty space for what the audience thinks.'[233] Lavender sets the record straight:

> live art combines various disciplines: dance, visual arts, conventional theatre, music and new technologies. It often boasts a sardonic, post-modernist wit. It can be repetitive and banal, poignant and beautiful, spectacular and bombastic.

Yeats would surely have allied himself with Diaghilev yet again in applauding such a confluence of artistic discipline. And once again, in late 1992, we find the obsession with words or body language, dance, gesture and the communication of meaning.

Lavender quotes John Ashford, artistic director of The Place, who was the first to bring Fabre's work to Britain when Ashford was director of the Instituted of Contemporary Art: 'In live art the meanings are multiple in the way in which the meanings of music or fine art are multiple.' We notice, and it is significant, that 'meaning' here is not language-based. Ashford goes on to explain:

> There is a completely different story to be had from each person who looks at it. Jan's show is extraordinary, and I will always carry the images from it with me. They meant things to me which they probably don't mean to Jan Fabre or to anyone else in the audience. That's fine.

Lavender questions whether such a look (backwards?) towards solipsism is indeed 'fine'. But this lack of consensus on what a piece may mean may well constitute the eventual fall-out from all these artistic explosions, not least the ones to which Yeats himself lit the fuse, during the first thirty years of the century and of the dance debate which still continues, as the discussion at the beginning of this chapter demonstrates.

British audiences are not enthusiastic because 'live art' is difficult and often, as Lavender admits, pretentious. On reading *The Times* review an impression of *déja vu* is inevitable for students of Yeats. We could, with some shifts of expression, be reading Joseph Holloway berating Yeats for his difficulty in 1904. And Fabre's tone is evocative of that of the Irish playwright himself when he, too, explained his theories:

> There are different metaphors and elements. A lot of my work is to do with an evocation of, and tribute to, the unnameable, the unspeakable, the invisible. It's not directly saying things, but I'm putting things next to one another. There's this gap, an empty space for what the audience thinks.

Yeats followed Mallarmé's thinking on dancers – they must be deciphered as Sign by those watching the dance in performance. If thinking about performance today in 1992 stimulates any hunches, let alone full-blown theories, they would express the recognition that the figures dealt with in this study haunt us with their extreme intelligence and prescience and that we have inherited a fascinating legacy which continues to challenge us and demand an equal degree of intelligence of our own.

NOTES

1. Fuller, *Fifteen Years*, p. 72.
2. Terence Gray, *Dance-Drama: Experiments in the Art of the Theatre* (Cambridge: W. Heffer & Sons, 1926), pp. 26–7.
3. Quoted by Michael Hamburger, 'Art as Second Nature', in *Romantic Mythologies*, p. 237.
4. *CP*, p. 694.
5. F. Nietzsche, *Also Sprach Zarathustra* (Leipzig: Alfred Kroner Verlag, n.d.), 'Das Grablied', p. 163.
6. Stéphane Mallarmé, 'Donner un sens plus pur aux mots de la tribu', from 'Le Tombeau d'Edgar Poe', *Oeuvres Complètes*, p. 189.
7. Lehmann, p. 235, quoting Mallarmé, *Divagations*, p. 142.
8. Plato, *The Laws*, trans.Trevor J. Saunders (Harmondsworth: Penguin, 1970; rpt. 1976), p. 308.
9. Aristotle, *Poetics*, trans. W. Hamilton Frye in *Aristotle XIII* (London: Heinemann, 1927; rpt. 1973), p. 7.
10. André Levinson, 'The Idea of the Dance from Aristotle to Mallarmé', *Theatre Arts Monthly*, August 1927, p. 572. Herafter cited as Levinson.
11. *Ibid.*, p. 572.
12. *Ibid.*, p. 572.
13. *Ibid.*, quoting Arbeau, p. 572.
14. Jean Georges Noverre, 1727–1810.
15. Jean Georges Noverre, *Lettres sur la Danse et sur les Ballets, a Facsimile of the 1760 Stuttgart Edition* (New York: Broude Brothers, 1967), Lettre II, pp. 28–9. Hereafter cited as Noverre.
16. *Ibid.* Lettre IX, pp. 275–6.
17. Labanotation, a term used by the Dance Notation Bureau, New York, to refer to the system of dance notation created by Rudolf von Laban, 1879–1958, in *Kinetographie Laban* (1928).
18. Ann Hutchinson, *Labanotation* (London: Oxford University Press, 1970), p. 12.
19. Noam Chomsky, 'Human language and other Semiotic Systems', *Semiotica*, vol. 25, 1/2 (1979), p. 32.
20. Michael Devitt and Kim Sterelny, *Language and Reality: An Introduction to the Philosophy of Language* (Oxford: Basil Blackwell, 1987), p. 4.
21. *Oeuvres Complètes*, p. 304.
22. Carol Barko, 'The Dancer and the Becoming of Language', *Yale French Studies*, No. 54; Mallarmé, 1977, p 187. All page references in parentheses are taken from the Pléiade edition, 1945.
23. Mary Sirridge and Adina Armelagos, 'The In's and Out's of Dance: Expression as an Aspect of Style', *Journal of Aesthetics and Art Criticism*, 36, 1977, p. 16. Hereafter cited as Sirridge and Armelagos, 'In's and Out's'.

24. *Ibid.*, p. 24.
25. Leroy Leatherman, *Martha Graham: Portrait of the Lady as an Artist* (New York: 1966) quoted by Sirridge and Armelagos, 'In's and Out's', p. 24.
26. *R I*, pp. 173–4.
27. Suzanne K. Langer, *Feeling and Form* (London: Routledge and Kegan Paul., 1953), p. 108. Hereafter cited as Langer.
28. *Ibid.*, pp. 174–5.
29. *Ibid.*, pp. 177–8.
30. Rudolf von Laban, *Welt des Tanzers: Funf Gedankenreigen*, p. 14, quoted by Langer, p. 178.
31. Langer, p. 180.
32. *Philosophical Essays on Dance, with Responses from Choreographers, Critics and Dancers. Based on a Conference at the American Dance Festival, Summer 1979 on the Campus of Duke University, Durham, North Carolina*, ed. Gordon Fancher and Gerald Myers (New York: Dance Horizons, 1981), Marshall Cohen, 'Primitivism, Modernism, and Dance Theory', pp. 144–5. Herafter cited as Fancher and Myers.
33. Thomas E. Wartenberg, 'Is Dance Elitist?'; Fancher and Myers, p. 118.
34. Wartenberg in Fancher and Myers, p. 119.
35. *New Directions in Dance, Collected Writings from the Seventh Dance in Canada Conference held at the University of Waterloo, Canada, June 1979*, ed. Diana Theodores Taplin (Toronto: Pergamon Press, 1979), Jacob Zelinger, 'Semiotics and Theatre Dance', p. 47. Hereafter cited as Taplin.
36. Selma Jeanne Cohen, *Next Week, Swan Lake: Reflections on Dance and Dances* (Middletown, Conn.: Wesleyan University Press, 1982), pp. 109–10.
37. Selma Jeanne Cohen, 'A Prolegomenon to an Aesthetics of Dance', (1962) in *Aesthetic Inquiry: Essays on Art Criticism and the Philosophy of Art, Essays from the Journal of Aesthetic and Art Criticism* (Belmont, Cal.: Dickenson, 1967), p. 274. Hereafter cited as 'Prolegomenon'.
38. *Ibid.*, pp. 275–6.
39. *Ibid.*, p. 280.
40. David Carr, 'Thought and Action in the Art of Dance', *British Journal of Aesthetics*, Vol. 27, No. 4, Autumn, 1987, p. 351. Hereafter cited as Carr.
41. *Ibid.*, pp. 352 and 354.
42. Maxine Sheets-Johnstone, 'Thinking in Movement', *Journal of Aesthetics and Art Criticism*, Summer 1981, Vol. XXXIX No. 4, p. 406.
43. Nelson Goodman, *Languages of Art, An Approach to a Theory of Symbols* (London: Oxford University Press, 1969), p. 65.
44. Paul Valéry, *Oeuvres de Paul Valéry* (Paris: Editions du Sagittaire, 1923; rpt. 1931), L'Ame et la Danse, p. 37. Hereafter cited as Valéry.
45. *Ibid.*, p. 42.
46. Levinson, p. 583.
47. Paul Ziff, 'About the Appreciation of Dance', in Fancher and Myers, pp. 70 and 78.
48. Sparshott, p. 385.

49. Mary Wigman, 1886–1973; Doris Humphrey, 1895–1958.
50. *The Modern Dance*, ed. Virginia Stewart and Merle Armitage (New York: Will Kistler, 1935; rpt. New York: Dance Horizons, 1970), p. xv.
51. *Collected Poems*, 'The Song of the Happy Shepherd', p. 7.
52. Denis Donoghue, *Yeats* (London: Fontana, 1971), p. 77. Hereafter cited as Donoghue.
53. *RI*, p. 94.
54. *CP*, p. 65.
55. *Ibid.*, p. 61.
56. *Ibid.*, p. 65.
57. *Ibid.*, p. 66.
58. *Ibid.*, p. 260.
59. *Ibid.*, p. 67.
60. *Ibid.*, p. 66.
61. *Ibid.*, pp. 69–70.
62. *Ibid.*, p. 70.
63. *Ibid.*, p. 70.
64. W. B. Yeats, *The Variorum Edition of the Plays of W. B. Yeats*, ed. Russell K. Alspach (London: Macmillan, 1965; rpt. 1966), p. 1124. Hereafter cited as *Variorum*.
65. *Ibid.*, p. 1126.
66. *Ibid.*, p. 1140.
67. *CP*, p. 415.
68. *Ibid.*, p. 414.
69. *Ibid.*, p. 416.
70. *Ibid.*, p. 653.
71. *Ibid.*, pp. 653–54.
72. *Ibid.*, p. 654.
73. *Ibid.*, p. 655.
74. *Ibid.*, pp. 653–54.
75. *Ibid..*, p. 661.
76. *Ibid.*, p. 666.
77. *Ibid.*, p. 662.
78. *Ibid.*, p. 251.
79. *Ibid.*, p. 254.
80. *Ibid.*, p. 224.
81. *Ibid.*, p. 262.
82. *Ibid.*, pp. 258–59.
83. *Letters*, p. 472.
84. *Ibid.*, 21 October 1910, to Lady Gregory, p. 554.
85. *CP*, pp. 214–15.
86. Taylor, *Readers' Guide*, p. 63.
87. *CP*, p. 216.
88. *Ibid.*, p. 217.
89. *Ibid.*, p. 217.
90. *Ibid.*, p. 217.
91. *Ibid.*, p. 217.
92. *Ibid.*, p. 220.
93. *Ibid.*, p. 442.

94. *Ibid.*, p. 443.
95. *Ibid.*, p. 443.
96. *Ibid.*, p. 443.
97. *Ibid.*, p. 444.
98. *Ibid.*, p. 434.
99. *Ibid.*, p. 444.
100. *Ibid.*, p. 442.
101. *Ibid.*, p. 445.
102. *Ibid.*, p. 290.
103. *Ibid.*, p. 290.
104. *Ibid.*, p. 290.
105. *Ibid.*, p. 291.
106. *Ibid.*, p. 291.
107. *Ibid.*, p. 291.
108. *Ibid.*, p. 291.
109. *Ibid.*, p. 291.
110. Worth, p. 175.
111. *CP*, p. 456.
112. *Ibid.*, p. 457.
113. *Ibid.*, p. 457.
114. *Ibid*, p. 457.
115. *Ibid.*, p. 454.
116. *Ibid.*, p. 456.
117. *Ibid.*, p. 455.
118. *Ibid.*, p. 455.
119. *Ibid.*, p. 455.
120. *Ibid.*, p. 455.
121. *Ibid.*, p. 456.
122. *Ibid.*, p. 456.
123. *Ibid.*, p. 456.
124. *Ibid.*, p. 456.
125. *Ibid.*, p. 456.
126. *Ibid.*, p. 455.
127. *Ibid.*, p. 455.
128. *Ibid.*, p. 456.
129. *Ibid.*, p. 456.
130. Donoghue, p. 27.
131. *CP*, p. 469.
132. *Ibid.*, p. 471.
133. *Variorum*, p. 805.
134. *CP*, p. 471.
135. *Ibid.*, p. 461.
136. *Ibid.*, pp. 462–3.
137. *Ibid.*, p. 461.
138. *Ibid.*, p. 463.
139. *Ibid.*, p. 471.
140. *Ibid.*, p. 472.
141. *Ibid.*, p. 580.
142. *Ibid.*, p. 587.

143. *Ibid.*, p. 593.
144. *Ibid.*, p. 593.
145. *Ibid.*, p. 594.
146. *Ibid.*, p. 594.
147. *Ibid.*, p. 594.
148. *Ibid.*, p. 594.
149. *Ibid.*, p. 594.
150. *Ibid.*, p. 594.
151. *Ibid.*, p. 594.
152. *Ibid.*, p. 622.
153. *Ibid.*, p. 622.
154. *Ibid.*, p. 627.
155. *Ibid.*, p. 627.
156. *Ibid.*, p. 627.
157. *Ibid.*, p. 627.
158. *Ibid.*, p. 627.
159. *Ibid.*, p. 627.
160. *Ibid.*, p. 628.
161. *Ibid.*, p. 628.
162. *Ibid.*, p. 629.
163. *Ibid.*, p. 629.
164. *Ibid.*, p. 629.
165. *Ibid.*, p. 629.
166. *Ibid.*, p. 629.
167. *Ibid.*, p. 630.
168. *Ibid.*, p. 630.
169. *Ibid.*, p. 630.
170. *Ibid.*, p. 630.
171. *Variorum*, p. 1311.
172. *CP*, p. 633.
173. *Ibid.*, p. 633.
174. *Ibid.*, p. 634.
175. *Ibid.*, p. 633.
176. *Ibid.*, p. 636.
177. *Ibid.*, p. 637.
178. *Ibid.*, p. 638.
179. *Ibid.*, p. 638.
180. *Ibid.*, p. 638.
181. *Ibid.*, p. 639.
182. *Ibid.*, p. 639.
183. *Ibid.*, p. 639.
184. *Ibid.*, p. 640.
185. *Ibid.*, p. 640.
186. *Ibid.*, p. 640.
187. *Ibid.*, p. 640.
188. *Ibid.*, p. 640.
189. *Ibid.*, p. 641.
190. *Ibid.*, p. 641.
191. *Ibid.*, p. 694.

192. *Ibid.*, p. 694.
193. *Ibid.*, p. 694.
194. *Ibid.*, p. 703.
195. *Ibid.*, p. 703.
196. *Ibid.*, p. 703.
197. *Ibid.*, p. 703.
198. *Ibid.*, p. 703.
199. *Ibid.*, pp. 703–4.
200. *Ibid.*, p. 704.
201. *Ibid.*, p. 705.
202. *Ibid.*, p. 705.
203. *Ibid.*, p. 704.
204. *Ibid.*, p. 705.
205. *Ibid.*, p. 704.
206 . Valéry, p. 57.
207. Saturday, 3 October 1931. *Joseph Holloway's Irish Theatre*, ed. Robert Hogan and Michael J. O'Neill, Vol. 1, *1926–1931* (Dixon, Cal.: Proscenium Press, 1968), p. 79. Hereafter cited as Holloway, *Irish Theatre*.
208. Joseph Holloway, *Impressions of a Dublin Playgoer*, the National Library of Ireland, Ms. 1802 (i), June to December 1904, pp. 564–5. Hereafter cited as Holloway, *Impressions*.
209. INTS (The Irish National Theatre Society), 'Una Ellis-Fermor argues that the Irish National Theatre Society was functioning as early as April, 1902, … and that the performances of *Kathleen* and *Deirdre* were under the auspices of the society formed "to continue the work done by the Irish Literary Theatre" [Una Ellis-Fermor, *The Irish Dramatic Movement* (London: Methuen, 1939), p. 202.]. A careful examination of evidence proves that the Irish National Theatre Society was not formed until after the April performances, that it was formed just before Samhain performances in October 1902 and that the actual name of Irish National Theatre Society was not used publicly until the performances of December 1902' (Brenna Katz Clarke, *The Emergence of the Irish Peasant Play at the Abbey Theatre* (Ann Arbor, Mich.: UMI Research Press, 1982), p. 22). The President, W. B. Yeats; vice-presidents, Maud Gonne, Douglas Hyde, George Russell (AE); stage-manager, W. G. Fay; secretary, Fred Ryan. Set up on an idea of the Fays to make a permanent society of Irish players, trained by the Fays, who would act in and produce only Irish plays. A popular theatre, blatantly nationalist in orientation, which stressed rural scenes from Irish life as opposed to the mystical, supernatural themes of its 'English' predecessor, The Irish Literary Theatre.
210. Holloway, *Impressions*, June to December 1904, p. 568.
211. *Joseph Holloway's Abbey Theatre. A Selection from his Unpublished Journal Impressions of a Dublin Playgoer*, ed. Robert Hogan and Michael J. O'Neill (London & Amsterdam: Carbondale and Edvwardsville Southern Illinois University Press, 1967), p. 58. Hereafter cited as Holloway, *Abbey Theatre*.
212. Holloway, *Abbey Theatre*, pp. 75–6.

213. *Ibid.*, p. 77.
214. *The Leader*, Vol. XIII, No. 15 (Dublin), 1 December 1906. Collected in W. A. Henderson's *Press Cuttings from the Abbey Theatre*, the National Library of Ireland. Mss. 1931–1773. POS 7271 (microfilm). Hereafter cited as Henderson, *Press Cuttings*.
215. Holloway, *Abbey Theatre*, 'Mrs Campbell's "Deirdre"', pp. 119–20.
216. *The Peasant*, 26 December 1908, '*Deirdre* in London.', in Henderson, *Press Cuttings*.
217. *The Times*, 28 November 1908.
218. Holloway, *Abbey Theatre*, p. 149.
219. *The Irish Times*, 18 February 1911.
220. Holloway, *Abbey Theatre*, p. 206.
221. Holloway, *Irish Theatre*,. Vol. 1: *1926–1931*, pp. 13–14.
222. Holloway, *Irish Theatre*,. Vol. 1: *1926–1931*, p. 50.
223. *The Independent*, 14 January 1930.
224. Holloway, *Irish Theatre*, Vol. 1: *1926–1931*, p. 70.
225. *Ibid.*p. 81.
226. Holloway, *Irish Theatre*, Vol. 2: *1932–1937*, p. 35.
227. *Ibid.*, p. 58.
228. *Ibid.*, 11 August 1937, p. 58.
229. Sam McCready, an unpublished MA thesis, University College of North Wales, 1975, 'The Stage-director's Approach to the Presentation of the plays of W. B. Yeats, with Special Reference to the Plays for Dancers; Together with a Detailed study of The King of the Great Clock Tower', p. 80.
230. Julian Hilton, *Performance* (London: Macmillan, 1987), pp. 33–4.
231. Katharine Worth, *The Irish Drama of Europe from Yeats to Beckett*.
232. See, for example, *The Independent*, 5 August 1992, p. 13; *The Times*, 5 August 1992, *Life and Times*, p. 3, *The Observer*, 9 August 1992, p. 92.
233. *The Times*, 27 July 1992; *Life and Times*, p. 3.

Conclusion

Even a dance which appears free and spontaneous to an onlooker is likely to involve an element of control, of balance. It is more knowing than it seems, for technique can do the work of prudence. Quite frequently, in Romantic writing, there comes a vertiginous moment where thought seems to be passing out of control. Romantic experience involves encountering the Infinite, but this is strictly beyond the scope of the human mind, and threatens it with a kind of chaos. If there are no boundaries to be established between the self and the rest of Nature, then the mind can be drawn with headlong speed to the very limits of the available world. From this it shrinks. ...

Spontaneity on its own, then, might dance itself out into chaos or exhaustion. In its pure form it was something which could not last. Technique, on the other hand, was the means of allowing freedom as much scope as possible, to the point where it became untenable, and adroitly and knowingly drew back. The element of deliberate control in this brought the conscious self back into the relationship, offering a kind of solution to Romantic estrangement. Yeats, using dance in this way, produced the same combination, while the separation of writer and dancer allowed the latter to be free from implication in the manufacture of that security.[1]

These issues raised by dance as aesthetic phenomenon were crucial to the concerns of late Romantic writers and to those of *Symbolisme-Décadence*. Such abstract concepts were rendered actual when portrayed through the Victorian predilection for the solitary female dancer, usually found on the music-hall stage and in the salon and through the vogue for Salome, with all the accompanying overtones of the threatening temptress, the *femme fatale* who incarnated original sin, the predatory woman who sapped her admirer's manhood and reduced him to waste and impotence. Yeats knew intimately and deeply these contemporary preoccupations of both his fellow artists and of *fin-de-siècle* society in general, and he crafted a symbolic system around them. He also, with confidence and panache, chose to follow another trend from the current fashionable obsessions in art, that of the Japanese Noh dancer, and this too he made his own by investing his version of the figure with a responsibility in the furthering of conflict and action in the drama in which she or he plays a crucial role. As Chapter 2 suggested, the authentic Noh dance, the 'mai', does not carry its burden in quite such a manner: the Japanese dance, rather, celebrates a lull in which true identity has been divulged or where conflict has been transcended.

In all of Yeats's registering and subsequent transforming of the contemporary *Zeitgeist* in aesthetic matters he discloses his fascination with dance because of its kinship with the poetic process. Mallarmé is of course his forerunner in this and it has been demonstrated superlatively by critics of Yeats's *oeuvre*, particularly by Frank Kermode, how the image of the dance as spontaneity controlled is analogous to the fact of the poem. To move from the recognition of this position to the crafting of a dance play, however, in which Yeats acknowledges the inadequacy of language for certain dramatic purposes and proposes dance as a transfiguration of words into another medium, is a brave step indeed, because the image, the emblem in the realm of poetry, the symbol, becomes metamorphosed and actualised through live performance on the stage. There it takes on a force of great potency, especially as Yeats's preference was for the dancer as abstraction – a hawk woman, a goddess – moving in a manner which subsumes aspects of humanity into the discipline of Art and Artefact, just those qualities which Loïe Fuller exhibited with such success and to the acclaim of the artists who desired an amalgam of emotion with intellect.

The dance plays of Yeats influenced several of his contemporaries, including Gordon Bottomley and Terence Gray and it would be interesting to pursue what happened thereafter and to wonder what will happen next. Is there a tradition of dance theatre or has it yet to be created ? The *prima facie* case is that there was indeed a tradition which included minor figures such as those cited above along with exponents of a far more major stature, like the Austrian poet Hugo von Hoffmansthal, who trod an aesthetic path very similar to that selected by Yeats himself in the early years of the century. Is there, however, a continuity of method or does each dramatist reinvent the rules? Is Yeats part of a continuum, not of dance-with-drama – Todhunter's contribution to the debate – but of drama through the dance? In the worst forms of the dance drama we are presented simplistically with a set of interludes. Yeats's plays are obviously never guilty of so doing; rather they provide an interreaction of media which mirror and comment upon each other to form a whole of tight integrity.

The preceding four chapters have exhibited Yeats's drama in the context of the aesthetic milieu in which he was situated and to which he responded with sensitivity and caution and wisdom. What is now needed is a larger exploration which would place the Irish playwright in the subsequent literary tradition of the dance play, if, as we speculate, such a tradition exists. A retrospective and informed glance may reveal the suspicion that Yeats seems to represent a dramaturgical dead-end, but this heresy provokes instant disbelief in admirers and students of his work. It is just such an enquiry that I would suggest forms the next logical step in the study so far completed: a close analysis of Yeats's legacy in terms of the dance play. This would be an interesting investigation on which to set forth in the secure knowledge that no figure immediately presents itself as at all comparable with the ablest proponent of the genre, W. B. Yeats himself.

NOTE

1. Joan Scanlon and Richard Kerridge, 'Spontaneity and Control: The Uses of Dance in Late Romantic Literature', *Dance Research*, VI: i, (Spring 1988), pp. 30–44.

Bibliography

In the treatments of the Herodias–Salome legend the date of the first publication of the work precedes later editions used.

PRIMARY SOURCES

Algeranoff, Harcourt. *My Years with Pavlova*. London: Heinemann, 1957.

Allan, Maud. *My Life and Dancing*. London: Everett & Co., 1908.

Anderson, Hugh Abercrombie. *Out Without My Rubbers: The Memoirs of John Murray Anderson*. New York: Library Publishers, 1954.

Aristotle. *Poetics*, trans. W. Hamilton Fyfe in *Aristotle XIII*. London: Heinemann, 1927; rpt. 1973.

Arnold, Sir Edwin. *Adzuma, or The Japanese Wife*. London: Longmans, Green, 1892.

Banville, Théodore de. *Les princesses*. Paris: Alphonse Lemerre, 1874.

—— *Poésies Complètes*. Paris: G. Charpentier, 1878.

—— *Oeuvres de Théodore de Banville*. Paris: no publisher, 1890.

—— *Choix de poésies*. Paris: Bibliothèque-Charpentier, 1923.

Baudelaire, Charles. *Oeuvres Complètes*. 'Les Fleurs du Mal' 1861. Paris: Gallimard, 1975.

Beerbohm, Max. *Around Theatres*. London: Rupert Hart-Davies, 1953.

Bowers, Faubion. *Japanese Theatre*. London: Peter Owen, 1954.

Cassirer, Ernst. *Language and Myth*, trans. Susanne K. Langer. USA: Dover Publications, 1946.

Chomsky, Noam. Human Language and Other Semiotic Systems. *Semiotica*. vol. 25, 1/2 1979.

Cochran, Charles B. *The Secrets of a Showman*. London: Heinemann, 1925.

Craig, Edward Gordon. *Craig on Theatre*, ed. J. Michael Walton. London: Methuen, 1983.

Devitt, Michael and Sterelny, Kim. *Language and Reality: An Introduction to the Philosophy of Language*. Oxford: Basil Blackwell, 1987.

Dresser, Christopher. *Japan: Its Architecture, Art, and Art Manufactures*. London: Longmans, Green, 1882.

Edwards, Osman. *Japanese Plays and Playfellows*. London: Heinemann, 1901.

Ellis, Havelock. *The Dance of Life*. London: Constable & Co., 1923.

Fawcett, Robin P., Halliday, M. A. K., Lamb, Sydney M. and Makkai, Adam. *The Semiotics of Culture and Language*. 2 vols. London: Frances Pinter, 1984.

Fenollosa, Ernest and Pound, Ezra. *'Noh' or Accomplishment. A Study of the Classical Stage of Japan*. London: Macmillan, 1916.

Flaubert, Gustave. *Trois Contes*. Paris: G. Charpentier, 1877.

—— Paris: Louis Conard, 1921.

Fuller, Loïe. *Fifteen Years of a Dancer's Life, with some Account of her Distinguished Friends*. Paris: 1908; London: Herbert Jenkins, 1913.

Goodman, Nelson. *Languages of Art. An Approach to a Theory of Symbols*. London: Oxford University Press, 1969.

Gray, Terence. *Dance-Drama: Experiments in the Art of the Theatre*. Cambridge: W. Heffer & Sons, 1926.

Grimm, Jacob. *Teutonic Mythology*, trans. James Steven Stallybrass, 4 vols. London: George Bell & Sons, 1882.

Hearn, Lafcadio. *Glimpses of Unfamiliar Japan*. London: Osgood and McIlvaine, 1894.

—— *Out of the East: Reveries and Studies in New Japan*. New York: Houghton and Mifflin, 1895.

—— *Japan: An Attempt at Interpretation*. New York: Macmillan, 1904.

Heine, Heinrich. *Atta Troll: Ein Sommernachtstraum*. Hamburg: Hoffmann und Campe, 1849.

—— *Samtliche Werke: Gedichte*. Munchen: Winkler Verlag, 1972.

Henderson, W. A. 'Press Cuttings from the Abbey Theatre'. The National Library of Ireland. Mss 1731–3.

Heywood, Joseph Converse. *Herodias: A Dramatic Poem*. New York: Hurd and Houghton, 1867.

Hollingshead, John. *Gaiety Chronicles*. Westminster: Archibald Constable, 1898.

Holloway, Joseph. *Impressions of a Dublin Playgoer*. Unpublished journal housed in the National Library of Ireland. Ms 1802 (i).

—— *Joseph Holloway's Abbey Theatre: A Selection from his Unpublished Journal, Impressions of a Dublin Playgoer, 1899–1926*, ed. Robert Hogan and Michael J. O'Neill. London & Amsterdam: Carbondale & Edwardsville Southern Illinois University Press, 1967.

—— *Joseph Holloway's Irish Theatre*, ed. Robert Hogan and Michael J. O'Neil, Vol. l. *1926–31*. Dixon, CA: Proscenium Press, 1968. Vol. 2, *1932–7*. Dixon, CA: Proscenium Press, 1969. Vol. 3, *1938–44*. Dixon, CA: Proscenium Press, 1970.

Honour, Hugh. *Chinoiserie: The Vision of Cathay*. London: John Murray, 1961.

Huysmans, Joris Karl. *A Rebours*. Paris: G. Charpentier, 1884.

Karsavina, Tamara. *Theatre Street: The Reminiscences of Tamara Karsavina*. 1930; London: Dance Books, 1981.

Kettle, Michael. *Salome's Last Veil*. London: Hart-Davies, Macgibbon, 1977.

Laforgue, Jules. *Moralités légendaires*. Paris: Librairie de la Revue indépendente, 1887; Paris: Mercure de France, 1964.

Langer, Suzanne. *Feeling and Form*. London: Routledge and Kegan Paul, 1953.

Lorrain, Jean. *La Forêt Bleue*. Paris: Alphonse Lemerre, 1883.

Mallarmé, Stéphane. *Oeuvres Complètes de Stéphane Mallarmé*. Texte établi et annoté par Henri Mondor et G. Jean-Aubry. Paris: Bibliothèque de la Pléiade, Gallimard, 1945.

—— *Les Noces d'Hérodiade, Mystère*, ed. Gardner Davies. Paris: Gallimard, 1959.

McCready, Sam. Unpublished MA thesis, University College of North Wales, Bangor, 1975: 'The Stage-director's Approach to the Presentation of the Plays of W. B. Yeats, with Special Reference to the *Plays for Dancers*; Together with a Detailed Study of *The King of the Great Clock Tower*'.

Mead, G. R. S. 'The Sacred Dance of Jesus'. *The Quest*. vol. II, Nos 1–4, October 1910–July 1911.

Michener, James A. *The Floating World*. London: Secker and Warburg, 1954.

Milliet, Paul and Grémont, Henri. *Hérodiade*. Lisboa: Typ. de Costa Sanches Fes., 1885; Paris: Calmann-Lévy éditeurs, 1911.

Miyamori, Asaturo. *Tales from Old Japanese Dramas*, revised by Stanley Hughes. New York and London: G. P. Putnam's Sons, 1915.

Nietzsche, Friedrich. *Also Sprach Zarathustra*. Leipzig: Alfred Kroner Verlag, n.d.

Nijinsky, Vaslav. *The Diary of Vaslav Nijinsky*, ed. Romola Nijinsky. 1937; London: Panther, 1966.

Noverre, Jean Georges. *Lettres sur la Danse et sur les Ballets: A Facsimile of the 1760 Stuttgart Edition*. New York: Broude Brothers, 1967.

Plato. *The Laws*, trans. Trevor J. Saunders. Harmondsworth: Penguin, 1970; rpt. 1976.

Pound, Ezra and Fenollosa, Ernest. *The Classic Noh Theatre of Japan*. New York: New Directions, 1959.

Ricketts, Charles. *Self-portrait Taken from the Letters and Journals of Charles Ricketts, R.A.*, collected and compiled by T. Sturge Moore, ed. Cecil Lewis. London: Peter Davies, 1939.

Stopes, Marie C. *A Journal from Japan*. London: Blackie and Son, 1910.

—— and Sakurai, Professor Joji. *Plays of Old Japan: The Noh*. London: Heinemann, 1913.

Sudermann, Hermann. *Johannes*. New York: I. Goldmann, 1897; Stuttgart: J. G. Cotta, 1898.

Symons, Arthur. *Images of Good and Evil*. London: Heinemann, 1899.

—— *The Symbolist Movement in Literature*. London: Heinemann, 1899.

—— *Studies in Seven Arts*. London: Martin Secker, 1906; rpt. 1924.

—— *Poems*, Vols. I and II. London: Martin Secker, 1924.

Valéry, Paul. 'L'Ame et la Danse'. *Oeuvres de Paul Valéry*. Paris: 1923; Paris: Editions du Sagittaire, 1931.

Valois, Ninette de. *Come Dance with Me: A Memoir 1898–1956*. London: Hamish Hamilton, 1959.

Waley, Arthur. *The No Plays of Japan*. London: George Allen and Unwin, 1921; rpt. 1950, 1954.

Wilde, Oscar. 'The Poets' Corner'. *Pall Mall Gazette*, February 15, 1888, Vol. XLVII: 7128.

—— *Salomé, drame en un acte*. Paris: Librairie de l'art indépendent, 1893.

—— *Complete Works*. London: Collins, 1948; rpt. 1967.

Yeats, W. B. *A Vision, 1925*; London: Macmillan, 1969.

—— *Collected Poems*. London: Macmillan, 1933; rpt. 1973.

—— *The Collected Plays of W. B. Yeats*. London: Macmillan, 1934; rpt. 1982.

—— *The Letters of W. B. Yeats*, ed. Allan Wade. London: Rupert Hart-Davies, 1954.

—— *Autobiographies*. London: Macmillan, 1955; rpt. 1973.

—— *Essays and Introductions*. London: Macmillan, 1961.

—— *Explorations*. London: Macmillan, 1962.

—— *The Variorum Edition of the Plays of W. B. Yeats*, ed. Russell K. Alspach. London: Macmillan, 1965; rpt. 1966.

—— *Uncollected Prose by W. B. Yeats, I. First Reviews and Articles 1886–96*, ed. John P. Frayne. London: Macmillan, 1970.
—— *Memoirs*, ed. Denis Donoghue. London: Macmillan, 1972.
—— *Uncollected Prose by W. B. Yeats, II. Reviews, Articles and Other Miscellaneous Prose 1897–1939*, ed. John P. Frayne and Colton Johnson. London: Macmillan, 1975.
—— *The Collected Letters of W. B. Yeats 1865–1895*, ed. John Kelly. Oxford: Oxford University Press, 1986.

SECONDARY SOURCES

Baker, Blanch M. compiler, *Dramatic Bibliography: An Annotated List of Books on the History and Criticism of the Dance and Stage and on the Allied Arts of the Theatre*. New York: H. W. Wilson Company, 1933.
Barko, Carol. 'The Dancer and the Becoming of Language'. *Yale French Studies*, No. 54. 1977.
Beardsley, Monroe C. and Schueller, Herbert M. ed. *Aesthetic Inquiry: Essays on Art Criticism and the Philosophy of Art. Essays from the 'Journal of Aesthetics and Art Criticism'*. Belmont, CA: Dickenson, 1962.
Beaumont, Cyril W. *The Diaghilev Ballet in London: A Personal Record*. London: Putnam, 1940.
Bland, Alexander. *A History of Ballet and Dance in the Western World*. London: Barrie & Jenkins, 1976.
Buckle, Richard. *Nijinsky*. London: Weidenfeld & Nicolson, 1971; rpt. 1975; rpt. with revisions 1980.
Caldwell, Helen. *Michio Ito: The Dancer and His Dances*. Berkeley: University of California Press, 1977.
Carr, David. 'Thought and Action in the Art of Dance'. *British Journal of Aesthetics*. vol. 27, no. 4, Autumn 1987.
Carter, Huntly. *The New Spirit in Drama and Art*. London: Frank Palmer, 1912.
Chiba, Yoko. 'Ezra Pound's Versions of Fenollosa's Noh Manuscripts and Yeats's Unpublished "Suggestions and Corrections"' in Masaru Sekine and Christopher Murray, *Yeats and the Noh: A Comparative Study*. Gerard's Cross: Colin Smythe, 1990.
Clarke, Brenna Katz. *The Emergence of the Irish Peasant Play at the Abbey Theatre*. Ann Arbor, Mich.: UMI Research Press, 1982.
Cohen, Selma Jeanne. *Next Week, Swan Lake: Reflections on Dance and Dances*. Middletown, Conn: Wesleyan University Press, 1982.
Crawford Flitch, J. E. *Modern Dancing and Dancers*. London: Grant Richards, 1912.
Dijkstra, Bram. *Idols of Perversity. Fantasies of Feminine Evil in Fin-de-Siècle Culture*. New York: Oxford University Press, 1986.
Donaghue, Denis. *Yeats*. London: Fontana, 1971.
Dorn, Karen. *Players and Painted Stage*. Sussex: The Harvester Press, 1984.
Ellmann, Richard. 'Overtures to Salome'. *Yearbook of Comparative and General Literature*, No.17, 1968.

Ellis-Fermor, Una. *The Irish Dramatic Movement*. London: Methuen, 1939.

Fancher, Gordon and Myers, Gerald. (eds) *Philosophical Essays on Dance: With Responses from Choreographers, Critics and Dancers. Based on a Conference at the American Dance Festival, Summer 1979, on the Campus of Duke University, Durham, North Carolina.* New York: Dance Horizons, 1981.

Feschotte, Jacques. *Histoire du Music-Hall.* Paris: Presses Universitaires de France, 1965.

Fielding, Daphne. *Emerald and Nancy: Lady Cunard and her Daughter.* London: Eyre and Spottiswoode, 1968. American title: *Those Remarkable Cunards. Emerald and Nancy: Lady Cunard and her Daughter.* New York: Athenaeum, 1968.

Flannery, James W. W. B. *Yeats and the Idea of a Theatre: The Early Abbey Theatre in Theory and Practice.* New Haven: Yale University Press, 1976.

Fletcher, Ian. 'Symons, Yeats and the Demonic Dance'. *London Magazine*, Ed. John Lehmann. London: June 1960, Vol. 7, No. 6.

—— ed. *Romantic Mythologies.* London: Routledge and Kegan Paul, 1967.

Frazier, Adrian. *Behind the Scenes: Yeats, Horniman, and the Struggle for the Abbey Theatre.* Berkeley: University of California Press, 1990.

Fréjaville, Gustave. 'Baladines et Bateleuses Illustres'. *Le Figaro Artistique.* Paris: November 1930.

Gordon, D. J. (ed.). *W. B. Yeats: Images of a Poet.* Manchester: Manchester University Press, 1961.

Grigoriev, S. L. *The Diaghilev Ballet 1909–1929.* Trans. and ed. Vera Bowen. London: Constable, 1953; Harmondsworth: Penguin, 1960.

Groos, Arthur. 'Return of the Native: Japan in *Madama Butterfly/ Madama Butterfly* in Japan'. *Cambridge Opera Journal.* Cambridge: 1989, 1.

Guest, Ivor. *The Ballet of the Second Empire.* London: Pitman Publishing, 1953; rpt. 1974.

—— *The Romantic Ballet in England: Its Development, Fulfilment and Decline.* London: Pitman Publishing, 1954; rpt. 1972.

—— *Fanny Cerrito: The Life of a Romantic Ballerina.* London: Dance Books, 1956; rpt. 1974.

—— *Adeline Genée: A Lifetime of Ballet under Six Reigns.* London: Adam & Charles Black, 1958.

—— *Le Ballet de l'Opéra de Paris: trois siècles d'histoire et de tradition*, trans. Paul Alexandre. Paris: National de l'Opéra, 1976.

Harbron, Dudley. *The Conscious Stone: The Life of Edward William Godwin.* London: Latimer House, 1949.

Highfill, Jr, Philip H., Burnim Kalman A. and Laughans, Edward A. *A Biographical Dictionary of Actors, Actresses, Musicians, Dancers, Managers and Other Stage Personnel in London, 1660–1800.* Southern Illinois: Carbondale & Edwardsville, 1978.

Hilton, Julian. *Performance.* London: Macmillan, 1987.

Hutchinson, Ann. *Labanotation.* London: Oxford University Press, 1970.

Hyman, Alan. *The Gaiety Years.* London: Cassell, 1975.

Kermode, Frank. *Romantic Image.* London: Routledge and Kegan Paul, 1957; London: Fontana, 1971.

—— *Puzzles and Epiphanies: Essays and Reviews, 1958–61.* London: Routledge and Kegan Paul, 1962. 'Poet and Dancer before Diaghilev'.

Kirstein, Lincoln. *Movement and Metaphor: Four Centuries of Ballet*. London: Pitman Publishing, 1971.

Kochno, Boris. *Diaghilev and the Ballets Russes*, trans. Adrienne Foulke. New York: Harper & Row, 1970.

Koegler, Horst. *The Concise Oxford Dictionary of Ballet*. London: Oxford University Press, 1977.

Kramer, Lawrence. 'Culture and Musical Hermeneutics: The Salome Complex'. *Cambridge Opera Journal*. Cambridge: 1990, 2.

Lazzarini, John and Roberta. *Pavlova: Repertoire of a Legend*. London: Collier Macmillan, 1980.

Lehmann, A. G. *The Symbolist Aesthetic in France, 1885–1895*. Oxford: Basil Blackwell, 1950; rpt. 1968.

Leslie, Peter. *A Hard Act to Follow*. London: Paddington Press, 1978.

Levinson, André. 'The Idea of the Dance from Aristotle to Mallarmé'. *Theatre Arts Monthly*. August 1927.

Lifar, Serge. *Serge de Diaghilev*. Monaco: Editions du Rocher, 1954.

Macdonald, Nesta (ed.). *Diaghilev Observed by Critics in England and in the United States 1911–1929*. London: Dance Books, 1975.

Macqueen-Pope, W. *Ghosts and Greasepaint*. London: Robert Hale, 1951.

Malone, Andrew E. *The Irish Drama*. First published London: 1929. New York: Benjamin Blom, 1965.

Maxwell, D. E. S. *A Critical History of Modern Irish Drama, 1891–1980*. Cambridge: Cambridge University Press, 1984.

McConnell, Joan. *Ballet as Body Language*. New York: Harper and Row, 1977.

Miner, Earl. *The Japanese Tradition in British and American Literature*. Princeton, NJ: Princeton University Press, 1958; rpt. 1966.

Money, Keith. *Anna Pavlova: Her Life and Art*. London: Collins, 1982.

O'Driscoll, Robert and Reynolds, Lorna (eds). *Yeats and the Theatre*. London: Macmillan, 1975.

Ogura, Shigeo. 'Ballet in Japan. A History of Fifty Years'. English version by Don Kenny in *Ballet Today*, March–April, 1970.

Oxford English Dictionary. Oxford: Clarendon Press, 1933; rpt. 1978.

Oxford English Dictionary, A Supplement, II: H-N, ed. R. W. Burchfield. Oxford: Clarendon Press, 1976.

Pearsall, Ronald. *Victorian Popular Music*. Newton Abbot: David & Charles, 1973.

—— *Edwardian Popular Music*. Newton Abbot: David & Charles, 1975.

Pessis, Jacques and Crépineau, Jacques. *The Moulin Rouge*, trans. Andrew Lamb. New York: Alan Sutton, St Martin's Press, 1990.

Priddin, Deirdre. *The Art of the Dance in French Literature, from Théophile Gautier to Paul Valéry*. London: Adam & Charles Black, 1952.

Qambar, Akhtar. *Yeats and the Noh*. New York: Weatherhill, 1974.

Rudorff, Raymond. *Belle Epoque*. London: Hamish Hamilton, 1972.

Scanlon, Joan and Kerridge, Richard. 'Spontaneity and Control. The Uses of Dance in Late Romantic Literature'. *Dance Research*, VI i, Spring 1988, pp. 30–44.

Seroff, Victor. *The Real Isadora*. New York: The Dial Press, 1971.

Sheets-Johnstone, Maxine. 'Thinking in Movement'. *Journal of Aesthetics and Art Criticism*, Vol. XXXIX, No. 4, Summer 1981.

Shelton, Suzanne. *Divine Dancer: A Biography of Ruth St. Denis*. New York: Doubleday, 1981.

Showalter, Elaine. *Sexual Anarchy: Gender and Culture at the Fin-de-Siècle*. New York: Viking Penguin, 1990.

Sirridge, Mary and Armelagos, Adina. 'The In's [sic] and Out's [sic] of Dance: Expression as an Aspect of Style'. *Journal of Aesthetics and Art Criticism*, Vol. 36, 1977.

Skene, Reg. *The Cuchulain Plays of W. B. Yeats: A Study*. London: Macmillan, 1974.

Spalding, Frances. *Whistler*. Oxford: Phaidon, 1979.

Sparshott, Francis. *Off the Ground: First Steps to a Philosophical Consideration of the Dance*. New Jersey: Princeton University Press, 1988.

St. Johnstone, Reginald. *A History of Dancing*. London: Simpkin, Marshall, Hamilton, Kent, 1906.

Steegmuller, Francis. *Your Isadora: The Love Story of Isadora Duncan & Gordon Craig*. New York: Macmillan, 1974.

Stewart, Virginia and Armitage, Merle. ed. *The Modern Dance*. New York: 1935; rpt. New York: Dance Horizons, 1970.

Stokes, Adrian. *Russian Ballets*. London: Faber & Faber, 1935.

Stokes, John. *Resistible Theatres: Enterprise and Experiment in the late Nineteenth Century*. London: Paul Elek Books, 1972.

—— *In the Nineties*. Hemel Hempstead: Harvester Wheatsheaf, 1989.

Taplin, Diana Theodores. ed. *New Directions in Dance: Collected Writings from the Seventh Dance in Canada Conference held at the University of Waterloo, Canada, June 1979*. Toronto: Pergamon Press, 1979.

Taylor, Richard. *The Drama of W. B. Yeats: Irish Myth and the Japanese No*. New Haven: York University Press, 1976.

—— *A Reader's Guide to the Plays of W. B. Yeats*. London: Macmillan, 1984.

Wilson, Edmund. *Axel's Castle*. London and Glasgow: Charles Scribner's Sons, 1931; London: Fontana, 1967.

Winter, Marian Hannah. *The Pre-Romantic Ballet*. London: Pitman Publishing, 1974.

Worth, Katharine. *The Irish Drama of Europe from Yeats to Beckett*. London: Athlone Press, 1978.

Zagona, Helen Grace. *The Legend of Salome and the Principle of Art for Art's Sake*. Genève: Librairie E. Droz, 1960; Paris: Librairie Minard, 1960.

Index